The Last Suffragist Standing

The Last Suffragist Standing

The Life and Times of Laura Marshall Jamieson

VERONICA STRONG-BOAG

UBC Press • Vancouver • Toronto

27 26 25 24 23 22 21 20 19 18   5 4 3 2 1

Printed in Canada on FSC-certified ancient-forest-free paper (100% post-consumer recycled) that is processed chlorine- and acid-free.

Library and Archives Canada Cataloguing in Publication

Strong-Boag, Veronica, author
The last suffragist standing : the life and times of Laura Marshall Jamieson / Veronica Strong-Boag.

Includes bibliographical references and index.
Issued in print and electronic formats.
ISBN 978-0-7748-3868-9 (hardcover). – ISBN 978-0-7748-3869-6 (pbk). – ISBN 978-0-7748-3870-2 (PDF). – ISBN 978-0-7748-3871-9 (EPUB). – ISBN 978-0-7748-3872-6 (Kindle)

1. Jamieson, Laura E, 1882–1964. 2. Politicians – British Columbia – Biography. 3. Suffragists – British Columbia – Biography. 4. Biographies. I. Title.

FC3824.1.J34S87 2018   971.1′04092   C2018-903301-0
C2018-903302-9

Canada

UBC Press gratefully acknowledges the financial support for our publishing program of the Government of Canada (through the Canada Book Fund), the Canada Council for the Arts, and the British Columbia Arts Council.

This book has been published with the help of a grant from the Canadian Federation for the Humanities and Social Sciences, through the Awards to Scholarly Publications Program, using funds provided by the Social Sciences and Humanities Research Council of Canada.

Printed and bound in Canada by Friesens
Set in Garamond by Apex CoVantage, LLC
Copy editor: Deborah Kerr
Proofreader: Kristy Lynn Hankewitz
Indexer: Cameron Duder

UBC Press
The University of British Columbia
2029 West Mall
Vancouver, BC V6T 1Z2
www.ubcpress.ca

For my almost daughters: Miranda, Meleyna, Jude, Natalie (Lai Leng), and Delilah (Turaluk)

Contents

List of Illustrations / ix

Acknowledgments / xi

Introduction / 3

1 The Girl from the Saugeen Peninsula, 1882–1911 / 12

2 The New Woman as Wife, Suffragist, and Activist, 1911–18 / 41

3 Still Bettering the World, 1918–26 / 62

4 Widowed Judge and Progressive Activist, 1927–39 / 80

5 The Challenge of Electoral Politics, 1927–39 / 102

6 Suffragist in the BC Legislature, 1939–41 / 120

7 Legislative Veteran, 1941–45 / 141

8 Taking on Post-war Misogyny and Vancouver Politics, 1945–64/ 162

9 Faithful Social Democrat, 1945–64 / 181

Conclusion / 211

Postscript from Four Granddaughters / 215
Dorothy O'Connell, Anne Jamieson, Karen Jamieson, and Marion-Lea Jamieson

Abbreviations / 221

Notes / 223

Selected Bibliography / 259

Index / 263

Illustrations

Map of Indian reserves on the Saugeen/Bruce Peninsula / 13
Laura as a child, Saugeen Peninsula, c. 1888 / 19
Souvenir of Owen Sound, Ontario, 1900 / 22
Fernie, British Columbia, c. 1902 / 26
Laura with the University College Women's Literary Society, c. 1908 / 29
Laura's graduation portrait, University of Toronto, 1908 / 32
John Stuart Jamieson, University of Toronto, c. 1908 / 39
The "Great Cause" in British Columbia, 1912 / 47
Champion of minimum wage, 1918 / 49
British Columbia as suffrage black spot, 1916 / 56
Vancouver Mother's Council aids the unemployed, 1935 / 99
Five women members of the BC legislature, 1941 / 143
British Columbia's CCF women champions, 1941 / 144
Vancouver City Council, 1947–48 / 171
Laura Jamieson, BC MLA, 1952 / 195

Acknowledgments

The Last Suffragist Standing has been improved by many fruitful exchanges with friends, notably the editors and the historians producing the volumes in the UBC Press series, Women's Suffrage and the Struggle for Democracy, for which I have served as the general editor since 2013 – Darcy Cullen, Melissa Pitts, and Lesley Erickson at UBC Press and Lara Campbell, Sarah Carter, Tarah Brookfield, Denyse Baillargeon, Heidi MacDonald, and Lianne Leddy. This volume also benefits from input from talented UBC Press editors Darcy Cullen, Lesley Erickson, Katrina Petrik, and Deborah Kerr. Georgina Taylor, the biographer of Violet McNaughton, has also been generous in sharing knowledge of that extraordinary feminist and her relations with Laura. Bailey Bjolin and Jed Anderson have proved invaluable research assistants for this project, and Cameron Duder has once again kept me sane, here with both the index and the endnote style. Canadian scholarship is the richer for their curiosity and industry, and for reminders about the value of feminist scholarship in refining the questions we ask.

I have also been fortunate in receiving the encouragement of Laura's surviving granddaughters, Anne, Karen, Marion-Lea, and Laura Jamieson and Dorothy O'Connell. They have long hoped for a biographer and retained a few private papers, though these offered far less than they believed or I hoped. The interviews that Laura's namesake conducted with her own parents, Stuart and Jean Jamieson, have influenced my approach even if they don't appear directly in these pages. Unfortunately, Kathleen Shannon (1935–98), the eldest granddaughter and the talented producer for the National Film Board of Canada's famed feminist Studio D, died prematurely, leaving only a few suggestive words on Laura's influence.

I am also grateful, as all Canadian scholars are, to the support and enthusiasm of librarians and archivists across the country. They are national treasures. So too is the Social Sciences and Humanities Research Council of Canada, which, in this project as in so many others, supports curiosity-driven research that helps us better understand the complex and demanding world we share.

The Last Suffragist Standing

Introduction

Risk-takers come in many guises. Even as myths of all sorts prefer them young, beautiful, frequently seemingly classless, and most often male, exceptions abound. *The Last Suffragist Standing: The Life and Times of Laura Marshall Jamieson* highlights just this alternative to fashion. This BC New Woman, suffragist, social democratic activist, juvenile court judge, Vancouver alderman, and CCF politician might have lacked the glitz attributed to much risk taking, but she possessed the requisite nerve. During a lifetime that began as a soon-to-be orphaned child on a marginal farm and ended as a frail veteran of Canada's struggles for equality, Laura, as she is often called in these pages, ventured where few contemporaries dared. She stayed loyal to a vision of a more just world.

Four broad stories percolate through *The Last Suffragist Standing*'s account of one extraordinary person. First, the tale of the girl from the Saugeen Peninsula (better known as the Bruce Peninsula) – who became in turn Miss Marshall, Mrs. John Stuart Jamieson, and finally Laura Jamieson – explores the evolution of political consciousness. Feminists, like feminism, are shifting products of particular times and places: some ideas and opportunities are nourished, whereas others are waylaid. Though political labels are frequently invoked to sum up individuals, the conditional nature of the journey that got them there is commonly left unsaid. From the beginning, however, I wondered how someone who was so connected with Canada's middle-class women's club movement and so generally represented as a respectable lady sufficiently questioned convention to become a suffragist, a birth controller, a peace worker, a champion of minimum wage, a social democratic activist, and British Columbia's fourth and Canada's tenth female parliamentarian.[1] Laura became far more than might have been predicted and far more than she often seemed to contemporaries and later scholars. Her trajectory, inspired and contained as it was by the times in which she lived, helped shape modern Canada.

At first glance, Laura's origins in rural Ontario, stints as a teacher, social worker, and juvenile court judge, not to mention her marriage to a Presbyterian lawyer, might have suggested a very different path. Indeed, during the First World War, Laura toyed with the promise of the provincial Liberal Party. On the other hand, her escape from rural poverty into study and a passion for mountaineering offered clues of different prospects. In her youth, Laura joined Canada's contingent of New Women to baulk at restraint and question tradition. She joined a remarkable cohort on the left who, as the biographer of Helena Gutteridge, another such radical, has suggested, "managed their personal lives without necessarily submitting to the social strictures that still fettered women. Essentially family women, they were not 'bohemian' and they did not believe in free love, but they believed in themselves and found their own kind of liberation."[2] Suffrage and economic justice campaigns sharpened Laura's dissension from the status quo.

By the end of the Great War, in taking up crusades for peace, internationalism, and socialism, she increasingly distinguished herself from the majority of her feminist contemporaries. The history she shared with suffragists who trusted in mainstream parties made Laura a highly suspect recruit for much of British Columbia's left, long associated with unions and working-class radicalism. Looking at this slim, well-spoken clubwoman, malestream socialists commonly took for granted her conventionality and their own radical superiority. Despite that reception, she remained a feminist champion of social democracy.

In sum, Laura's life offers ample reminders of the constructed, fluid, and uncertain nature of political allegiances.[3] Whatever her contemporary critics believed, Jamieson was not frozen in ladylike aspic. In response to evolving challenges to conscience, from the early twentieth-century factories of Stratford, Ontario, to the Great Depression and the internment of Japanese Canadians, she kept enlarging her vision of democracy, albeit incompletely. In 1945, she could insist, as she had not done during the suffrage campaigns, that crusades for equality required the inclusion of "new immigrants, racial minorities and others." Only "equal opportunity for all" satisfied her expanding feminist agenda.[4] In making sense of its subject, this biography seeks to illuminate the "dialectical relationship between women's experience and the creation of oppositional ideas," as recommended by Joan Sangster in the recovery of Canada's non-conforming women.[5]

A second big question to inspire this volume is the nature of the first women's movement and the follow-up to the initial suffrage victories. Many scholars have been transfixed by the middle-class and racist prejudices of suffragists and have paid too little attention to women's rights coalitions, post-suffrage results, or the persisting resistance to gender equality.[6] Despite that response, feminist visions were in fact diverse and uncertain even as the vote became a common goal. In the years before women were partially enfranchised in 1917 and 1918, British Columbia produced an eclectic band of women's rights activists, some of whom found inspiration in its strong socialist and labour movements. Vancouver feminists forged broad-based partnerships in campaigns for political equality. Those networks did not quickly disappear. They provided inspiration into the 1920s and 1930s, notably in non-partisan support for Mary Ellen Smith, British Columbia's first female MLA, and, later, for the Mother's Council and Vancouver Women's Emergency Committee to Aid the Single Unemployed.

Although Mary Kinnear's observation in *Female Economy: Women's Work in the Prairie Provinces, 1870–1970,* that "only a small handful of the suffragists were later candidates for election" and that most "women who became candidates were drawn from a new and different generation" is for the most part true across Canada,[7] exceptions were important. In fact, a significant group of BC suffragists persisted in politics, especially in municipal affairs, well after they won the vote for themselves. Mary Ellen Smith was one important example but so too was British suffragette and Canadian suffragist Helena Gutteridge, who finally won office on Vancouver City Council in 1937. In 1939, Laura Jamieson became the last suffragist in British Columbia and in Canada to be elected to a provincial or federal legislature. Her victory drew on the feminist networks that survived from the enfranchisement campaigns.

Laura was often self-conscious about her membership in that broader community. Even as she recommended feminist foremothers such as French socialist Flora Tristan, she reflected on the different political options taken up by her contemporaries. She emphasized that the great causes of justice and freedom led herself and a select group from suffrage activism to left-wing politics. She also sought to explain other choices. Her review of Catherine Cleverdon's pathbreaking *The Woman Suffrage Movement in Canada* (1950) stressed the disappointment that "socialist women" felt when "so few of the original suffragists" developed "a vision of the kind of society that could be achieved by continuing the campaign to include social, economic and political changes." She faulted many enfranchised women as too wedded to the status quo. She did not spare leaders such as Nellie L. McClung and Emily Murphy, seeing McClung as too narrowly preoccupied with temperance and the franchise, and dismissing Murphy for her senatorial ambitions.[8]

In stark contrast, Jamieson, Gutteridge, and radical friends such as Saskatchewan's Violet McNaughton and Ontario's Agnes Macphail interpreted the drive for the vote as only one stage in the inevitably long struggle for full democracy. Suffrage was neither the ultimate nor the sufficient goal. Once enfranchised, Canadian women required inspiration and education in families, schools, co-operatives, and unions. Only lifelong consciousness raising and community building could counter patriarchy and capitalism. Just as there had been no shortcuts for suffrage, there was none to a feminist or socialist future. The fact that all women and racial minorities eventually achieved the vote signalled to Laura that socialism might advance in the same incremental fashion. The alternative was backlash and setback, just what was sometimes attributed to British suffragettes. In the life that is explored in these pages, a politics that might be termed "radical caution" emerges as one legacy of the first women's movement.

A third significant concern running through this book is the relations of feminism with Canada's left. Since both vary significantly in their makeup, interaction has always been extremely complicated and often contentious. Most former suffragists who hoped for political office sought progressive options in Liberal parties or in diverse parties on the left, such as Alberta's Non-Partisan League or the Federated Labour Party, which Laura endorsed in 1920. The fragmentation and internal conflicts of the communist and non-communist left, like those of the BC Liberals and Conservatives, made choices all the more difficult in the post-war decades. Not surprisingly, some suffrage veterans opted out of electoral politics altogether to commit themselves to the radical solutions for peace and co-operation offered by the Women's International League for Peace and Freedom or the Women's Labour League. The pioneering feminist MP Agnes Macphail was typical in exploring various options, shifting from the Progressive Party to the Ginger Group and eventually to the Co-operative Commonwealth Federation (CCF).

By the Great Depression that latter party, with its partnership of farmers, socialists, labour activists, and progressive intellectuals, offered justice-seeking women far more than its mainstream competitors. Although its recognition of exploitation rarely highlighted gender or, for that matter, race, its condemnation of class privilege addressed concerns that had mobilized more radical suffragists such as Laura. Whereas BC Liberals could promise a "little New Deal," the CCF focus on working people and social security attracted far more outspoken feminist recruits. They trusted the sympathetic reception they received from men such as the first CCF leader, James Shaver Woodsworth, who had endorsed suffrage campaigns. When she became a BC MLA, Laura joined an ongoing effort to establish the CCF as a champion of the rights of women as well as workers.

Yet if the CCF was more promising than conventional parties, priorities and prejudices always troubled its relations with feminists. The influential Second Socialist International (1889–1916) set the stage when it viewed "feminism as a rival enterprise and attempted to counter its attractiveness by smear and counterclaim, by allegations that feminism was irremediably 'bourgeois,' that capitalism was the fundamental problem, that class conflict was the motor of history, and that only socialism could resolve the 'woman question' – but only after the victory of the proletariat."[9] Though they have largely let far more egregious mainstream political offenders off the hook, most scholars have confirmed this distrust. Socialists in the CCF, like members of other progressive parties, frequently preferred to sidestep the radical message of gender equality. This meant treating Laura and other feminists as suspect interlopers on terrain that belonged above all to male labour socialists and progressive intellectuals.

The feminist writers of columns variously titled "Women's Views," "The Women's View Point," "Mainly for Women," and "A Word to the Wives" in the CCF newspaper highlighted hostility. One 1939 contributor captured the recurring clash: "I find that among men of my acquaintance I am said to 'carry a torch' ... for women ... A few years ago and it was only men who stuck together, women supposedly selling each other out with every breath ... We have travelled far in the right direction."[10] Few early feminists would have been happy with subsequent histories of the Canadian left. Many repeat the original disrespect. Historian James Naylor's key recognition that the BC CCF was never homogeneous and always diverse has been more honoured in the breach than in the observance.[11] Recent fascination with supposed populism or labour socialism in the CCF typically does little more than re-enact original indifference to feminism and gender analysis.[12] The struggle of Laura and others to win recognition of feminism as essential to a truly radical politics is, however, a central part of the story that follows.

The final current animating *The Last Suffragist Standing* infused the entirety of the years under scrutiny. Only recently have Canadians begun to consider racism as a fundamental flaw, and recognition of the magnitude of gender prejudices has been equally slow. Misogyny and antifeminism have always crippled parliaments and assemblies, churches, schools, professions, employments, and the media. My research for this biography supplied ample reminders of the steady assault on women's self-respect and material well-being, and this is essential to understanding Canada in these years. Reading the determinedly conservative *Saturday Night* magazine from its inception in Toronto in 1887, soon after Laura was born, provided only one lesson in male disparagement and too often as well in women's apparent self-hatred. The usually less reactionary *Maclean's Magazine, Chatelaine,* and mainstream and labour, socialist, and communist newspapers were frequently little better. Leading anti-suffrage intellectuals from Goldwin Smith to Andrew Macphail and Henri Bourassa had many misogynous heirs who found ready audiences across the dominion.[13] Few commentators fit Agnes Macphail's description of "men who think a woman should get a fair break."[14]

Patriarchy's champions frustrated feminist activists and corrupted parties in the years that Laura was active politically. On the left stood many men like Tom Uphill (1874–1962). A former coalminer in Wales, long-time labour and socialist alderman, mayor, and MLA from Fernie, British Columbia, Uphill was an irrepressible misogynist. From the beginning, he unfurled his standard as "one of the boys," with "hundreds of 'nieces'" and an office featuring "pictures of pin-up girls on the walls."[15] Between 1939 and 1945 and from 1952 to 1953, Laura had to endure his presence in the Victoria legislature. Uphill's arrogance was easily matched on the respectable right. In 1930, one of Canada's many supposedly "grand old men" of political life, Conservative journalist and senator Grattan O'Leary (1888–1976), comfortably pontificated, "Men, too, especially the old-line, hard-boiled partisans, are suspicious of the woman politician, disdainful of her efforts, and often openly contemptuous of her achievements."[16] Like Fernie's good old boy, O'Leary viewed women as incapable of playing the legislative game, which had to follow male rules. No wonder Laura declined to run in the 1930 federal election. Despite their pragmatic endorsement of women suffrage, Liberals proved little better. Even as Laura battled for a second term on Vancouver City Council, Bruce Hutchison, the reputable dean of BC journalists, flaunted his derision for half of humanity. Writing in the *Vancouver News-Herald* in 1949, he mocked women as "the all-powerful, unknown, deified, glamorized and unintelligible, riddle" who "will spend anything" and "believe anything." Far from ideal democratic subjects, such creatures could only be inferior legislators.[17] Such blatant bigotry, like wandering hands and taken-for-granted domestic violence, undermined all pretensions to equality. The persistence of that deeply immoral landscape ensured that Laura's choices to seek education and professional employment, to demand suffrage and peace, to insist upon economic justice, and eventually to enter politics always trespassed on dangerous territory.

Such feminist trailblazers, with all they mean for the state of democracy, merit far better treatment than they received in their own time. Biographies, such as the appropriately titled *The Struggle for Social Justice in British Columbia: Helena Gutteridge, the Unknown Reformer,* by Irene Howard, and *Rose Henderson: A Woman for the People,* by Peter Campbell, offer the obvious redress to faulty observation and memory. Fortunate biographers have access to significant personal papers and/or the iconoclasts themselves as well as those who knew them well. No scholar investigating Canadian suffragists, with the conspicuous exception of the path-breaking Catherine L. Cleverdon who was able to interview suffrage veterans, has yet been so lucky. Few private or personal records survive of that critical generation. This study of Jamieson is no exception: like those of Gutteridge and Henderson, her papers are minimal, indeed misleading, and memories of her are scant. Few expressions of her innermost thoughts survive. The BC Provincial Archives holds the pages of her unpublished autobiography, but they portray a rose-tinted life that is often at odds with reality. Much information in her papers at the archives can be found elsewhere, and the limited correspondence tells little.

Lacking a treasure trove, *The Last Suffragist Standing* relies heavily on a diverse array of evidence and spotlights particular historical contexts and places to make sense of Laura. Autobiographies and biographies of her contemporaries, histories of Ontario and British Columbia, accounts of suffrage campaigns and female politicians, studies of the CCF, and investigations of the employments and causes she took up set the stage on which her life unfolded and illuminate her contributions. Magisterial and doctoral theses, first of all the compelling assessment by my former student Susan Walsh of the CCF quartet Jamieson, Gutteridge, Dorothy Gretchen Steeves, and Grace MacInnis – but many others as well – proved a godsend in charting activism and political movements that Laura joined or opposed.[18] Foundational scholarship on women activists, the Canadian left, and British Columbia by Joan Sangster, Linda Kealey, Irene Howard, James Naylor, Benjamin Isitt, Robert A.J. McDonald, Mark Leier, Peter Campbell, Jean Barman, Lisa Pasolli, and Thomas Socknat, among others, has mapped the critical terrain on which Laura tried to make a difference.

Primary materials in archives, periodicals, and the Internet provided other clues to reconstructing a largely forgotten activist. Though all too scarce, useful archival sources appeared in CCF and related papers at the University of British Columbia, in clubwomen's holdings at the Vancouver City Archives, in student records at the University of Toronto Archives, in Violet McNaughton's papers in the Saskatchewan Archives, and in Kathleen Shannon's at Library and Archives Canada. Newspapers and magazines added substantially to the emerging portrait. First of all, Laura's extensive writings, notably in CCF publications, offered a running commentary on many battles. Newspapers in Fernie, Burnaby, and Vancouver similarly did much to compensate for the lack of key records, such as a BC *Hansard* for the years that Laura was an MLA (1939–45, 1952–53), official minutes of Vancouver City Council on which she served (1948–49), and reports of the juvenile court overseen first by her husband (1923–26) and then by Laura herself (1927–38). A raft of local and popular histories had much to teach about settler farming on the Saugeen or Bruce Peninsula in the late nineteenth century, Kootenay mining towns where she taught, and Burnaby, a Vancouver suburb where she lived as a wife and ventured forth as a widow. I have also been repeatedly grateful to the Internet. One afternoon, for example, it unexpectedly produced a picture of Eliza Marshall, Laura's indispensable and far more forgotten nursing sister, without whom she would have been hard pressed to escape rural poverty.

With much help, *The Last Suffragist Standing* tells its complex story of a single individual and her times in nine substantive chapters. The first examines Laura Emma Marshall as a farm child, student, teacher, mountain-climber, and YWCA secretary from 1882 to 1911. Progress was marked by hard work, scant money, and stubborn accomplishment in an environment where Anglo-Celtic hegemony and the displacement of the First Nations were taken for granted. In testing settlers' boundaries of education and employment for her sex, she became one of Canada's New Women. Chapter 2 considers Laura as a middle-class wife, mother, suffragist, and activist from 1911 to 1918 in the BC Lower Mainland, increasingly the centre of the province's feminist protest. Married to John Stuart Jamieson, a University of Toronto classmate and liberal lawyer, she shared with him a commitment to the social gospel and women's empowerment even as she gave birth to three children. Both Laura and John joined the BC suffrage movement. Chapter 3 turns to the years after the First World War, when Laura balanced marriage to a rising legal professional with her embrace of radicalism in the Women's International League for Peace and Freedom, the Parent-Teacher Association, and socialist politics. No longer part of the liberal mainstream, she forged a post-enfranchisement activism that was committed to raising feminist consciousness and expanding democracy. In 1926, John Jamieson, her stalwart anchor into the middle class, unexpectedly died. His death ushered in the next chapter in Laura's evolution. Chapter 4 considers her experience as a widow, juvenile court judge, and steadfast reformer from 1927 to 1939. As her children grew to maturity, she supported her family and joined other activists in tackling the Great Depression's deepening of domestic and global injustice. Chapter 5 sets forth the challenge of electoral politics that increasingly engaged her during those years. With gender and class her central concerns, she joined the social democratic wing of the newly formed CCF, which was led by her early mentor James S. Woodsworth. In 1939, she became the successful CCF candidate in a provincial by-election in Vancouver Centre. Chapter 6 then turns to Laura's first term in the BC legislature (1939–41). Joining the other female MLAs, CCFer Dorothy Gretchen Steeves and Liberal Helen Douglas Smith, she quickly made her own mark as a dedicated advocate for women and workers. In addressing issues from juvenile delinquency to childcare, female employment, and housing, she emerged as an effective parliamentarian. Chapter 7 continues the legislative story to focus on Laura's second term, from 1941 to 1945. She proved herself a distinguished member of the largest group of women elected to any Canadian parliament until the 1970s. Commitment and skill in promoting social justice did not protect her from defeat in 1945. Chapter 8 describes the reactionary climate that created the conditions for her spirited engagement as a city councillor and activist in Vancouver's post-war municipal politics. Civic democracy was her banner. Chapter 9 then addresses her efforts as an MLA during 1952–53 and as a CCF activist until her death. Her opposition to doctrinaire Marxism and emphasis on the centrality of women's rights to the overthrow of capitalism during the Cold War placed her firmly on one wing of Canada's left politics. Old age and the conservatism of her times slowed Laura down, but disabilities never extinguished her passion for justice. She survived to become a founding member of the CCF's successor, the New Democratic Party. Ultimately, Canada's last suffragist standing remained an irrepressible champion of greater democracy.

1
The Girl from the Saugeen Peninsula, 1882–1911

Nearly three decades moulded Laura Emma Marshall before she became Laura Jamieson. Though largely forgotten and now hard to retrieve, those years supplied the staging ground for the advent of a feminist activist and social democratic politician. From 1882 to 1911, Laura was linked to critical shifts in the history of Canada and modern women. Her life began on December 29, 1882, in a settler community north of Toronto and extended briefly into the prairies and then to British Columbia; she returned east to Toronto and finally moved to the busy industrial centre of Stratford, Ontario. Laura went from a poor farm child to an ambitious pupil, teacher, university coed, and social worker, with many of the markings of the age's New Women. This geographical and occupational voyage fashioned a complex figure.

Until very recently, this chapter might have boasted the title "A Girl from the Bruce." Possible alternatives could have included "A Girl from the Queen's Bush" or "A Girl from the Indian Peninsula."[1] All such invocations foreground the imperial history of her birthplace, the postal village of Park Head, Bruce County, Ontario. Even when she appeared little conscious of her home region's heritage of dispossession, she was critically shaped by its influences. Placing her on the Saugeen Peninsula, as it was sometimes titled in the nineteenth century, reintegrates her into a protean political landscape of losers and winners that included the marginalization and exploitation of the Ojibwa-Chippewa, Potawatomi, and other Indigenous peoples.

The Saugeen is not a platform that the younger Laura would have claimed. Her emerging vision of fair dealing initially sidestepped injustice

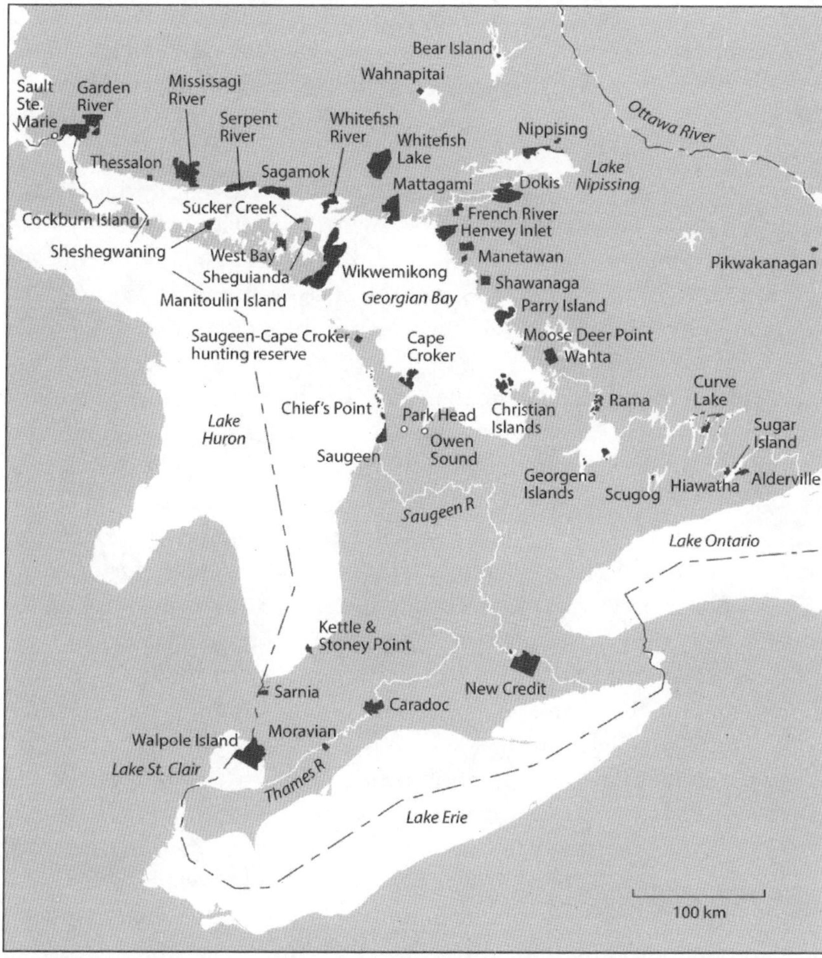

Indian reserves on the Saugeen/Bruce Peninsula | Cartography by Eric Leinberger

based on race. As an Anglo-Celtic girl and young woman from a poor family, she focused first on the obvious restraints that a patriarchal and capitalist society imposed on people much like herself. Even such recognition was difficult and not widely shared. Laura stood with the vast majority of her settler peers in failing to question Europeans' right to rule, but she gradually set herself apart in questioning the privileges of gender and class. Only later in the course of an international education in human rights would her vision expand to include injustices done to non-Europeans, though Canada's Indigenous peoples rarely attracted her close attention. In the Saugeen/Bruce, she was far from alone. As late as the twenty-first century, "poor, rural, and working class settlers" continued to take for granted their dispossession of the "sovereign indigenous peoples of Turtle Island."[2] However, Laura's ignorance should not be repeated by her biographer. Her story properly begins, and indeed continues, with recognition of racial privilege as well as the constraints of gender and class.

In 1837 and 1857, imperial treaties alienated Indigenous rights to the Saugeen Peninsula – the long tongue of land that runs between Lake Huron and Georgian Bay in Canada West, later Ontario.[3] In the catastrophic course of three decades, the bands of the region surrendered some 98 percent of their territory.[4] Though they fought hard to develop strategies of successful accommodation and resistance, they had ultimately to accept paltry acres on the margins of the peninsula or on Manitoulin Island. That loss made it possible for Laura's maternal and paternal relatives (the Smiths and Marshalls, respectively) to move from Ireland and King County, Ontario, to claim affordable farms and a better life. In a few decades, these newcomers would in turn contribute to another settler wave that would extend farther west, both to the prairies and British Columbia, where Laura would live and work. That migration once again depleted resources and forced Indigenous peoples onto inadequate holdings.

By the time they arrived in the region, Laura's kin could reap the benefits of dispossession from predecessors who frequently became effectively invisible to their mainstream replacements. The newcomers' own toehold on economic survival was sufficiently precarious to leave most with little inclination or opportunity to question the displacement on which their own hopes for a better life rested. Like many reform-minded women and men of her era from the region, the child Laura saw little of the Ojibwa-Chippewa and Potawatomi, who were segregated on reserves as she grew up. Indeed, until she attended high school in Owen Sound, she met few non-relatives.

Laura Emma Marshall experienced childhood and adolescence in a settlement dominated by Scots and Anglo-Irish. Despite a sprinkling of Germans, Americans, and blacks, there was no doubt as to pre-eminence. Park Head was named after the Scottish birthplace of the wife of its first postmaster; Amabel Township, in which it was located, memorialized a female relative of Sir Edmund Walker Head, governor general of British North America (1854–61), and Bruce County itself recalled James Bruce, the Earl of Elgin and governor general of the Canadas (1847–54). That nomenclature, just like Laura's later designation as "Mrs. John Stuart Jamieson," reminded everyone of who really mattered.

As would be true in British Columbia, recent arrivals to the peninsula liked to congratulate themselves that the "condition of the Indians residing in the reservations within the county of Bruce" was "a highly satisfactory state of affairs, complimentary to all who have worked for the uplifting and civilization of our native tribes."[5] The herculean efforts of local Ojibwa-Chippewa to use both the Catholic and Methodist Churches and the short-lived federal promise of support for farming to forge an effective counter to settler pressure went unacknowledged and often unknown. This included ignorance of Indian women's histories, which ironically could have offered feminist newcomers further proof of the female agency that they continually sought as a response to pervasive misogyny. In the case of the Saugeen Peninsula, this history would have highlighted Nahneebahweequa (1824–65), the Ojibwa Methodist Catherine Sutton, who took claims for the land rights of wives and Indians to the court of Queen Victoria. Until her premature death in 1865, at much the same time that Laura's maternal family, the Smiths, arrived in Indian country, this crusader challenged "wholesale robbery and treachery" and "the shameful injustice" that lay at the heart of new communities. Like the younger E. Pauline Johnson (1861–1913), who would appear on the national scene in the 1880s, Sutton denounced settler encroachment as "might makes right."[6]

As modern science increasingly shored up faith in a hierarchy of the world's so-called races, Indigenous visions of partnerships and inclusion lost purchase on the evolving national vision of Canadians. No wonder then that it was "hard to overestimate the excitement felt" by the Saugeen/Bruce's eager recruits to the Canadian forces that were raised to quell the North-West Rebellion of Metis Louis Riel and his Indian allies in 1885.[7] By this time, the family of Joseph Marshall (1836–92) and Lucinda Smith (1840–92) was complete, with three-year-old Laura following two boys and two girls. One other son died in infancy. The 1881 and 1891 censuses list virtually no Indigenous residents in Amabel or the adjacent township of Keppel, where most of Lucinda's family lived.

Although rare, African Americans, most of them refugees from US slavery, were somewhat more visible than the First Peoples. Indeed, the nearby port city of Owen Sound (originally the village of Sydenham, so-titled after another British governor, then incorporated in 1857 and renamed for a British admiral) was the northern terminus of the Underground Railroad. Black women and men laboured as sailors, farmers, and artisans, as well as the occasional lawyer, publisher, and musician before the First World War.[8] Although an annual Emancipation Picnic, celebrating first the 1834 British Emancipation Act and then the 1863 US Emancipation Proclamation, began in about 1862, the region's black history received scant attention until the end of the twentieth century. Like the

Indigenous people of the Saugeen Peninsula, black residents presented alternative, but largely unappreciated, outcomes of the early Canadian experiment. Laura's eventual endorsement of a more inclusive national vision could only begin to restore an earlier vision that her families had resisted or had not known.

For decades, that alternative was muted amid the din of European concerns and contests. Like those of other progressive contemporaries, such as Nellie Letitia Mooney (1873–1951, later McClung), Norman Bethune (1890–1939), and Agnes Campbell Macphail (1890–1954), all of whom grew up on the Saugeen, Laura's sensibilities were initially aroused by the hardship and exploitation associated with class, notably the rural-urban divide, and, in some cases, by gender. This prioritization confirmed racial privilege, relative isolation from Indigenous peoples, the presence of patriarchy, and the era's limited understanding of human rights.

Most white settlers concentrated on their own difficulties. Many found themselves on marginal holdings, dealing with bad harvests, grasshopper swarms, rocky soil, deadly epidemics, and political nepotism. Hardships helped explain the willingness of some male voters to break with traditional parties: in 1894, Bruce County chose a candidate from the progressive Patrons of Industry for the Ontario legislature.[9] The Patrons were sometimes allies of the Woman's Christian Temperance Union (WCTU), another challenger to conventional politics, and many local Patrons endorsed women suffrage. In the 1894 provincial election, the Patrons demonstrated a further affinity for connecting causes. In declaring their commitment to "labour as the creator of wealth," they chose to link themselves with the Trades and Labour Congress of Canada to elect seventeen MLAs.[10] Though both the alliance and their impact were limited, the Patrons helped "electors to break away from mere party lines and think and vote in an independent manner." Their introduction of co-operative stores and buying programs, and sponsorship of events and entertainments designed to build community feeling – exactly the agenda that the adult Laura would later endorse – similarly reminded residents on the Saugeen/Bruce and elsewhere that capitalism did not have to be taken for granted.[11]

Federal politics proved a different matter. From 1882 to 1900, the Bruce North riding elected Alexander McNeill, a Conservative MP from the Anglo-Irish immigrant gentry, as the champion of both local mill-owners and desperate small farmers. A "leading figure in the Imperial Federation League in Canada," McNeill erected a mansion outside Wiarton, the only peninsula town to rival Owen Sound.[12] Though he might have seemed little more than a remittance man, he offered the reassurance of familiar imperial relations of patron and client.[13] McNeill's wheeling and dealing over timber and Indigenous rights did not, however, secure prosperity for the settlers for whom he presumed to speak. By 1881, Grey-Bruce's arable land had all been claimed and its population had peaked.[14] Many offspring of those who had displaced the Ojibwa-Chippewa and others had to look elsewhere for subsistence. Sometimes this meant fishing and shipping on the Great Lakes, but frequently it was the Canadian prairies, where newcomers once again dispersed the Indigenous inhabitants. This was the choice of the Irish Methodist Mooneys, who with their youngest child, Nellie, left Grey County for Manitoba in 1880.

Other politics arose from women's oppression under patriarchal institutions. Commonplace Anglo-Celtic experiences of hard drinking and financial difficulty, when combined with customs and laws that privileged men, left many women and children particularly battered and exploited. Their plight readily became one of the key causes of the "emancipating theology" of the era's Protestant evangelism, itself closely associated with the Methodist Church, to which the Marshalls belonged.[15] The WCTU entered Ontario from the United States in 1874 and established an autonomous provincial organization in 1877; a World WCTU was founded in 1885 and a Canadian one in 1888. In 1874, Owen Sound produced the Women's Prohibition Society. Soon renamed the WCTU, it campaigned to remove liquor licences from grocery stores. Its temperance crusades, with their embedment in global activism, "taught women the power of effective collective action and provided them with a rationale to take progressive action against male vices" even as they celebrated "the ideology of the central place of home and family."[16] Such feminist-infused evangelical Protestantism offered women a strong sense of righteousness that quickly moved to reject second-class citizenship. Ontario's all-male government nicknamed the WCTU as "Women Constantly Troubling Us," communicating just how its determination to "do everything" and commitment to consciousness raising offended the patriarchal state.

Nor was it alone. The tiny hamlet of Park Head might not have been large enough to support a WCTU branch, but it did rally behind the International Organization of Good Templars. Dedicated to temperance and abstinence, this North American fraternal organization accepted both sexes and all races as members. In 1893, its Lodge No. 211 joined Laura's home Township Council of Amabel and activists elsewhere to petition the Ontario legislature for a plebiscite to put the "question of importation, manufacture and sale of intoxicating liquors" to the voters.[17] Such grassroots mobilization was precisely what Laura would later endorse for the promotion of Canadian social democracy.

Laura's family had plenty of reason to question the status quo. It was clearly economically marginal. Her mother's relatives, the Methodist Smiths, had arrived from Ireland, via Toronto, to settle small holdings on the peninsula in the 1860s. Lucinda's widowed maternal grandfather parented three daughters, of whom she herself was the eldest, and three sons. Laura's father, Joseph Marshall, another Methodist, arrived alone from King County, just north of Toronto, to homestead nearby a few years later. No one was notably prosperous. Joseph Marshall's choice, Park Head, was some thirteen miles west of Owen Sound and ten miles south of Wiarton. In 1882, it provided the junction of Grand Trunk Railway branches to both these centres. By the end of the nineteenth century, the village possessed a Methodist church, a store or two, saw- and shingle mills, and a public park. In 1906, past its glory days, its population was reported as seventy-five.[18] Subsequently, it barely survived on the map of Ontario.

In 1871, Lucinda Smith, who was then thirty-one, married Joe Marshall, aged thirty-five, in a quiet ceremony. In a foretokening of the value of maternal kin, it was witnessed by one of her sisters and one of her brothers. The couple's first child, Eliza, was born in 1873, followed by two daughters (Ellen and Laura) and three sons (Edward, Gilbert, and Stanley, who died in 1883). Born in 1882, Laura was their last child. Shortly before her death in 1964, she wrote about her memories as a young farm girl. A resolutely cheerful account rejected by a publisher, it left hardship largely unmentioned, though it did hint at mind-numbing labour in noting that her brothers picked stones out of the peninsula's heavily glaciated fields, a typical employment for the young. The "rigid economy and self-denial" that were required to survive, even when maple sugar, game, and fish were plentiful, virtually disappeared from her story, as did the family's Methodism, which she deserted as an adult.[19] Laura did, however, remember temperance meetings, a reflection of the costs of cheap whiskey and commonplace taverns, with their special temptations for men, who held the purse strings in most families. She also appreciated her sisters for teaching her to read before she entered the local one-room school.[20]

In early 1892, flu and pneumonia swept the peninsula. Nine-year-old Laura's mother and father died intestate within days of each other, leaving neither insurance nor cash. The husbands of Lucinda's two sisters administered the estate on behalf of their nieces and nephews. Nearby farmers, they knew how to run a marginal operation of a hundred acres. The land, along with a few horses, cattle, sheep, and pigs, altogether valued at

Laura as a child, Saugeen Peninsula, c. 1888 | Courtesy of the Jamieson family

$2,559, remained to support five children, the eldest (Eliza, 1873–1941) not yet twenty. In a pattern that more often characterized the distaff side of families, farming aunts, uncles, and cousins rallied to help the offspring of a sister, who, as the eldest in her family, had taken charge of her own siblings when their mother died. A bachelor uncle, Tom, came particularly often to lend a hand and typically took scarce money out of his pocket to convey Laura to a dentist in Owen Sound.[21] Later on, another maternal uncle served as her official guardian when she was a student at the University of Toronto. As one contemporary observer of borderline holdings on the peninsula noted, "where all were poor it was felt that mutual assistance, when possible, must be rendered, so the meager supplies of the necessities of life were cheerfully shared."[22] Cheerful or not, such aid confirmed the value of the grassroots co-operation that an older Laura would champion.

Being orphaned reinforced the message that all the Marshalls were expected to work. Though Edward eventually appeared to take on the family homestead, he tried his luck farming in Saskatchewan. Gilbert explored the prospects in British Columbia. He would join the Canadian Army during the First World War and wed an Englishwoman. Many of his last years were spent chronically unemployed and dependent on Laura in Vancouver. The second daughter, Ellen, married a farmer near Wingham, just to the south on the peninsula. In time, she seems to have stood at the centre of the Ontario family network, with Gilbert citing her as his next of kin during his enlistment, Eliza living with her from the 1920s to the 1940s, and Laura in touch and occasionally visiting from Vancouver.

The eldest sister, Eliza, became a teacher (with a third-class certificate), then a trained nurse, and eventually a Methodist missionary to China. Except for her choice of a religious career, she fit the typical portrait of the New Woman, choosing a path of professional expertise and independence.[23] After a stint in private practice in Buffalo, she nursed and trained as a deaconess at Toronto's Methodist Fred Victor Mission.[24] Her photograph figured in a fundraising pamphlet celebrating mission work in Toronto, where she was praised for her "human charity and Christlike service."[25] In 1926, after a career in China that included the principalship of girls' schools, Eliza returned to convalesce with her sister Ellen and her family. She drowned in a nearby river, while walking alone, in 1941. Eliza's service to Methodism reflected that denomination's significant shift in the last decades of the nineteenth century from missions that targeted Indigenous peoples, including those on the Saugeen, to the evangelization of Canadian cities and immigrants, and then to the search of foreign fields for recruits to Christ. In teaching, nursing, and evangelization, Eliza took a path associated with the social gospel, with its application of Christian precepts to social problems. As the eldest Marshall child, she may have acquired more religious training from her parents, and perhaps too, faith proved a special anchor in raising the younger orphans and making her way as a single woman with limited resources.

Laura's links to the church would prove less durable. She may well have been influenced by critiques such as those of Manitoba feminist and Methodist Alice Chown (1866–1949), who in 1911 "roundly criticized the deaconess movement for its inattention to the structural roots of poverty." That year has also been identified as the beginning of the movement's decline.[26] The New Women of the twentieth century often demanded more than the paltry wages and subordination to male authority that the deaconess movement originally enshrined.

Though Eliza became a respected professional, Laura alone of the orphaned siblings graduated from high school. Much later, she remembered the challenge:

> It had been pretty well agreed in our family that I, being the youngest of five, should have a High School education; our farm income, in a pioneer community not having been able to give that privilege to any of the other four. However, the High School Entrance examination came, and I passed it; but there were no prospects that the family could afford to send me to town, to pay for my board, books and clothes.

Providentially, the youngest Marshall had impressed the teacher in Park Head's one-room school. He taught her the first-year high school curriculum without charge. His pupil summed up its demands:

> It was heavy going. No one else was doing it. My former classmates had all stopped at the Entrance Exam. I sat alone all day, trying to make out what algebra was all about with those strange little figures. The teacher would try to give me 15 or 20 minutes after school. I had no books to read, except the few texts. I began to wonder if Higher Education, beginning with High School, was all that I had been led to believe. Was it worth the struggle, and when would the struggle end?[27]

Like many ambitious young people who had few books at home, she ransacked the hamlet's Sunday School library to feed her passion for reading. Good luck took another form as well. Eliza's American wages

Souvenir of Owen Sound, Ontario | Grip Printing and Publishing, 1900, Toronto Public Library

grubstaked Laura at fee-paying Owen Sound College Institute (OSCI). The eldest Marshall sibling did not "give it outright" lest Laura take "education too lightly." There was small likelihood of that.[28] Eliza's loan was still registered against the estate when Laura's husband, John Stuart Jamieson, died in 1926.

Laura first appears in the OSCI attendance registers in September 1897 at age fourteen. Although most local collegiate records have been destroyed by fire, the remnants suggest that she advanced quickly, while paying tuition as a city non-resident.[29] One of the province's premier secondary schools, OSCI was marked by a massive Victorian-style brick structure that lorded over the obstreperous lake port. In 1896–97, the school advertised its attractions:

> Town of Owen Sound has many advantages to offer to students ... Its clear atmosphere and pure water render it a most healthful and desirable resort. Its citizens are characterized by industry and push ... Students who come here will find the combined advantages of country and city life, with none of the disadvantages of either.

> The cheapness of the accommodation afforded to students is a point of no less importance. Board averages – for ladies $1.75 per week, and for gentlemen $2.50 per week, and this in Christian homes where students will not be shut out from the family life.
>
> The educational and religious influences by which students are surrounded are unsurpassed. There is in the town a well-stocked Public Library and Reading Room. The Y.M.C.A. and the churches of the town have classes for religious instruction; and special attention is given to students, that healthy religious influences may surround them.
>
> The Collegiate Institute affords particular advantages in every department. The building is among the finest and best adapted for school use in the Province. It is heated throughout by steam, whereby an even temperature is preserved ... It is beautifully situated and conveniently planned; the grounds surrounding it are tastefully laid out. The staff consists of nine teachers, and all departments of study are under the charge of Specialists, who cannot be excelled in attainments, teaching ability, or in personal character; and parents may feel safe in committing their sons and daughters to their charge.[30]

Such facilities were beyond anything familiar to a girl from a struggling farm. OSCI's high-minded aims would have proved equally inspirational and congenial, namely,

> To give a sound, liberal, practical education, useful in every walk in life – the Home, the Farm, the Trades, Business, Teaching, the Professions, and the University;
>
> To impart useful information, but always to subordinate this to the knowledge of principles and the training and development of the faculties of mind and heart;
>
> To promote bodily health and vigor by encouraging exercise in field sports, and by training both sexes in calisthenics or gymnastics;
>
> Incidentally, to cultivate a literary taste, to lead to the formation of business habits, and to teach the lessons of a sound morality – self-discipline, submission to authority, reverence for what is sacred, and a love of things honest and of good report.[31]

Left unmentioned was the fact that Owen Sound, the so-called Chicago of the North, was a tough, hard-drinking harbour town.[32]

Despite the temptations of Owen Sound, the determinedly studious Laura kept to her books and her boarding house. The close scrutiny of her relatives reinforced the message. She nevertheless grew up fast, rushing home after the first classes to lower her hemline and braid her hair after critical comparison with urban classmates suggested that her watchful older sisters had tried to keep her a little girl "as long as possible." A further promise of maturity was the luxury, available only in the early morning, of a borrowed bicycle, one of the defining signs of the freedom claimed by New Women. As a collegiate student, Laura initiated a lifelong enthusiasm in joining the literary society, where members read beyond the curriculum and debated the ideas of their age.[33] Such experiences helped sustain the young Marshall in her regular return to farm chores.

Like many others from the rock-strewn peninsula, Laura found little to retain her when she finished at OSCI in 1899. Her brother Gilbert was probably already west, as was another male cousin, teaching his way through medical school. Eliza would soon be employed in Toronto. After a few months, perhaps spent teaching in the North-West Territories, the Saugeen's young New Woman was escorted to Vancouver by a paternal aunt, Kezia Marshall Carter of St. Catharines, Ontario. One of Laura's brothers purchased her railway ticket. She began her BC stay teaching outside of Vancouver, where, like other young teachers, she remembered her situation boarding with a local family as "sort of a dungeon."[34] In June 1901, she went to live with her newly married cousin Albert E. Carter and his wife, Cassie, in Vancouver's West End.

The Vancouver kin connection publicly affirmed the new arrival's middle-class status. Carter was a comfortably established building constructor, an original director and executive officer of the city's Builders' Exchange, which was founded in 1899 to control competition. In terms typical of a monopoly capitalist, though notably inclusive with regards to race, he robustly defended the exchange in the *Canadian Architect and Builder,* a professional journal:

> We decided that in these days of trusts, unions and combinations, organization was necessary in order that we might hold our own and keep abreast of the times ... We notice that in almost all progressive cities in Eastern Canada and the United States the builders had some kind of association ... There are rumors afloat to the effect that the exchange, by resorting to questionable methods, will attempt to limit competition or secure a corner on the building business ... but the public may rest assured that the members of our exchange are too shrewd to adopt any such short-sighted policy ... We consider that we are quite justified in limiting competition

> ... and that no one will suffer thereby. Any man, however, be he white or black, who can show our membership committee that he is prepared to do a legitimate business may become a member of the exchange by paying the same fee.[35]

Equally significantly, in 1909, Carter would become secretary-treasurer of the city's Employers' Association and would join the executive of the Good Government League two years later.[36] In 1917, he would assist the unsuccessful re-election campaign committee of Mayor Peter McBeath, who was also known as a supporter of woman suffrage. In testimony to the continuing significance of Ontario connections in Vancouver, McBeath hailed from Allenford, Bruce County, very near Laura's birthplace.[37] The estimable cousin Albert further testified to respectability by publicly supporting temperance, Methodism, and the YMCA. In 1920, Cassie Carter took the stage as a director of the Vancouver Children's Aid and three years later represented the Local Council of Women at a Methodist meeting for world peace.[38]

The Carters' only child took a different route into the middle class. Born soon after Laura's visit, Neal Marshall Carter (1902–78) would earn a PhD (1928) in organic chemistry from McGill and become a marine biologist at the University of British Columbia. Even as Albert encouraged Laura to act on the "adoration" she felt on first seeing the BC mountains,[39] he fostered similar feelings in his son. Neal would become an enthusiastic mountain climber, an early president of the BC Mountaineering Club, and a prominent member of the Alpine Club of Canada.[40] Such Vancouver relatives, with their respectability and authority, suggested that Laura would have a choice of politics when she arrived to stay.

Boarding with the Carters had the additional advantage of close proximity to the new Provincial Normal School that had begun operating out of the Vancouver High School in January 1901. Its free summer program had obvious appeal for the Carters' poor relation. The Model School for practice teaching ran in nearby Lord Roberts Elementary School.[41] The majority of would-be teachers in attendance were women, attracted by prospects for independence offered by one of the few professions open to their sex. By July 1901, with 1,077 marks out of 1,850 (the highest was 1,187), Laura had earned a third-class teaching certificate – grade B.[42] In October 1902, after she became a Normal School graduate with experience, her certificate was extended to three years.[43] Thus credentialed, she presented herself as a New Woman, committed to education and economic independence.[44]

Miss Marshall immediately started teaching in the province's hard-pressed primary schools, beginning with a few months in Webster's Corners, a village later absorbed in the Lower Mainland's eastern suburb of Maple Ridge. When wages there proved low and uncertain, she turned to the Rockies. Between 1902 and 1904, Laura took jobs in the new coal settlements of Michel and Fernie, the latter dubbed "the Pittsburgh of Canada,"[45] at about sixty dollars a month. At Michel, she taught in a one-room school "in a valley so narrow that, in winter, the sun came up behind one mountain at 12 noon, and went down behind another mountain an hour later," but the work helped her to "save money to pay for a course in University."[46]

Both Michel and Fernie were company towns, with a male majority drawn from all over the world. Their inhabitants stood on the front lines of the tough class politics of Canada's resource frontier. Militant male unionists battled low wages, brutal bosses, and underground disasters. In tiny towns, they shared close space with a diverse minority of black, Indigenous, and European women who could challenge conventions. The local press dubbed some of them "scarlet," "sporting" women or "soiled doves," the "object lesson of painted vice flaunting itself at every corner."[47] Such sights offered an Ontario farm girl further education in

Fernie, a BC Resource Town with Mountains, c. 1902 | Fernie Museum, FMP.00236

gender relations. In contrast, attendance at the local Methodist church and membership in the Fernie choir attested to what marked respectability for women.

Laura's students, younger girls and boys, and sometimes illiterate adults, provided other lessons in the life of mining communities. The mine manager had asked the Fernie principal for help in training his labour force since workers "who were unable to read the safety warnings were a great danger."[48] The sons and daughters of miners, commonly poorly clothed and fed, normally had brief childhoods. Boys might well go underground before they hit adolescence, and girls were often chained to the endless chores of poor households. Schooling did not release them from toil. Laura's workplace in Michel was inadequately heated by a potbellied stove, and it lacked plumbing; students who lived nearby brought water from home. Fernie's situation was demonstrably better, as the province had funded a new building, but improvements came glacially as parents and local ratepayers, including the dominant Crow's Nest Pass Coal Company, paid operational costs and generally resisted additional expenses. Children's ambitions were kept further in check since the valley lacked a high school until 1913. Hard-won knowledge of recurring privation for children and young people would not have been far from Laura's mind when she eventually presided over a juvenile court in 1927.

In 1903, the Fernie Public School boasted a multilingual enrolment of nearly four hundred, but its regular attendance was "the lowest of any school in the province."[49] For the next two years, two other mining communities stole this abysmal distinction, but it was never out of reach. Such learning and teaching conditions were sufficiently intimidating to deter even the brave. Few of the district's frequently inexperienced teachers stayed long. Only in 1921 did British Columbia make education compulsory for youngsters aged seven to fifteen and finally somewhat extend prospects for poorer pupils.

Boarding in private homes in the Kootenays gave Laura a heightened perspective on the class politics of the region. These were summed up by a *Fernie Free Press* journalist: "Low wages always mean discontent on the part of the worker and lead to the very evils which are most to be avoided in the interests of capital and labour ... a starved community, poor business men, and dull miserable towns ... bad for all alike."[50] Deaths from a 1902 explosion in underground operations that were commonly reckoned "among the most dangerous in the world" and the recurring threat of typhoid from unsanitary water offered similar edification.[51] The young refugee from agrarian poverty could also observe organized labour's frequent antipathy to Asians (matter-of-factly referred to in the local press as "Chinks" and "Japs") and Italians and eastern Europeans (similarly deemed "dagos" and "slavs"). Such economic rivals, who were assumed to make drudges of their own women, loomed as suspect intruders to hard-pressed British immigrants, many of whom were Scottish, and Canadian workers who sought to wrest a fair deal from a hard land and harder employers.[52] Unions, like organized women, had much to learn about inclusion and diversity, even as they crusaded during Laura's time in BC coal towns.

Brutal class relations underpinned radical politics. In 1908, the new coal-mining constituency of Rocky Mountain elected the first socialist to the new Alberta legislature. The continued re-election of former coal-miner Tom Uphill as Fernie alderman, mayor, and eleven-term MLA, first for the Federated Labour Party and later for the Fernie and District Labour Party, similarly spoke to class tensions. He flaunted himself as a man of the mines, someone who embodied labour's masculinist heritage.[53] As part of this portrayal, Uphill condemned wage-earning wives and female judges as ill-suited, ignorant, and nosey.[54] In other words, independent-minded and economically independent women should not question either his pre-eminence or that of others like him.

But during Laura's sojourn in the Rockies, there was more to observe than class, race, and gender politics. Although the Kootenay communities were surrounded with mountains scarred by stumps and fallen logs, the Elk Valley offered trails into high country that was still largely untouched by modern industry. A sympathetic ranch family occasionally loaned Laura and her pupils horses and ponies kept for the "big game hunters, coming from the East, New York and Pennsylvania."[55] Though less destructive than coal mining, such moneyed interlopers offered further reminders of the economics of resource exploitation. Fernie's attractions for an intrepid spirit were nevertheless profound. As Laura remembered, it "possessed the ideal setting. The mountains were not breathing down our necks. They were kept at a discreet distance, but most of them were very beautiful."[56] Wearing a shorter skirt and hobnailed boots, she was soon climbing with her students. By 1903, she was scrambling up the Lizard Range southeast of the coal mines, with elevations touching 2,360 metres. Those bright prospects stood in stark contrast to the human conflict and misery that flourished below.

In 1905, Laura's employment in western coal towns was put to good use subsidizing a degree in philosophy from the University of Toronto. Nor did she immediately leave teaching. Summer 1906 found her joining her homesteading brother Edward, who helped her secure a job at a nearby school in Saskatchewan. There, hardship went beyond isolation and water fouled with alkali to include "an absolute dearth of books in the community." This time, the new university coed turned to her Toronto church to acquire reading material from its Home Missionary Department.[57]

The ambitious orphan with a taste for reading was the sole member of her immediate family to attend university. She did not register at the Methodist Victoria College, which might have been expected to welcome her. Her choice, the officially non-sectarian University College (UC), enrolled Presbyterians, Anglicans, and other Protestants including many Methodists, but it also accepted a few Jewish coeds and the Catholic young women who were not admitted to Toronto's St. Michael's College until 1911. Laura's anomalous choice hinted at the ecumenicalism that she would publicly endorse as a more mature woman. UC had begun to admit female students in 1884, an integration that has been fairly described as a "path not strewn with roses."[58] In 1895, its female undergraduates participated in a controversial anti-administration college-wide boycott of classes that suggested a continuing willingness to contest notions of propriety for their sex.[59] Part of the second generation

Laura, far left, University College Women's Literary Society, probably before or after a skit, c. 1908 | Courtesy of the Jamieson family

of Canada's university coeds, Laura and others were still on trial in male-dominated space. "Ideas of both manliness and womanliness" that had been contentious upon women's admissions remained "in a fluid state of uncertainty."[60]

Over three years, Laura did very well in arts classes that included Latin, English, German, French, ancient history, mathematics, philosophy, psychology, logic, physics, and metaphysics. Religious knowledge, by which was meant Christianity, was also a prescribed course for all undergraduates. Although UC men benefitted from college residences, women were expected to lodge at home or in boarding houses until the first "makeshift" building became available in 1905. Nothing permanent would exist until the 1930s.[61] Nor were all of Toronto's faculties officially open to women when Laura arrived, with medicine, for example, barring coeds until 1906. Until then, the alternative was the Ontario Medical College for Women, founded by feminists in 1884. Female faculty were rare everywhere, and there is no evidence that Laura ever had a female instructor.

Nor had long-standing resistance to coeducation disappeared. Indeed, it resurfaced officially in Laura's last year, 1907–08. Women's growing numbers and their overcrowding in limited space, not to mention their success in winning prizes, roused familiar reservations. A 1908 Senate report by history professor George M. Wrong repeated old calls for separate provisions for women. In the face of strong opposition from female alumnae, administrators, and the city's University Women's Club to any hint of inferior funding and second-class status, the proposal quickly disappeared, but its odour remained.[62] Even superior students such as Laura had to know that their interests were not ultimately central to the institution they adorned.

Despite prejudice, women students increased their proportion of Toronto's arts faculty from about 30 percent (250) in 1900 to 49 percent (574) in 1911.[63] Elsewhere, in science and the professional faculties, other than education and household science, they were far fewer. Students of colour were still more unusual. Only one such woman has been identified during Laura's tenure at Toronto. This African West Indian, the daughter of a barrister, was admitted before the administration at the Anglican St. Hilda's College realized that she was black.[64] Laura's university world was far whiter than the community she had surveyed in the Kootenays and readily confirmed a worldview centred on Anglo-Celts.

For all its limits, Toronto offered its coeds critical access to knowledge and credentialing, invaluable resources for the era's New Women, with their hopes for economic independence. In the social sciences, a strain of thought promised empowerment. Like many others, including Ishbel Aberdeen, a leading global activist with close ties to Canada, Laura seized upon the theories of the British sociologist Benjamin Kidd (1858–1916), whose influential writings, *Social Evolution* (1894) and, later, *The Science of Power* (1919), stressed the role of both religious faith and women in human progress. "Because women were the bearers and rearers of children, and so were primarily responsible for the continuation of the race, so he said," as she recalled much later, "they were bound to be creative in their mental and emotional outlook, once they were enlightened, and would take the long view in their work for society." That belief bolstered lifelong optimism. Even as she moved away from traditional religion, Laura would credit women with the capacity to "do something concrete and constructive" in contributing to human betterment.[65] Never extinguished by personal tragedies and public setbacks, such confidence was at least the match for other socialists' reliance on the awakening of the proletariat.

From the start, despite her limited funds, Laura proved a notably active member of her graduating class. It is not clear whether she boarded with a respectable family or resided in the renovated private house, Queen's Hall, which in 1908 became UC's first female residence but could hold less than a quarter of its coeds. Boarding with a family, generally a cheaper option, was more likely. It did, however, involve the inconvenience of finding new housing every year. It is also possible that she shared premises with her sister Eliza, who was employed nearby.

The disparity between accommodation for female and male students was repeated in facilities in general. Women would not gain access to the University of Toronto Historical Club, created in 1903, until the 1960s. Celebrated by the *Toronto Globe* in 1906 as "the best known and most prominent of the departmental societies," it met "in the homes of prominent men and professors and entertained prominent male visitors."[66] The similarly prestigious Hart House, with its prized social, cultural, and athletic opportunities, remained closed to women until 1971. The message of second-class status for female challengers was clear.

Undeterred, Laura made the most of her associations "with other women in the multitude of religious, literary, athletic, and social clubs and societies within which they created what they liked to call a 'little sphere' all their own," a counter to "their status as relative newcomers to the male-dominated colleges."[67] She quickly proved a keen debater and fencer, both relatively recent skills for Canadian coeds. During the years that Laura was at Toronto, "the UC Women's Literary Society debated against the Round Table Club [probably from the city's Conservatory of Music] that the women of Canada should have the same franchise rights as the men of Canada (affirmative), and against St. Hilda's College on nationalism and on whether there should be a separate college for women (negative)."[68] She was vice-president of her class in 1907, on the board of the *Torontonensis,* the university yearbook, the following year, and a member of the YWCA and the University College Women's Literary Society – the latter which engaged students in debates, theatrical productions, and musical performances.[69] It built community and introduced many coeds to self-government, all very useful for young women

Laura Marshall, graduation, University of Toronto, 1908 | Courtesy of the Jamieson family

who were committed to making their way in the world and changing it as they advanced.[70] In 1905, UC activists were among the Toronto group that established the University Athletic League (for women students).

Coeds also looked to the YWCA for sociability and action. Originating in England in 1855, it arrived in New Brunswick in 1870 and became a Canadian national organization in 1895. It focused an uncertain mix of Protestant evangelicalism and feminism on education, employment, and housing for young women. Its largely middle-class employees and volunteers set out to demonstrate the benefits of discipline and industry to working-class and immigrant girls and women. In an age when democracy was expanding, this clientele's potential for immorality was seen as threatening the very foundations of social peace and the "future of the race," a term that generally meant Anglo-Celts. Inspirational leadership in programs that emphasized domestic training, healthy bodies, and practical Protestantism was intended to make female beneficiaries into good Christian citizens on the model of the middle-class workers and volunteers. Y programs were closely tied to the social gospel, designed to engineer "a new Christian social order" in which women would have an honoured place.[71]

Many coeds found the Y's affirmation of female value and ability a powerful counter to pervasive misogyny. Its programs, essentially a form of internship or apprenticeship in social work, provided critical sources of authority. UC recruits and others with similar social backgrounds were expected to "take charge of two meetings a month, in one of the city missions" and "to prepare to send representations to the conference of hundreds of women of the Universities, great and small, of the Eastern States, who meet every year."[72] Family ties often reinforced their commitment. Laura could take personal inspiration from her sister Eliza's outreach at the nearby downtown Fred Victor Mission, which ministered to the poorest residents of Toronto. As a nursing deaconess, Eliza offered one career model for ambitious young women.

In joining other coeds to volunteer for Evangelia House, Canada's pioneering city settlement addressing urban poverty and distress in the east end of Toronto, Laura participated in one of the Y's remedies for the so-called girl problem.[73] Founded in 1902 and modelled on London's Toynbee Hall and New York City's Christadora House, Evangelia initially concentrated on rescuing girls and young women who were believed to be at moral and physical risk in the new industrial and retail jobs. By 1905, it had broken its formal links to the YWCA when it extended services to boys and men. British Protestants formed the majority of early clients, but by the time Laura graduated in 1908, more suspect southern and eastern European newcomers were using settlement clubs and services in much the same way as they did in the Winnipeg All People's Mission, organized by Methodist minister James S. Woodsworth, who would later be a friend of Laura's.[74] Such missions were "expected to provide leadership to working class women, and later men" and to ensure "women's domestic role inside the home, and men's role as breadwinners," with "middle-class family forms, social relationships, lifestyles and attitudes to work" the desired result.[75] Much like schools and many youth organizations, the settlement houses concentrated on "citizenship training," intended to foster "the ideals of democratic citizenship, and the norms of class and gender relations in a capitalist parliamentary democracy."[76]

Like many classrooms, Evangelia House offered concrete benefits. It set up Toronto's "first supervised playground, penny savings bank, a kindergarten, a three bed infirmary, a free dispensary, a pure milk depot, and a well-baby clinic."[77] Frequently consigned to cramped and unsanitary spaces, and unsafe food and drink, city dwellers had good reason to join, if not agree with, their would-be saviours. The observation from one Toronto volunteer that "for some portion of the week at least, the sordidness passes out of their lives, and they begin to comprehend the idea of culture, in a limited and primitive form certainly, but the seed is sown" reflected both the desire to help and the sense of entitlement that inspired many volunteers.[78] Such inspirations continued into the emerging profession of social work for which some coeds were effectively interning.[79]

Settlement house influences, like those in teaching, could go both ways. Much later, Laura remembered a mentor's suggestion that Y clients had much to offer volunteers:

> You must know about how they earn their living; the condition under which they live and work; the wages they are paid. You women must know these things before you can do much to help them. Women who have the education and ability must know about the hundreds of thousands of other women in this country before they can help the latter to live a good life, a happy life to which they are entitled. These women may be closer to you than you think.[80]

Laura's retention of this advice suggested receptivity to diverse perspectives. Girls and women who lived in difficult circumstances were not necessarily inferior. That message may have helped prompt Laura's graduating year poem, which embraced the search for "Truth."[81]

Fernie's schools might have been left behind when Laura entered university, but the Rockies were not. The University of Toronto yearbook identified her as one of a select group of women who were active members of the Alpine Club of Canada.[82] In fact, in the first decade of the twentieth century, the Alpine Club proved a treasure trove of New Women. Elizabeth Parker, a *Winnipeg Free Press* journalist and YWCA activist, partnered the surveyor Arthur Oliver Weaver in founding it in 1906. Laura recalled spending ten days in July 1906 at its first camp in Yoho Park, British Columbia. Rules made it very clear that only women who were prepared to reject convention were welcome: "No lady climbing, who wears skirts, will be allowed to take a place on a rope, as they are a distinct source of danger to the entire party. Knickerbockers or bloomers with puttees or gaiters and sweater will be found serviceable and safe." This version of dress reform, a long-time suffrage cause, proved no deterrent to Laura. Alongside fifteen other "ladies" and twenty-seven men who climbed Mount Vice-President (10,049 feet above sea level), she graduated to active membership at the 1906 camp.[83] A year later, one-third of Alpine Club members were female, confirming the lure of physical challenges for New Women.

In the summer of 1907, the Toronto coed used an office job in the new mining town of Taber, Alberta, to finance her final year of studies. Again, she felt the pull of the Rockies. Along with a female friend from Fernie, she made up a group of four men and three women to climb Crow's Nest Pass Mountain, putting her name with the others in the cairn at its peak. Laura eventually proudly claimed the ascent of ten mountains, "2 of them in the 10,000 foot class," between 1901 and 1907.[84] The experience was sweet. Back in Ontario's Queen City in the fall, she "would take out my blue and white sweater and hold it to my face. It smelt of fir feathers, pine needles and wood smoke. It was months before I could bring myself to wash it."[85] Such memories anchored her when she tackled academic and professional summits.

A comparison of the brief biographies of women graduates in the 1908 Toronto yearbook shows that Laura stood out from the throng. Her diverse accomplishments, ranging from excellent grades to leadership in student athletics, societies, and debates, as well as volunteering at Evangelia House, made her "one of the few possessing sufficient energy and skill to play a leading part in every activity open to women students."[86] That impressive record was maintained even when, unlike most of her peers, she worked during the summers to finance her education and laboured from time to time on the Saugeen family farm.

None of the official coed biographies reveal suffrage sympathies. This omission suggests their still controversial nature. In fact, Laura's UC class had won a debate favouring votes for women, and the YWCA and settlement houses regularly attracted suffrage loyalists as professionals and volunteers. This was hardly surprising. Activists such as Toronto's Emily Howard Stowe had forced universities to open to female students, including Laura's alma mater. In the years before the First World War, Toronto itself was a centre of Canadian suffragism. Debates were ubiquitous in the press, as were petitions to the Ontario legislature. Laura's direct involvement cannot, however, be glimpsed. Explanations for this probably owe something to her outsider and economically marginal status. Dominated by middle-class professionals who had established roots and networks, the Toronto suffrage movement was far removed from a young newcomer who was hard pressed to pay her tuition.

Immediately after graduating in 1908, Laura has proven difficult to find. She may have worked for the Y, probably at Evangelia. With the governor general as guest of honour, it had opened a new building in downtown Toronto in October 1907, which required additional staffing. Few executive members of University College's Women's Literary Society took up social work; most graduated into teaching or marriage, the latter a choice that forced the great majority to forego paid employment.[87] The Y's 1907 decision to extend operations into work with female factory operatives nevertheless opened up new opportunities.[88] They attracted ambitious New Women who accepted Christian doctrine but wanted greater independence and a more autonomous female community than labours within traditional Christian churches, such as Laura's sister Eliza had chosen, usually permitted.

A small group of middle-class women activists in Stratford, Ontario, the home of railways, furniture making, and food processing, seized the initiative and appointed Laura as the general secretary for the new Y they organized in 1909–10. This choice would have been highly unlikely if she hadn't come recommended by Evangelia's reform-minded leaders. In entering, as she said, upon "a whole new set of social duties,"[89] Laura found herself far from Toronto's resources and soon, like the local Y itself, at odds with factory owners who counted on nearby farm girls for cheap and docile labour. Women's success in making Stratford the first city in the province to introduce domestic science as integral to schooling, in effect recognizing the dignity and skill of much female labour,[90] was not matched by victories in the paid labour force. Employers' hold on the community became all the tighter after the Grand Trunk Railway expanded its major repair shops in the downtown area in 1909. That powerful corporation, with its insistence upon an open shop, affirmed its civic authority by paying a third of the costs of the new YMCA and providing the electricity from its powerhouse to heat the pool.[91] Like the International Association of Machinists, a union that started Canadian operations in Stratford in 1890, feminists, even camouflaged as Christian activists, were strained to challenge entrenched relations that kept female workers in line in candy, paper box, biscuit, and other factories.[92] Despite the machinists' resort to a lengthy strike in 1905–07 and admission of women to equal membership in the union in 1911, relations were hard to shift.[93]

In comparison with that of Toronto, the Stratford Y seemed unable to find critical support for its message of middle-class responsibility for girls and young women, and it stumbled during its first decade. Laura's stint in its service from 1910 to 1911 was not, however, wasted. It sharpened her appreciation of the difficulties facing both working-class Canadians and progressive reformers. In addressing Stratford's labour conditions, she, like Mildred Osterhout Fahrni, another feminist similarly associated with the Y's industrial programs whom she met in Vancouver, found cause to look beyond the resources of evangelically minded, if sometimes feminist, philanthropy when it came to assisting women and workers.[94]

In any case, like most young working women of all classes, Miss Marshall would not spend her lifetime in paid employment. When she married at age twenty-nine in August 1911, she was expected to leave waged work behind. As a wife, she was to support her husband in his labours, run the household, and produce children. Training in teaching and social service was to be directed to volunteer efforts in the wider community, not to bringing the economic independence so much prized by New Women. In the context of wedlock, the meaning of freedom needed to be negotiated.

After marriage, female opportunities very much depended on the choice of husbands. As far as surviving records allow us to know, Laura Marshall selected well. Like many others, she chose a man whose background resembled her own. John Stuart Jamieson (1877–1926), known by family and friends as Jack, was born to a farm family similar in size to the Marshalls but located on better land just outside Galt, Ontario. His Presbyterian Scottish household was typical of those who assumed they had the moral and physical resources to run Canada. His very name invoked the leading liberal theorist of the day, John Stuart Mill. It was a good fit with the politics he would pursue. Jack's sisters, like Laura's, included a nurse as one expression of New Womanhood. Money was not abundant on the family farm, but ambition was.

Jack and Laura had ample occasion to meet as activist students at University College during 1905–08, but family lore suggests that they encountered each other as ambitious teachers in the Canadian west. In any case, their courtship evolved slowly. Immediate marriage would have been very difficult as both had to work their way through university and took time to establish themselves in employment. The wait undoubtedly tested their relationship, even as it enabled Jack to demonstrate his commitment to equality for women and to generally more liberal views. It also permitted Laura to gain experience in the extent of urban problems and solutions that empowered women.

As a teenager, Jack had earned a third-class teaching certificate from a prestigious local institution, Galt Collegiate Institute. Employment in small schools in Ontario, Nova Scotia, and the west financed his degree in philosophy from University College. Though his grades did not match those of his future wife, the graduating yearbook singled him out as a varsity athlete, president of the Class Debating Society, and vice-president of the Literary and Scientific Society (familiarly known as the Lit).[95] The goals of the latter were to produce excellent public speakers and promote "gentlemanly conduct" among young men who were intended to join Ontario's, indeed Canada's, elites in business, religion, and the professions.[96]

Even as he applied himself to the arts curriculum, Jack simultaneously attended theology classes at Knox College, the leading training school for Canada's Presbyterian clergy. At this time, Knox was well known for liberal theology and as a noted centre of progressive Christian thought.[97] Key influences were the Scottish idealist theologians T.H. Green and Henry Drummond, both of whom supported higher education for women and more inclusive citizenship.[98] Drummond was also the Glasgow academic whose insistence on God's abundant love and the inevitability of human progress assigned a prominent place to women in creating a more humane, Christian, and liberal order. That inspiration helped mobilize many contemporary feminists, including Ishbel, the Countess of Aberdeen, who in 1893 as an international feminist reformer and wife of the governor general founded the National Council of Women of Canada, to which Laura would later belong.[99]

In Toronto, Jack seemed destined for the ministry. Indeed, he served for a few months as an assistant minister at Montreal's Crescent Street Presbyterian Church and was ordained in the Ottawa-Montreal Presbytery in 1909, a year after his graduation with a bachelor's of arts. In 1909, however, Jack joined a tiny pool of University College Lit officers (some 4 percent of them between 1891 and 1921) in setting out for British Columbia.[100] Until he joined the United Church of Canada when it emerged in 1924, he remained an active Presbyterian, serving as an elder at Gordon

John Stuart Jamieson, University of Toronto, c. 1908 | Courtesy of the Jamieson family

Presbyterian Church, which was founded in November 1911 in Burnaby's Edmonds neighbourhood.

By 1910, however, Jack Jamieson had chosen the law, not the church, as his primary instrument for earning a living and improving the world. That year, the provincial Law Society welcomed him as a Quebec barrister and solicitor who stood highest in the BC bar admission examinations. By 1911, he was employed in private practice in downtown Vancouver with Alex D. Wilson, a fellow University of Toronto graduate and member of the prestigious Seaforth Highlanders (itself established only in November

1910 by H.O. Bell-Irving and other prominent Scots in the young city). Wilson would be one of the witnesses at Jack and Laura's wedding. A newly established Vancouver practice did not prove sufficiently lucrative, and Jack soon enhanced his income as a police court prosecutor for the City of Burnaby. The scene seemed set for his entry into the comfortable professional circles of the Lower Mainland.

However, Jack's liberal principles were also on early display. In April 1911, he went on record as a defence lawyer, albeit unsuccessfully, asking for a suspended sentence in a criminal case involving the theft of cattle, arguing that it would be better not "to leave the stigma of a term in prison hanging over the two young men for the rest of their lives."[101] The same month saw him speaking to a joint gathering of the Local Council of Women, the University Women's Club, the Women's Canadian Club, and the Political Equality League on "legal points in the laws affecting women and children." Very much the liberal idealist, the newcomer to the province saluted British laws and justice as "the finest" in the world and declared his faith in evolution and "fair play" for their improvement. "There was no place," he asserted, "for discouragement" in the campaign for reforms in matters such as dower rights and child custody.[102]

Such views marked Jack Jamieson as a man who was "sufficiently free from prejudice and old world trammels to consider with dispassionate common-sense and freedom from arrogant egotism, the possibility of advanced legislation" and to value "the worth, comradeship, and good judgment of the women." Local suffragists hailed such figures as crucial supporters of the rights of women in "an age of progress."[103] In other words, well before Laura married him, Jack was already at home with the arguments of the province's first women suffrage conference that met in Vancouver on May 5, 1911.

Almost three decades had taken the girl from the Saugeen Peninsula on a voyage of significant self-discovery and accomplishment. This passage may have been unique in its details, but it corresponded to trajectories marked out by many New Women. Unlike their mother, Laura and her sister Eliza would have significant educational and professional opportunities. Even as they did not question the privileges of European settlers, they challenged the constraints of a marginal rural economy and tested themselves in broader worlds. Though Eliza stayed with her church, the better-educated Laura strayed. By turning from teaching to social work with the YWCA, she staked out claims in secular society. As a young spinster with few financial resources, she became dependent on a labour market that rarely favoured outspoken women. The precarious post in Stratford offered uncertain traction in bettering the world. She would next test women's opportunities in a modern marriage of educational and professional equals.

2

The New Woman as Wife, Suffragist, and Activist, 1911–18

On August 1, 1911, Laura Marshall and Jack Jamieson exchanged vows in Vancouver. Only two unrelated people stood as witnesses, and no family members, such as Albert and Cassie Carter, appeared in an official capacity. That ceremony, which publicly decoupled the key players from their kin, raised the possibility of a fresh start on gender relations. In a modern marriage, reform-minded wives and husbands such as Laura and Jack might find freedom to pursue both hopes for domestic intimacy and a meaningful contribution to public life. Not to be forgotten in this evolution were middle-class and Anglo-Celtic privileges that, despite the Vancouver couple's initial struggles for security, placed them within the mainstream elite of the dominion.

Soon after their wedding, the Jamiesons set off to hike Haida Gwaii (then known as the Queen Charlotte Islands). There, they were photographed before the villages of the Haida, whom the 1911 *Encyclopedia Britannica* described as "the finest race" and "most advanced in the arts, of the entire west coast of North America" but "reduced in number and spirit."[1] What the visitors made of this experience has not survived. Laura, like other suffragists, showed little public interest in Indigenous rights.[2] Indigenous petitions and organizations for justice were nevertheless active in British Columbia. Su-á-pu-luck, popularly known as Squamish chief Joseph Capilano (1854–1910), had long campaigned for land, hunting, and fishing rights. He would die just before Laura and Jack set up house, but his friend E. Pauline Johnson, the well-known Mohawk English performer and writer, whose work Laura prized, would live in

Vancouver until her death in 1913. Her best-selling *Legends of Vancouver* (1911) provided critical reminders of the people whom the newcomers had displaced. The destruction of the city's Kitsilano Reserve and dispossession of the Squamish similarly backdropped the early years of the Jamieson marriage. Although Laura came to sympathize with Indigenous communities, real engagement from her family awaited her son Stuart, who became the first Canadian economist to co-write with an Indigenous collaborator, and later her granddaughter, choreographer-dancer Karen Jamieson, who collaborated with First Nations artists.

Injuries such as British Columbia's 1874 disenfranchisement of the Chinese and First Nations, the 1885 federal "head tax" on Chinese immigrants, the 1907 anti-Japanese riots in Vancouver, or the 1914 exclusion of the *Komagata Maru* carrying Punjabi migrants rarely disturbed assumptions of the British right to set the rules. Newcomers Laura and Jack entered a highly racialized and taken-for-granted world of exclusion and entitlement.

Like others, they drew deeply on both religious faith and a pervasive belief in racial hierarchy. Jack, the former Presbyterian minister, found inspiration in Methodist social gospeller James S. Woodsworth. At the August 1913 meeting of the missionary committee of Vancouver's Grandview Methodist Church, Jack led a discussion of Woodsworth's influential 1909 study of immigration, *Strangers within Our Gates.* Many progressive Canadians shared its exaltation of the Scots, misgivings about the English and southern and eastern Europeans, and suspicion of Asians, blacks, and Indians. In teaching the girls' Sunday School class at Gordon Presbyterian Church, Laura drew similarly on beliefs that often took superiority for granted.[3] Ethnicity's significance in claims to leadership was affirmed by her "Scotch readings," a recitation of poems by Robbie Burns, in the same church, and by an early twentieth-century photograph showing her in a Highland kilt.[4] Religion and ethnicity went hand in hand in confirming respectability for such British settlers and, equally, in denying it to others.

Upon their return to the Lower Mainland from Haida Gwaii, the newlyweds soon moved to the suburb of Burnaby, which another arrival in the same year recalled as a "wild frontier" that lacked municipal water services.[5] Their California bungalow home on two and one-half acres was relatively cheap, with easy access to the new interurban railway that ran between Vancouver and New Westminster. Settlers' tickets, at $3.50 for fifty rides, connected passengers to Vancouver streetcars.[6] Jack, Laura, and visitors easily commuted from and to downtown employments and entertainments. Soon enough, their residence was a lively hub of progressive debate and planning. In the settler habit of erasing Indigenous spaces, they called it Thrums, referencing *A Window in Thrums* (1889) by popular Scottish novelist James Barrie, the author of *Peter Pan.*

Laura's family duties quickly accelerated. As a wife and mother, she managed, with the help of one or two white female servants, an increasingly busy household, which initially lacked electricity and running water. She gave birth to Laura Jean in 1912, Stuart Marshall in 1914, and Angus Bruce in 1917. Early in 1918, she collapsed and entered the Kamloops Tranquille Sanatorium for treatment of tuberculosis.[7] Still worse was the death in March of that year of ten-month-old Angus. Such events help explain why, when she corresponded with Catherine Cleverdon, the author of the classic study *The Woman Suffrage Movement in Canada* (1950), she placed herself on the margins of suffrage action. As she explained, "I wish I could give you more of the information you wish; but at the time we got the suffrage in B.C. I had young children & did none of the recording or business of organization. My contribution was mainly public speaking at meetings that were arranged by those who had more leisure."[8] In fact, her summary was misleading. Vancouver newspapers show that Laura's Burnaby home was a centre for reform agitation. Offspring did not immobilize a determined New Woman.

As Laura and Jack began housekeeping as part of a growing population of young professionals,[9] the suffrage movement in the BC Lower Mainland shifted into high gear. Provincial expressions of that great cause had existed since the 1870s, when the BC government introduced the municipal franchise for property-holding spinsters and widows (revoked 1908). Between 1884 and 1890, some eleven women suffrage bills were introduced in the BC legislature, and Victoria feminists presented their first petition to the legislature in 1885. In 1889, female householders won the urban school board franchise (revoked 1892). Only the bill for the provincial suffrage presented by Labour MLA Ralph Smith came near to success, but it too was defeated on second reading in 1899. These early efforts, which focused on votes for white women, cited justice as they commonly assumed female moral superiority and the need to remake the masculinist imperial frontier.[10] Momentum in British Columbia and elsewhere proved hard to maintain after Prime Minister John A. Macdonald failed to bring in federal enfranchisement for women (or Indians or Asians) in 1885.[11] Patriarchy's defenders – west coast Conservative politicians among them – frustrated, enraged, and exhausted activists. Feminism was never for the timid. Just as in the United States, in Canada and British Columbia, "everyone was brave."[12]

When Laura and Jack arrived, insult and injury remained omnipresent in settings from banks to schools, professional societies, and churches. Vancouver women could not so much as possess a library card without a man's approval. Mothers had limited rights to the custody of their daughters and sons. Female job-seekers were barred from many employments, including the legal profession until 1912; those they could enter offered less reward. And everywhere women were subject to the sexual double standard and were vulnerable to violence. In response, in a clear expression of the personal as political, settler activists, most of whom were middle class, readily prioritized their own oppression and passed over the suffering of others.

The pioneering BC feminist novel *Is It Just?* (1911) set out the dominant perspective in its tragic tale of Mary Pierce, a respectable white woman whose husband squanders resources and causes her death. The author was Minnie Smith. Born in Peachland, British Columbia, she graduated from Ontario's McMaster College in 1894 and was a member of the WCTU and the Women's Institute.[13] Indignation was fanned by a series of pamphlets written between 1913 and 1939 by Vancouver suffragist Helen Gregory MacGill (1864–1947), which disclosed laws that injured BC women and children.[14] The pervasive acceptance of inequality was confirmed in the January 1914 referendum that Victoria suffragists had the city put to the propertied male electorate after some forty years of intense effort. Its question, "Is it desirable that the Municipal, Provincial and Federal franchise be extended to women on equal terms with men voters?" garnered less than 54 percent support, revealing the misogynist bedrock that would long frustrate Laura and other feminists. By the beginning of the twentieth century, Victoria suffragists no longer captained provincial agitation. Laura and Jack arrived just as the Lower Mainland became the political heart of the BC franchise campaigns.

Early suffragists were handicapped by the initially non-partisan policy of Local Councils of Women, which were established throughout the province beginning in the 1890s, but this stance was shifting during the first decade of the twentieth century. By the time of the Jamiesons' marriage, the National Council of Women of Canada and its local councils had publicly endorsed suffrage, and University Women's Clubs (UWC) had emerged in both Victoria and Vancouver to mobilize well-educated activists, many with personal histories of professional and educational discrimination. Laura would find an immediate community in such groups. Left-wing political parties, such as the Canadian Socialist League, the Social Democratic Party, and the BC Socialist Party, further strengthened the cause. Though rarely prioritizing the vote, such radical allies supported universal suffrage and raised consciousness about women's rights. A few activists, such as the English-born suffragette Helena Gutteridge (1879–1960), who also arrived in Vancouver in 1911 and later became Laura's friend, influentially connected suffrage and working-class politics.

In Burnaby, the Jamiesons found themselves immersed in an early and continuing stronghold of the left. Progressive networks, which included unionists, public health nurses, social workers, teachers, and politicians, quickly informed life at Thrums. A few visitors were socialists; others were liberals, some of whom, in the fluid politics of the day, retained working-class sympathies.[15] Local activists would figure significantly in Laura's future. In January 1914, Social Democratic Party candidate Ernest Winch, later a long-serving CCF MLA and Laura's colleague, ran for Burnaby council and school board, calling "for the public ownership of all public utilities, the initiative, referendum, and recall, and scientific accounting, efficiency, and 'fullest public service' in government." What would have been of special interest to Laura was Winch's support for sex education and "equal pay for equal work, irrespective of sex."[16] His endorsement of these causes helps explain why the Burnaby suffragist found the BC left increasingly attractive.

Laura encountered other kindred spirits among the New Women who abounded in the Lower Mainland. The unionist Gutteridge was a veteran of the militant Pankhurst-led Women's Social and Political Union. Before arriving in British Columbia, Helen Gregory MacGill and her mother had joined campaigns in Minnesota and California. Elite Liberal and co-founder of the Vancouver UWC, Evlyn Fenwick Farris (1878–1971) discovered early inspiration as a coed and teacher in New Brunswick and New England. At the same time, BC newspapers covered global campaigns, including the 1910 victory in adjacent Washington state, and British and US suffragists joined Canadian sympathizers as regular visitors. Vancouver may have been on the margins of the British Empire, but it was not a political backwater to many of its residents, who knew full well that New Women in diverse guises claimed respect and freedom.

Although history and morality largely justified imperial and middle-class rule for many suffragists, dissenters also appeared. In particular, the frequently polarized nature of provincial politics kept the injuries of class regularly in view. Although Liberal-Labour alliances were at best uncertain, provincial Liberals sometimes embraced working-class voters in an "anti-elitist" effort to distinguish themselves from more conservative rivals for power.[17] The careers of Liberal-Labour suffragists Ralph and Mary

Ellen Smith were grounded in just those links.[18] Occasional sympathy "laid the foundation for co-operation between the primarily middle class suffrage societies and working class suffrage groups."[19] Race proved a hardier barrier. Only very slowly after the First World War would anti-racism mobilize a significant group of settler women, notably in the Women's International League for Peace and Freedom under Laura's leadership. In the suffrage crusade, however, partnerships between progressive women and men, and sometimes between classes, were far more likely to question gender and class privilege.

In 1910 and 1911 respectively, Victoria and Vancouver established the first suffrage groups – the Political Equality Leagues (PELs). They welcomed both sexes and have rightly been designated "the commencement of the second and the final phase of the woman suffrage movement" in British Columbia.[20] In August 1911, the very month that Laura and Jack married, the Vancouver PEL set out to register female property owners and tenants entitled to the municipal franchise.[21] A year later, the Victoria PEL launched *The Champion,* the province's first suffrage weekly. Its slogan, "The Woman's Cause Is Man's," which it borrowed from the British poet Alfred, Lord Tennyson, aligned both sexes in the ascent of civilization.[22] Soon its front-page sketch of a young white woman with an early version of the provincial shield, featuring "Fiat Justitia" (let justice be done) just above the setting sun, highlighted its racialized vision of human rights.[23]

The 1911 and 1912 election defeats of the federal and provincial Liberals stimulated reflection on recruiting voters and the meaning of liberal principles. The recalcitrance of Conservative premier Richard McBride, memorably captured by contemporaries and later historians as the "People's Dick," spurred activism.[24] Little wonder that British visitor Bessie Pullen-Burry concluded in 1912 that "nowhere in the Dominion are the intellectual and sociological interests of the sex more to the fore than they are on the Pacific coast."[25] Ranged against McBride and William John Bowser, his successor from 1915, was a movement increasingly headed by New Women.

In the course of rapid growth, the suffrage movement became more complex. In 1913, some members left the Victoria PEL to form the Women's Freedom Union, known as the "Go Aheads." In Vancouver, Gutteridge led the BC Woman's Suffrage League when it broke from the Pioneer PEL to link to the Labor Temple. And though mainstream newspapers featured middle-class activism, the *British Columbia Federationist* proudly counted "Miners Wives [as] Keen Suffragists."[26] Mounting working-class

The "Great Cause" in British Columbia | *The Champion*, August 1912

mobilization was demonstrated in the formation of the BC Home and Domestic Employees Union in March 1913, the very day that clubwomen sold a special women's edition of the *Vancouver Sun* newspaper in support of a Women's Building. How such heterogeneity could be harnessed for practical purposes challenged would-be leaders, including Laura.

Like many elsewhere, BC suffragists emphasized two different, albeit related, approaches. The most familiar stressed women's essentially maternal or altruistic nature and the need for its protection and extension into the public sphere. This was the origin of the "militant mothering" ideology that inspired some women in the Canadian left during the twentieth century.[27] The second claim focused on justice, what would later be called human rights, and targeted women's paid employment. That latter perspective, very much associated with New Women, but not restricted to them, was evident in the first issue of *The Champion,* with its insistence that the cause was "not a Woman's Movement, not even a Feminist Movement, but a Humanist Movement."[28] Distinction between the two perspectives was not necessarily that between conservatism and radicalism. Maternalism's insertion of gender and domestic labour into the political narrative could question patriarchal (and even class and race) authority, and humanism's "same rights" orientation often did little to reorient values that prioritized male, and white, ways of being. More significantly, suffragists' ability to claim and even blend both justifications broadened their appeal.

Whatever their orientation, BC feminists constantly contended with charges that they were becoming "unsexed" or "unwomanly." The Victoria suffrage leader and co-editor of *The Champion* repudiated slurs even as she conceded that "several of our English members became militant under the conditions of the women in England." She was nevertheless sympathetic: "Personally, I am not a militant and abhor the methods used in England. I stand, however, with uncovered head and without censure before the brave women who are fighting so fearlessly, so fiercely for imprisoned womanhood and childhood, which have nothing but poverty, misery and degradation to call their own."[29] Though public censure continued to curb many British Columbians, Laura arrived just as unprecedented numbers questioned malestream conventions about proper womanhood.

When the Great War broke out in August 1914, suffrage initially took a back seat to other forms of patriotism. This did not, however, require forgetting rights for women. Laura, generally identified as Mrs. J. Stuart Jamieson, soon spoke for the UWC on the board of the Women's Employment League, founded in October 1914 at the Labor Temple. Set up "to find work for all, and to give financial aid," it insisted "that any woman or girl, out of work may register without hesitation, and without feeling that she is in any way asking for charity." Applicants were sent to the league secretary, Helena Gutteridge.[30] Though girls and women soon found plentiful jobs in the burgeoning wartime economy, neither Gutteridge nor Jamieson forgot their cause.

Like many liberal-minded contemporaries, Laura had high hopes for cross-class efforts. As she explained to the Pioneer PEL a few days after the creation of the employment league, "present conditions should open the eyes of women generally to the fact that woman's political equality and her economic status are inseparably bound up ... The suffrage societies should appeal to the women upon their economic status."[31] Taking up her own challenge in January 1915, she assumed the presidency of the new Burnaby Women's Forum, with its goals of "equal pay for equal work and an equal moral standard for all," a revealing mix of socialist and bourgeois causes.[32] Like its Vancouver counterpart (1912), the group targeted

INTRODUCED FIGHT FOR MINIMUM WAGE

Burnaby Women's Forum Has Been Aotive in Impressing Importance of the Measure Before Legislators.

MRS. J. STUART JAMIESON, who first introduced the minimum wage question in the Burnaby Women's Forum several years ago, and who has been untiring in her efforts to secure the passing of the important measure.

Champion of minimum wage | *Vancouver Sun*, March 10, 1918, reproduced by Supra Design, Victoria

legislators.[33] The forum anticipated the demands of the Minimum Wage League, led by Gutteridge from 1918. Nor was fair pay its only economic demand: in December 1915, Laura toasted a successful eight-year crusade for shorter holiday hours in stores. She trusted that "the troubles of the past year have softened people's hearts and awakened their consciences to such an extent that they will be glad to cooperate in bettering conditions of workers in industrial lines. We cannot do better service in preparing for the period of readjustment which must inevitably follow the war than securing the best possible conditions of work."[34] From the start, the recent BC resident made economic reform key to social improvement.

During the global conflict, suffragists may have spent less time petitioning for the vote, but as Laura remembered, "we still got good publicity, for the newspaper women in British Columbia were very sympathetic. They always announced any war work done by us as being done by the 'Equal Suffrage Society' or 'Political Equality League.'"[35] That visibility was evident in January 1915, when the *Vancouver Sun* and the *Vancouver World* organized a mock election among readers. Nineteen candidates stood before this electorate. The result put Conservative prime minister Robert Laird Borden and Liberal leader of the opposition Wilfrid Laurier at the top, but Nellie L. McClung, the nation's best-known suffragist and a regular BC campaigner, placed a good third. Public space became even more of a battleground when yet another women suffrage bill was defeated in Victoria in February 1915. The Political Equality League from Vancouver's Cedar Cottage neighbourhood quickly rallied irate champions with a play titled *How the Vote Was Won*.[36]

Laura contributed to the rising tide of protest. Thrums buzzed with hope when it hosted the inaugural lecture of the Burnaby Women's Forum by Mrs. Ralph (Mary Ellen) Smith, who spoke on the municipal franchise.[37] After a 1918 by-election, Smith would become British Columbia's first female MLA. The quick affiliation of the local Women Ratepayers' Association encouraged the forum to organize candidates for municipal office.[38] In May 1915, the British Columbia Equal Franchise Association elected Laura vice-president and arranged public lectures by McClung and Lord and Lady Aberdeen.[39] McClung's presentation, "Should Women Think?" drawn from her suffragist best-seller *In Times Like These* (1915),[40] attracted a full house at Vancouver's Wesley Methodist Church. By 1916, Laura and other suffragists were listening to spirited advocates of proportional representation, another popular remedy for Canada's flawed democracy.[41]

By the time she gave a talk titled "Woman Suffrage" to the Central Park Woman's Institute in July 1916, Laura was in good spirits.[42] As she remembered,

> Well! Were the Liberal and Conservative MLA's annoyed! Here they were in the fine progressive province of British Columbia, just working out how they would give women the vote, and behold, the three prairie provinces had got ahead ... Why, it was just like a Sputnik! What could the legislators of B.C. do, except recognize that woman's suffrage now instead of being a mill-stone round their necks, was a band-wagon, upon which they had better clamber as unobtrusively as possible, and try to pretend they had been there all the time.

Called to heel by Prairie pioneers, BC Liberals hastened to the suffrage camp, albeit "not ostentatiously, you understand, lest it might frighten some voters."[43] Mounting skepticism in the face of such tardiness encouraged Laura and others to emphasize principles rather than parties when considering political candidates.[44]

In another indication of a turning tide, the UWC pledged in March 1916 "to do all in its power ... to further the enfranchisement of women" and agreed to be guided by the suffrage societies.[45] That March affirmed the close ties of diverse suffragists when Conservative Helen Gregory MacGill gave a presentation to the Burnaby forum titled "Laws for Women in British Columbia."[46] Connections were equally clear when Laura presided over the UWC's September 1916 endorsement of prohibition.[47] The demands of wartime production had strengthened the long-standing WCTU arguments against alcohol. The forum's November 1916 discussion of the failure of the provincial Workmen's Compensation Act to include clerical labour, a field increasingly dominated by women, also confirmed broad alliances.[48] In the same month, Laura addressed the Vancouver Women's Liberal Association to affirm "unparalleled opportunities for reform in all the social and economic problems that confronted humanity." Women were "to solve forever the problems that have called for palliating measures in the past."[49] Radical solutions appeared everywhere. In June 1917, no longer a Conservative, MacGill again addressed the forum as it passed "a very comprehensive resolution," asking Ottawa "to nationalize all the Canadian resources to prosecute the war to a successful finish."[50]

As prospects were debated, Laura, the former teacher, always stressed education. She remembered,

> we didn't speak on street corners. We did better than that. With the consent of the owner of a restaurant ... we would hold a meeting of women, about a dozen or so at a table at lunch time. We would go early and choose a table where our speaker could be heard plainly all over the room. We would have our lunch early, and when the large room was well filled with men we would introduce our speaker. Her main point would be the various injustices now done to women and children by our obsolete laws, which could only be removed by women getting the vote and changing some of the laws ... Later they would come over to our table and ask questions and we would give them literature.[51]

Such enthusiasm for outreach would distinguish her activist and political career.

Determination to seize the moment was obvious when suffragists linked emancipation to the war. In 1916, the Burnaby Women's Forum invited everyone, "especially soldiers' wives," to meet at Laura's Presbyterian church. Even as the forum's Christmas parcels to servicemen confirmed its patriotism, guests received progressive instruction, namely, how to vote on the basis of their husbands' municipal franchise.[52] At the same time, Laura led the forum in extending its municipal program to consideration of "the larger franchise shortly to be placed in the hands of the women of British Columbia,"[53] and she encouraged the YWCA along the same lines. In December 1916, she shared these hopes in her talk "Reconstruction after the War" with the BC Methodist Woman's Educational Club.[54] A few months later, she marshaled forum forces to condemn the Canadian Patriotic Fund, a private national charity created to assist military families. Alongside servicemen's wives and mothers, the forum firmly informed Ottawa and Victoria

> that the present system of raising the Canadian Patriotic Fund is inadequate and inequitable, and that this meeting favors the adoption of a system whereby the soldier is paid a proper living wage for himself and family and that the money be raised by a graded taxation on incomes and a greater conscription of profits from manufacturing and industrial plants.

The forum's endorsement of a living wage and progressive taxation made it clear that capitalism was far from sacrosanct.[55]

Laura's involvement in the wartime women's movement extended beyond economics and suffrage. In September 1915, she presided over the UWC when it proposed a Parent-Teacher Association (PTA). By April

1916, she was addressing Vancouver's King Edward High School PTA on "the relationship between the school and the home," and the need to co-operate "in the development of the ideal citizen."[56] Her rising repute led to her consideration in 1916 as a candidate for Burnaby school trustee.[57] That did not happen, perhaps due to the birth of her second son, Angus, in 1917 or because Laura was preoccupied with a UWC investigation into prison life. Its special committee studied health, diet, sanitation, medical services, pregnant prisoners, tubercular and venereal infections, and segregation.[58] Once again, the revelation of distress showed the need for political action.

As debates about wartime Canada heated up, the Jamiesons initially sided with both the provincial party and the federal Liberals under Laurier. In April 1916, Jack became vice-president of South Vancouver's Liberal Ward Association, in December, president of the Edmonds and District Liberal Association, and in January 1917, second vice-president of the New Westminster Federal Liberal Association.[59] By summer 1917, he was hailed as a possible reeve for Burnaby.[60] In November 1915, Laura addressed the Women's Liberal Association, publicly identified by its president as "avowedly a suffrage organization," advancing women's "own cause."[61] After confessing that she had not expected male listeners to attend, Laura delivered a spirited call for a new politics. First, she took it "as assured the approaching triumph of the Liberal party and in consequence the conferring of the suffrage upon women." Belonging as she did "to the class of those who think that permanent social reform can be brought about, and seeing like many others an especial opportunity for bringing about social changes after the conclusion of the present war," she "naturally took a confident and hopeful view of the changes." The moment was ripe for introducing a

> new social order that should not be a continuous patchwork of compromise and make-shift ... That power lay in the collective will of the voting public and if their influence was not of the most intelligent and sagacious character, mistakes would again be made. Unscrupulous powers such as the big commercial interests and the yellow journalists would get the upper hand and things would settle down again into the old ruts. It was necessary, therefore, that women should prepare themselves to take up these problems of national and civic bearing and help to solve them ...
>
> Women had been foremost in charitable and philanthropic works, but all present could testify of the palliative and alleviative nature of what was accomplished. There was no cutting down to the root cause of the conditions

> that led to such states, with a view to grappling with the situation and making recurrence impossible ...
>
> Women had not been encouraged to use their intellects. The work they had carried on had been according to the plans and procedure laid down by men. They all knew from present experience with philanthropic organizations etc. that this division of work still prevailed. Men did the planning women the carrying out.

Drawing on her own frustrating experience with the Stratford YWCA, Laura charged that

> one of the largest of women's organizations had its hands tied ... In the east ... it was impossible for women to reach the working girls without getting in the way of the big business interests. Stipulation was made that the organization in return for being able to work among the young women employees should not interfere with their working life. This made it impossible for any improvement ... since their main troubles sprang from the meager wages on which they subsisted and the adverse conditions under which they work.

From the perspective of this advanced Liberal, who showed no sign of embracing the Union Government of Liberals and Conservatives proposed by Prime Minister Robert Laird Borden, new voters should "deal with every section of the community, for it was only when the good of each part was kept in view that the well being of the whole was attained." Laura closed with the invocation of a favourite progressive principle: "The needs of humanity must be studied. A comprehensive survey must be made by the woman voter of the social and economic world. It was necessary to read as much as possible ... Too much stress could not be laid upon the value of this knowledge of the woman voter, or indeed the voter of either sex."[62] A year later, Vancouver Women Liberals heard her reaffirm the need for root-and-branch reform "in all the social and economic problems that confronted humanity."[63] Such radical talk suggested a move beyond conventional liberalism, one that became all the more likely as the provincial party shifted to the right to encompass "commercial interests" and to marginalize critics of the status quo.[64]

Partisanship did not stop Laura from addressing other parties. In February 1916, as UWC president, she explained to Conservatives that a "great reconstruction ... must follow the war owing to the crumbling of so many institutions." It was essential to give her sex "better control of the conditions which affect the home." She dismissed "the indirect influence of women," which was, after all,

> gradually passing away and the demand for universal suffrage as a principle of democratic government is becoming firmly established ... Women were not satisfied to be bound by tradition when they saw many evils which they felt they could do something to remedy if they possessed the power of the ballot ... Women have proven their ability to use with discretion the municipal franchise and ... they should [not] be deprived of the full franchise.[65]

As long as British Columbia remained a "black spot" on the suffrage map, a bright future was unlikely. When an old opponent, Conservative premier Richard McBride, stood down in December 1915, a new day seemed possible. His replacement, Bowser, soon disappointed. In March 1916, Helen Gregory MacGill renounced her Tory allegiance, declaring that Conservative women should join with Liberals to defeat the government.[66] In April 1916, suffrage societies met Bowser to reject his proposed suffrage referendum and demand immediate enfranchisement. A referendum wasted energy that was better devoted to the war effort, and they resented "being forced to beg for" the vote.[67] Soon enough, they found an ally when the Vancouver Trades and Labour Council endorsed the cause in June 1916. Another boost occurred that month, when the Pioneer PEL hosted English suffragette Emmeline Pankhurst. Laura moved a vote of thanks to the visitor, claiming, "it a privilege to look into the face of a woman who could not be frightened into abandoning a cause which she believes to be well nigh sacred."[68] The table of honour at the PEL banquet linked local notables such as Laura, Mary Ellen Smith, and Helen MacGill with the admired suffragette.[69]

The suffrage referendum, together with one on prohibition, was held during the September 1916 provincial election. British Columbia was the only Canadian province to put female enfranchisement to male voters. Misogyny was not the only bigotry on view. Fingering foreigners, the *Vancouver Sun* ignored the fact that the majority of the male electorate was Anglo-Celtic:

> If it should then turn out that more than half the electors, consisting partly of male foreigners, are willing that Canadian women should vote in their own country, the measure will become law. A referendum will entail upon the women an active campaign and a serious expenditure of money, when all their time and money should be devoted to helping their men at the front.[70]

Tells Why Women Should Vote

British Columbia Is One Remaining "Black" Spot

Has Established Right to Ballot Since War Began

Even Premier Asquith Concedes They Should Vote

By MRS. J. A. CLARK.
Chairman Central Suffrage Committee.

The map here depicted shows a vast tract of country reaching from Behring Sea on the north to Mexico on the south, and extending hundreds of miles eastward, with British Columbia the one black spot. This means that this province is the only place on the western half of the American continent where women have not equal suffrage with men. This discrimination against women—while those of the surrounding territory are enjoying political equality—should alone be sufficient argument to induce even those men who have been opposed to the cause of suffrage to change their attitude.

Woman's suffrage is no experiment. For years it has been in operation in many of the states to the south, while from Norway, Sweden, Denmark, Tasmania, Isle of Man, Finland, New Zealand and Australia—where women have the vote—constantly come reports of good results of woman's influence in the political arena. In our own Dominion the Provinces of Alberta, Saskatchewan and Manitoba have, within the last year, placed their women on an equality with the men.

Not Political.

Woman's suffrage is based on the principle of right and justice, and as all political parties in British Columbia are agreed on the justness of the cause, voters are free to express themselves favorably upon the issue regardless of party affiliations.

The position of woman's suffrage in this province is most unique, as it has met with no opposition, either organized or otherwise. This tends to an optimism on the part of our women workers which might lead to over-assurance if not guarded against.

Man's Question As Well.

Since the bringing down of the referendum at the last session of the Legislature the question of woman's suffrage has become man's question as well—inasmuch as it is in the hands of men to decide rather than the women.

As woman's suffrage is world-wide, other nations that are considering this question will watch to see how the men treat it on Sept. 14.

What women are asking for is very simple, viz., that they might be self-governed citizens so as to be able to express themselves intelligently on questions of the day and to be able to say who may represent them in the Legislature.

Co-operation Desired.

Women do not wish to exceed men.

British Columbia as suffrage black spot, 1916 | *Vancouver Province*, September 12, 1916, reproduced by Supra Design, Victoria

Given their uncertain public reception, suffragists feared that rights won in a referendum might later be confiscated. By June 1916, a Provincial Women's Suffrage Referendum Association nonetheless appealed to both civilian and military voters. However, an important labour ally, the *British Columbia Federationist,* went sour, suggesting on April 14, 1916, that "the master class" only intended to co-opt enfranchised women. Even as it offered a salutary reminder that not all leftists could be trusted, betrayal did not stop British Columbia's leading working-class suffragist Helena Gutteridge from defending suffrage as a human right.

Among civilian voters, the 1916 referendum passed, with 43,619 in favour and 18,604 against. Vancouver counted 63 percent support overall, but Ward II, an east-side working-class community, voted 61 percent against. In Victoria, the heart of so many decades of campaigns, only 59 percent of male voters gave the thumbs-up. If many rural areas and small towns were won over, others resisted.[71] Canadian-based military voters counted 4,499 in favour and 2,528 against, but the overseas returns were disappointing. In March 1917, the old anti-suffrage warhorse, Richard McBride, now British Columbia's London representative, finally reported, no doubt gleefully, 3,999 votes for enfranchisement, 4,033 against, and 409 rejected ballots.[72]

The newly elected Liberal government ultimately ignored the referendum and opted for legislation. A women's suffrage bill received Royal Assent on April 5, 1917, making British Columbia the fourth province to enfranchise white women. What then did the BC referendum achieve? The final count, especially among military voters, who presumably were younger on average than civilians, was grudging. Claims of "fair play on the part of men" by the *Victoria Colonist* were bloated. As Nellie McClung foresaw in July 1916, "it will be many years before there are [many] women legislators in Canada; for there will be a heavy weight of prejudice against women which only patient years can dispel."[73] In the following decades, female candidates found no level playing field in British Columbia. A meaningful proportion of the electorate long viewed women as illegitimate political actors.

That future lay ahead for Laura. Amid a crowd of speakers from the feminist elite at a September 1916 Hotel Vancouver luncheon hosted by the Women's Liberal Association, the ever-buoyant New Woman foresaw systemic change:

> Having achieved the franchise ... women can look forward to more fruitful service to the community. They may hope in some cases to remove

> the causes of distress, instead of merely relieving that distress temporarily: they may hope to solve problems permanently instead of only ameliorating conditions. But in solving problems for the social betterment of the community they must always keep in mind this fact – no problem can be solved as an isolated and detached factor in the life of the community ... They must think through each problem and its interrelations and get down to the basic principle beneath ... Too often they have been forced to work in a piecemeal fashion in any reform undertaken ... One has only to look at the work done by the women of British Columbia in seeking to improve the laws affecting women and children. Time was when they asked for whole new laws, and got nothing. Then, they learned to ask for very little at a time – amendments to the most important laws, which were granted only in part, or refused. If they had had to go on many more years gaining such small amendments as in the past, the laws for women in British Columbia would have come to look like one of their grandmothers' crazy patchwork quilts. There was no hope of constructive legislation in this realm – only an amelioration of the most distressing examples of unjust laws. This ... was one reason why my heart had been warmed by the offer of the Liberal leader of a piece of constructive legislation – not a patchwork – in an equal guardianship law, which places a wife on exactly the same footing as her husband with regard to their children. Such a law assumes that great basic principle ... of absolute community of interest between husband and wife. This same principle must undoubtedly be applied in the case of laws regarding property. Women want no privileges but only an equal share in the property accruing to husband and wife after marriage ... This is an appropriate time for women to drop for once and all that malicious word "dower," for it smacks of privilege and that is not what women want. As wives and mothers they must ask no privileges or favours in the laws which govern them, but only equal rights, and in return they must be ready to accept equal dues and responsibilities.[74]

With Victoria's new Liberal government declaring itself "ready for change,"[75] a progressive agenda seemed in sight.

Even as the western provinces led in suffrage, Ottawa proved more recalcitrant.[76] Since provincial voting lists had determined the federal franchise since 1898, BC suffragists anticipated casting ballots in the 1917 election. The restrictions imposed in Prime Minister Borden's Military Voters Act and Wartime Elections Act, both designed to return his government in the December 1917 election and to secure military conscription, soon dashed hopes. The first act enfranchised all British subjects, male and female, ordinarily resident in Canada and serving in the allied armies. This included some two thousand nurses. The second enfranchised all spouses, widows, mothers, sisters, and daughters of anyone in the military while disenfranchising those who were unlikely to support the government, notably conscientious objectors and anyone born in an enemy country who had been naturalized after March 31, 1902. Borden's legislation ended the previous federal practice of accepting provincial voters' lists, which would have enfranchised most women in the Prairies, British Columbia, and Ontario for 1917.

Such discrimination divided suffragists. Conservatives and Liberal supporters of Borden's Union (or coalition) government cheered; pragmatists accepted the legislation as better than nothing; and critics condemned it as illiberal and undemocratic. Vancouver Conservative MP Harry Stevens defended the restrictions: the absence of so many men required that "the voice of their immediate relatives should be heard as a measure of compensation." Furthermore, "he could not bring himself to vote for the enfranchisement" of women from enemy countries. Such arguments roused fierce opposition. The city's United Suffrage Societies demanded the vote for "all women ... or none." Meeting with Stevens before the 1917 federal contest, they condemned his bankrupt promises to the suffrage societies.[77] A local feminist journalist bluntly labelled the restrictions "unjust" while agreeing "that the 'alien' menace should be guarded against by every possible means."[78] In the end, however, the election put Borden's Union Government in power. Only on May 24, 1918, did most Canadian women get the federal vote independent of provincial regulations. In 1919, enfranchised women won the right to run for federal office. Conspicuously absent were many Indigenous and Asian women, who waited far longer for full rights.

Even as she won the right to vote, Laura became much less publicly visible. Although her sympathies appear to have coincided with those of Liberals loyal to Wilfrid Laurier and opposed to conscription, it has proved impossible to find any public statements from her about the federal election. Personal tragedies took over her life. She was fighting off the tuberculosis that confined her to the Kamloops sanatorium for months, and she grieved the death of her son Angus in March 1918. She also mourned cousins: in September 1916, Aubrey Milton Marshall, a former student at the University of Toronto, died serving in the Princess Patricia's Canadian Light Infantry, and sapper Harry Attwood Stevenson fell in April 1917, fighting with the 12th Field Company, Canadian Engineers. Well after the 1918 armistice, war's ongoing costs haunted life. Laura would regularly shelter her brother Gilbert, who returned from overseas service "very disillusioned" with the world fit for heroes.[79] A Burnaby neighbour recalled the familiar sight of "many recuperating soldiers walking by our house on Douglas Road ... Some ... were gas victims on a rehabilitation program."[80] Little wonder that Laura later found much to admire in Vera Brittain's anti-war memoir, *Testament of Youth* (1933).[81]

Canada as a whole had been deeply tested by the war. Many observers found the nation wanting, not on Europe's killing fields but in the halls of government. The conscription of men but not of capital, the restrictive franchise legislation, and evidence of war profiteering and inflation fuelled dissent. In 1918, the editor of the *Western Methodist Recorder* spoke for social gospel critics in fearing Canada's surrender to the power of "a privileged class" of war profiteers.[82] Laura's 1918 article on novelist John Galsworthy likewise raised doubts about the status quo.[83] *The Forsyte Saga: The Man of Property* (1906), by this British suffrage ally, uncertain supporter of the Great War, and later Nobel laureate for literature (1932), had portrayed "the destructive ethos of an owning class through the tragedy of an unhappy marriage, where a sense of material possession destroys love," and has been judged "the nearest approach to a great socialist novel" in English literature.[84] In hailing such critics, Laura once again positioned herself as skeptical of the mainstream.

Even as wartime debates grew more passionate, Jamieson focused on working from within for reform. This could mean starting at the top. In February 1916, she became an early supporter of the Vancouver Institute, established in association with the new University of British Columbia (1915). Recognized at its inauguration as the wife of a lawyer and a member of the Alpine Club and the UWC, she joined Helena Gutteridge, identified on this occasion as "Tailor, Vancouver Trades & Labour Council," to champion an educated leadership ready to build bridges between otherwise warring classes.[85]

Even as it assembled British Columbians who were committed to diverse causes, from public health to labour and women's rights, the institute also "embodied the educational efforts and interests of a wealthy and influential segment of Vancouver's population."[86] The mix remained uneasy. The February 1919 executive decision "to reject the discussion of contentious or otherwise unsuitable topics" suggested the limits of collaboration.[87] Notably, only Laura, not the more intimidating union activist Helena Gutteridge, joined two other middle-class women – the UWC's Evlyn Farris and an activist teacher named Anna Jamieson – on the institute's first council. After her February 20, 1919, institute lecture,

"Women's Relation to the Labor Movement," Gutteridge left little trace, and the Vancouver Trades and Labour Council quickly disappeared as an official patron. Laura's own tenure on the council was brief, perhaps cut short by pregnancy, illness, and her baby's death. In 1917, she failed as the UWC candidate for the UBC Senate. Much like Gutteridge's "Women's Relation to the Labor Movement," her institute lecture "Recent Tendencies in Socialism," delivered on January 17, 1918, shortly after the Bolshevik Revolution (November 1917) and before the Vancouver General Strike (August 1918), also demonstrated views that jeopardized popularity among the conventionally minded. When in 1920 Laura gave another institute lecture on the Fabian Society, headlined in the UBC student newspaper as "Come on Reds,"[88] and then stepped forward as a member of the Federated Labour Party before a UBC club, her reception could only be frostier. In post-war British Columbia, the Burnaby New Woman would have to take the suffragist legacy not into the mainstream but into the left. The Vancouver Institute proved no vehicle for Laura's vision of a better Canada.

3
Still Bettering the World, 1918–26

Laura's political experiment with the Vancouver Institute represented the effective climax of a liberal effort to forge a wartime consensus in British Columbia about the nature of the brave new world that was to arise from sacrifice and suffering. In the institute's early days, female activists and labour representatives symbolized the Vancouver elite's efforts at accommodation. Provincial initiatives such as the creation of a Department of Labour and experiments with proportional representation similarly aimed to blunt discontent. So too in 1919 did Ottawa's establishment of the Royal Commission to Inquire into and Report upon Industrial Relations in Canada (the Mathers Commission) and the selection by the Liberal Party of William Lyon Mackenzie King, a labour economist and grandson of the 1836–37 rebel, as federal leader. The promise of accord proved fragile. The soaring cost of living, wartime profiteering, and the determination of employers to discipline workers told another tale. The October 1917 Bolshevik Revolution, the 1917 and 1918 provincial and federal enfranchisement of most BC women, the 1918 and 1919 general strikes in Vancouver and Winnipeg, the 1919 election of Ontario's farm-labour government, and the 1919 creation by the BC Federation of Labour of the Federated Labour Party, like the wartime appearance of the Canadian wing of the Women's International League for Peace and Freedom, signalled other possible politics. Now released from the shared crusade for the vote, Laura had once more to navigate challenging times.

The Jamiesons emerged from the armistice as a couple prominent in Vancouver's progressive middle class but with political choices to make.

In the 1920s, Jack would continue to hoist the liberal standard in criminal courts and in child welfare. Laura's trajectory was less straightforward. Hard wartime lessons of unequal sacrifice and her resistance to the economic status quo undermined her potential leadership in mainstream groups such as the University Women's Club (UWC), the Liberal Party, and the Women's Canadian Clubs. Her status as the mother of young children and the financially dependent wife of a man committed to a professional career further shaped her post-enfranchisement options. As provincial Liberals increasingly jettisoned progressive sympathies, the new voter considered other choices.

In short, Laura had to figure out how to combine radical sympathies with the maintenance of a middle-class household led by a liberal breadwinner. Her situation recalled the trap vividly evoked by Nellie L. McClung: "The one who has the greatest temptation not to think at all, is the comfortable and happily married woman – the woman who has a good man between her and the world, who has not the saving privilege of having to work. A sort of fatty degeneration of the conscience sets in that is disastrous to the development of thought."[1] Time would test the effect of a comfortable marriage on Laura.

After the war, Jack's career seemed to position the family for conventional success. The couple readily took their place in elevated professional circles. In February 1921, for example, they attended a dinner dance hosted by the Vancouver Law Students' Society, whose patrons included Lady Tupper, a local Conservative Party maven.[2] In 1923, Laura presided as a hostess – "at the supper table, centred with lovely single pink chrysanthemums" – of a "distinctly social affair" arranged by "one of society's leaders," Evlyn Farris, a UWC suffragist and wife of the provincial Liberal attorney general and minister of labour.[3] On other occasions, the Jamiesons joined a reform-minded elite at concerts performed by the inmates at the reformed Girls' Industrial Home.[4] Laura's own social prestige as a female university graduate allowed her a role in a play written by English man of letters Maurice Baring, staged by the UWC.[5] Such routine engagements conveyed social respectability and standing.

Jack was not, however, merely an ambitious lawyer making a good living in private practice and presiding as a magistrate over police and juvenile courts. He allied himself with the local League of Nations Society, one of the foremost indicators of post-war liberal internationalism,[6] and proved sympathetic when accompanying Laura as a Canadian delegate to the Washington meetings of the Women's International League for Peace and Freedom (WILPF) in 1924.[7] The Vancouver YMCA regularly benefitted from his voluntary services. He helped plan and teach at "an attractive summer school in which swimming, gymnasium work and class drills will be combined with the work of 'brushing up' on school work" for some fifty boys who were failing in school.[8] As "one of Vancouver's well known lawyers," he told the Y campers that

> a boy might get all the learning it was possible for school or college to give him, but if he did not develop character at the same time he would never amount to anything worth while. Character was worth more than piling up dollars. He advised the boys to do with their whole will anything they set out to do ... Don't stall your engine with bad habits; don't put any cheap stuff into your life; acquire the habit of reading; let the voice of the great dead speak to you; master that subject that's beating you, that temptation which pulls you under; worry about character ... [He] then spoke of the particular requirements for entering the legal profession.[9]

The popular magistrate also appeared on the PTA speakers' circuit. His 1922 talk, "The Questions Asked by Youth," typically emphasized careful parental listening.[10] Another talk the following year stressed post-war changes:

> The youth of today were challenging many ideas ... and could only see that the past was dark, the future uncertain and the natural development was ... living intensively in the present. Mr. Jamieson gave several instances which came under his jurisdiction as magistrate and brought out the rights of boys and the duty of the community toward them. He advised the parents to keep young with their children in order to understand their psychology and stressed the importance of character building.[11]

A few months later, he applauded maternal influence. In urging that every boy should "feel he had a pal to whom he could come for advice and confidences," he echoed Canada's surging child study movement, a progressive cause of the day.[12]

Though evidence from the provincial courts is scanty, what does survive puts Jack Jamieson firmly within the reform tradition. In 1922, in a rare publicly reported trial, he tore into a defendant who was charged with assaulting his wife and two children: "This is the worst case of raising hell in the home through the drunkenness of the father that I have ever heard of. There is not one redeeming feature about the man. You are a most contemptible creature." Summing up the defendant's testimony as "pathetic in its revelation of their home life," he made it clear that male violence was inexcusable.[13]

Jack's support for what the era termed "mental hygiene" was equally typical of its liberal reformers. In 1925, the Royal Commission on Mental Hygiene held public sessions in Victoria and Vancouver, and Jack has been assessed as generally supporting its conclusions that "60 to 70 per cent of all mental problems were inherited."[14] Though further evidence of his views has not been recovered, such assumptions of biological or eugenic inferiority later helped inspire British Columbia's 1933 Sexual Sterilization Bill as a possible solution to poverty and crime. By then, however, his widow would be left to make independent choices about how best to address inequality and injustice.

While Jack stuck with the BC Liberal Party, Laura contemplated different prospects after the war. She was inspired by the first elected female MLAs, beginning in Alberta with Louise McKinney, an activist with the left-leaning Non-Partisan League, and Roberta MacAdams, a Canadian Army Medical Corps dietician and independent representative of overseas military voters (both 1917–21). Nor could the Burnaby matron miss the debates about an independent feminist politics that quickly followed enfranchisement across the country. In 1917, the University of Toronto professor who had advocated segregated classes when she was a student argued in *Woman's Century*, the official magazine of the National Council of Women of Canada (NCWC), that women should not join political parties until the latter reformed themselves.[15] The following year, feminist journalist Anne Anderson Perry proposed "the most careful attention" to creating a women's party as "a temporary means of focusing the woman's vote," although she ultimately concluded that women and men should collaborate.[16]

In 1918, the editor of the *Western Woman's Weekly*, the sole BC feminist magazine to survive the suffrage campaigns, called for independence:

> The salvation of your country depends upon united womanhood ... We must start clean as a Woman's Party. We must learn to sink personal differences, petty jealousies and overcome the reputation which women have for quarrelling ... Men are proud of strong men. Women should be proud of strong women ... A Woman's Party would be all the stronger in that, like a girl with two beaux, we could keep both political parties guessing. We would have it in our power to play the men, whereas if women divide into political parties the men will and are now playing the women to their own purposes ... They will become submerged in the party machine ... The franchise would be as good as lost to them.[17]

A few months later, the *Weekly*, which featured the endorsement of leading BC women's groups on its front page, reiterated that

> our great strength will be in a non-political stand, and in our ability to command both parties. Women cannot take political sides with advantage. We do not come by politics either by tradition or inheritance. We should do in the larger life as we do in the home, – put aside all self-interest and self-advancement in the interests of the great human family as we do for the private family ... Peace will bring many radical changes. It rests with the women to preserve a sane balance, and thinking men know it, and are fervently hoping we will be equal to the occasion ... Organization is the answer.[18]

In a similar spirit, with input from the Vancouver Local Council of Women (LCW), the NCWC proposed a women's platform in 1919.[19] In sum, many watchful observers assumed that Canada's new voters faced big questions: Should they become non-partisan, searching all platforms for good policies and voting accordingly; should they form a separate women's party and negotiate with other parties; or should they join traditional parties and aim for reform and influence? This passionate debate questioned old partisanship.

In January 1918, feminists were encouraged by the Vancouver provincial by-election victory of Mary Ellen Smith, Laura's prominent suffragist ally and widow of the Liberal-Labour MLA Ralph Smith, who had moved the second reading of an 1899 suffrage bill in the Victoria legislature. Emigrating from Britain in 1892, Mary Ellen had built an impressive record in the women's movement. Running as an Independent and invoking the non-partisanship later embraced by Nellie L. McClung in an Alberta provincial election, she campaigned for "women and children first."[20]

Though British Columbia produced no equivalent of the Women's Party that was founded in Toronto in September 1918,[21] Mary Ellen claimed significant autonomy. She intended to

> go to the house as a free lance and that hundreds and thousands of men were going to stand behind her in the election, whether Conservative, Liberal, Laborite or Socialist ... She did not believe that one sex could get along without the other and ... men had already shown that they had been too long in the legislature by themselves.

In lamenting "girls ... working in stores and not getting enough to keep their bodies and souls together," she sought female and male supporters.[22]

As she highlighted greater supervision of factories and workshops, mothers' pensions, reforms to education and the treatment of juvenile delinquents, and a minimum wage for women, Smith was clearly searching for shared progressive space.

Expressing the racism of mainstream politics in British Columbia, Smith also sought to counter rumours that she had

> stood on the public platform [in Ontario] and advocated the bringing into country of 20,000 Chinese. My attitude toward Chinese labor has been a consistent one. I never employed a Chinaman in my life. I do not believe in bringing in people we cannot assimilate. Mr. Smith [her husband] was responsible for getting the Chinese head-tax increased from $100 to $500. Is it likely that I am going to degrade his memory by going to Toronto and advocating the bringing in of 20,000 Chinese coolies? Let me tell you that whatever help I have needed in my home I have always obtained from girls and I paid them union wages.

Smith also had to repudiate gossip that she had failed to vote in the 1917 federal election, that she was about to remarry, that her children were not hers, and that she had failed the Imperial Order Daughters of the Empire (IODE) as its president.[23] Such slings and arrows, as Laura would learn, were the special burden of female trespassers on male political territory.

Upon election, Smith paraded her colours as a suffrage champion, leading a March 1918 Vancouver delegation to the legislature in quest of mothers' pensions. In April 1920, she did much to ensure that the province adopted the most extensive program in the country. Its relative inclusiveness (providing for mothers who had been deserted or were parenting only one child) and rights-based rhetoric were nevertheless compromised by its exclusion of Asians and non-British residents.[24] Only its refusal to include the unmarried, except under a discretionary clause, was firmly condemned by Mary Ellen: "May God forgive us for brand[ing] a mother who has not gone through a marriage ceremony [as] different [from] ourselves."[25] Following her arrival in Victoria, other legislative gains drawn from the pre-war feminist agenda proved significant, notably the Registered Nurses Act (1918) and the Testator's Family Maintenance Act (1919), which authorized the provincial Supreme Court to improve maintenance and support for widows or children when husbands' wills proved insufficient. In her new role, Mary Ellen remained determinedly cheerful. She professed to believe that "men [were] ready and anxious to help" and that they promised to take up "equal pay for equal work ... in order to protect the returned soldiers and other wage-earners, as well as women."[26] Her dedication kept some suffragists loyal to liberalism.

In the early 1920s, many BC feminists foresaw better times. Vancouver magistrate Helen Gregory MacGill updated her compendium of BC laws regarding women and children to conclude "the belief of the suffragists that the ballot is the proper and only effective means of expressing public opinion has been amply demonstrated in the case of British Columbia, which, from being the most backward of Provinces, today leads in social legislation."[27] As Laura later reflected,

> I think that working for the suffrage, and using ingenious methods of educating the public gave us a zest and impetus that carried over into the period when we were able to get good legislation passed, and we felt that we should get as much passed as possible, for it was all very much needed. Besides we realized that we were in a very favourable position, with a woman in the cabinet who was very much interested in what we were trying to do, and willing to give us the greatest help. And we didn't know how long this would last, for politics in British Columbia has never given the province a stable government that lasted for a very long time.[28]

For a moment, great things seemed possible.

There were, however, shadows on the horizon. In 1919, Mary Ellen Smith identified women's prejudices against their own sex, "especially when allied with party bias," as a serious handicap. She warned that

> if women are going to divide into the old parties ... and carry on in this same picayune party spirit, then of necessity women in parliament, to be effective, must line up with one or other of the old camps. But what a pity this is. And the weakness of it!
>
> We, who worked for suffrage, always hoped that at least for a time until they found their political feet, women voters would remain independent, would support on all sides their representatives in parliament and would go single mindedly after the things for which women have struggled unsuccessfully as nonvoters for years and years ... For the support, advice and encouragement of the many, many women in B.C. who do place principle before party and the public good before party advantage, I am most grateful, and would like to assure them ... that the present session has seen the beginning of a thoroughly satisfactory programme of social legislation.[29]

The independent-minded constituency for which she hoped consisted of just the voters that Laura later sought to recruit.

Smith herself had early cause for anxiety. The *Western Woman's Weekly*, which had endorsed both her and non-partisanship, all too quickly retreated to celebrating party allegiance. In November 1919, its editor favoured "one of Vancouver's most prominent women, Mrs. A.J. Paterson," soon to be president of the Women's Canadian Association (1920–22), whose husband was a member of the nativist Vancouver Pioneers' Association. Revealingly, Paterson was not noted as a suffragist. She was an entirely safe choice for the heady heights of third vice-president of the Conservative Association. The *Western Woman's Weekly* nonetheless saw her elevation as

> a tribute, not only to herself, but to womankind generally, and it is a matter of gratification to all to know that it is due to Mrs. Paterson's brilliant intellect and executive ability that they have at last yielded a long contested group and given open recognition of the right of women to have a voice in public affairs.
>
> Mrs. Paterson has always been a woman's woman and has had their cause deeply at heart. But she also believes in women being well qualified to perform whatever public duties they undertake.

In return for such accolades, the paragon insisted that she did not believe in a Woman's Party. Instead, the sexes should

> stand shoulder to shoulder in politics as in everything else, and since men have established party government and found it good, that women should go into politics along the same lines and in the same high-minded manner.
>
> She would like to see women play the game to each other in the same fair-minded way that men do, and she feels that they must learn to give and take and stand true to one another before they can hope to be a power for good.[30]

Such homage to male fair-mindedness could only raise the hackles of women who had long been frustrated by the "People's Dick," his predecessors, and successors. The concession of a subordinate Conservative vice-presidency was hardly a sign of great things to come.

Other clouds gathered as well. Although feminist activists had demanded that women be given a joint interest in family property, early legislative advances notably failed to take this step.[31] Even apparent victories proved uncertain, with the new BC Minimum Wage Commission quickly charged with favouring employers.[32] Municipal politics also proved a minefield. At the close of the war, the Vancouver LCW appeared to have won the battle for a woman's division in the police department.

Soon enough, there was trouble. In 1921, the chief constable fired the LCW nominee, who ascribed her termination to her call for female magistrates. During the resulting official investigation, the chief constable engaged in a smear campaign, charging the veteran suffragist with "Bolshevici talk" and raising doubts about her Christian faith.[33] Close to the heart of antagonism was LCW determination to represent organized women in public affairs. City elections similarly shut down hopes. After Vancouver's charter was amended in 1917 to permit the election of female mayors and aldermen, the Women's Forum looked forward to equal representation, but the persisting property-based franchise kept male voters in charge.[34] In 1919, none of the three female candidates was elected to Vancouver city council. That record went unbroken until Helena Gutteridge triumphed as an alderman in 1937 and then Laura in 1948.

The new decade also simmered with anti-liberal sentiments regarding race. Feminists could be complicit in this. In December 1920, Laura attended a lecture hosted by Vancouver's Political Equality League. The speaker, veteran Ontario suffragist Dr. Augusta Stowe-Gullen, insisted that new immigrants "should be obliged to become Canadian citizens and adopt our habits, customs and language. If they are allowed to do as they please, Canada will have foreign nations within her dominion, and will be in danger of being overthrown by the people in her midst."[35] The same year introduced the Native Daughters of British Columbia, whose nativism excluded Asians from the provincial and national community. Its founding president, Helen Douglas Smith, would go on to become British Columbia's second female MLA in 1933 and would share the legislature with Laura in 1939. Racism also surfaced in controversies about Asian competitors in the labour market and Asian store-owners employing white women. The Vancouver Women's Forum and the New Era League (NEL, the successor of the Political Equality Leagues) were typically divided about how to respond.[36] The 1922 publication of the best-selling *The Black Candle,* an exposé linking drugs, the abuse of women, and Asian immigrants, written by Alberta suffragist and judge Emily Murphy, similarly fostered long-standing prejudice.

Class supplied the other great dividing line in Canadian politics. When the editor of the *Western Woman's Weekly* hailed the "dawn of a new era" for 1919, she warned of the crippling effect of class, even as she ignored the race divide:

> Autocracy, in its traditional form, has crumbled into dust. But commercialized autocracy still stalks through the land. Until this autocracy, which

> is as truly greed of power as if it were on an autocratic throne, – is vanquished, true democracy will not exist. The principles of democracy fail utterly as long as there are very rich people and very poor people. Autocracy will persist as long as the kings of finance have it in their power to "profiteer," and are able "to live and not let live."
>
> True Democracy means a living for everyone ... It means a purifying of the state and a doing away with the necessity of criminal institutions ... Let us hope that Vancouver and British Columbia will be foremost in the movement for the bigger and nobler life that paves the way to a Democracy which will make every man, woman and child an asset to the community and the state.[37]

Revealingly, however, such noble sentiments in this women's magazine never extended to any sustained consideration of the injuries of class or any appreciation of labour or socialist politics. Such alternatives remained on the fringe of respectable society in British Columbia, or more often beyond it.

When she contemplated substantive change in the political status quo, Laura had to search beyond the mainstream women's movement for allies. In looking left, she saw a familiar Canadian social gospeller, James S. Woodsworth. He had attracted growing public attention in opposing the Great War, being fired as director of the prairie provinces' Bureau of Social Research, resigning from the Methodist ministry, and working as a stevedore on the Vancouver waterfront. In 1919, his manifesto, "The Dawning of Labor's Day of Economic Freedom," set out a creed that resonated for Laura: "The Labor Party leaves the 'scientific orthodox' group and the revisionist groups to fight out their theories, but takes the great underlying principle stressed by Marx, viz., the collective ownership and democratic control of the means of wealth production. Men may differ widely in theory and yet unite to fight a common foe."[38] Joining a small socialist study group under Woodsworth's mentorship, Laura readily took up his pragmatic approach to theory and his emphasis on unity. This perspective, a logical continuation of the lessons she had learned as a suffragist, informed her evolving vision of justice and social democracy. Inspiration was reinforced by her friendship with Lucy Staples Woodsworth, also a graduate of the University of Toronto, who campaigned alongside her husband. That couple became Laura's model of a progressive partnership in life.

Integral to Woodsworth's appeal was his feminism, an aspect of his philosophy that has been largely ignored by commentators then and later.

In 1919, he summed up his sympathies in a pamphlet that originated in the *Western Labor News:*

> We agree that women should receive equal pay for equal work. The practical difficulty is that frequently a man has "a wife and family to support."
>
> That does not however make it right that he should get more for his work of teaching school or operating a machine. As a matter of fact it is the wife who should be paid for bringing up a family ...
>
> A woman before she is married is perhaps earning as large a wage as her husband. When she is married he gets no more aid and her wage stops altogether. Yet she works harder than ever – long hours and work that most women couldn't be paid to do. If she wants a quarter she must beg it from her husband.
>
> After all who has the benefit of the family! As soon as the children are old enough to care for themselves they become part of the great industrial army ... In war time, the State steps in and claims the worker as its own. Yet it rewards the mother not a cent for the years of care and expense involved in producing a citizen.
>
> The State can never repay the mother ... It can, however, and it should assume the financial burden involved. A mother's work is as necessary and valuable as that of an office or factory girl. She should receive at least equal pay.[39]

He went farther to endorse "equal rights of citizenship irrespective of sex, class origin, religion or property qualification."[40] Such sentiments help explain why a New Era League representative chaired a 1920 public meeting of the Federated Labour Party candidates, including Woodsworth.[41] That year also saw Laura offer a definitive public statement of her evolving views. Standing beside Woodsworth, she addressed UBC's Student Socialist Society on "the aims of socialism and the work of the Federated Labour Party," directly repudiating the liberalism with which she and Jack had been associated during the suffrage campaigns.[42]

Immediate hopes for left-wing success were dashed when Woodsworth was defeated in Vancouver in the 1920 provincial election. He stood fifteenth with 7,444 votes (3.68 percent of ballots), and the Independent Liberal Mary Ellen Smith topped the polls with 17,510 (8.66 percent). Overall, the Liberals took twenty-five seats, the Conservatives fifteen, Independents three, and Independent Labour one. Disappointment did not stop a member of the Parent-Teacher Association, where Laura was increasingly prominent, from acknowledging the Federated Labour Party a year later as the "Real Woman's Party."[43] Optimism rebounded when

Woodsworth was elected to the Commons as an Independent Labour Party MP for Winnipeg North Centre in 1921, with the slogan "Human Needs before Property Rights." Even as their base shifted back to the Prairies and onward to Ottawa, James and Lucy Woodsworth continued to inspire BC admirers. The influence deepened after 1932, when their daughter Grace, who later became Laura's colleague in the BC legislature, married Vancouver CCF MP Angus MacInnis.

The 1921 federal election was equally noteworthy for producing Canada's first female MP, Agnes Campbell Macphail (1890–1954) of Grey County, Ontario, the adjacent county to Laura's birthplace. Eight years younger than Laura, she was not known as a suffragist, but she came from the progressive farm politics that had become ubiquitous in the Saugeen/Bruce Peninsula. In a foreshadowing of the fate of many female legislators, she quickly found herself "an alien novelty, commented upon and scrutinized by other MPs, by the public, and the press." Not surprisingly, she remembered her first terms as "intensely unhappy. Some members resented my intrusion, others jeered at me, while a very few were genuinely glad to see a woman in the House. Most of the members made me painfully conscious of my sex."[44] Such hostility encouraged Macphail to rally to the feminist Women's International League for Peace and Freedom (WILPF), where Laura became an admirer.

Even with the support of the Woodsworths and Macphail's growing allegiance over the 1920s, socialism remained an uncertain home for feminists. Gender justice was not central to its arguments, and it valued women less as candidates and more as workhorses, both at home and in politics. In the 1924 provincial election, the Federated Labour Party, campaigning as the Canadian Labour Party (CLP), had support from socialists and communists as well as the Vancouver Trades and Labour Council, but it ran only two women, neither victorious. Its Vancouver candidate was Ontario-born Priscilla Janet Smith (1879–1954). A protégé of Woodsworth, Smith had graduated from the Toronto General Hospital and the Toronto Deaconess Home and Training School (1902). She was also a former superintendent of Winnipeg's Methodist Deaconess Home and a Burnaby nurse with the Victorian Order of Nurses, which put her into direct contact with Laura.[45] Though the CLP took 11 percent of the popular vote and won three seats, provincial Liberals, helped by their promise of an eight-hour day, returned to power. In the federal election of October 1925, the CLP put up five BC candidates, including Ontario suffragist and socialist Rose Henderson (1871–1937), who ran in New Westminster. Henderson was the CLP's strongest vote-getter, but she too fell short.

A few weeks after that disappointment, the re-elected Woodsworth returned to Vancouver to stress that his Ginger Group held the balance of power in Ottawa. Indeed, in 1927 it would force King's Liberals to concede old age pensions. In the meantime, the Winnipegger encouraged Pacific Coast loyalists to focus on building municipal foundations. Hopes rose in December 1925, when Angus MacInnis was elected Vancouver alderman. Buoyed by that outcome, the BC Independent Labour Party emerged in February 1926. In the September 1926 federal election, however, no BC labour candidate was successful.

Unlike Smith and Macphail, Laura stood on the electoral sidelines in the 1920s as she managed her household and family. Nor did she continue to captain mainstream women's groups such as the University Women's Club and the Liberal women's associations. As socialism and labour seemed to fail electorally, she concentrated her post-war energy on internationalism, notably in WILPF, and education, particularly in the Parent-Teacher movement. These became her primary tools for bettering her community.

Canadians who endorsed internationalism during the 1920s faced rising intolerance and racism. In 1922, New Westminster's MP found plenty of local support in urging a complete ban on Asian immigration. A year later, dissident Conservatives formed the Provincial Party, which opposed both Oriental labour and the wartime income tax. The BC British Progressive League emerged with an Asian exclusion platform, and Ottawa passed a still more restrictive Chinese Immigration Act. The 1924 murder of a young Scots nursemaid, Janet Smith, in a Shaughnessy home similarly rallied bigots who, despite lack of evidence, accused the Chinese houseboy. By 1927, thirteen thousand British Columbians had joined the Ku Klux Klan, eight thousand of them in Vancouver. The decade's efforts to segregate Chinese students in Victoria and Vancouver reflected the same prejudice. "Spectacular healing and evangelistic campaigns" in the province during the mid-1920s merely confirmed the period's conservatism.[46]

Contemplating that challenge, Laura linked global and anti-war sympathies to progressive voices in the socialist and labour movement and women's groups. In 1921, the Federated Labour Party typically hosted Dr. Hardikar, director of New York's Bureau of Information on India, whose lectures "Bolshevism in India" and "British Rule in India" played to packed houses.[47] Charging the British Empire with culpability for terrible industrial conditions, he urged unionization.[48] In contrast, the new League of Nations was hailed as portending an end to imperialism, narrow nationalism, and global conflict. In 1921, the grieving mother of

Angus and cousin of young men buried in Europe directed her listeners to *The Great Illusion* (1910), a best-seller written by the English Labour Party activist Norman Angell, with its argument that war never made economic sense.[49] She also gave lectures titled "The Economic Futilities of War" and "The Will to Peace and the Will to War."[50] British imperialism received her ready censure. In a 1922 letter to the *Vancouver World,* she condemned the malicious ignorance of a contributor to the rival *Vancouver Province,* who had suggested that British taxpayers bore the costs of pensioning Indian civil servants. In pointing out that India paid all its own administrative costs, Laura concluded there was "a more dangerous species of 'illiteracy'" than that suffered by those on the subcontinent – namely, the stupidity of would-be governors.[51] Her sympathy soon extended to Mahatma Gandhi's pacifist nationalism. Laura's efforts to connect British Columbia to international pacifism showed as well when she hosted meetings on philosopher Bertrand Russell's *Why Men Fight* (1916), with its overview of the roots of war, and encouraged discussion about the League of Nations as a force for good.[52]

Such opinions confirmed her friendship with Dr. S. Mack Eastman, a war veteran and prominent socialist who was UBC's first professor of history. When super-patriots attacked W.L. Grant's *A History of Canada* as "anti-British, anti-Protestant, pro-French Canadian and pro-Catholic," Eastman defended it as an approved text for BC schools, and Laura stood with him.[53] The importance of education for the decade's internationalists was similarly demonstrated in 1923, when she faulted an IODE gift of "War Pictures" to schools as little more than warmongering. Because she signed her public denunciation as "L.E. Jamieson," opponents assumed that she was male: "His contentions are most ridiculous. They sound like the vaporings of a crank."[54] She remained unrepentant, soon urging the UBC Women's Literary Society to exchange its outdated slogan "Teach man so that he may do his duty" for "Let man know and then trust him." In the modern world, she insisted, an older "narrow nationalism" should be replaced by "honesty and frankness."[55]

The Canadian operations of WILPF provided Laura with her major platform for the promotion of women's rights, pacifism, and internationalism. In Canada and globally, WILPF stood on the front lines against racism and capitalism.[56] Although a Toronto branch of WILPF was formed in 1919, Laura headed the BC chapter and quickly ensured its survival nation-wide. In 1922, she set out her agenda in a revealing letter to American Emily Greene Balch, WILPF's international secretary-treasurer and a future Nobel peace laureate. She intended to position

WILPF very cautiously as an avant-garde organization in a conservative nation. Above all, it had

> to avoid becoming "a middle class organization with a middle class mind." Becoming a working class organization would be easy ... because some of their most "ardent" members were labour people with radical views. "So we aim to be middle class externally, while we strive with all our might not to be middle class internally, that is, to be far in advance of the general middle class in outlook, in information, and in leadership of ideas."[57]

These few words captured the strategic tightrope that Laura chose to walk.

As part of her efforts to broaden the appeal of WILPF, she strove to connect it to other progressive groups. In 1922, this meant supporting the Trades and Labour Council and Helena Gutteridge in hosting a talk by international birth controller Margaret Sanger. Liberty for women required reproductive choice. Laura also took peace and disarmament arguments to UBC's Student Christian Movement summer camps.[58] At the dominion level, she encouraged WILPF's alliance with the prairie Grain Growers, previously a proven suffrage ally. Such efforts aimed to realize her conclusion that "our greatest work is not in building up a large membership in our own organization but in working through other groups."[59] Her prominence made her an easy choice as a Canadian delegate to the 1924 WILPF conference in Washington and again in Geneva in 1927.

Seemingly more mainstream than efforts in WILPF was Laura's leadership of the provincial Parent-Teacher Association (PTA), formed in 1922 with the assistance of the UWC. Former teachers, Laura and Jack enthusiastically promoted its attempt to introduce child-centred education throughout the province. Between 1925 and 1926, as a parent representative of Burnaby School District 41, Laura became provincial president. Her contribution occurred in the midst of what has been identified in Ontario as the PTA's transition from an "essentially reformist and innovative" response to an emphasis on modern theories of child study, such as IQ testing, that sometimes wandered far from original progressive ideals.[60] Laura, however, followed its older tradition. In writing to the sympathetic Violet McNaughton, women's editor of the *Western Producer* and soon a trusted confidant, Laura stressed concerns about the link between education and militarism, and worried that many Parent-Teacher groups were indifferent to the danger.[61] She nevertheless felt quite "perky" in using the group's letterhead rather than WILPF's. She had taken on the PTA presidency because she believed that the group's greater "prestige" might better promote internationalism. Its programs could look "innocuous" but they could foster "a 'peace background' for children's minds." Though sensitive to opposition, she remained typically upbeat, concluding that the Parent-Teacher "members must be liberal minded or they would never have elected me President."[62]

Laura's prominence in the Parent-Teacher movement led to her December 1926 appointment by the Liberal provincial government to the three-person Public Library Commission.[63] The commission quickly initiated an investigation of provincial library services, which was reckoned "the most ambitious project of its kind ever attempted in Canada."[64] In fact, the British Columbia Library Survey, 1927–28, dubbed the "King James Version," proved singularly effective in obtaining a $100,000 grant from the Carnegie Corporation to demonstrate the value of local libraries.[65] Like the farm girl from the Saugeen, isolated British Columbians with books in hand were better equipped to improve themselves and the world. Here was the democratic route to political transformation.

By the mid-1920s, Laura had assumed a significant role in trying to educate the province in matters that started at home but spanned the globe. Unlike some British Columbians, whose outlook was bounded by the Rockies, the Ontario-born activist imagined the country as a whole. In 1926, she published a piece of nationalist doggerel, "Canada First," in the *Canadian Trade Unionist,* the official organ of the Canadian Federation of Labor. It lacked elegance and originality, but it expressed a heartfelt commitment to a reformed nation.[66] Here was the persisting faith of the generation that trusted in a new day, beginning with women's enfranchisement. Both WILPF and the Parent-Teacher movement exemplified Laura's belief that internationalism and education stood at the heart of solutions to global problems and a fair deal for women. They also shared a commitment to building broad alliances on the earlier suffrage model of consciousness raising. In other words, they offered the hard step-by-step route to constructing a better world while living in an imperfect one:

Canada First

Not merely in breadth of expanse and wealth or resources, but in things of the spirit;

Not merely in natural beauty, but also in ideals, principles and character;

Not merely in national prosperity, but in the happiness and contentment of citizens;

Not merely in the assertion of rights, but in the willing assumption of duties;

> Not in splendid isolation, but in courageous co-operation;
>
> Not in arrogance and disdain of other peoples, but in sympathy, love and understanding;
>
> Not in treading again the old, work-worn, blood-stained pathway which ends inevitably in chaos and disaster, but in blazing a new trail along which other nations will follow, where wars shall be no more.
>
> Some day one nation will be honored above others for blazing such a trail. That honor I covet for my beloved Canada.
>
> And so, in that spirit and with these hopes, I say with all my heart and soul – "CANADA FIRST!"[67]

Less positively, Laura's post-war history suggests that the larger reform coalition that had sustained the suffrage crusade was in decline. No women's newspaper existed after the *Western Woman's Weekly* collapsed in 1924, and discussion of women in major newspapers such as the *Vancouver Sun* and the *Vancouver Province* shifted from activism to "increased coverage of the social activities of Vancouver's elite."[68] When she came out as a socialist and promoted WILPF and the Parent-Teacher movement as internationalist and anti-war organizations, Laura hoped to build for a progressive future, but she also placed herself on the periphery of women's political activity in the province.

The ups and downs of the women's movement and the left were not the only dilemmas of the decade. For Laura personally, its second half was tragically darkened by the death on November 28, 1926, of forty-nine-year-old Jack. In the era before antibiotics, he died from blood poisoning linked to an abscessed tooth. In a matter of days, Laura lost her economic anchor to the middle class and all that marriage to a man of larger sympathies and the father of adolescent children represented. Unfortunately, no reference survives to the emotions thrown up by sudden widowhood. We are left only with suggestions of its impact. Jack's death prompted tributes. The *Chilliwack Progress* praised him as a "man of sterling worth and incalculable influence for good, and the boys and girls of Greater Vancouver, in particular, have lost an understanding friend and helper who will not easily be replaced." As a judge, he had "brought to bear on the cases before him a great understanding of human nature and a great kindliness and many a boy and girl owe a happy and useful life to his assistance and aid."[69] *The New Outlook,* the magazine of the brand new (as of 1925) United Church of Canada, reprinted an accolade from the Vancouver *Province* hailing Jack as a Juvenile Court magistrate who "was markedly successful in getting the confidence of delinquent youth and in assisting in their restoration."[70]

Jack Jamieson's last will and testament, dated November 9, 1917, mere months after the birth of Angus, spoke to his respect for and confidence in Laura. Even as BC laws were slowly reformed to do justice to widows, and two years before the Testator's Family Maintenance Act, he left her all his "Real and Personal Estate and effects whatsoever and wheresoever situated for her sole use and benefit absolute, knowing full well that she will provide for the maintenance, education and needs of my said infant children."[71] In other words, this New Man treated Laura with esteem and due regard for the situation she would face as a single parent.

The proceeds of the Jamieson estate reflected the status of a family that lacked inherited wealth and whose male breadwinner was still relatively new to his professional career. The only debts were those acquired in the course of Jack's illness and death, as well as the significant sum of $1,120.26 that was owed to Eliza Marshall, the sister who had helped finance Laura's education. The bulk of inheritance came from two insurance policies ($7,000) and Burnaby real estate ($6,600), not to mention a Chevrolet and goats, estimated at $600 and $125 respectively, for a net worth of $14,639.56. There was no pension. In 2015 dollars, the estate represented nearly $200,000. Though very significant, this sum could not long support a three-person family in middle-class comfort. In the years to come, Laura would need to generate income, both to support herself and to assist her children. As a widow, the left-leaning New Woman had entered another stage in life, with new responsibilities and opportunities.

4
Widowed Judge and Progressive Activist, 1927–39

After Jack's death, Laura stayed in Burnaby for almost three years and then in 1929 moved westward to the main road in Point Grey, the interwar residential suburb that lay just east of UBC. Her modest house would welcome kin, guests, and boarders for more than a decade. When jobs evaporated in the 1930s, her brother Gilbert and his English wife, Elizabeth, came and went. From there, too, Laura would connect with more distant relatives, including married sister Ellen Johnston and her husband, who were active in the United Farm Women and the United Farmers of Ontario, as well as close friends such as the prairie activist and journalist Violet McNaughton. Intimate ties did much to offset the loneliness of widowhood.

Laura's 1937 condolence to a dear friend, the Vancouver activist Lilette Mahon (d. 1956), whose husband had died, nevertheless seems suggestive of what Jack's loss also meant: "The freedom he gave you was so generous." As Lilette herself reflected, after widowhood left her with few resources, she went "out of circulation" as a reformer.[1] Jack may have remained a Liberal after the Great War, but he supported his progressive wife, both financially and emotionally. Without him, life for an independent-minded woman, now no longer young, would be far more insecure. She, however, did not share Mahon's fate.

After a stint at UBC, Laura's daughter, Laura Jean, went off to teach primary school in Kimberley. In February 1935, she married mining engineer Jack Shannon from Vancouver Island in her mother's home before a United Church minister. Her mother and her new mother-in-law served as witnesses. In November, Jean would give birth in Vancouver to Kathleen, later a producer with the National Film Board. She was the first of four daughters for Jean and eight granddaughters for Laura. During the 1930s, Laura would visit the Shannons in remote mining towns, as Jean and Jack struggled to find a foothold in the Depression economy.

Between 1931 and 1935, Laura's son, Stuart, studied sociology and economics at UBC, taking his bachelor's degree in 1935. In 1933, Laura proudly reported to Violet McNaughton that the nineteen-year-old had "finally realized that economics and world affairs are most engrossing subjects" and had become an avid reader of Saskatoon's *Western Producer.*[2] Soon Stuart wanted to join the anti-fascist Mackenzie-Papineau Battalion, fighting for Spanish Republicans against General Franco, but a childhood injury kept him out of both that conflict and the Second World War. Instead, he moved on to graduate studies in sociology at McGill and then economics at the University of California. His 1938 master's thesis, titled "French and English in the Institutional Structure of Montreal: A Study of the Social and Economic Division of Labour," demonstrated his interest in the intersection of "race," as it was understood at the time, and class. His mother worried about the influence of Montreal, a suspect metropolis for many Anglo-Canadians. In a 1936 letter to McNaughton, she wrote, "It is a terrible city – our biggest industrial centre. What poverty! What graft! What ignorance on the one hand & hypocrisy on the other!" However, she reassured herself that "fortunately Stu has had a radical upbringing, or he might have been submerged."[3] Her son's summer jobs in fishing camps and sawmills offered further inspirations to his critical thinking.

As Laura's children transitioned to adulthood, her household expenses increased for some years. Though part-time employment as a Burnaby Juvenile Court judge, beginning in 1927, netted a small monthly stipend, Laura initiated an ongoing strategy of taking in boarders, as many CCFers did. As she explained, "I liked having young people about me, especially since my husband had died; and it helped to pay the taxes and upkeep of the house."[4] In describing the tasks involved in looking after the students and business people who lodged with her, she joked that "hard work agrees with me."[5] When Stuart won a McGill scholarship in 1935, thus reducing the cost of his support, she nevertheless confessed how "tired I am" and said that it was a relief to "ease up a bit," even as all her bedrooms were regularly rented. The current affairs study groups, which she started up soon after moving to Vancouver, similarly provided additional income. She charged more for the afternoon lectures "because those attending are fairly well off," but she appreciated the steady, similar, though less well paid, work for the Vancouver School Board.[6] Only her 1939 election and salary as an MLA curbed such strategies for increasing her income, temporarily at least.

Once Laura became an independent woman, her public identity began to shift. For some time, the press continued to refer to her as Mrs. J.S. Jamieson. Increasingly, however, as a sign of her changed status, she was noted as Mrs. Laura or Mrs. L.E. Jamieson. Once the spouse of a rising lawyer, she now had to rely on her own strengths to take on the era's related challenges of child welfare, internationalism and peace, economic justice, women in politics, and the BC left. Unlike friends who formed a monthly "belles-lettres" reading club to shelter from the problems of the world, Laura didn't "find it so necessary to have an 'escape.'" Though she enjoyed its gatherings, she teased that it should be titled the Bourgeois Club.[7] She preferred to focus on solutions.

Early in 1927, Laura succeeded Jack to become the province's second female magistrate. Her appointment by the Liberal government as Burnaby Juvenile Court judge was not a singular event. It represented an emerging Canadian tradition of widows or wives succeeding dead or incapacitated husbands in politics and appointed office. In British Columbia, this had happened with Mary Ellen Smith's 1918 nomination as an Independent to succeed her husband, Ralph, in a Vancouver constituency. After the 1935 federal election, it would be employed with Yukoner Martha Black (1866–1957), who held a parliamentary seat as an Independent Conservative for her indisposed MP husband, George. As with both those cases, the wives' reputations mattered. The *Toronto Globe and Mail* opined that the "signal honour" of Laura's appointment was entirely appropriate since she had been for some time "President of the Provincial Parent-Teacher Association of British Columbia, and, in addition to her own important activities, kept in touch with her late husband's work, and was his constant advisor." It noted approvingly that "in assuming her new duties, Mrs. Jamieson has relinquished the Presidency" of the PTA.[8] The new magistrate was expected to demonstrate neutrality. That expectation, much like her marriage to a Liberal, would cramp her political expression until she resigned from the bench in spring 1938.

Laura's more than decade-long engagement as a judge has left few records. The local press had paid little attention to Jack's court, and Laura's fared no better. In 1929, *Chatelaine* published an article that discussed female magistrates, but it omitted Laura. Instead, it focused on Vancouverite Helen Gregory MacGill's emphasis on rehabilitation and her firing by the BC Conservative administration.[9] A year later, *Chatelaine* briefly singled out Laura in the first of a series of articles titled "Women and Their Work." The only British Columbian among the six women whom the series scrutinized, she was also the only legal professional. She was described as "one of the most interesting women in Canada today," a "noted speaker" on juvenile delinquency and peace, as well as a judge.[10] For all such praise, the Toronto-based *Chatelaine* subsequently ignored Laura in both areas of expertise.

The new magistrate was reimbursed for the part-time sittings of the court at $50 a month, which in 2015 dollars would amount to some $675.[11] She joined a small number of such female appointees in these years, all in family, juvenile, women's, or domestic relations tribunals.[12] They lacked law degrees, drew heavily on experience with the clubwomen's movement, and left scant records. The Vancouver and Burnaby press appeared minimally interested in Laura's court. Certainly, the *Burnaby Broadcast* rarely mentioned it. It seems to have proceeded somewhat informally, with Laura holding many meetings of the Juvenile Court Committee at her home. This powerful group was composed of Thomas Corbett, the city's chief probation officer, Miss Amy Leigh, the prominent Burnaby Girl Guide leader and mountain-climber as the junior probation officer, and Dr. J.W. McIntosh, the court's medical adviser and future medical health officer for Vancouver. Its additional members included one other man, a 1923 candidate for Burnaby civic office, and three more women, one of whom was an activist in the Ladies' Aid of the local Presbyterian church and a supporter of the Victorian Order of Nurses (VON). This roster, which when complete was to include four representatives of Protestant churches and three for the Catholic, captured the reformist hopes of the juvenile court movement in North America.

Young people who came before the court were commonly medicalized. That is, they were seen as fit subjects for cure rather than punishment and were preferably redirected away from the adult penal system.[13] J.W. McIntosh, as is suggested below, was a significant presence on the committee but so too was Amy Leigh, who has been described as "a strong advocate for the indigent when she worked as a welfare worker in Vancouver's City Relief Department during the early years of the Depression and [who] left because her championship was met only by 'contempt.'"[14] In 1958, critical of the degradation of public services by the Social Credit government, she would again resign as a matter of principle, this time as provincial superintendent of child welfare. In short, she, like Laura and the Burnaby VON nurse Priscilla Smith, who ran for the Canadian Labour Party in 1924, represented Burnaby's left-leaning middle class.

Such progressive professionals were sometimes enthralled by conservative solutions to problems, a fact that surfaced at the first meeting of the Canadian Conference on Child Welfare in Vancouver in 1927. Dr. McIntosh presented a paper on the sterilization of the supposedly unfit. Under his leadership, Burnaby's Juvenile Court Committee resolved to make a recommendation on that subject to the provincial legislature. Unfortunately, the particulars of its advice haven't been located.[15] Support for sterilization would not have been unusual. In 1925, Victoria had appointed the Royal Commission on Mental Hygiene to investigate how a perceived increase in "mental defectives" could be combatted. Its recommendations found expression in the province's 1933 Sexual Sterilization Act.[16]

Laura also addressed the 1927 conference. Her talk, "Sex Education in the Child Welfare Programme," was given under the auspices of the Canadian Social Hygiene Council, one of the nation's leading advocates of eugenics. This paper, published as a pamphlet in 1928 and 1936 by the Provincial Board of Health, would have a long life. Whereas sterilization was a negative approach to human sexuality, Laura saw sex as a natural interest: even in young children, its proper management was essential to "their future happiness." Up-to-date parents could turn to groups such as the BC PTA for appropriate instruction. Her fears were particularly directed at harder-to-reach mothers and fathers: "It is from the homes of the indifferent and ignorant parents that the problem children and delinquents come." Remedies, the new judge felt, rested with sympathetic caseworkers and child welfare clinics as well as educational materials. She praised writers "who place sex on a high plane – Maude Royden, Edward Carpenter, and, greatest of all, Havelock Ellis," in short, the pioneers of contemporary sex education. Once suitably taught, parents could answer their children's questions "not timidly and reluctantly, but freely and enthusiastically, so that the impression may be given that sex is something normal and beautiful, not furtive or ugly." Instruction should begin before children entered school so that adolescents would "have the right adjustment toward those of the opposite sex." Like other professional authorities, Laura insisted that the teenage years should properly elicit "the greatest sympathy and understanding on the part of parents." Warning about venereal disease as "the darker side of sex" and "a crime against childhood," she recommended that "instruction should be positive, not negative; constructive, not destructive ... based on hope, not fear." As a feminist, she spoke of the injustice done to women and poor families who lacked reliable birth control. No wonder that she supported the creation of the city's Birth Control Association in 1928.

Near the end of her conference presentation, Laura shifted into a discussion of direct personal relevance. She had, after all, been admitted to the Kamloops TB sanatorium less than a year after giving birth to her third child, who died in 1918. She described the many women who

> contract tuberculosis while bearing children. When the disease is arrested, the usual procedure is for the doctor in charge to warn such a woman not to have any more children: but without giving her the proper instruction. She goes back to her husband and family with the best of intentions; but frequently she fails for lack of the necessary sex knowledge; she gives birth to another child, which has a tendency to tuberculosis all through life; while the mother herself has a break-down as a result, and perhaps leaves her children motherless.[17]

Unfortunately, we can only speculate on how closely these remarks reflected what happened to Laura or what she observed as a sanatorium patient during the First World War.

British Columbia's interwar juvenile justice system has been described as focusing "on parents as the source of child maltreatment" and as revealing "the two often-conflicting purposes of child welfare: supporting parents to care for their children and removing children from families where the parents failed to measure up." It did not incorporate "correctional facilities for children, institutions for the mentally challenged or disabled, or the Indian residential schools" into overall planning for the welfare of youngsters. The result was "a Eurocentric and urban-centred view," and a confirmation of "separate and unequal child welfare services in British Columbia."[18] For a suburban magistrate such as Laura, Aboriginal children were a rarity, and no record has been found in which she mentioned them. Like Helen Gregory MacGill, Laura also encountered few Asian children: their families were credited as both effective and protective in raising offspring. For other unfortunate children and teens who appeared before the bench, progress meant diversion from adult correctional institutions. This could require placement in foster care, but it more commonly entailed community oversight by professionals. In 1930, even as she observed that crimes against property were increasing among boys, Laura asserted that the majority were not guilty of "any real criminal intent." Most had no criminal experience, and the best treatment was supervision by "friendly" probation officers.[19] In this measured response, Laura stood within the progressive mainstream of criminal justice and child welfare reformers.

The Burnaby Juvenile Court was only one part of contemporary efforts to address concerns about child welfare and the breakdown of the family. In 1927, the BC Child Welfare Survey, conducted by prominent Ottawa social worker Charlotte Whitton of the Canadian Child Welfare Council, mobilized the same anxiety. It quickly proved a provincial landmark in "measuring public opinion for change, scrutinizing carefully the credentials and practice of the social workers of the day, and giving wide publicity to the results."[20] Although Whitton's later opposition to improved social security would draw Laura's ire, she approved of her emphasis on research, professionalism, and foster care rather than institutions. For the next several decades, celebrated "wise women" social workers, such as Laura Holland, former director of social work for the Toronto Public Health Department,[21] would lead Vancouver in engineering some of the survey's recommendations. In the process, they confirmed female professional leadership in child welfare. In 1932, working under a Liberal government as BC superintendent of neglected children, Holland became the ally of juvenile court judges such as Jamieson and Helen Gregory MacGill.

In the 1930s, now resident in Vancouver, Laura turned her attention to its provision for children. Together with an energetic group of progressive citizens, she helped found the West End Community Centre, eventually chairing its board of directors and making child services her major concern.[22] As was her practice with all her causes, she read widely to stay abreast of modern developments and sought opportunities to observe best practices. In spring 1938, she toured California's early childhood education efforts while visiting her son Stuart at Berkeley. Back in Vancouver, she reported approvingly to the Nursery School Association that the initiatives "developed as a relief project under the [US] Federal Works program are incorporated into the school system with the domestic science or home economics classes operating to provide lunches."[23] The overall progressive orientation of Vancouverites who were committed to improving children's services was suggested in 1939, when the PTA lobbied Victoria to introduce "an adequate health insurance scheme, vocational training in prisons, and adequate care for unemployed youth."[24] In the same year, Jamieson's standing as a prominent defender of youngsters was recognized when she became honorary president of the Vancouver Nursery Schools and Kindergarten Association.

Even as she won kudos as a local child welfare expert, Laura continued to make her name as a passionate public advocate of internationalism and peace. And once again, she linked these causes to economic justice and equality for women. The Women's International League for Peace and Freedom (WILPF), for which she was either president or an executive member until the Second World War, channelled these arguments, as did the Current Events Club that she ran as a small business. Tight finances kept her efforts largely concentrated in Vancouver and western Canada. Her unusual attendance at WILPF meetings in Geneva in 1927 and Prague in 1929 nevertheless kept ties close with global activists and Canadian friends such as Agnes Macphail, Violet McNaughton, and Mary McGeachy, the latter serving in the League of Nations secretariat.[25] When she ventured out of province, however, Laura usually went to the prairies, often as the guest of farm groups, to speak on peace and international relations.

As global conditions worsened in the 1930s, enthusiasm for peace mobilized increasing numbers of Canadians, but agreement on the relations among pacifism, internationalism, and social justice proved hard to find. When Ontario's Communist-aligned Women's Labour Leagues criticized Jane Adams, a founder of WILPF, as insufficiently attuned to the economic causes of war, Laura dismissed them and their newspaper, the *Woman Worker,* as "bad-tempered": they think "the worst about everyone else than just themselves." In a 1928 letter to Violet McNaughton, she contrasted such "bad policy," by which she meant the failure to reach out, with the generous reception given to WILPF by female labour leaders in Alberta and Manitoba. She summed up her preferred response for the sympathetic McNaughton: "I should like to tell these people that only by showing a better spirit than the capitalists will they ever get anywhere. 'You can build nothing upon hate!'"[26] That approach to coalition politics helped make Laura WILPF's leading public speaker in western Canada and the bane of more doctrinaire radicals.

A collaborative spirit was especially important because, as she lamented, "The fact that I am known in Vancouver as a Radical, and even to many as a 'dangerous woman,' mitigates against the popularity of my club."[27] Finding progressive allies was essential. In spring 1927, she was working with the Vancouver committee of the "Hands Off China" campaign, organized by British socialists and unionists, to demand that Western empires recognize the right of Chinese nationalists to an independent state.[28] By the autumn of that year, Laura was trusting that a prairie lecture series under the auspices of the Canadian Club signalled "that pacifists were no longer persona non grata to the establishment."[29] She likewise hailed as a victory for the art of persuasion that year's successful WILPF campaign "to de-militarize schools," when British Columbia finally eliminated cadet drills for boys.[30] In June 1928, she and MP James S. Woodsworth found appreciative audiences in the United Farmers of Canada for their arguments "that war was caused by the existing world economic system" and that alternatives were available. Laura saw this as justification for hope.[31] In August 1928, history seemed all the more on their side when Canada joined fourteen other nations to sign the Kellogg-Briand Pact (the General Treaty for Renunciation of War as an Instrument of National Policy) and the General Act for the Pacific Settlement of International Disputes.

In the dominion, WILPF's strength nevertheless remained locally concentrated, notably on the prairies and in Vancouver and Toronto, and staging national events remained difficult. Laura considered its operations as essential to the times because "only a few women's organizations are really and actively interested in Peace." WILPF's most effective role was to work with local partners and build bridges from there.[32] In Vancouver, this meant ongoing interaction with diverse groups. In November 1928, WILPF typically hosted a city conference on education and peace in co-operation with nineteen other societies. The inclusion of a "young East Indian" who brought a "peace message from the young people of India" as poster child for interracial co-operation was a common ploy.[33] In June 1929, Laura was building alliances at the Saskatoon Peace Conference, delivering a talk titled "How to Make the Kellogg Pact a Reality" and approving Woodsworth's condemnation of the armaments industry. Her lecture subsequently circulated as a pamphlet among the Saskatchewan Live Stock Pool, the Saskatchewan Poultry Pool, the Saskatchewan Registered Seed Growers, and the United Farmers of Canada, exactly the prairie groups whom she regarded as allies. By November, she was helping to organize Vancouver's second annual peace conference with some thirty societies on the theme of "Education and Peace." She optimistically assessed the initiative as "practical and realistic," with peace being "spoken of, not as a pious hope but as an objective which must have some assurance of attainment if any other form of social service is to be worthwhile."[34]

Jamieson's 1929 trip to Europe for meetings of WILPF, the World Federation of University Women, and the World Federation of Educational Associations subsidized her peace gospel lectures in Winnipeg, Toronto, and Montreal. There she characterized Canadian women as lucky "daughters of a country, free, wide and unembittered by old hatred," who ought to see "the point of view of the women in the older, battle-scarred parts of the world." They should stand with WILPF, which she proudly saluted, in an explicit reference to Woodsworth and the Labour MPs, as "the 'ginger group' of the League of Nations Society." Clearly expressing her sympathies with Western protest, she told Toronto audiences of "magnificent" prairie women who were more informed "about the new methods of education than many university graduates," and she referred to wheat pools as "the greatest experiments in co-operation which the world has ever seen." Women were also applauded for excellent work in League of Nations Committees in the Local Councils of Women, Home and School Clubs, the WCTU, and other women's societies.[35] Better than most men, they understood that advances in child welfare and education would be wiped out by war. She was less charitable about the peace efforts of Canadian churches, and expressions of religious faith were notably absent in her talks.[36]

Everywhere she went, Laura stressed personal effort. Her core principle held that "when informed people meet together face to face on social equality and discuss international questions, greater and finer things will be done than by diplomats standing a great distance apart with much clicking of heels." In grassroots practices, from improved housing to playgrounds and parks, and multilingualism, citizens learned to co-operate.[37] A new faith in people was needed to replace the reliance on violence that fuelled the armaments industry and wars. Ultimately as well, a peaceful world required that governments devote as much attention to "struggle between classes" as diplomats paid to conflicts among nations.[38] A fair deal for workers stood at the core of both good social policy and a peaceful future.

A 1930 appeal from Violet McNaughton typified their mutual hopes for consciousness raising: "I am taking the liberty of sending you an S.O.S. call [for] ... poems, human interest stories, little simple summaries of world conditions at this time or anything which you personally think would make an appeal to those who are not so keenly interested in the work for peace."[39] In the same vein, Laura directed the program of her Current Events Club particularly at local teachers and toured her lectures province-wide. Here she found occasions to express sympathy for the Soviet experiment, admitting its mistakes while insisting on its advances, and to champion reorganizing the Canadian economy co-operatively on the Scandinavian model.[40] The mounting despair of the 1930s gave her confidence that her listeners knew the right answer to her rhetorical question as to "whether a planned economy could be carried out under the capitalistic system or whether a change is required."[41] The sympathetic *Western Producer* furnished her "with a lot of ammunition."[42] The "monthly review of current events pertaining to war and peace" that she wrote for WILPF was acclaimed by McNaughton as among "the most statesmanlike documents to be found in Canada."[43]

By the early 1930s, WILPF's prospects seemed to be on the ascendant. The 1931 Japanese invasion of Manchuria, the 1935 Italian assault on Abyssinia, and the 1936–39 Spanish Civil War extended its appeal beyond the conventional left. In spreading the message, Laura had high hopes for Fraudena Gilroy (Mrs. Rex) Eaton (1892–1973), an executive member of the Local Council of Women (LCW). Later president of the National Council of Women of Canada and associate director of Ottawa's National Selective Service during the Second World War, she became WILPF president in 1936. Laura celebrated this "new blood" and anticipated stepping back.[44] Such tactical withdrawal accorded with WILPF internationally, where "socialist and anti-capitalist attitudes may have been common, but at the end of the day pluralism and the ability to work with many groups of different colours trumped all other ideologies."[45] Optimism was fuelled by WILPF's achievement of "an official status akin to the NGO status" after the Disarmament Conference of 1932–33.[46]

Other signs seemed to augur well. In January 1934, the editor of *Chatelaine* appealed to readers in a spirit reminiscent of the suffrage campaigns:

> It is NO LONGER true that Woman's place is only in the home.
>
> For these are times of stress: and, as always, women must get beyond their particular home interests and problems to help their men-folk in the world outside ... For there is much work to be done that only women can do.
>
> There is the challenge to battle for peace.
>
> A united womanhood could stop wars. An intelligent, understanding womanhood must educate the coming generation to be peace-minded.[47]

A month later, the same editor promised to run a series on peace, written by "leading thinkers."[48] Although plans for the series soon fizzled out, Laura's friend Irene Parlby, a former Alberta MLA, did get a chance to slam the "made-in-Canada" movement favoured by conservative politicians:

> Carried to its logical conclusion, it [autarky, or the resistance to imports] is a policy comparable to living by taking in each other's washing ... face to face with the crude facts of economic imperialism, economic nationalism, the whole ugly warfare of a competitive capitalist system and its fight for markets, its ruthless methods of exploitation and its claims for the protection and intervention of governments, ... [autarky will] lead to trouble in all countries to which it penetrates.[49]

Parlby's accompanying condemnation of the "great unthinking body of womanhood" underlined the continuing difficulties of recruitment and suffragist disappointment.[50]

Months later, with little to show for her call to action, *Chatelaine*'s editor could only invoke the past. Her November 1934 editorial, titled "Home Women in the World," turned once more to the club movement, specifically the venerable International Council of Women and the relative newcomer, the Pan-Pacific Association of Women. She hailed their meetings as attracting "women of every race and creed and type, learning to see beyond the confines of the world."[51] After that date, however, *Chatelaine* went missing in action on the peace front. It printed only occasional reminders of anti-war sentiments, as when it introduced readers to the noted English feminist writer and pacifist Vera Brittain, whom Laura was also recommending for her study groups.[52] No wonder the Canadian world secretary for the YWCA and president of the Women's International Labor Organizations berated audiences in 1935 Vancouver "for their general indifference to questions of world economics, peace and equality."[53] Jamieson attributed some of the apparent lack of interest to the media: for instance, she described the editor of the *Vancouver Province,* who routinely ignored WILPF, as "very imperialistic."[54] The more mainstream groups with which she was affiliated could also be frustrating; she castigated the League of Nations Society for resisting a strong stand on peace lest it appear unpatriotic or anti-British.[55]

From irrepressible Jamieson's perspective, such resistance existed to be overcome. March 1937 typically saw her celebrate both International Women's Day and the World Peace Congress. Along with Dorothy Steeves, a female officer of the League of Nations Society who was elected to the BC legislature for the Co-operative Commonwealth Federation in a 1934 by-election in North Vancouver, Laura foresaw better times as she listened to a "symposium of anti-war poems" given by radical poet Dorothy Livesay.[56] WILPF's strategic use of First World War anniversaries to stage children's peace pageants, school "Good Will Days," essay contests, and radio programs offered the additional gift of global "friendship and co-operation ... [which] strengthens ... groups in countries where the war spirit is perhaps stronger. It tends to make *friends* of possible enemy nations, which is the strongest defense against war yet devised."[57]

By the mid-1930s, however, all was not well in Canada's premier women's peace group. Disagreement mounted between resolute pacifists and anti-fascist advocates of pooled or collective security. WILPF "found itself in an inescapable dilemma; its commitment to non-violence was in danger of being compromised by its commitment to social justice, which some inter-war pacifists had already begun to equate with the necessity to resist fascism, if need be, by armed resistance."[58] By the end of the decade, Laura had made her own hard choice: neither Canada nor the United States could "afford to let Europe fall by remaining aloof." She denied deserting WILPF's core principles, arguing that its founders had not been "composed of pacifists, but of women who would prevent war and settle difficulties without killing."[59] She sided with international WILPF leaders such as Emily Greene Balch, who concluded that security required "democratic collective defence against fascism."[60] One common argument, however, did not change: as Laura reminded a WILPF audience in 1937, peace-makers had to eliminate the material causes of conflict. Without economic justice, wars would continue.[61] By 1939, she was campaigning for the embargo of belligerents such as Italy and Japan, and was appealing to Ottawa to give besieged China financial assistance "so that [it] might buy Canadian foods and have more resistance against the [Japanese] aggressor."[62]

The determination to address the root causes of war engaged WILPF in fostering cultural diversity and respect. The preferred approach was to initiate multicultural pageants, festivals, and workshops, and then hand them over to other organizations to carry on.[63] The Vancouver Folksong and Dance Festival was a significant strategic foray into intercultural communication that Laura highlighted in 1933 for the *Canadian Forum,* the dominion's leading left-wing monthly. She argued that a better introduction of immigrants could counteract the reception of "the foreigner" as a rather unlovable "specimen of mankind." In 1925, this ambition had inspired her when she joined the new Vancouver International Club, with its mandate to create a "happy social milieu for members of many of the national groups in the city." Under the direction of her friend Nellie McCay (Mrs. John T., 1884–1971), previously president of the LCW, the club partnered with WILPF in hosting events. In September 1933, they produced the first Vancouver Folksong and Dance Festival, including an Arts and Crafts Exhibition, to encourage "Anglo-Saxons to appreciate more strongly the art of the new Canadians; and ... the latter to preserve and continue the arts of their motherlands."[64] The YWCA and the LCW were similarly minded supporters of the festival, and MLA Steeves and Garfield King, a labour lawyer, former Liberal, and executive member of the Vancouver Proportional Representation Society, with links to the Communist Party, served as patrons. More mainstream credentials were confirmed when the festival received useful assistance from the Canadian

Pacific Railway, which anticipated that it would enhance global tourism. In deference to volatile passions, festival celebrations sidestepped many contemporary antagonisms, leaving unmentioned the Spanish Civil War, for example. Moreover, the festival was selectively global. In 1933, very typically, the only non-Europeans to appear were Japanese women who offered flower arrangements and tea making, and "a Chinese gentleman" who demonstrated "seal-cutting."[65]

In a host of venues, such as the folk festival, culture emerged as a key battleground for BC hearts and minds. Soon after its founding in 1932, the Vancouver CCF supported ten play-reading groups.[66] By 1936, New Westminster had hosted a workers' drama festival. When Laura addressed the annual 1937 CCF summer camp on the meaning of the proletarian literature of her age, she voiced sympathies that were evident in the 1935 Vancouver Progressive Arts Club staging of *Waiting for Lefty*, an agit-prop play that focused on a New York City taxi strike.[67] Many of its crew and cast members were jobless workers, and the production was heavily scrutinized by the Vancouver Police, the BC Provincial Police, and the RCMP, but it played to packed houses and ultimately won the 1936 Dominion Drama Festival Prize for best English-language play.[68] The link between the arts and radical politics was visible as well when Laura and poet social worker Dorothy Livesay shared stages and co-operated in establishing the West End Community Centre.

Under Laura's leadership, WILPF also championed anti-racist activists from minority communities. In 1933, she typically endorsed Jerry Hundal as a speaker. A Sikh who had been admitted to Canada in "an act of grace [effectively on humanitarian grounds] back in 1913," Hundal was a UBC graduate, a member of the Greater Vancouver Student Christian Movement and the International Club, and an advocate for Gandhi and the Indian National Congress.[69] In 1934, WILPF and the Canadian Institute for International Affairs hosted UBC professor H.F. Angus, who called for the enfranchisement of Canadian-born Japanese and urged women's clubs to admit Japanese women.[70] In March 1937, WILPF demanded "full rights of citizenship" for these same Canadians.[71] A year later, Laura praised "a very fine East Indian," Dr. Anup Singh Dhillon, who had spoken to WILPF on India's constitution. She judged him "very broadminded & fair," even as she warned Violet McNaughton that "he wouldn't suit your Canadian Club perhaps but would certainly suit your friends."[72]

Pervasive hostility sometimes encouraged tactical backtracking. In 1937, according to a Vancouver newspaper, Laura suggested that "family limitation for Orientals in British Columbia would be a means of relieving some of the resentment caused by their population pressure." That extraordinary idea, tabled for study and subsequent discussion at WILPF, disappeared almost immediately.[73] What it signalled at the very least, however, was Jamieson's caution in the face of widespread hostility regarding Japanese residents in British Columbia, especially at a time when progressive observers were horrified by the Japanese assault on China.

Efforts to combat racism nevertheless persisted. Jamieson and WILPF sometimes found allies in the Woman's Christian Temperance Union (WCTU), that early suffragist stalwart. Shared sympathies surfaced in 1934, when the local WCTU voted two to one in favour of "civic rights" for Canadian-born Asians and heard its president urge it to "disregard racial prejudice."[74] Opposition to Japanese expansionism in China and Korea accompanied the repudiation of local bigotry, even as it complicated it. Like other peace workers, veteran WCTU members condemned the export of copper and scrap metals to Japan as strengthening the Japanese war machine. Reflecting its diminished status in interwar Canada, the WCTU asked Laura to suggest "efficient" organizers for a march to protest the exports. She supplied names, admitting later that her choices were probably "fellow travellers," in effect either communists or advocates of a common front. Such a selection showed the strength of the Communist Party in staging anti-war protests and its close links with a broad range of progressive women.[75]

Less controversial were WILPF links to the Pan-Pacific Association of Women. Created to foster regional understanding, it began to meet in 1928. Its 1937 Vancouver conference started with great expectations, seeing both "friendly exchanges between the Japanese and Chinese delegations" and hope for "women's cultural internationalism."[76] Again, however, certain silences were deafening. Notably, Canada's own mistreatment of racial minorities and exclusion of Asian migrants went largely unmentioned. As a local delegate to the 1937 conference, Jamieson could offer only an "oblique reference to White Canada" policies, expressing "the hope that the part played by Chinese and Japanese delegates at the conference would help extend goodwill for the nationals of those countries living in Canada."[77] Her nomination by the Canadian Federation of Business and Professional Women as a delegate to the anticipated Pan-Pacific group's 1940 conference in Wellington, New Zealand, was scuppered by the Second World War.[78] Before that outcome, Laura joined Helena Gutteridge to work with women members of Vancouver's Chinese community to welcome a female student activist from China who toured North

America in 1939, urging support for her country.[79] Concerns about the deteriorating situation in Asia were matched by horror at events in Europe. As WILPF representative, Laura found allies in the LCW to urge Ottawa to admit Jewish refugees.[80]

Laura and WILPF's efforts at global co-operation always ran up against pervasive racism. This was nothing new and feminists were sometimes complicit. The conclusion of Judge MacGill that laws should not be based on "race prejudice or suspicion, but on moral as well as industrial protection" could not dislodge ready bigotry.[81] In 1924, MLA Mary Ellen Smith had introduced a bill to eliminate the Chinese employment of "white or Indian women or girls," and economic collapse merely strengthened the desire to discriminate. Even relatively progressive Burnaby was not immune: in 1930, some of its residents were up in arms about what they designated an "Oriental Colony," or more correctly land purchases by local Chinese buyers. In a typical expression of paranoia, whites were portrayed as victims of "a more virile and calculating race of a different colour."[82] Such bigotry flourished. By 1933, Vancouver had given birth to the Fascists of Canada, which claimed nearly 1,300 members.[83] In 1937, the Asiatic Exclusion League and the Native Sons of British Columbia launched a campaign to "clean up" Vancouver's Chinatown. Once again, they targeted Chinese-owned restaurants as moral threats to white female employees. The waitresses themselves defended their honour and their jobs, and mustered significant support from the Hotel, Restaurant and Culinary Employees and the Bartenders Unions, the Women's Labour League, the Vancouver Mother's Council, and WILPF. That confrontation, like many others, exposed the explosive racial politics that inflamed BC public life.

Laura's activist agenda readily linked opposition to racism with condemnation of mounting economic inequality. Nor could the two issues be separated. Canadian WILPF members, like those elsewhere, committed themselves to a 1934 declaration that made it their duty "to work for social change and economic justice." Peace and racial harmony were impossible without the redistribution of wealth.[84] In considering the soaring unemployment, evictions, malnutrition, and defaults of the 1930s, Laura saw the "end of an era" and once again the need for a very "different type of economic life."[85] Governments' recurring use of martial law and the police and military against the unemployed, unionists, and their allies continued the class warfare that Laura had seen in the general strikes after the First World War. Global and national peace required raising "the standard of living, making manufactured articles available to the masses and higher wages."[86]

As she faced the Great Depression, Laura retained her emphasis on the grassroots. The first step toward solutions was to reinforce practices of working together. Confident that "co-operative associations are the intermediate steps between the present order & the Socialist State,"[87] she joined Burnaby's Army of the Common Good, composed of the unemployed and their sympathizers. This group printed its own money, popularly dubbed "lulus," established a co-operative store, farmed, logged, and built furniture in the quest for self-sufficiency and respect.[88] Its members took a secret personal pledge to support "the Army of the Common Good and the Cause of Humanity ... to think, and act and speak constructively, and to count the interests of the common good as dear as life itself" – exactly the vision favoured by WILPF.[89] The army itself drew inspiration from a utopian anti-capitalist polemic titled *A War on Poverty: The One War That Can End War* (1925), written by prairie radical and co-operator Edward Alexander Partridge, whom Laura admired.[90] Such initiatives offered essential training. As Laura explained to McNaughton, "co-operatives in some form are simply indispensable to any form of Socialism; and of course should be used whenever possible under capitalism also."[91] As members learned the methods and values of solidarity, they took "the intermediate steps between the present order and the socialist state."[92] As she sought out the like-minded in British Columbia, Laura envied McNaughton the farmer co-operators of the prairies. She in contrast had to look to allies in settings such as the UBC continuing education program, which readily endorsed internationalism and progressive politics.[93]

In all her efforts, Laura highlighted the gendering of hard times. As always, reactionaries, drawing on prejudices that defined all women as properly dependants of men,[94] reckoned that good jobs were the particular prerogative of one sex. Both employers and unionists often agreed that wives should rely on their husbands and that unmarried daughters should be kept by their fathers. As in the past, looming directly below such rhetoric was the reality of prostitution. Canadian Morley Callaghan used his popular realist (and moralist) novel *Such Is My Beloved* (1934) to depict young women who were forced to sell themselves. It was a regular on Laura's reading lists. In Vancouver, WILPF stalwart Mildred Osterhout used a radio broadcast to sum up other brutal costs:

> A girl of 26, whose husband of 41 is a proven degenerate, with several jail records, and who has beaten her unmercifully on 3 occasions, left him. They were on relief, but when she applied for her allowance separately she was refused and told she must go back to the vicious brute. If she didn't that was so much saved to the capitalist coffers.[95]

Far from the independence and freedom that suffragists had championed, such heartbreaks worsened throughout these years.

Organizations such as the Vancouver Women's and Girls' Club and the Single Unemployed Women's Protective Association put their rights before unions and progressive women to demand "equal treatment for the unemployed regardless of marital status or sex."[96] Female workers joined with jobless men to demand relief, resist evictions, condemn the high cost of living, and set up picket lines. These were claims for economic justice that Vancouver WILPF members understood and championed.

Pervasive resistance to economic equality for women kept activists frequently defensive. In 1930, Helen MacGill used *Chatelaine* to explain that only women's lower wages kept them trapped in jobs that men often refused and that daughters supported entire families.[97] Vancouver clubwomen's mobilization on behalf of their sex during the 1930s ultimately offered a mixed message. An early assessment of the BC Conference of the YWCA, the LCW, and the Women's Missionary Society of the United Church was scathing: these groups left unquestioned "the social and economic system which had produced the Depression."[98] Although the Vancouver YWCA opposed cuts to relief rates in 1932 and established an accommodation annex and a club for single unemployed women, with classes in typing, sewing, stenography, and gymnastics, its assistance was readily compromised. It eventually concentrated on directing the unemployed into domestic service. On the other hand, CCF sympathizers such as Jamieson, Gutteridge, and Steeves kept the LCW challenging malestream agendas.[99] It joined with the New Era League (NEL, successor to the Political Equality Leagues) in a "women's coalition that took on relief issues in Vancouver on a broad scale."[100] In 1933, the LCW led in campaigning for women appointees to the advisory board of the city's relief committee and in arguing for the restoration of provincial mothers' pensions.[101] A year later, the NEL demanded that a proper provincial welfare department be established.[102] Such agendas readily brought feminists into conflict with elite men in the Vancouver Welfare Federation, founded in 1929 in co-operation with the board of trade.[103] The federation had little sympathy for clubwomen's preferred solutions, such as foster care, mothers' pensions, and welfare services. From its business-minded perspective, poorer citizens were not to be trusted but disciplined.

As Laura remembered, the era's crippling misogyny repeatedly compromised claims for justice:

> Oh, we believed that women should have the RIGHT to work, just as men have, and that women should be left to make their own decision as to

> whether they SHOULD work, or should not, just as men are left to decide. Not to let them decide for themselves would be treating them like children, not grown up adults. Only a few of us said this, however; and we felt that this was not the time to campaign for legislation protecting married women from dismissal, because there would be too little support for it.[104]

Her fears were confirmed in the anti-equality sermons that littered the popular press. *Saturday Night* magazine typically regaled readers with Benito Mussolini's denunciation of independent women as failing Western civilization in their refusal to bear numerous offspring.[105] In *Chatelaine,* established in 1928 to speak for modern women, former Montreal mayor Médéric Martin found a platform to demand that women surrender paid work to the more deserving sex, and prominent McGill behavioural psychologist William Dunlop Tait used the *Dalhousie Review* to blame feminism and woman suffrage for most errors of the contemporary world.[106]

Still more serious was the wholesale assault on social services by both Conservative and Liberal governments. Despite the grandiose title of the Sex Disqualification (Removal) Act (1931), which removed, retroactive to 1871, sex or marriage as a basis for job discrimination, it had nothing to do with equality and everything to do with a post-facto legalization of early (and rare) state appointments of women to boards and judicial positions.[107] The *CCF News* later summed up the law as constituting no more than "paper rights for women."[108] Other assaults on women's rights were more obvious. The cornerstone of the suffragist agenda had been mothers' pensions, but like minimum wages and employment in teaching, nursing, and social work, they could not be taken for granted. The 1932 *Report of the Committee to Investigate the Finances of British Columbia* proposed massive cuts, including ending education at age fourteen, capping funding for social services, and cutting civil servant salaries.[109] In the same year, Victoria transferred half of the costs of mothers' pensions to already desperate municipalities. Nor were municipal politicians friendly to women. In 1939, Vancouver alderman Helena Gutteridge had to fight a proposal to limit the employment of wives.[110] The city's anti-vice campaign of that year similarly victimized women. Siding with Gutteridge, Jamieson summed up the bankruptcy of municipal campaigns: "Society is creating prostitutes so rapidly that all the social services and welfare organizations and all the churches can not possibly care for them, and supposing they could take them all in and give them useful training of what use would that be when there are no jobs for them when they come out?"[111] Ultimately, feminists such as Laura and Helena stood with a small group of concerned citizens in recognizing the decade's fundamental threats to women's human rights.

In December 1933, the *Vancouver News-Herald* confirmed Laura's importance as a feminist advocate in selecting her as one of twelve "prominent club women" to reflect on prospects after the election of the Liberal administration of Dufferin Pattullo. Her response was blunt:

> We are told prosperity is returning. What prosperity? That of 1928 and 29? The question, we as women and mothers should face on the eve of 1934 is this: Do we want a prosperity based on the same old, sordid foundations, with the same disillusionment of youth; or do we want a new prosperity, not so big perhaps, in material things, but built upon a basis for which our youth can work with eagerness and admiration?[112]

In short, better times required a fundamental shift in politics, much more than that offered by the new Liberal premier in his "little New Deal."

In 1935, the creation of the Mother's Day Committee to assist the desperate male unemployed who increasingly crowded Vancouver streets depended on the long-standing cultivation of shared sympathies. Using the familiar trope of "militant mothering," with its claims to universalism, to counter conservatives' stress on laissez-faire survivalism, the committee provided food and clothing and supported rallies and petitions.[113] Male

Vancouver Mother's Council aids the unemployed, 1935 | Glenbow Archives, NA-3634-10

relief camp workers became its putative sons.[114] In such efforts, Laura co-operated with communist women.[115] On April 28, 1935, the committee mobilized some two thousand women, who led about fourteen thousand men to the city centre to condemn all governments.[116] The prominent participation of women did much to reduce violence, but by May 1935, as reactionary forces centred on the BC Citizens' League tarred all resistance as a "Red" threat, government became more antagonistic to the inhabitants of relief camps.[117] On July 1, the On-to-Ottawa Trek of the unemployed, which had set out from Vancouver, met a bloody end at police hands in Regina. That incident deepened the divide between advocates of the economic and political status quo and their opponents on the left, and it further discredited the Conservative government of R.B. Bennett.

Vancouver's ongoing feminist protest brought continuing surveillance by the Royal Canadian Mounted Police. Its "Reports on Revolutionary Organizations and Agitation in Canada" provided a nervous government with details about a March 8, 1937, meeting to celebrate International Women's Day, chaired by Margaret Delmage, an eminently respectable PTA activist and secretary of the League of Nations Society.[118] That stalwart introduced Laura Jamieson, who, in what was hardly a revolutionary claim, described women's use of the franchise as an essential force for good. MLA Dorothy Steeves followed with a condemnation of the Department of National Defence and relief camps. Dorothy Livesay then read anti-war verse. A United Church minister preached on the text of "Thou Shall Not Kill," an evocative admonition at a time when police forces were assaulting the jobless. The audience also heard from CCFer Elizabeth Kerr, who was departing for the Soviet Union, and from the communist Peggy Harrison of the Women's Labour League and the Mother's Council, who had just returned.[119]

In May 1938, the communist-dominated Mother's Council, formerly the Mother's Day Committee, took to the streets in support of sit-down strikers, many from provincial work camps, at the Vancouver Post Office, art gallery, and Hotel Georgia. Laura joined CCF women in supporting the broader-based Vancouver Women's Emergency Committee to Aid the Single Unemployed. Though it collaborated with the Mother's Council, it deliberately reached out to diverse groups, including the Imperial Order Daughters of the Empire (IODE), the SPCA, and the Liberal Women's Association, to demand fair federal work programs and to organize assistance. When the police arrested the city's jobless panhandlers, known as "tin-canners," Laura united with the emergency committee and the Mother's Council in denunciation.[120] Soon she chaired an emergency committee meeting to hear Dorothy Steeves support strikers and Helena Gutteridge endorse a federal works scheme at union rates.[121] When the mayor condemned these interventions as a communist plot, the committee rejected his red baiting.[122] Laura faced similar charges when, speaking as a representative of WILPF, she "strongly deplored the action of the authorities" in tear gassing protesters.[123] These recurring battles with obdurate governments at all levels fostered Laura's growing support for the CCF and her eventual decision to resign the Burnaby judgeship and test the world of electoral politics. That is the story of the next chapter.

5
The Challenge of Electoral Politics, 1927–39

After the initial elation of the early 1920s, feminists found no ready welcome in any political party. Fractured and male-controlled institutions strengthened the appeal of women's groups, whose disagreements Laura at least found familiar and sometimes moderated by personal histories of collaboration. The continuing crises of the 1930s, nevertheless, once again demonstrated the limits of civil society protest. There was only so much that groups such as the Women's International League for Peace and Freedom (WILPF), the Parent-Teacher Association, and the Mother's Day Committee could do. Significant change required electoral power. Just how this could be secured challenged Laura and her contemporaries.

All parties courted women as dutiful volunteers while simultaneously resisting their equality. The Liberal Party's refusal to promote MLAs Mary Ellen or Helen Smith, and its regular backtracking on reform measures, confirmed its retreat into its own reservoir of middle-class male entitlement during the interwar years. Farther to the right, the Conservatives, with their particular opposition to the franchise and social legislation, were never an option for Laura. Pretensions to "new deals" in the 1930s by provincial Liberals and federal Conservatives were ultimately meaningless. British Columbians also confronted new contenders and other promises on the right. The 1920s saw the rise of the ardently pro-business Provincial Party. In the next decade, Social Credit clubs offered a confused program of hostility to and accommodation with capitalism, whereas breakaway Conservatives set up the Reconstruction Party in opposition to Prime Minister R.B. Bennett.[1] Also of concern for Laura and other democratic champions were efforts to unite Vancouver Liberals and Conservatives in the municipal Non-Partisan Association, which later blocked her anti-poverty efforts as a city alderman. In short, even as they crowded politics and distracted voters, no centre or right-wing program offered any realistic base for addressing electoral or other forms of unfairness.

Nevertheless, even as Laura's commitment to child welfare, internationalism, and human rights located her in the midst of Canada's democratic socialist culture, voting alternatives on the left were similarly fractious and fluid. In 1926, the Independent Labour Party (ILP) emerged from a battered Federated Labour Party, which had first captured her loyalty. Modelled on the British Labour Party, which formed a government in 1924, the ILP coalition linked many BC progressives, with the conspicuous exception of the old Socialist Party of Canada, which feared a dilution of Marxist principles. Both the ILP and the Socialist Party battled with the Canadian Communist or Workers' Party, and the issue of a common front on behalf of the unemployed and against fascism was persistently contentious. Divisions were so great that one authority has concluded that "by 1928 the political left in BC seemed barely to register a pulse."[2] With the Great Depression's deepening of class conflict, however, the ILP arose as a reinvigorated Socialist Party of Canada (SPC) in 1932. Its members, proud "labour socialists," such as Ernie and Harold Winch, relied on a self-conscious working class and credited it and themselves with a special radical authenticity, as well as the right to set the standards for socialist orthodoxy.[3]

In 1932 and 1933, however, while the Co-operative Commonwealth Federation (CCF) was being formed, the new SPC had to share radical space with a progressive think-tank named the League for Social Reconstruction (LSR), its ally the BC Reconstruction Party, and the local CCF clubs that spread throughout the province. Unlike the SPC, both the league and the clubs could generally be described as broadly social democratic, with a preference for parliamentary action. Their relations with the SPC could be chilly. Dismissing league members as counterfeit socialists, the SPC was strong enough to ban the LSR's *Social Planning for Canada* from approved reading as nothing but "muddled thinking," no more than "barely distinguishable from the proposals of present-day radical liberals."[4] The CCF clubs were judged equally unsound, drawing on many British Columbians' deep disillusionment with conventional politics rather than serious investment in socialist doctrine. When charismatic membership recruiters such as the CCF's own Lyle Telford strayed into anti-bank orations reminiscent of Social Credit's William Aberhart in Alberta and populist investment in anti-statism and strong leaders, doubts seemed confirmed.[5]

Nor was possible populist fervour the only source of questionable neophytes for the left. Technocracy, an American group born out of the Great War, arrived in British Columbia with proposals to redistribute wealth and eliminate corruption and inefficiency by replacing politicians with scientists and engineers.[6] Sometimes judged a cult, it sufficiently questioned capitalism to inquire about affiliating with the CCF, which allowed the CCF clubs to form technocracy study groups.[7] In 1933, Jamieson devoted a speech to its arguments, which occasionally resembled those of the League for Social Reconstruction, not a comparison that she made explicit.[8] Though this alternative quickly faded, Technocracy's presence confirmed the confused state of much Depression-era politics.

As it endeavoured to set the ideological benchmark for the BC CCF, the SPC readily appeared dogmatic, unwelcoming, and masculinist. In its view, the social democratic constituencies cultivated by Laura in Vancouver's International Club, WILPF, the Theosophical Society, and church groups, all of which were likely to supply members for the CCF clubs, were little more than second best. The good "labour credentials" of feminists such as Helena Gutteridge could not offset the suspect class origins of Jamieson and others, and could not correct what was regarded as an inadequate appreciation of socialist theory.[9] Even as the nascent provincial CCF sought a common platform for its disparate elements, differences about the best way to confront capitalism produced bitter struggles and departures. Such conflicts probably disproportionately deterred female recruits, socialized more often than men to avoid conflict.

Distinctions between the two founding wings of the CCF survived into the 1960s. Determined members who were associated with the SPC perspective continued to treasure their "mission of providing the working-class ideological direction to the CCF,"[10] even as their social democratic compatriots stressed a broad-tent socialism that would include middle-class as well as working-class voters. In 1936, the SPC faction's role in dispatching the provincial CCF leader, Anglican clergyman Robert Connell, who was termed "a very conservative radical," confirmed that a socialism invested in much Marxist orthodoxy would dominate the provincial party.[11] After she became a CCF MLA in 1939, Laura tacitly acknowledged the power of the SPC grasp on legitimacy by self-consciously aligning herself at public events with the working class and playing down her bourgeois identity. Later still, however, in the context of the Cold War, she helped mobilize the CCF's moderate wing in curbing and expelling doctrinal hard-liners, who from her perspective threatened electoral success. Above all, her commitment was to democratic and parliamentary socialism.

In the end, despite all their differences, co-operation among the CCF factions was guaranteed by the spectacular growth of the CCF clubs in 1932–33, which promised to mobilize a wider pool of voters. As Dorothy Steeves, herself a founder of the LSR in British Columbia but soon a powerful recruit to the SPC argument that capitalism must be rooted out, concluded, suspect middle-class allies might well be "genuine converts to socialism" and even long-time voters for labour candidates. Much like Steeves herself, they could be rescued for the greater cause.[12] In emphasizing redemption, she could also have been describing Laura. Such conclusions, reflecting an ultimately shared commitment "to both revolutionary change and to parliamentaryism and gradualism," ensured that the CCF produced significant consensus about day-to-day operations.[13] That agreement set the foundation for the allegiance of many feminists.

Laura's socialism, like that of the SPC, pre-dated the recruits of the 1930s. It drew on her early attachment to the Federated Labour Party and her sustained commitment to WILPF. However, because she shared the LSR faith in progressive policy research and favoured the CCF clubs' inclusive pattern of recruitment, they supplied her point of entry as a democratic socialist or social democrat (the terms were relatively interchangeable) into the CCF partnership of socialists, radical farmers, and progressive intellectuals. The leadership of her friend James S. Woodsworth made the transition into party loyalist all the easier. The *Vancouver News-Herald*'s description of his summer 1933 lecture to the local Rotary Club underscored his influence in enlarging socialism's tent:

> Socialism has arrived in Canada ... The applause was directed as much to the man himself – in appreciation of his integrity and sincerity and steadfast intellectual honesty – as to the ideals he represents ... What is important, however, is that Socialism is now something that can be discussed by anyone, in any circles, without incurring [the] danger of being dubbed "Red" or "Bolshevik."[14]

Even as rivals jockeyed for influence on the left, the North Winnipeg MP promised activists such as Laura a long-desired progressive coalition that could finally challenge the old parties on parliamentary terrain, where decisions on human welfare were actually made.

Although she did not attend the founding convention of the CCF, Laura had joined Vancouver's CCF Club No. 26 by October 1932. As she explained to Violet McNaughton, it was "a local movement, mostly young people," which workshopped key Fabian and social democratic texts such as G.D.H. Cole's *The Intelligent Man's Guide through World Chaos* (1932).[15] Though *Social Planning for Canada* was anathema to the SPC, it also became a staple on Laura's reading lists for her Current Events Clubs, which readily served as recruiting grounds for progressive allies. As her support for many recommendations of the Royal Commission on Dominion-Provincial Relations (the Rowell-Sirois Commission, 1937–40) would indicate, she shared the LSR's hope that expanded government, staffed by specialists, would assist a peaceful transition to a socialist state.[16]

While working with WILPF and parent-teacher groups, Laura championed education, an emphasis she brought into the CCF. In particular, she worried lest newcomers to left politics were joining "in an emotional reaction; and the great majority of them will not do any serious study & hence cannot give an intelligent contribution. Such a movement is apt to have a severe setback later unless we can educate the individuals."[17] Rather ironically, she shared this concern with labour socialists, who likewise feared members with inadequate training in history, politics, or theory but who viewed her credentials with skepticism.[18] Her trust in consciousness raising provoked a humorous retort from veteran suffragist CCFer Susie Lane Clark, who could not resist observing that the Conservatives and Liberals had "flourished for a good many years" without "intelligent & informed members."[19]

After joining the moderate arm of the CCF, Laura further distinguished herself by embracing enthusiasm for agrarian radicals, whose cause she had supported since the 1920s, and counting on a rising feminist consciousness. In the 1930s, the woman who had grown up on a marginal homestead still hoped to see the farmers' movement supply "the back-bone of any large movement toward a co-operative state."[20] On the west coast, however, agrarian radicals were few in number and ultimately inconsequential to the provincial party. Though regular visits to the prairies and communication with Violet McNaughton of the *Western Producer* kept Laura a loyal admirer of left-wing farmers, other allies were always far more important in British Columbia.

Progressive women were the obvious source of additional talent and energy. Laura's advocacy of feminist issues and networks attempted to link the older tradition of suffragist radicalism to the new party. However, unlike the Communist Party, established more than a decade earlier, the CCF lacked a platform statement on women's rights, although it did endorse equal pay, not a choice of either free-market Liberals or Conservatives.[21] Whatever their varying interpretations of socialism, the CCF's partners all favoured their own (largely male) communities when it came to leadership and liberation. Members in general took for granted men's right to shape the new party, with the unglamorous tasks of fund-raising, catering, and building libraries, such as Laura performed for the LSR, delegated to women.

Across Canada, opportunities for public speaking and leadership were far fewer for CCF women than for their male counterparts. The common reception was signalled at the 1936 CCF national convention, when Winnipeg feminist activist Beatrice Brigden's report on "the establishment of women's groups to discuss birth control ... was greeted with 'chortles' of amusement by the assembly."[22] In 1938, the election of three women to the BC CCF executive was typically derided in many circles as a sign of "feminist control," an aspersion rejected by the women's columnist for the party newspaper. Laura would have shared her conclusions: "Why shouldn't that womanly view be expressed in our movement? For a movement boasting no differences in race and creed, some of our Marxian socialists are pitifully mid-Victorian."[23] Ultimately, however, for all the CCF's persisting misogyny, feminist members had to trust to long-term awakening and a broadening awareness of oppression.

Laura's remedies for CCF limitations emphasized the potential of existing independent women's groups and the value of separate organization within the party itself. Ultimately, self-conscious women, like the working class, could be trusted and mobilized through an active program of education to counter the abuses of capitalism. That response explains why she and other feminists established the Women's Lyceum, later called the CCF Women's Council, as a forum to recognize and reward contributions. Friendships among outspoken feminists, such as Laura, Violet McNaughton, and Agnes Macphail, fuelled determination and loyalty. So too did close observation of women's politics elsewhere. When British Labour politician, unionist, and women's rights advocate Margaret Bondfield lectured in Vancouver in June 1938, Laura recognized a kindred spirit. In saluting female MPs across the Atlantic, who kept "their heads and their independence of action in spite of party lines" in foreign policy debates, she shared feminist hopes that women would have a key role as full members as democracy matured.[24]

Political maturation nevertheless proved disappointingly glacial. The years after Jack's death and Laura's judicial appointment were depressing for female activists everywhere. Only three women contended the July

1928 BC election. The sole Liberal was pioneering MLA Mary Ellen Smith, who ran in Esquimalt just outside of Victoria rather than in her previous Vancouver riding. Unable to mobilize the broad feminist constituency that had brought success on the Lower Mainland, she lost. Two relative unknowns – Gladys Elspeth Cross of Golden, an Independent running for the constituency of Columbia,[25] and Mrs. J. McGregor as an Independent Conservative in Victoria – both seemingly without significant allies among organized women, also went down to defeat. The Liberal Party's unwillingness to build on its inheritance of fielding the province's first female legislator and the socialist and labour movement's failure to recruit women, as it had in the 1924 BC election, were particularly unedifying. As a result, the BC legislature was entirely male between 1928 and 1933, and the new one-term Conservative administration of Premier Simon Fraser Tolmie was left all the freer to ignore the distaff side of the electorate.

Journalist Anne Anderson Perry's coverage of the first national conference of Liberal women in April 1928 conveyed the divisions and exclusions that, alongside male hostility, thwarted hopes. Like Laura, she feared that too many women accepted the status quo. As the feminist veteran noted with disapproval, the Ottawa convention left entire "classes of women" inadequately represented, including "wives of laboring men, factory and store workers, the armies of stenographers and other business women now in our midst, and the farm women." Equally pointedly, she answered her own question as to why Laura's friend Agnes Macphail had not been invited despite her "liberal views on many subjects, as well as her alignment with the Progressives."[26]

Perry might also have wondered why neither *Chatelaine* nor *Maclean's Magazine,* two of Canada's leading magazines, published any serious treatment of the nation's first female MP. No wonder Helen Gregory MacGill titled a September 1928 article "Are Women Wanted in Public Life?" Her answer emphasized that her sex's "depressing" sense of inferiority, in concert with inadequate funding, could not rival men's prodigious lack of "doubt as to their own ability."[27] The Persons Case of 1929 did constitute a victory, which forced Liberal prime minister King to appoint the first female senator a year later and his successor, Conservative R.B. Bennett, to name the second in 1935.[28] But gains were few. No more female senators appeared until 1953, making them almost as rare as female MPs. Perry's gloomy 1930 conclusion that Canada favoured "Stag Politics" and that women had "meekly" accepted "the rule of thumb of the male politicians,"[29] backtracked on even the faint hope permeating her earlier coverage of Liberal women.

In 1930, R.B. Bennett became prime minister with 135 seats and 47.79 percent of the popular vote. The Liberal incumbent, W.L. Mackenzie King, was defeated with 89 seats and 45.50 percent of the vote. The United Farmers dropped to 9 seats and the Progressives to 3. James S. Woodsworth survived for Labour in Winnipeg North Centre. Only ten women contested ridings across the nation: three identified with the Liberals, two for the United Farmers, two as Independents, one as a Progressive, one as an Independent Conservative, and one as Labour. Once again, Agnes Macphail was the only woman elected. Few male commentators seemed concerned. In a *Chatelaine* article, conservative Ottawa journalist Grattan O'Leary defended the virtual monopoly of men. He opined without apparent fear of contradiction that politicians had no interest in courting women voters or addressing their issues. Lacking influence and now without the status of "angels," they counted as no more than political "window dressing." Even as he expressed contempt for female politicians, he blamed the victim and validated the offender. Women, he suggested, wanted "immunity from criticism and attack," despite the fact that most men were chivalrous.[30] Little wonder that Jamieson rejected the opportunity to run federally as a "sacrificial lamb" in 1930.[31] By 1933, the *Vancouver News-Herald* could assert the common anti-feminism of the day in concluding "Freedom of Women Now Unwanted Toy." The conclusion was brutal: there was "no single, lasting piece of legislation in Canada today that can be attributed to the influence of the women's vote." When they had lacked the vote, "downtrodden" women had been defended by male champions, but "the fighting Amazon," which meant Macphail and suffragists such as Jamieson, had none.[32]

Just as they did with the right to waged employment, feminists challenged such political misogyny. In 1933, a panel of leading Vancouver clubwomen, all well known to Jamieson and many numbered among her friends, collectively rebutted opponents to political equality. MacGill pointed to legislative gains, including minimum wage and equal guardianship, and insisted that relying on "influence gives unfair, unjust advantage to wealthy social position and sex appeal" while "the poor, the humble and the plain people are robbed and oppressed." The president of the Local Council of Women (LCW) and convert to WILPF, Fraudena Eaton argued that because women were so diverse, it was "short-sighted and stupid" to expect them merely to elect their own sex. The suffragist Mary Norton, president of the New Era League (NEL), conceded women's laxness "in making full use of their hard-won freedom" but anticipated that "present economic conditions are forcing them to take an active interest in politics – a sphere which they have been taught and trained to consider beyond their accepted domain." Alice Townley, president of the League of Women Voters and a journalist who had campaigned for the vote, was still more forthright, maintaining that she would not "admit that carelessness and neglect of our opportunities are universal failings of my sex today. I believe that women are much more alive to the fact that the vote is a privilege and a duty."[33] Notably, none mentioned being welcomed by any BC political party. In fact, Mary Ellen Smith, who had been narrowly defeated in the 1928 provincial election, was later eased out of consideration as a Liberal candidate by Pattullo and his Little New Deal campaign.[34] Less than two decades after the provincial enfranchisement of most women, progressive liberalism lacked a female or suffrage face in the legislature.

During the November 1933 provincial contest, eleven women ran for office. Most had significant links to the club movement or suffrage. One, Alice Townley, the first of her sex to serve on the Vancouver Parks Board, was the long-time League of Women Voters president and a regular speaker at Laura's home during the First World War. Two candidates – Mrs. Laura MacKay and Mrs. Nora Leavy – recollected early suffragist hopes in standing as Independent Non-Partisan candidates. In a similarly liberated spirit, two others sought election as representatives of the United Front (or Communist Party) and one more as an Independent. In a revealing indication of shared politics, an open meeting in Vancouver saw eight female candidates agree unanimously "on one common point – the betterment of conditions for women and children." WILPF member Mildred Osterhout, a CCF admirer of Mahatma Gandhi, veteran of Kingsley Hall settlement house in London, and manager of the Vancouver unemployed girls' co-operative club, attracted "the most attention by her Socialistic attitude."[35] Two years later, she would win a seat on the Vancouver School Board, where she fought to protect educational opportunities.

In the 1933 election, only Liberal Helen (Mrs. Paul) Douglas Smith won her constituency.[36] She would sit alone in the Victoria legislature for over a year. Like many female candidates for elected office at every level, Smith was a former teacher, but she had many other advantages. She was the first supreme factor of the Native Daughters of British Columbia, former president of both the University Women's Club and the Provincial Council of Women, and chairman of the Vancouver Board of School Trustees. As the grand-niece of former premier John Robson, she possessed additional credentials for traditional voters. When she advocated for old age pensions, health insurance, and unemployment relief, she also found progressive allies. After her solitary victory, clubwomen chose to close ranks in non-partisan support. The League of Women Voters, presided over by the defeated Townley, lobbied for Smith's immediate appointment to cabinet.[37] Within a few weeks, the NEL endorsed her as minister for a new public welfare portfolio that would address the deepening gulf between rich and poor.[38] Nonetheless, Smith would never enter the cabinet of Liberal Dufferin Pattullo. Despite earning a second term in 1937, she effectively disappeared from provincial public memory.

The disappointing returns in the federal elections of the 1930s spurred *Chatelaine* editor Byrne Hope Sanders to urge women to "banish, once and for all, the suggestion that they are lethargic" and to leave their homes to "raise such a storm of protest that you cannot be ignored."[39] An ad-filled publication, *Chatelaine* nevertheless contradicted that call to action. During much of the Great Depression, it focused on romance, fashion, and homemaking, with occasional backtracking into reactionary consideration of domestic service as the solution to female unemployment and outright misogyny from both male and female contributors.[40] No wonder that, in 1934, *Maclean's* declared politics "a man's world."[41]

The arrival that year of a new force in BC politics nevertheless questioned that dispiriting conclusion. Dutch-born lawyer Dorothy Gretchen Steeves, a Vancouver neighbour of Laura's, rose out of the same circle of progressive middle-class professionals who favoured CCF clubs, the BC Reconstruction Party, and the LSR. Her membership in WILPF, the Overseas University Graduates' Association, the International Club, and the League of Nations Society likewise signalled the value of local ties.[42] Steeves was an immigrant bride who joined her Canadian soldier husband, soon a Vancouver school principal, after the First World War. Her links to local feminism did not include suffrage. Backed by the security of her husband's salary, she could attend the Regina founding of the CCF as a BC delegate. Unlike Laura, Dorothy soon aligned with the Socialist Party wing of the CCF and would later write an admiring biography of one of its stalwarts, CCF MLA Ernest Winch. Celebrated as "a brilliant European scholar, full-fledged barrister and heroine of a Canadian war romance,"[43] she ran unsuccessfully in Vancouver-Point Grey during the 1933 provincial election. One year later, she benefitted from the split between Conservatives and Liberals to take a North Vancouver by-election. With this victory, British Columbia became the second Canadian jurisdiction to boast two female legislators (the first was Alberta in 1917). Steeves and Helen Smith had already crossed swords at meetings of the Vancouver LCW, when they disagreed about solutions to the Depression, and their differences persisted. In Victoria, the Dutch lawyer soon outpaced the first supreme factor of the Native Daughters of British Columbia, quickly establishing herself as a tough and informed debater much feared by mainstream opponents.

Liberal premier Pattullo had campaigned on putting British Columbia back to work, with enhanced government action and better terms from Ottawa. His ready introduction of a Special Powers Act (1934) gave "the cabinet most of the powers of the provincial legislature" and promised quick remedies that did not require the consent of MLAs. The outcry from champions of civil liberties prevented its invocation, but it embodied the era's ever-present threat of authoritarianism.[44] In other moves more calculated to cultivate progressive support, Pattullo increased school funding, teachers' salaries, and relief scales, and introduced a new apprenticeship system. However, by the 1937 election, when they lost four seats, the Liberals had dissipated much promise in fights with Ottawa about jurisdiction and funding. The party was also weakened by internal dissension about reforms to employment laws and social services. It fielded a health insurance plebiscite that year, and though the measure was approved by a majority, the proposal disappeared, confirming the Liberal tendency to campaign from the left and govern from the right. Meanwhile, the desperate situation of the unemployed was unfolding in work camps throughout the province and would soon spill into the streets of Vancouver.

The failure of the old parties was similarly evident in federal politics. Despite Prime Minister Bennett's sudden conversion to greater state intervention in the economy via another so-called New Deal, the Conservatives collapsed in the October 1935 election, which one Vancouver editorialist characterized as a battle of the "Left, Lefter and Leftest."[45] W.L. Mackenzie King's Liberals returned to power with 171 seats, leaving the Tories with a paltry 39. The Progressive Party and the United Farmers of Alberta disappeared, to be replaced on the left by the CCF. Led by Woodsworth, it took seven seats, three of them in British Columbia. Agnes Macphail was elected nominally for the United Farmers of Ontario, but she caucused with the CCF, which won 9.3 percent of the total popular vote. Seventeen Social Creditors arrived in Ottawa with 4.1 percent of the popular vote. Across Canada, sixteen women had taken to the hustings.[46] Only two triumphed, Macphail and the Conservative Yukoner Martha Black, who ran to retain the seat for her indisposed husband. One of Laura's friends, Lilette Mahon, well known locally from the League of Nations Society and the BC School Trustees Association, ran unsuccessfully in Vancouver Centre for the conservative Reconstruction Party, as one of its four female candidates.[47]

A feminist journalist credited the victory of Macphail and Black as a near "Act of God." In contrast, "the rest of their sex" caught only "a glimpse of the Promised Land which they may gaze upon, but never enter into possession of." Lamenting the fact that female candidates were fewer than in 1920, the writer foresaw threats to women's right to jobs and independence, and even feared that "great bodies of men will approach the law-makers to bring in Hitler-like legislation, relegating women out of their chosen professions, out of office and the store, back to the home."[48] Shortly after the federal result, the observant Laura condemned the failings of the electoral system, particularly the "disparity between the total number of votes cast for the various parties" and "the actual number of candidates elected for those parties." Without proportional representation, a remedy that had interested her since the enfranchisement campaigns when she had hosted discussion of its merits, many Canadians would be "left unrepresented."[49] She must also have been thinking of the unemployed on the streets of Vancouver, whom she had been championing in groups such as the Mother's Day Committee.

Female candidates were not the only losers: all parliamentarians were white. In British Columbia, the politics of race were especially visible. In a significant foretaste of future conflicts that would engage Laura and the CCF, BC Liberals used Woodsworth's endorsement of votes for Asians to launch a crusade of race hatred. Liberal posters shrieked, "A vote for any CCF candidate is a vote to give the CHINAMAN and the JAPANESE the same voting right you have. A vote for the Liberal candidate in your riding is a vote AGAINST ORIENTAL ENFRANCHISEMENT."[50] Post-election politics did not temper that bigotry. In 1936, despite pleas from a Japanese Canadian delegation, the Liberal majority in Ottawa rejected the universal equal citizenship bill proposed by Angus MacInnis, the CCF MP from East Vancouver.

By the 1937 provincial election, as the Liberal government in Victoria rapidly retreated from its promises to improve old age pensions, labour protection, and mothers' pensions,[51] the need and the electoral space for a progressive alternative were all the clearer. The contest produced eleven female candidates: four Liberals, two for the Social Credit League, two for the BC Social Constructive Party (a CCF breakaway group led by former leader Robert Connell, which fielded fourteen candidates), two for the CCF, and one Independent (previously a 1933 Liberal candidate). In a revealing indication of much generational change, none had a clear identification with earlier suffrage campaigns, though several had club affiliations.[52] The Liberals returned to office, winning thirty-one of forty-eight seats and 37.37 percent of the popular vote. The Conservatives recovered somewhat from their 1933 disaster to jump from two to eight seats and gain 28.60 percent of the vote. The CCF remained at seven seats, with 28.57 percent. One Labour and one male Independent (Conservative) MLA were also returned. The Conservatives formed the Official Opposition. For women, the tally was two. Steeves retook North Vancouver with 32.23 percent of the popular vote, and Liberal Helen Smith was returned in Vancouver with a plurality of 17.95 percent.

At much the same time, municipal politics provided another site for women to seek some traction in the battle between left and right. In 1937, the Vancouver LCW, whose roll call included the CCF Women's Group, the Domestic Workers' Union, and the Ukrainian Women's Association of the Labor Temple, together with long-standing members such as the Woman's Christian Temperance Union (WCTU), the Imperial Order Daughters of the Empire, and the YWCA, called on members to "Vote Women Candidates and Don't Betray Those Who Got the Vote for You." In an ecumenical spirit, it cheered on all five CCF and Liberal women who ran for civic office, a group that included suffragists, notably but not only Helena Gutteridge. It also approved a resolution prepared by its WCTU affiliate, "deploring the fact that no women were named to the citizenship committee" of the conservative civic Non-Partisan Association (NPA), which had been founded that year. Setting out to unite pro-business Liberals and Conservatives against the CCF municipally, the NPA portended the malestream coalition politics that would eventually engulf the province.[53] Such danger on the right explains why Laura continued to view the LCW as a valuable forum in which critical voices could make their case for change. In contrast, Steeves felt that the Liberals had far too much influence in LCW ranks.[54] The civic results saw Gutteridge repeat her earlier by-election victory to return to city council, where she continued the battles for democracy, housing, and employment that would mobilize Laura in the same role about a decade later.

As she watched parties vie for power and saw that the popular vote too often counted for little, Laura warned that the economic conditions and uncertainty of the Depression were threatening the foundations of democracy.[55] And once again, she urged the development of community resources to foster self-respect and democratic agency. In Burnaby, she struggled to use the authority of the Juvenile Court Committee to wrest concessions from the provincial Department of Physical Education and Recreation. Her proposed community centres in the north and south of the CCF-dominated municipality were intended to empower young people and offer constructive training for the future.[56] Such enhanced opportunities could lift spirits and foster democratic revival.

By 1938, the Burnaby judgeship had clearly become an insufficient and confining platform from which to tackle community problems. The Pattullo Liberals surely welcomed the resignation of so outspoken a local critic, but Laura's departure, which took effect on March 31,[57] also reflected the failing trajectory of women's judicial recognition. During this decade, women lost the jobs that had come with much suffragist hope.[58] More than ever, Canadian courts functioned as a male bailiwick, handing out justice that paid little attention to women's needs and vulnerabilities.

Unleashed from the judiciary, Laura soon sought political office. As she explained in 1939,

> eleven years as a Juvenile court judge in Burnaby had shown her juvenile delinquency is the result of economic conditions.
>
> "When I resigned from that court I decided to devote my time to getting to the root of the trouble" ... Describing how she had devoted her energy to the work of recreational and cultural centres for youth ... [she noted that they were] not really effective as long as young people are without "food and clothing."

She concluded with the keywords, "I have been a Socialist for a long time."[59]

The moment proved auspicious. By the end of the 1930s, she could draw on both her own tested strengths as an organizer and speaker and on many women's mobilization against the Depression and government shortcomings in groups such as the Mother's Council and the Women's Emergency Committee. Her long history of commitment to the welfare of women and children, and her extended international affairs training in WILPF and the Current Events Clubs were widely appreciated. Her ability to attract bipartisan support across a diverse range of liberal and socialist voters was an especially attractive asset. A reputation for expertise in global affairs helped explain her initial approval as a possible CCF candidate for the next federal election in Vancouver South. That opportunity, however, became irrelevant when a provincial by-election was called to replace a Liberal MLA for Vancouver Centre, who had suddenly died in office.

Endorsement by the federal CCF leader Woodsworth confirmed Laura's merits. In April 1939, perhaps in a gesture designed to appease suspicions about middle-class intruders in a struggle that the SPC felt properly belonged to the proletariat, he vouched for her as no "newcomer": after the First World War, she had studied socialism at his home. Only Laura's subsequent judicial service had prevented her from engaging more actively with the party (her marriage to a Liberal lawyer went unmentioned). However, "as soon as the opportunity came," she had thrown "herself actively into the work of the CCF." This "well-grounded and exceedingly well informed" woman was just right for the voters of Vancouver Centre, a stronghold of the CCF clubs and the LSR.[60] Later, not surprisingly, the *Vancouver Sun* hailed Jamieson as "a Socialist of the school of J.S. Woodsworth."[61]

Despite the CCF leader's powerful endorsement, the local nomination meeting was fiercely fought. Some members, most identified with the SPC, clearly considered neither Laura nor her Point Grey CCF club to be quite legitimate. Her eligibility was finally settled by the party's provincial president, who sided with Woodsworth.[62] For some reason, Laura did not attend the nomination meeting. Despite her absence, she was elected on the third ballot from a pool of eight. Her closest rival was the former editor of the CCF newspaper *The Federationist*.[63] Ultimately, Laura's success owed much to her own reputation, to the loyalty of CCFers who were associated with the largely middle-class CCF clubs and the LSR, and to a progressive network of women who were willing to contest bad times and governments.

Despite its internal conflicts over the nomination, the CCF badly wanted to challenge the disappointment of the 1937 election. Veteran BC journalist Bruce Hutchison described the party as mounting "its big guns" and laying "down a barrage" in Vancouver Centre. From his mainstream viewpoint, the CCF would "make a desperate effort to capture this key seat. It believes that the working people of British Columbia are turning to it and Vancouver Centre is full of working people. If the C.C.F. cannot win Vancouver Centre it certainly cannot claim to be gaining ground in the territory where its main hope lies."[64] He also put the moment in perspective by invoking the tragic global conflict that would soon preoccupy Laura and her contemporaries: "Vancouver Centre, to tell the cold truth about it, will be no great event in the history of our race. Even the label and political stripe of the Government of British Columbia is not a very exciting question for the public when it is wondering about the future of civilization itself."[65]

Whatever the significance of the by-election in the grand scheme of world affairs, nothing stopped the new BC CCF leader Harold Winch, MLA Steeves, and Councillor Gutteridge from heading noisy meetings in support of their candidate. Alongside Laura, they attacked the two Vancouver aldermen who were her main rivals – Halford D. Wilson for the Conservatives and H.L. Corey for the Liberals. Wilson had enraged

Gutteridge a few months earlier when he proposed that married women who worked for the city should be laid off. He was also singled out for his racism. CCFers condemned him as essentially proposing

> to conduct a pogrom against the Japanese – as the Nazis had done to the Jews – a pogrom against Japanese merchants who make a precarious living selling a few oranges and loaves of bread ... He would, in effect, do as the Nazis have done in Germany where Jewish stores are labeled: "No business here – Jew!" Tell Ald. Wilson on election day that we want none of that sort here![66]

The Liberal Corey, who described himself as a "labour man" in his quest for votes, was chastised as anything but. In particular, Jamieson accused him of not supporting workers during the occupation of the Vancouver Post Office by the unemployed and during a bitter Texada Island strike conducted by the International Woodworkers of America.[67]

These attacks on the reactionary politics of opponents were accompanied by insistence that the CCF offered the only constructive opposition in the legislature, where it initiated most progressive bills, including those on silicosis among miners, minimum wages for male and female workers, hours of work, and the right to unionize.[68] As Laura put it, "if you are willing to continue under capitalism, support the Siamese twins: the Liberals and Conservatives, but if you want to go forward to a planned, democratic socialist economy," vote CCF.[69] She told voters that she had become a CCFer to fight "for the decent necessities for our people," to develop a low-cost rental program for Vancouver, to create employment, and to clean up the causes of prostitution. She also reminded listeners of her stance on global affairs when she attacked the provincial government for "refusing to lift its voice in protest against the shipment of war materials from B.C. to Japan and other aggressor countries."[70]

Jamieson's campaign, during which newspapers started to call her "Laura" rather than "Mrs. J.S.," perhaps because that name appeared on the ballot paper, was boosted by long-standing friendships grounded in nearly two decades of activism. Seemingly innocuous non-partisan teas hosted by her "many friends and admirers throughout the city" spread the good word.[71] To the dismay of her adversaries, her hostesses included Conservatives, Liberals, and independents, as well as CCFers.[72] A *Vancouver Sun* headline highlighted this spirit: "Women Sink Political Differences to Get behind One of Their Own Sex."[73] As Laura's publicity insisted, to vote for her was to "vote for yourself."[74]

Laura's cause was further served by a relatively low turnout of 56 percent among eligible voters. Many Liberals were said to have stayed home. Some who did venture out found Laura's appeal sufficient to cross party lines. This was clearly the opinion of the *Vancouver News-Herald*, whose editor applauded what he judged as the CCF's electoral retreat from "doctrinal theories," an assessment that would have horrified old-line SPC CCFers and merely confirmed their suspicion of the ladylike candidate.[75] Whatever her advantages, Laura did not lead definitively until after 100 of the 124 polls were counted. Once enough voters had shared Alderman Gutteridge's hopes for "a girl," she passed Wilson to win the night.[76]

As the results came in, Laura's gender once again took centre stage. The *Vancouver News-Herald* described her as "one of the best known and best liked women in the city – and in the country for miles around, for during the last 15 years she has made a host of friends as she has worked quietly, but thoroughly, in the interests of all."[77] The paper also commented that she was "a woman of capacity and clarity of thinking, who is widely known as a close student of public affairs. The legislature will be strengthened on its intellectual side by her membership."[78] Her appearance very typically drew far more comment than was the case for male contenders. Laura's gender might depart from the norm for a politician, but her appearance was reassuringly ordinary: "neat in a green wool suit and white hat," she was a "lithe, slender woman with a cheery 'all-in-the-day's-work' smile."[79] She embodied a socialism that was polite and respectable.

The candidate herself seems not to have been entirely confident that she would win her seat, a caution suggested by the fact that she had scheduled herself to spend the subsequent three days at a Student Christian Movement camp on Gambier Island, just north of Vancouver, where she would lead study groups on peace and social change.[80] Election night, however, brought celebration as she was "carried at the head of the crowd." She could not repress her elation, confessing that "a movement like the C.C.F. that lives and works for the brotherhood of man is going to win steadily, and is going to rule." She thanked not only her CCF supporters but significantly "those other groups who voted for me." After that, she joined the parade, linking arms with Winch and Steeves while a crowd of spectators "ran alongside and congratulated" her.[81]

Laura's victory in "a former Liberal stronghold brought joy to the labor and socialist movement throughout Canada" and was hailed as revitalizing the entire party.[82] It also provided a concrete reminder to the CCF's SPC wing of the value of its social democratic comrades in ensuring wider appeal in British Columbia. In contrast, her mainstream opponents worried that their voters were no longer loyal. One of his more progressive cabinet ministers told Premier Pattullo that "many Liberals had refused to vote because they felt the government had developed a paralysis," that this explained the election result, and that "very probably not a Liberal candidate would be elected in Vancouver in the next provincial election."[83] In fact, the race had been a close one: 3,774 votes for Laura, 3,617 for the Conservative, and 3,535 for the Liberal. Like the earlier results for Steeves in North Vancouver, this demonstrated that divisions within the mainstream parties contributed to CCF success in general. One bitter consequence of Laura's triumph was to encourage the two old-line parties to reconsider their options. As Liberal journalist Bruce Hutchison emphasized in surveying what he regarded as a disappointment,

> What the more intelligent politicians are asking today is how to prevent the same thing happening on a larger scale in a general provincial election two years from now? ... Eventually the logic of this situation is almost certain to force union of those who believe in the present system of society and a union of those who want another system. When this realignment appears we shall have realistic party politics in Canada and British Columbia but not before.[84]

The emergence of that coalition on the right would dog Jamieson's political career into subsequent decades.

In April 1939, however, the sun shone. Laura's thank-you to her supporters was typically upbeat, ecumenical, and linked to class politics: "We have lighted one more lamp for the cause of the workers and the common man ... the brotherhood of man."[85] In the fall, she would enter the legislature to join Dorothy Steeves and Helen Smith, making British Columbia the first province with three female representatives of the people, one of whom had been an active suffragist who had rallied a diverse cross-section of female activists to her standard.

6
Suffragist in the BC Legislature, 1939–41

Election to the BC legislature changed Jamieson's life. She transitioned from the significant community of Canadian feminists who were active in progressive causes to the small crew of seasoned suffragists who tested elected office. She was the last Canadian suffragist to serve in a legislature. During her two terms in Victoria, she explored what it meant to be a social democrat in a male-dominated parliament and in a party that seemed to be on the verge of breakthrough, especially in British Columbia.

In her late fifties when she arrived in the capital, Laura was largely freed of pressing daily domestic duties, but her life was enriched and complicated by the evolution of her family and household. Her daughter, Jean Shannon, lived in Vancouver during her husband's wartime enlistment with the Royal Canadian Air Force. At that time, Jean had three daughters – Kathleen, Dorothy, and Mary Ruth. A fourth, Elizabeth, was born later. Grandchildren would call Laura "Mama J." The eldest granddaughter, Kathleen, showed early signs of rebellion from convention, initiating a precedent for siblings and cousins. During the war, she "started a club for little girls in order to fight the Ku Klux Klan," which she had learned about in *Readers' Digest.* Although Jean tried to convince her daughters to "devote ourselves instead to collecting pencils and toothbrushes for the Unitarian Services Committee to send to postwar Europe," Kathleen preferred militancy.[1]

Stuart completed his doctorate in 1943 at the University of California, Berkeley. During investigations for the US Department of Agriculture and the Senate Committee on Violation of Free Speech and Rights of

Labor, he interviewed "Okies" and "Arkies," the agricultural migrants made famous in John Steinbeck's *Grapes of Wrath* (1939). Their stories informed his doctoral thesis, "Labor Unionism in American Agriculture" (published 1946).[2] In 1943, he married Jean Collins of Bowen Island, a resident of his mother's co-operative business girls' house in the West End of Vancouver. Between 1945 and 1960, they too would produce four daughters (Anne Marie, Karen, Marion-Lea, and Laura). Stuart Jamieson's American investigations confirmed his commitment to progressive labour economics.[3] In 1944, he became research director for the national CCF, and in 1945 he moved to the UBC Department of Economics, where he helped found the Institute for Industrial Relations. Though Stuart and his mother weren't always in agreement, they shared progressive politics.

Laura's living arrangements were complicated by the need to be in Victoria for the intermittent sittings of the legislature. Vancouver remained her base, but she acquired short-term digs across the strait. As an MLA, she eventually gave up the struggle to maintain her Point Grey home. In 1941, she worked with women of various ages to set up a communal residence in the city's West End, a downtown location ideal for many clerks, secretaries, and retail workers. It began with ten occupants, some of whom were Vancouverites, whereas others were newly arrived to take up war-related jobs.[4] Since everyone was employed and was "old enough to understand the ordinary rules of living together," few explicit regulations were deemed necessary. By June 1942, a second house with thirteen girls and a "house-mother" extended the first initiative. By spring 1943, four such houses operated, and a Co-operative Society included all residents. Food and other supplies were purchased at a consumer co-op. The MLA settled into the Business Girls' Co-operative House on Barclay Street.[5]

Laura took pride in these experiments. Though admitting that they did not suit "extreme individualists," she hailed the potential diversity of the women whom they attracted, including mothers with children. Residents could develop the good habits that would serve them well in community life if they wished "to advance beyond the little portion of political democracy which so far has been our lot in Canada."[6] Attending a dinner for the Business and Professional Women's Club, the mature New Woman applauded such shared options, arguing that "women can only make contributions to democracy when they are living democracy in their own lives."[7] In living with nine others, "just like a family," Laura claimed to have realized one of her dreams: "We share the work of the house and the expenses and the girls have a large comfortable house to live in instead of crowded single rooms."[8] The feminist CCF editor of "Women's Views" admired her choice, asking readers if they could "imagine a Liberal MLA willing to live with working girls in the low income group, and able, not to solve their problems for them, but to set them on the road to solving their own problems." Here was someone who didn't "just talk about social pioneering" but lived it.[9]

Duties in Victoria nevertheless forced Laura to leave the housing co-operative, and by late 1944 she was living in Kitsilano when she wasn't in the provincial capital. Again, however, she rarely lived alone. Now a more informal community of working women, her household remained busy. Her enthusiasm for collaboration flourished as well when she joined the board of directors for the New Vista Society, which was dedicated to comfortably housing the elderly poor. In June 1945, she succeeded another CCF MLA, Ernest Winch, as the New Vista president. In choosing co-operative living and such volunteer service, Laura gained ongoing insights into the challenges that low-income people faced in Vancouver's persistently difficult housing market.

When Jamieson won the 1939 by-election, she raised CCF legislative numbers to eight. Her arrival to join Dorothy Gretchen Steeves and Helen Douglas Smith secured British Columbia's status as possessing the Canadian provincial legislature with the largest number of women. Although two-term Smith had not won a reputation as an effective parliamentarian, Dorothy Steeves most definitely had. Younger than Laura by almost a decade, the Dutch-born lawyer had far fewer ties with the women's club movement. Though details remain scant, the two were not intimate friends. Indeed, they regularly disagreed over CCF policy, with Dorothy the champion of Marxist socialists and Laura of democratic socialists. While in Victoria, however, Dorothy and Laura supported each other in contests with patriarchy and capitalism. Both were widely recognized as effective debaters who infuriated government MLAs. Steeves, whose physical attractiveness was frequently remarked upon in the press, was especially feared for her rapier-like sallies, which readily evoked the courtroom. The more matronly Jamieson was likely to intimidate with a retinue of facts, all the while shaking her finger like an admonishing teacher. Although Laura was interested in international affairs, Dorothy's obvious knowledge and capacity for the topic left little room for a contribution from her. Her commitment to child welfare, women's rights, and workers kept her busy, though she never entirely resisted commenting on global affairs.

Given that British Columbia lacked a *Hansard* in these years, and mainstream newspapers appeared little interested, Jamieson's early months in

Victoria are best recovered from the pages of the CCF newspaper, *The Federationist.* In underlining her significance, the prominent socialist journalist Elizabeth Kerr, who sometimes wrote as Constance Errol, stressed the value of the women's movement to the young party. She singled out Jamieson in the Vancouver Local Council of Women, arguing that its CCF women's group was influential there, outperforming Conservatives, Liberals, and union auxiliaries. At the monthly LCW meetings, its representatives made an effective case on a wide range of concerns. Though Kerr admitted that the LCW had its share of reactionaries, she insisted that "much good work has been done ... and more radical ideas cannot be expressed on the floor of the meetings unless there are radical women present to express them." Gutteridge, Steeves, Susie Lane Clark (a CCFer on the Vancouver Parks Board), and Jamieson were her models:

> The CCF delegates, because of their courtesy, their regular attendance, the obvious interest, and their unswerving stand on all matters of public good, have won for themselves the respect and confidence of the large delegation of other women's organizations. Of course their resolutions do not always go through though they get a hearing, in many cases representing often a new point of view, and following the meetings, many women, formerly strangers, come forward and agree with or further question their ideas.[10]

In the ecumenical setting of the LCW, socialism might be advanced beyond the converted and new electoral support mustered for the party.

The CCF's persistent uneasiness with feminism nevertheless meant that such recommendations upset some *Federationist* readers. In December 1939, Kerr referred to charges by

> men of my acquaintance [that] I ... "carry a torch" ... for women. Also the other day I heard one of them say, "My God, how these women do stick together." A few years ago and it was only men who stuck together, women supposedly selling each other out with every breath. I don't quite agree with this old idea but if it was so, then we have travelled far in the right direction ... The defeat of Alderman Helena Gutteridge and Commissioner Susie Clark at the recent Vancouver civic election was not regretted in the movement as I felt it should have been. The fact that the first woman on the city council should lose her seat was more than just a lost seat for the CCF. It was a loss to socialists who make no distinction between sex, race, color or creed, and yet who are so prone to elect men to every office save that of social convener or unpaid secretary.[11]

Less than a month later, the indefatigable Kerr again endorsed independent organization. She welcomed the Vancouver CCF Women's Central Group as the forerunner of a much-needed nation-wide movement. Laura had spoken at its January 1940 gathering, skewering the "Ideal Woman" or the "Womanly Woman" of the past, who, "content to worship," had left "lords and masters" unchallenged in public space. The "machine age" that had "brought women out of their homes, and mechanized wars," meant that women were better able than ever to defy old stereotypes.[12]

Steeves and CCF MLA Colin Campbell spoke at the same event. The latter drew Kerr's condemnation when, in a good example of victim blaming, he "maintained that men did not consciously discriminate against women because they were women, but that women themselves discriminate against other women." In reply, Kerr made two points: First, men subconsciously discriminated all the time. Second, some women did need to "brush up" their thinking. She nevertheless agreed with Campbell that they were likely to be more "ruthless" than men in protecting children. In an argument that might have come straight from the suffragists, she added that men

> deal in theories but there is little theory about birth, or death, or getting the meals on time, or paying the milk-man or the grocer. These are facts that won't wait for settlement till another day or hour. Woman has to deal with such facts in her every day life, and she carries her practical outlook into the larger sphere of provincial, national or international affairs. Her viewpoint is not necessarily better than man's, but she has a viewpoint that is different, and as she is half of humanity, and has the teaching of a large portion of the other half ... it would seem that in the best interest of all humanity she should be listened to after the same manner as her consort, man.

Like Jamieson, Kerr worried that the party relied on too few people. In a revealing use of the first person plural, she concluded, "We regret that no more women were willing to accept office at the Annual Meeting. We have tried to rotate responsibility, each person occupying one position for only one year. Unfortunately the willing workers, who are not already overburdened with work, are in only a few clubs, so that too few [CCF] clubs are represented on the executive."[13] She described empowerment strategies that sounded very much like those of later twentieth-century feminists. That consciousness-raising task had long been key to Jamieson's work in the Women's International League for Peace and Freedom (WILPF), and it remained her approach in the CCF.[14]

Kerr's observations highlighted women's uncertain claims to legitimacy. Laura's pragmatic feminism never made her an easy fit with the ubiquitous masculinist theorists of the CCF. She was typically dismissive of George Weaver (1908–86), sometimes dubbed the BC party's "foremost Marxist theoretician."[15] He was more than two decades younger than Laura, but in a 1940 letter to Grace MacInnis, she described him as "trying desperately to become more modern-minded ... But the poor old chap's mentality is so firmly imbedded in the Marxian dialectic that, with all his attempts, he is not getting very far."[16] Nor was she shy in summing up the limitations of Karl Marx himself. Very much a product of the nineteenth century, Marx "could not see ... the necessity for the workers, while struggling for their rights, to lay the basis for co-operation and lead other classes into it." In modern Canada, education and co-operative programs, not revolution, would topple capitalism. Citizens of parliamentary democracies should employ "all the early Socialists as guides," but "we in Canada must make our own Socialism."[17] That home-based creed, with its confidence in gradualism, should embrace both democracy and feminism. Such views explain why the CCF labour socialists, with their well-developed suspicions of both liberal democrats and bourgeois feminists, sometimes treated Laura as an interloper.

Despite all such reservations, Laura's arrival as an MLA was celebrated. In the context of rising union numbers and favourable public opinion polls, CCFers of all persuasions foresaw that capitalism would soon be brought to heel via successful appeals to voters.[18] The parliamentary road to that outcome required the education and good practice, not to mention the respectability, that Laura represented. As leader of the BC CCF, and frequent representative of the Socialist Party of Canada founders, Harold Winch admitted that "our work is to make Socialists – founded upon a clear understanding of Marxian principles – not doctrinaire high priests of hairsplittingdom. This, however, is not enough. A theoretical socialist who does not strive at all times to act as a practical one might as well never have been made for he is neither use nor ornament."[19] What he didn't say was that few of the people who were in charge or in the rank-and-file accepted feminism as part of necessary practice in growing the CCF.

Though keen to advance women's cause, Laura made her own concessions to the pervasive ethos in the party. Even as she presented her credentials as a representative of organized women, she often publicly aligned with the working class, the preferred source of revolutionary consciousness among classical Marxist theorists. During the 1940s, notably in articles for *The Federationist* and the *CCF News,* she regularly distanced herself from the middle class. This positioning is visible in her August 1939 reflections on federal politics and the rise of the New Democracy movement, a short-lived phenomenon that linked supporters of Social Credit, dissident Conservatives, and a few communists, whom Laura suggested "provided any backbone." Correctly predicting a short life for the party, which died in the 1940 federal election, she concluded, "truly, the way of those who would co-operate with middle-class movements is hard."[20] Whatever New Democracy promised about cross-class alliances, Laura placed her hopes in securing feminist socialist space in the CCF.

After 1939, CCF life, within and without the legislature, often turned on the waging of the Second World War. Canada's official declaration of war on September 9, 1939, was addressed by Laura before the legislature convened. On September 14, speaking as a WILPF veteran of peace campaigns, she reminded CCF *Federationist* readers that Canada had supplied combatants "with war materials right up to the last minute. As in the last war, Canadian soldiers will be killed with bullets tipped with Canadian nickel. Canada is still supplying Japan with copper and other war materials. These are facts which make the military music at the recruiting stations give out a hollow sound." And she concluded bleakly, "the present war marks the complete bankruptcy of our civilization."[21]

The CCF suffered much the same divisions over the worsening international situation that wracked WILPF, which had effectively operated as the party's feminist peace arm for much of the 1930s. Both included advocates of collective security and equally passionate pacifists who dismissed the League of Nations as "little more than an imperialist cabal and ... naïve dupes."[22] Dorothy Steeves was a powerful champion of the latter. In 1935, soon after her by-election victory, she set out her standard: "The slightest hint of militarism or imperialism sends an unpleasant chill down my spine."[23] During the Dirty Thirties, however, the threat of fascism became clearer, and a majority of CCFers agreed with Laura and one of her favourite Fabian authors, G.D.H. Cole, that "Hitler cured me of pacifism."[24] Even as fascism spurred the party's national executive to vote in support of the Allies in September 1939 and soon for the deployment of troops,[25] CCF leader James S. Woodsworth nevertheless refused to acquiesce. He had BC supporters. Immediately after Canada entered the conflict, Steeves "denounced the imperialist character of the war to a CCF mass meeting."[26] A few weeks later, she expanded her condemnation in terms that Laura understood:

> Political democracy in itself is not enough. It must be accompanied by economic democracy which would lead to social justice. As long as you

> have poverty and exploitation out of which the privileged group makes profits, you are going to have war, Hitler or no Hitler. Democracy is not synonymous with the British Empire or British traditions. It is certainly not so in this part of the British Empire ... It is no use to destroy Hitler in Germany and leave alive Hitlers in our own country ... Empire means Imperialism and the apostles of imperialism are the arms manufacturers.[27]

Whatever her sympathies, however, Laura had decided that pacifism was not a realistic option in 1939. Disarmament had to come in stages, and "peace workers should not refuse to consider any sincere move toward partial disarmament. The first essential in a Peace worker is tolerance, a willingness to co-operate with every agency sincerely interested in Peace, and to accept as feasible other methods besides our own."[28] A military response to Hitler and the Axis powers could not be avoided. Steeves' warning of domestic Hitlers remained nevertheless a powerful reminder of the need to protect civil liberties and the working class, causes that preoccupied the wartime CCF.[29]

Jamieson defended those arguments in the BC legislature. In November 1939, she dismissed war-mongering government hawks with the derisive summary that "hell hath no fury like that of a non-combatant." In particular, she accused future Conservative leader Herbert Anscomb of "sadism" due to his earlier support for the "physical punishment administered to a female Communist," pointing out that "she was not a foreigner and there was no war on at the time."[30] During her wartime days in the legislature and in spreading the CCF message province-wide, Laura dedicated herself to "hammer[ing] away at the welfare of the people" and taking officialdom to task for civil liberties violations that targeted the left even as "proven" fascists received light sentences.[31]

Jamieson's legislative career confirmed her pan-Canadian approach to politics. Much like CCF leaders such as Angus and Grace MacInnis, she endorsed connections to progressive groups elsewhere and hoped for action at the federal level. Seeing the 1940 report of the Royal Commission on Dominion-Provincial Relations (the Rowell-Sirois Commission) as an opportunity to improve Ottawa's record in health and welfare, and a step toward greater social democracy, she condemned Victoria's failure to engage with its recommendations for greater co-ordination of spending powers. In particular, she felt that Ottawa should assume responsibility for the unemployed and for contributory old age pensions. Instead, all the Pattullo Liberals did was foster "an anti-Eastern prejudice."[32] Such narrow-mindedness elicited the recurring outrage of the Ontario-born legislator, who never forgot the other provinces.[33] In taking up domestic issues, Jamieson typically placed them in a larger comparative context. Her solutions regularly looked beyond British Columbia, Canada, and the Commonwealth. And always she derided obsequiousness: "We do so love to be colonial and try to be more British than the British."[34] Her preferred inspiration came instead from democratic socialist strongholds in New Zealand and elsewhere.

In November 1939, Laura's maiden speech to the legislature addressed the plight of juvenile offenders, an obvious subject for a former judge. With fathers in the armed forces or preoccupied with war production and mothers hard pressed as parents and often as wage-earners, the war fed long-standing fears about the moral and physical corruption of children and young people.[35] Few commentators in Victoria shared Laura's direct experience with girls and boys who were in trouble with the law. Her obvious expertise made it difficult to contradict her insistence that "beyond all prevention is the fact that most delinquency comes from poverty stricken homes. From my eleven years as a Juvenile Court Judge I have found this to be true over and over again. Until there is employment for the fathers of the families and the young people coming out of school we shall have more delinquency."[36] Bruce Hutchison, leading BC journalist and rarely an advocate for the CCF, gave her speech a thumbs-up:

> Evidently the C.C.F. has a brace of ladies in this House who know how to take care of themselves. You would have thought from her ease of manner that Mrs. Jamieson had been speaking in the House all her life ... Most young members are flushed, breathless and speechless when they have completed a maiden speech. Mrs. Jamieson sat down and calmly began to peel an apple with a blunt paper knife while notes of congratulation poured in from other members.[37]

Equally significant was the fact that Laura's initial entry into the legislative fray inaugurated what would be an unrelenting assault on mainstream poor bashing.

Wherever she looked, what would later be termed the "social determinants" of public welfare took centre stage in her agenda for change. Halfway through her first term, she condemned the direction of Burnaby's Borstal home for boys, established with high hopes in 1937, as misunderstanding the forces that created its charges. In 1942, it would close under the weight of scandal, not to reopen until 1947. For Laura, Scandinavia, as well as New Zealand, pointed the way to humane rehabilitation.[38] At the heart of all good policy for youngsters lay broad-based community support for good parenting. The pre-school groups of Vancouver's West End Community Centre, which she had helped found, remained a source of inspiration: "Here were mothers who did not merely want to get their small children 'out of the way.'" Such women secured Canada's democratic foundations as nursery school programs offered training in "practical" socialism.[39] Their practices were the best guarantee against juvenile crime.

From the beginning, Laura's commitments were never restricted to the legislature. She proved a popular guest of both mixed and women's groups in British Columbia and beyond. February 1941 saw her addressing a Chilliwack audience that included farmers from the Fraser Valley. She urged them to seize the

> opportunity to build a new socialist democracy. What little bit of democracy we have left in the world is better than fascism, but others prefer fascism to the capitalistic democracy we have to offer. If we want to shorten this war, we will have to offer the peoples of Europe something better than our capitalistic democracy to get them to turn in rebellion against their fascist masters.

While praising agriculturalists and condemning the impact of tariffs on manufactured goods, she recommended the Rowell-Sirois Report as an opportunity for British Columbians and Canadians to invest in community well-being.[40]

During a week spent in Prince Rupert a few months later, she again positioned the CCF as the common-sense answer to the shortchanging of working people. Speaking to the Gyros men's social service club, the Junior Chamber of Commerce, the Canadian Club, and the CCF, she tried to calm potential fears by presenting social democracy as the logical extension of municipal government: "There was nothing new in community ownership ... Schools, playgrounds, water systems, telephones, electric power and such like were provided on a community basis. This type of management could be extended to transportation, utilities, banks and even motion pictures."[41] In short, the CCF was no Red menace but a familiar part of the political landscape.

Though she cast her net widely for audiences, female listeners were Laura's obvious target. Sometimes this meant crossing borders, as with a May 1940 speech that she gave before Washington state's federation of business and professional women's clubs, just the type of activists who supported her at home. They heard her endorse the principles of a more co-operative and just citizenship for every nation.[42] As the war deepened, she became all the more anxious to encourage such groups to act as critical bulwarks of democracy. When it came to women's rights, their continuing vitality offered the real test of the difference between fascism and socialism.[43]

Women's clubs were not, however, always entirely satisfactory. In February 1941, the CCF Women's Central Group had succeeded in getting the Citizenship Committee of the LCW to study a proposed amendment to Vancouver's charter to entrench the principle of one person one vote. The resulting April report, with its opposition to extending the electorate, proved deeply disappointing. Ultimately protective of the status quo, it highlighted the danger that "young people with no property sense ... would vote for people with expensive tastes that might not be in the best interests of the community."[44] In 1943 and 1944, CCF members' championship of a broad municipal franchise similarly failed to sway the LCW. For all Laura's high hopes, collaboration between socialists and women's clubs was not assured.

But full enfranchisement at every level remained central to her vision of meaningful democracy. In particular, women needed to look well beyond their own oppression to recognize "the lack of opportunity and liberty for the masses." Those in the middle class should accept the equal claim of others "to lead the same kind of lives." Laura admitted that prospects for an expanded vision were too often crippled by self-interest. This was the obvious explanation for the recurring failure of women's clubs to recognize the rights of household employees: "The claim is inconvenient to a lot of middle class people." No wonder, she stated, that "domestic servants and women were the last classes to claim successfully the equal right to happiness enunciated" by American democrats in 1776.[45]

Like the Liberal suffragist Nellie McClung in *In Times Like These,* Laura continued to concede some failings of her sex. Some women possessed an impenetrable "middle class feeling" that fostered "the patronizing atmosphere which drives loyalty out of the picture." In one such example, she highlighted the shortcomings of "the wife of a leader of one of the old-line political parties" who denied "that if poverty stricken people were given better economic conditions they would quickly improve their position." That privileged madam insisted that the poor must be taught to better themselves. Laura's response was firm: "In the vast majority of cases, give them better economic conditions and they would teach themselves; that is, unless they had been pauperized so long that they had lost all ambition." Laura then asked the same woman if she had attended the recent Vancouver showing of American writer Clare Boothe Luce's *The Women,* a satirical 1936 comedy that savaged bourgeois Manhattanites. As it turned out, neither wife nor husband had liked it. On first reflection, Laura saw only another woman's disloyalty to her sex. She then recalled the play's main target, the leisured middle class, and remarked, "Well, I thought it was a jolly satire on women, and surely women laugh at themselves occasionally. But my companion was as solemnly humorless as her husband's political party."[46]

Laura returned to her critique of the middle class in describing a woman who attended a Business and Professional Women's Club meeting. Upon hearing a defence of nationalists and anti-imperialists on the Indian subcontinent, she stated that she was "sick of the word 'capitalism.'" Once again, Laura's comment was direct: "Some of us were sick of the reality, not only the word, but we didn't press the point." In seeking to explain reactionary views among clubwomen, she concluded that "our Canadian universities are turning out these as supposedly educated women," though she conceded that a university education didn't create fools – it merely perfected them. She drew on popular psychology to account for female limitations: "Perhaps too, the women are not altogether at fault. Frequently women who express such ideas have some strong frustration or complex which they are trying to hide; and at a time of crisis it comes out in anti-social and anti-democratic sentiments."[47]

She also referred to birth control, which she and Steeves defended in the legislature, to indict the self-satisfied and self-centred behaviour of their sex: "I have often felt that one of the greatest demonstrations of selfishness among middle class women was their willingness to use birth control methods themselves; but their unwillingness to make the information on the methods available to their poorer sisters. Middle-class women, generally speaking in Canada, have remained utterly silent and inactive in this regard." She derided such inadequate representatives of womanhood as often seeking to evade responsibility by citing spousal disapproval: "What a convenience a husband is to a middle-class woman who wants to avoid some useful activity in the community which might also bring upon her the slightest criticism." Such passivity did not have to be. Laura commended aristocratic Spanish women who challenged "false modesty and false religious scruples" in campaigns for contraception.[48] Eleanor Roosevelt, long-time activist and wife to US president Franklin D. Roosevelt, provided another example of "those rare women, who although they have always belonged to the middle class, and have held the highest positions that class has to offer, have never had the 'middle class' mind."[49] In short, class, or race or gender for that matter, was not destiny. Politics, like principles, involved choice.

Even on the left, however, organized women never had a free pass to illumination. A week after praising Roosevelt, Jamieson addressed cliquishness, a defect shared by both sexes in the party: "Some members in the CCF tended to keep it a small charmed circle of clubs where members can speak their grievances freely; but that such a circle is not likely to be enlarged. Whereas members with the cause really at heart should be seizing every opportunity to get out into other groups and carry the message."[50] The net for members needed to be cast well beyond existing circles. In a typical recommendation, she urged that seasonal workers, such as the province's fishers, be welcomed. Although the fishermen's union possessed "a very active women's section," and "union members and CCF members" were often one and the same, the party had not engaged in active recruitment.[51] Too often only old loyalists were courted.

In 1940, Jamieson's determination to mobilize her sex led her to take regular responsibility for the women's column in the CCF newspaper. She wanted it

> to voice the woman's points of view, not only in the abstract, interpreted by the writer, but in the concrete – the actual point of view of individual women in the CCF. I have met women doing splendid work in the CCF from Kimberley and Fernie in the east of the province, to the west on Vancouver Island. Their point of view, their suggestions as to how women can further still more the work of the CCF will be most valuable ... Today, when great economic forces seem to be causing convulsions that make or mar whole continents, we are apt to minimize the power of the human will, and to become fatalistic. Women who know what it means to bring human life into the world and protect it ... can never forget the power of the human will and of human love. Against the tendency to take the negative attitude they must always take the positive stand, and do something concrete and constructive.

Urging her readers to write with specific suggestions, Laura set out to establish a dialogue to address the urgent questions facing the legislature.[52]

In speaking to party members and the public, Jamieson reiterated familiar suffrage arguments that women's domestic skills were readily transferable to public life. More than twenty years after partial enfranchisement, she answered the question of why so few women took up politics. Her responses emphasized that her sex did a disproportionate share of home-based labour: "Most women when they come into the CCF, have used up so much physical and emotional energy organizing their households and families that they are tired. What they need most of all is recreation and rest."[53] The prospect of Christmas in 1940, with an "SOS from a male relative" already in her hand, provided a personal example. Why, she asked, were women the custodians of family festivals? "To be sure, Santa Claus is of the male sex; but a very shadowy male at that ... All the real preparation, for weeks ahead, and the hard work of the day before, and of the day itself, is done by the women of the household." And when times were hard, as they often were especially in wartime, one sex bore disproportionately "the heavy task of cheering faint hearts."[54]

In addressing such impediments to public life, Laura recommended ongoing targeted preparation and support: "There is a place in our movement, I believe, for a sort of 'experimental station,' where women can experiment and work out some special medium for their talents, as well as keeping up the well-tried methods of the past."[55] Women-only spaces offered safe environments to practise democracy and gain parliamentary skills. Though some CCF feminists such as Dorothy Steeves dismissed same-sex organizing as retrograde, Laura saw it as a necessary response to discrimination in most male-dominated arenas.

Just as she had done with WILPF, Laura gave explicit direction on encouraging female members. Although most women would favour a legislative agenda focused on community well-being, "gentle reminders" would not forge activists. Most already had too much on their plates. Unlike men, who "frequently" had "nothing to do, and [were] just looking for a meeting to go to, women had to be impressed with its importance – and its importance FOR THEM. This can be done, but it requires hard work."[56] Raising consciousness could require the recovery of what would later be termed "women worthies" – "outstanding women who have been pioneers in the field of Labor and socialism, coming down to the women who are doing the same thing at the present time." Laura's own examples included the writer Olive Schreiner, the Fabian socialist Beatrice Webb, the settlement and peace activist Jane Adams, the birth controller Margaret Sanger, FDR's secretary of labor Frances Perkins, and Eleanor Roosevelt. She also recommended inspirational texts, including John McCormac's *Canada, America's Problem* (1940), which targeted Canadian colonialism; Leonard Woolf's *After the Deluge* (1931), on the psychology of violence; George B. Shaw's *Intelligent Woman's Guide to*

Socialism and Capitalism (1928); John Steinbeck's *Grapes of Wrath*, the classic account of dispossessed Americans in the Great Depression; and African American author Richard Wright's *Native Son* (1940), with its indictment of US racism. Readers of a particularly practical persuasion were directed to advice pamphlets provided without charge by the Canadian Council on Child Welfare and the BC Department of Labour.[57]

In her heady early legislative days, when the CCF seemed in sight of power, Laura credited women with the necessary energy to take it over the top. Organizing on the Sunshine Coast met with her approval. She judged Powell River's "new women's groups" as "the best symptom of a healthy movement," giving "it a distinctive character and atmospheres ... that warmth and friendliness which woman's hospitality in the home leads them to extend naturally in the clubs."[58] While praising the English feminist socialist and pacifist Winifred Holtby in *The Federationist*, Jamieson made the same case for grassroots organization. Holtby's novel *South Riding* (1936) demonstrated how involvement in local government provided "the first-line defense thrown up by the community against our common enemies – poverty, sickness, ignorance, isolation and social maladjustment."[59] Here was the field where women could test their mettle and secure the foundations of better policy.

To spur them on, Laura tried to connect CCF readers to contemporary women who were making a difference. In reviewing Hitler's *Mein Kampf* (1925), she praised courageous anti-fascists. Brave souls, like those whom she had met in peace groups and the British Labour Party during visits to Europe and the United Kingdom in the 1920s, represented her sex's "creative courage," a quality "much superior to passive endurance."[60] She applauded Agnes Macphail as an inspirational Canadian figure. Defeated in the March 1940 federal election, Macphail would not return to elected office until winning a seat in the Ontario legislature in 1943. In the interval, she barnstormed the country for the CCF. Her resilience was embraced as the guarantee of eventual victory. Setbacks merely "deepened" Macphail's "sense of strength and singleness of purpose."[61]

Another gallant example of resistance, left unnamed in Laura's column, was very clearly Anna Helene Arkanasy, a Jewish refugee in Vancouver. A WILPF member and niece of composer Gustav Mahler, she had been brutally widowed by the Gestapo. Together with the refugee psychiatrist Dr. Elda Lindenfeld,[62] Arkanasy had founded the Women's School for Politics in Vienna before the Nazi triumph. Laura told *Federationist* readers that she had a brain "packed full of constructive ideas for women to follow" in a new land that still offered "unbounded possibilities, especially for women." In 1941, Arkanasy and Lindenfeld co-operated with Laura and other progressive women to establish the Vancouver Women's School for Citizenship. Still another outstanding woman was Isobel Cripps, the wife of Sir Stafford Cripps, an economic architect for the British Labour Party. She briefly visited Vancouver in 1940 and would become president of the British United Aid to China Fund two years later. Her time on the Pacific coast allowed Laura to highlight the Cripps family's capacity for solidarity. Though Sir Stafford and Isobel supported the war, one of their sons was a conscientious objector, a choice that Laura presented as understandable and acceptable.[63] In short, there were many ways to be a good democratic socialist.

The new MLA returned to an equally familiar refrain in recommending consumer co-ops. They constituted "democracy in action" and meaningful "practice in socialism."[64] In contrast, the "preaching of abstract socialism in the home," a sly kick at more doctrinaire CCF colleagues, was unhelpful – far better to link domestic everyday consumption to the real world of industrial injustice. Offering the concrete example of stockings that were made in the factories of Drummondville, Quebec, Jamieson described a town with "open sewers," "poorly paid workers," "rickets in the children, [and] stunted and deformed adults." Restricting one's purchases solely to "union made goods," a crusade taken up in 1939 by the New Westminster and District Trade Union Label Council, would address such blights far more effectively than dreary sermonizing.[65]

In describing co-operative experiments, Jamieson defended her sex against charges that it lacked solidarity. There was nothing inevitable about rivalry among women. It originated in economic dependence: "So long as the meal ticket remains such a large factor in marriage, as it still is in all capitalist (and fascist) countries, women are competitors with each other for their living."[66] This could change as they left domestic restrictions behind. In co-ops and other joint enterprises, women would become more loyal to each other and more than ever the source of social betterment. Laura reproved uninterested party dogmatists: "I know that by hair-splitting arguments it can be proved that co-operatives are not real socialism." Such narrow-mindedness ignored grassroots training in the fundamentals of democracy that would "prevent our theory turning to dust." Any preoccupation purely with politics was "extremely limited in scope."[67] Laura used a February 1940 visit to Mexico, where she reconnected with a UBC international student and former boarder, as an opportunity to point to co-operative farms and nationalized railways as democracy in action.[68] Such initiatives, with their benefits for ordinary people, were a world away from the UBC fraternities and sororities whose embodiment of privilege drew her denunciation in the same years.

Half-way through her first term in Victoria, Laura summed up her female colleagues. When measured against most male legislators, who were likely to "mumble" and talk "town-pump politics generally," they shone. She had her favourites. Despite her university degree, public experience, confidence, and good speaking voice and appearance, Liberal MLA Helen Douglas Smith disappointed. Ultimately, she simply had "nothing to say," offering little more than government reports "almost verbatim," without "originality" or "imagination." And despite having "more brains than several of the Cabinet Ministers" as well as "executive ability," the Liberal loyalist remained unrewarded even as "second rate men" rose. Laura caustically noted that Smith's poor treatment by her own government did not stop women in the old parties from

> aspiring to a similar role ... coming up through the same women's organizations; learning a little bit about everything in the process; but not much about any one thing. They are careful never to make a wrong move, never to get any unfavourable publicity. They are patriotic in just the right way. But to have to watch one's step every foot of the path kills all originality and makes of one just a good politician, nothing more.

Once again, she invoked the example of Eleanor Roosevelt to remind readers that no one need be a prisoner of class privilege.[69]

Unlike their Liberal opponent, the female CCF MLAs met suffragist standards. Laura depicted Dorothy and herself as resisting the irrelevant social events that preoccupied others. From their perspective, the legislative entertainment schedule strayed far from proper wartime "restraint." Worse still, invitations to social functions were part of women's exclusion from "useful work for serious lawmakers."[70] Steeves and Jamieson were far more interested in parliamentary business. This required investigation and consultations with British Columbians who were suffering the consequences of exploitation, not canapés and social chitchat at elite gatherings.

Beyond British Columbia, a new left-wing Canadian politician soon attracted Laura's scrutiny. The March 1940 federal election returned Dorise Nielsen (1902–80), the United Progressive candidate from North Battleford, Saskatchewan, as Canada's third female MP. In fact, Nielsen, a hard-pressed farmer, had already joined the Communist Party. Like Laura, she had lost an infant son. His death in 1930 had helped radicalize his desperate mother. In January 1941, as a guest of the Canadian Liberties Union, she addressed a capacity crowd at UBC, where Laura, who was a member of the union, joined her on the platform to speak briefly. For her readers, Laura identified Dorise as "a political phenomenon worthy of study." Repeating her concerns regarding her own BC colleagues, she wondered at Nielsen's "lack of interest in the democratic processes" and her preoccupation with political action. She attributed Nielsen's indifference to lack of involvement with Prairie women's and co-operative movements. She concluded that Nielsen had "read political books and economic treatises constantly, without an economic laboratory in which to work over her political and economic theories and test them. For the burnt grass and sterile ground of the Prairie breeds desperation, and acceptance of political theories without testing."

But, as was often the case, Laura remained determinedly optimistic: "She can learn and learn quickly. Her future depends upon those she chooses for her political tutors and companions. If she chooses wisely she may play a significant part in Canadian life, and be honoured, whether in victory or defeat, like Agnes Macphail."[71] However, Laura's hopes were destined for disappointment. Moving farther left, Nielsen ran for the Labor-Progressive Party (Communist Party) in 1945 and was defeated. In 1957, she went to the People's Republic of China and never returned permanently to Canada.[72] Such alienation was the price, Laura would have felt, for Dorise's refusal to embrace grassroots activism.

Although she concentrated on domestic policy in the legislature, Laura's commitment to international co-operation and dialogue surfaced repeatedly. As she watched performances in Vancouver's 1940 folk festival, she "could scarcely keep from tears as my mind came back suddenly to the world in a shambles of hate and destruction, the very antithesis of what I had been watching." Far more than mere entertainment, such occasions offered women a chance to "practice freedom" and ensure democracy's vitality. They helped foster a "very special courage to persist in the unending work of trying to rouse people politically to the sense of their danger of losing democracy altogether, and of carrying on the drab duty of meetings to further study of political and economic subjects." She nevertheless finished on a cynical note: "Don't expect any of your legislative members to come home from the next session with the proceedings recorded in blank verse and set to music. Why? Because there is no democracy there, drab or otherwise."[73] Ultimately, women needed to commit themselves to "war work" that would "preserve democracy, which is being demolished rapidly in our own country."[74]

To this end, Laura helped found the Vancouver Women's School for Citizenship in spring 1941. This group, officially non-partisan like the LCWs, aimed to be "purely educational, with no restrictions in membership because of race, religion or political creed ... Since human problems, not only local but national and international would be studied, it was hoped that the School would help equip and encourage women to deal intelligently with these problems." Classes in public speaking and reviews of recent books were designed to appeal to "every sort and age of women, with every point of view," and to promote "World Peace and World Brotherhood." Mothers were to be tempted beyond the home by stimulation and support, and those who "formerly spent their leisure solely in social pursuits [would] find more important channels."[75] Amid serious world conditions, the school might nurture "a second women's movement," embodying "not only freedom for women but for all."[76] It looked backward to some suffragists' hopes for non-partisanship and forward to experiments in consciousness raising that a later feminist generation would take up.

The wartime moment seemed opportune. Laura Jamieson gave the school's third lecture, speaking before a packed house on a topic that inspired suffragists – "Are men women's equals?" Reported as "restrained, fair, and reasonable," she ranged from wives' right to paid employment, to wage differentials, to what would later be termed the "glass ceiling," and male fear of women. The evening was hailed as fun and friendly, offering the potential for concrete concerted action.[77] A few weeks later, another meeting of the school saw former suffragist, teacher, and policewoman Evelyn LeSueur suggest that many modern women, unlike feminist pioneers, knew "nothing of courts or laws, or of how people really live." A good dose of history, followed by more female politicians, was her remedy. Again, the non-partisan spirit prevailed, with congratulations to Liberal Cora Casselman, newly elected MP for Edmonton East and the fourth woman to enter the Commons. *The Federationist*'s feminist commentator nevertheless worried about "wildly voting women into office who may simply be feminine editions of our present politicians. For women can play politics, and we must insist on a higher standard of honesty and sincerity from women than we have had from so many of our men."[78] Such aspirations should properly be directed to the CCF.

Groomed in the anti-imperialism of WILPF, Jamieson felt that Canadian slights to democracy in war and peace owed much to the persisting romanticization of the British connection. She condemned the best-selling Jalna novels of Canadian writer Mazo de la Roche as promoting this wrong-headedness, with their "distorted picture of life"; they could only keep "young people living in day dreams instead of grappling with reality." Empires built on the privileges of race, class, and gender, as in the

Jalna saga of the Tory Whiteoak family, betrayed ordinary people. Jamieson recommended the work of BC realist writer Hubert Evans, with its repudiation of jingoism.[79] In novels such as *No More Islands* (1943) and *Mist on the River* (1954), the admirable Evans, a Quaker, would make common cause with Japanese Canadians and Native peoples.[80]

Jamieson shared Evans' sympathies for Asian British Columbians. In 1941, before Tokyo's assault on Pearl Harbor, she visited the pulp and paper company town of Ocean Falls, reporting on the merits of its Japanese residents for readers of *The Federationist.* Despite their segregation "in extremely crowded quarters," they were a musical, "literate and intelligent group," deeply committed to improving life for their children and to birth control, both signs of civilization. The men had proved themselves solid members of Local 312 of the Pulp, Sulphite and Paper Mill Workers Union.[81] They paid their dues and raised funds for union causes even when their basic wage was significantly less than that of white workers. The union had protested on their behalf, but employers hid behind the federal Wartime Wages Policy, "which limited wage increases to the highest rate established in the late 1920s."[82] Good will between white and Japanese residents extended beyond the workplace, and Laura noticed "no great divergences in attitudes or opinions." The Japanese residents also appeared equally patriotic in "Victory Loan drives, war certificate sales, and Red Cross work," and some wished to enlist. She suggested that such loyalties characterized the BC Japanese population as a whole.[83]

As the war lengthened, Jamieson's concerns over threats to social welfare and human rights deepened. Telling legislative opponents that "government services have failed to keep pace with changing conditions," she questioned their commitment to a better tomorrow. Where were the "war aims" that justified losses and costs?[84] In the *Canadian Forum,* she outlined her fears about the curtailment of civil liberties and the rise of police surveillance.[85] Her questions extended to a future peace agreement. As she told MLAs in November 1940, "You can beat Hitler by offering the German people more than they've got now. Don't just offer them the status quo of capitalist democracy."[86] The Treaty of Versailles had taken this approach and had merely guaranteed future conflict.

Even as Jamieson brandished a higher standard, the mainstream media compromised consciousness-raising by printing nostalgic depictions of harmony in the home. In 1941, *Chatelaine* published the account of a young wife, centred on "finding marriage a thrilling adventure in co-operation between a man, a woman, and God." War, the economy, and politics went unmentioned.[87] Though some appalled readers condemned the writer's "egotism,"[88] her story was common fodder. Indeed, even Laura herself could not entirely escape the pull of fantasy. In particular, her admiration for her friend Lucy Woodsworth sometimes resembled a paean to convention. She applauded Woodsworth as a "woman with splendid qualities for public life who subordinates all else to the care of her husband and children." To be sure, Lucy "had reaped a fine harvest from that decision; and by her ability and good management, has been able not only to share in her husband's public life, but to give leadership to various community groups as well, besides making the care of her family the paramount work of her life."[89] Ultimately, however, this paragon remained first and foremost a wife. As it demonstrated the power of the era's dominant assumptions, even for ardent socialists, that conclusion may also have hinted at widowed Laura's continuing sense of loss. Whatever the explanation, her first term in the legislature revealed an independent woman who enjoyed public life, someone who could match and outperform the best of the old boys, so many of whom were subsidized by helpful wives.

7
Legislative Veteran, 1941–45

In the course of her first term, Laura Jamieson had found a secure footing in the legislature as an active campaigner for the CCF and an advocate for women's greater public participation. Her links to the club movement had proved a strength, and she had become a formidable debater. This record, together with rising popular support for the CCF, seemed to herald good prospects for both women and the party. The October 1941 election, which occurred just before the bombing of Pearl Harbor, tested that promise. Harold Winch led the BC CCF against Premier Pattullo's Liberals and the Conservatives headed by Royal Lethington Maitland. Red baiting blackened a bitter campaign. Running in Vancouver Centre, the Liberal attorney general typically warned that a CCF victory "might plunge the province into bloody revolution resembling the overthrow of Kerensky's regime in Russia." Even the "mild socialism" of the CCF would "destroy confidence of investors in the province's industries, as Social Credit" had done in Alberta.[1] For all his dire warnings, he went down to defeat, as did his Liberal teammate, both succumbing in the double-member constituency to Laura and Wallace Lefeaux, a Marxist theoretician and former member of the Socialist Party of Canada. The overall result, however, was nearly a dead heat in the popular vote, with the CCF at 33.36 percent, the Liberals at 32.94 percent, and the Conservatives at 30.91 percent. The seat count stood very differently, with fourteen, twenty-one, and twelve respectively. When Pattullo refused to align his minority government with the Conservatives, he was ousted by a Liberal-Conservative Coalition led by John Hart, who then became premier. This strategy effectively kept the

CCF – referred to as the "Reds" – out of power. Applied throughout subsequent decades, it eventually brought the Social Credit Party to office in 1952 (future Socred premier W.A.C. Bennett was elected as a Conservative in 1941). Briefly unseated by the New Democratic Party (successor to the CCF) in 1972, Social Credit kept its hold on power until 1991.

All three female incumbents – Helen Douglas Smith, Dorothy Steeves, and Laura Jamieson – contested the election. So did a further nine women, including, for the CCF, Clare Nulalinda McAllister in Victoria City, Felicia Snowsell in South Okanagan, Grace MacInnis in Vancouver-Burrard, and Helena Gutteridge in Vancouver-Point Grey. Gutteridge faced Conservative clubwoman Tilly Rolston and Liberal UBC dean of women Mary Bollert. Mary Douglas McBride ran for the Conservatives in New Westminster, and Liberal clubwoman and journalist Nancy Hodges campaigned in Victoria City. A noteworthy addition to their numbers was Catherine Emily Ling, the first Chinese Canadian female candidate in any election, who set the standard for the Emancipation Party in Vancouver-Point Grey. Though little is yet known about Ling or her party, its title was significant in highlighting the disenfranchisement of her community.

Women of all parties were vulnerable to caricatures, but those on the left were the special targets of mainstream newspapers. Though acknowledged as an "effective" debater, MacInnis was typically summed up as follows: "good cook, has a keen eye for home furnishings and looks forward to the day when she and Angus are going to buy a farm and build a home. In fact she has all the wifely characteristics – including that of back seat driving in the MacInnis' little English car."[2]

The veteran Steeves was described as a "pleasant-looking, genial woman ... Despite her three-way job – marital, maternal and political – Mrs. Steeves still finds time for her hobby – gardening. She raises super delphinium from seed, and she also writes a lot; and wants to write more."[3] Laura was reintroduced as a former teacher and judge with a "love for children," who "fill[ed] her home with young people." She was also a "Charter member of the Alpine Club of Canada," a veteran of the Crow's Nest Mountain climb, and soon resident of a co-operative house.[4] All the female candidates could be asked about feminism. Rolston, who claimed that she had "been too busy with club work" to be active politically, emphasized that she was not "a feminist" but added that "it takes the brains, the judgment and the wisdom of both men and women to run a government."[5] When Laura was interviewed, she bluntly summed up her two years in Victoria: "It's a man's world ... and in parliament it is never more evident ... so if the women want to be heard above the masculine tenor of things, they've got to be better than men." Like other female candidates whom the press interviewed, she prioritized "human welfare."[6]

The election returned five women. MacInnis joined Steeves and Jamieson on the CCF benches, whereas Rolston and Hodges eventually pledged themselves to the new Liberal-Conservative Coalition. Together, they constituted 10 percent of the BC legislature, the highest in Canada and a percentage not matched or beaten in the province until 1972, when six women made up 11 percent of BC MLAs.[7] Despite having done nothing in support of them, the *Vancouver Sun* preened: "In contrast to the women of Nazi Germany, whose activities have been increasingly restricted to home and children since Hitler came to power, women in this Canadian stronghold of democracy took a flying leap from kitchen

Tops in Canada until the 1970s in number of women representatives. Left to right: Nancy Hodges (Victoria City, Liberal), Tilly Rolston (Vancouver-Point Grey, Conservative), Dorothy Gretchen Steeves (North Vancouver, CCF), Laura Jamieson (Vancouver Centre, CCF), and Grace MacInnis (Vancouver Burrard, CCF) | *Victoria Daily Times*, December 5, 1941, reproduced by Supra Design, Victoria

British Columbia's CCF women champions, 1941: Laura Jamieson, Dorothy Gretchen Steeves, and Grace MacInnis | Image E-00045 courtesy of Royal BC Museum and Archives

to public platform as a result of yesterday's elections."[8] Even *Chatelaine*, which likewise paid scant attention to female politicians, briefly featured the five candidates.[9] In thanking voters, Laura emphasized the significance of women: "I am particularly grateful for the women's vote which I believed played a big part in my re-election, and I am glad to see women taking a greater and greater interest in public life." However, she stressed that women were "not the only ones in whom I am interested. I particularly want to carry on the work of helping the industrial workers."[10]

Mere weeks after the provincial contest, the Vancouver municipal election again tested party prospects. Hopeful as always, Laura believed she had glimpsed "evidence of greater activity among women" in the earlier campaign. Ultimately, however, she had to accept the voters' choice of an all-male city council dominated by the Non-Partisan Association. She attributed that disappointment in large part to the restrictive franchise.[11]

She also forthrightly condemned an electorate who "preferred to let the children of the city live in wretched shacks and vermin-infested houses, since they have voted in again the aldermen who have persistently refused to do anything about a housing scheme." Voters further betrayed democracy in favouring candidates who had not opposed having "copper, nickel and scrap iron go to Japan," where it would be used against China and, though that was not yet clear, soon against the Allies. Laura pointed to the guilty parties. They were not

> the main body of the adult population of Vancouver, [since] only a minority of the population, the people who own property and the people who pay certain rentals [could vote]. All the rest, no matter how much indirect taxes they pay, no matter how intelligent they may be, no matter how much they have done for Vancouver in public service or otherwise, are disenfranchised ... The great proportion are women.[12]

As an alderman later in the 1940s, she would continue to protest that discrimination.

In the meantime, Laura found much to occupy her in the BC capital. Provincial CCF leader Harold Winch refused an invitation to join an all-party government, trusting that "a non-socialist coalition would demonstrate to the public ... that there was no difference between the Liberal and Conservative parties."[13] Many CCFers foresaw a bright future. Dorothy Steeves insisted that "labor is on the march." Rather noticeably, however, even as she named many CCF MLAs in her roll call of victors, including newcomer Grace MacInnis, she did not mention Jamieson. Steeves was a leader of the party's staunch Marxists, whereas both Grace and Laura aligned with the gradualist social democratic wing.[14] Due to her pedigree and ability, Grace could not be ignored, but Laura's ties with women's and the early CCF clubs did her little favour in Steeves' calculation of the proper future of the party as a revolutionary agent for change.

Such divisions were nevertheless regularly offset by common concern about the impact of war on the economy and society. In 1941–42, the Allies were not doing well. British and Canadian forces were defeated in Hong Kong on Christmas Day 1941, and the Japanese bombed Pearl Harbor in the same month. In mid-1942, the tragedy of the Dieppe Raid raised the prospect of defeat. Pressure mounted on military recruitment and industrial production, in the process fuelling British Columbia's long-standing anti-Asian prejudice. The entry of the United States into the war, like the end of the German-Soviet entente in June 1942 and the re-establishment of Canadian-Soviet diplomatic relations, did little to curb pervasive fearmongering and assaults on civil liberties.

Wartime British Columbia sucked in male and female workers to fill jobs created in agriculture and in plywood mills, packing houses, shipyards, and factories. Between 1939 and 1944, Vancouver's population grew by forty-four thousand, straining already inadequate infrastructure and services. In 1944, the report of the BC Post-War Rehabilitation Council described a province-wide housing crisis. In some cases, as with woodworkers in Port Alberni, wartime employment lit a feminist consciousness and new unionization.[15] In short, the province seemed ripe for new political solutions.

It was not alone. High hopes on the left and terror on the right unsettled politics all across the nation. In the 1943 Ontario election, Conservatives only narrowly bested the CCF, winning thirty-seven seats to the latter's thirty-four. That fall, the CCF stood first in Canadian public opinion polls.[16] In June 1944, the party took Saskatchewan. In British Columbia, journalist Bruce Hutchison observed that the ruling Liberal-Conservative Coalition "is drifting, or rather pushing, to the left, as it must if it is to survive the growth of the CCF." As evidence, he pointed to Nancy Hodges and Tilly Rolston: "Both lady speakers were guilty of grand larceny of the C.C.F. platform ... The C.C.F. members watched them grimly, with granite faces and the collective look of Robespierre before the Terror ... It all goes to show how women think alike and think in general along more advanced lines than men."[17] Nor was theft restricted to Rolston and Hodges. Busily borrowing wholesale, the coalition reformed industrial relations, boosted education spending, expanded mothers' pensions, and produced a "Bill of Rights" for civil servants.[18]

As the war dragged on, Laura's dismissal of theory that was untethered to practical application became ever more a leitmotif of her politics. In the summer of 1942, the visiting British penal reformer Marjory Fry offered a concrete example of what her sex should do. Despite her "good" family and unlike other middle-class women who were hobbled by position and propriety, Fry didn't shy away from difficult subjects. Laura rebuked other contemporaries who took up "radical lines of thought," felt "genuine moral indignation at social injustice," and linked "themselves with radical movements" but subsequently did little more than pontificate. She suggested that these Canadians, frustratingly unnamed but apparently communists or some within the CCF, became "incapable of an impartial estimate of a social situation, or of constructive action toward a solution of problems." Perched on the lofty pinnacle of theory, they ignored the practical search for solutions by women such as Fry. Laura feared that

> we in Canada are not used to impartial analysis. And those who have repudiated completely the capitalist point of view are often very susceptible to skillful propaganda from the other extreme. Moreover, few of us understand human psychology well enough to realize the change that is taking place in a country like England ... lessons we, especially radicals, must learn. The women I have mentioned do not seem to feel, nor wish to feel themselves an active and necessary part of our nation. They like to remain apart, so that they can criticize. But unless the criticism is constructive, unless they are willing to pull their weight in positive effort toward change and reform, they lower the whole standard of women's contribution to social advance. The same state of mind is formed in many men also.
>
> This gives the CCF a double task which it is striving manfully to perform. It has to make itself, as a Socialist movement, an active and necessary part of the nation; and it has to create in its individual members the same feeling of participation in national effort and national life. Is it too much to ask that all its members should recognize the double task and strive to perform it?[19]

No doubt those on the left, whether members of the CCF or the Communist Party (known as the Labor-Progressive Party from 1943 to 1959), understood whom she was singling out.

During her second term, Laura renewed her commitment to diverse causes, but women workers, internationalism and racial justice, post-war reconstruction, and improvement of women's prospects in the CCF topped her agenda. In 1943, she summed this up for *Chatelaine:* she aimed to encourage women to "train themselves for public life at a high standard." This required "personal contact" with "underprivileged women and children," and personal investigation of housing, health, wages, working conditions, poverty, legislation, and the causes of war. Women needed to "realize the present war is a revolutionary period and that bold policies for a better world must begin now." They could "become sincere and vocal advocates of necessary changes."[20] Near the end of her term, Laura reiterated much of this message in her thirty-five-page election pamphlet, *Women Dry Those Tears,* published by the CCF Women's Council of BC, with assistance from "Ontario CCF Women."

In short, Jamieson continued her pursuit of serious change. During a post-election tea for women MLAs, she was typically irritated when Rolston rambled on about the feminine pleasures of washday. Jamieson asked, "If an elected representative boasts of her household accomplishments on the platform, her constituents may well say, 'Is that what we elected her for?'" Time spent over the teacups was much better employed in studying factory conditions and wages.[21] Women must offer remedies, not adorn tea parties. In the same spirit, Laura inquired as to how the federal Committee on Post-War Reconstruction, made up entirely of men, could deal with national issues.[22]

To realize her hopes, Laura returned to the educational potential of organized womanhood. After the 1941 BC election returned five female MLAs, the Women's School for Citizenship brought them together with women's groups in a two-day conference. This launched an annual discussion of matters ranging from health insurance, housing, family and juvenile courts, and libraries to day nurseries. By the end, female legislators knew more about the opinions of organized women. This recurring event was augmented by the school's weekly panel discussions, where audiences might debate "Women and World Citizenship" and meet representatives of China, Austria, and the Soviet Union or learn about the "History of Women." Historical thinking was deemed essential since "it is very necessary for women to see themselves in the light of history before they can plan intelligently the part they wish to play in the future." The history session also inspired discussion of continuing limits on women in employment and the pervasiveness of "a strong inferiority complex." That unfortunate psychology encouraged women "to shrink from many of the tasks which would enlarge their perspective and enrich their characters," in the process impoverishing the entire nation.[23]

In speaking to the school near the end of her second term, Laura acknowledged the "valiant" struggle for the vote but suggested that her sex had ultimately been ignorant and divided in dealing with a world ruled by men. The school offered another chance to realize suffrage hopes:

> All forms of democracy, particularly those affecting women and children, are our texts. We have enacted court scenes to show how neglected and delinquent children are dealt with and also we have demonstrated the working of the Minimum Wage Act ... We gather groups of our women students ... and take them on field trips to visit the Women's Gaol, Detention Home for Juvenile Delinquents, and other institutions. We have women attend the Police Court and the Assize Courts when cases involving women are being tried. We want to have the School interpret groups of women to each other and show one group how they can help others of their own sex when they are in difficulties.[24]

The school's 1944 conference on women and employment was designed to introduce "club women and housewives" to "women on the job (or just off the job) in industry." Laura could only wish that farmwomen had been included among the invited female workers. In short, the school's programs embodied the "conviction that being a citizen entails a broad understanding of the problems of all women, and not merely of one's own group or class."[25]

Labour's exclusion from key decisions left female workers especially ill-served in wartime policy making. As Laura told legislators in January 1942, some eighteen thousand of the estimated twenty-four thousand women who worked in the province received "less than $14 a week, while thousands of girls were at work as beginners at $9 a week," an amount insufficient "to maintain proper living." The female employees in some canning and jam factories faced especially hard times, with the denial of overtime rates.[26] In the summer of 1942, Jamieson visited the Okanagan to check on its canneries. In addition to describing women's exploitation, she used the occasion to call for tolerance among workers and Canadians in general. She singled out a "Doukhobor woman, kerchief on head, skirts around her ankles," who seemed "to have stepped out of the sixteenth century." Her future would be far different from her past. Once employed in industry, she could "cover those four centuries and catch up to her twentieth century sisters." Although such a woman might be used "to undercut" wages, soon enough she would "be as good a union member as the others." In time, as well, she would marry and integrate into the mainstream. Her "broad face and high cheek bones will appear, modified, in succeeding generations, and the 'Doukhobor problem' will be a thing of the past."[27] Such previously excluded groups and Canada itself would evolve, not as a nation of ghettoized communities arranged hierarchically by race, class, or gender but as a pluralistic whole. Although she left unquestioned the right of the Anglo-Celtic community to define the terms of inclusion, Jamieson emphasized both the future Ukrainian contribution and the critical role to be played by unions in securing a fair deal.[28] Before a Vancouver audience of nearly a thousand in spring 1942, the energetic CCFer made the specific case for the Retail Clerks' Union. Its crusades undergirded progress for white-collar workers.[29] A brave new world required a better deal for both minorities and unions.

In her defence of female workers, Jamieson, like Steeves and MacInnis, recognized that the largest number of women were engaged in unpaid household labour. In 1944, the trio championed a domestic minimum wage. Their bill was defeated on second reading by an unfriendly legislature. Investigation and evidence provided by the YWCA counted for nothing when Conservative Tilly Rolston insisted that the "time was not ripe" and demanded that more study be undertaken. Jamieson, who never had much patience with the Point Grey MLA, cited a BC Security Commission survey of households that wished to employ Japanese Canadian women as domestics as proof of the benefits of official oversight.[30] Her 1945 election pamphlet, *Women Dry Those Tears,* championed the same employees as a central part of an advanced labour policy: their protection would "help considerably to raise the wage standards of all women." Since governments had uniformly failed this group, Laura advanced the Vancouver Trades and Labour Council's support for a Household Workers' Union as a model for unionists everywhere.[31]

As the war in Europe ended, Laura highlighted the implications for female employment. No Canadian government offered women "protection against exploitation" or layoffs. Although Jamieson didn't refer to women as a reserve army of labour, she identified them as a routinely abused group that was "used only as a pool of cheap labor under capitalism, along with Orientals and new immigrants."[32] They would be fired or pushed into domestic service so that the better jobs could be reserved for men. Once again, organized labour was more reliable than legislators. Along with their other benefits, unions offered lessons in "living democracy." At their best, they produced "a spirit inflation," an encouragement to contest the constraints that so commonly curbed women.[33] In the meantime, Laura joined Grace and Dorothy in campaigning in and out of the legislature for equal pay for equal work, a long-time CCF goal.[34]

Central as well to their agenda for women's economic well-being were day nurseries. British Columbia had refused to join Ottawa's wartime day nursery scheme, claiming that its female war workers were too few to justify the expense. Jamieson responded that nurseries offered a solution to historic difficulties. Speaking in the legislature in March 1943, she made the following general case:

> The day of "barbarism" in the home, when the economic life did not permit proper care of children is gone ... Day nurseries ... will not only be for the duration of the war but will have their place after the war, when women will refuse to return to the economic instability of some homes, when they can supplement husbands' incomes with earnings of their own and go home, after work, to pleasant children.[35]

She was strongly rebutted by Rolston, who claimed that day nurseries were "an insult to British Columbia mothers" and that they represented "the thin edge of the wedge for regimentation," by which she meant communism. Ignoring her own escape from domesticity, Rolston insisted that women found "a career full and satisfying" in their homes, indeed a "sacred" endeavour.[36] Unsurprisingly, Jamieson asked, "I wonder if Mrs. Rolston actually knows many of these women [workers] and has talked to them." Perhaps her opponent had "forgotten so soon the depression years when women couldn't get enough food for their children."[37]

Laura's quest for realism when it came to domestic life similarly appeared in her insistence on the need for a highly trained provincial social welfare department. Equipped with a knowledge of law and civil administration, such professionals could do a far better job than the untrained magistrates who commonly ruled on family matters.[38] In particular, Jamieson ridiculed judges for "delivering platitudinous sermons on domestic relations when granting divorces."[39] Like Rolston, such amateurs offered no answer to the real-life problems that began with inadequate income and male privilege.

CCF women's crusade for working women and domestic reform irritated the coalition government, but equally significantly it found little support in the popular press, where economic independence and opportunity were commonly trivialized or disappeared altogether in the preoccupation with romantic outcomes. *Maclean's,* English Canada's largest circulation magazine, was a typical offender. Only too regularly, its trite observations diverted attention from women's real lives, as the following passages show:

> Rumors are trickling over from England that, with the help of a clever little tailor, a girl can get a very dashing suit from her fighting husband's civvies.[40]

> Most women don't worry a great deal about not having a chance to rise to the top of the heap and not getting equal pay with men. They've never had it and they don't look for miracles.[41]

> One of the hot spots of discussion groups all over Canada today, and everyone has an opinion as to the lasting effect of khaki, Air Force and Navy blue, or well-worn denim and slacks on the softer side of womanhood.[42]

And as it pointed out, military women "haven't forgotten dancing, perfume, moonlight ... and men."[43] Such pervasive flippancy simply undermined women and feminist politicians.

Jamieson's campaigns for internationalism and tolerance similarly found little mainstream resonance. Throughout the war, she joined Steeves in condemning the failure of the British Empire and the Commonwealth to live up to professed principles of fair play and democracy. Laura also repeatedly defended her colleague, whose legislative orations on imperialism's responsibility for the horrors of war, all the more impassioned after Dorothy lost her only child on a flying mission over Europe, drove jingoists to demand her removal from the legislature.[44] And just as with women's work, Laura believed that modern technologies and education offered freedom from past mistakes in international relations. Thus, "the exploitation of so-called backward nations for profit – is as unnecessary as it is suicidal. With all the scientific discoveries and technological inventions, any nation can produce at home all the things that far-away countries have provided in the past."[45] Co-operation, not competition and exploitation, was the best way forward in foreign relations, as it was in life generally.

Anti-racism was part of the brave new world that Laura trusted could come into being. *Women Dry Those Tears* set out the inclusive standard demanded by feminist socialism:

> If women wish equality of opportunity in Canada, realizing that low income women are a depressed group, along with new immigrants, racial minorities and others, they will have to work for equal opportunity for all. In achieving equality of opportunity for all depressed groups they will achieve it for themselves. So long as there are depressed groups anywhere, so long as there are people in want and fear, we shall have wars.[46]

Here was WILPF's familiar message of linked oppressions and oppressions linked to war. Laura stood with Grace MacInnis, who denounced racism in a *Canadian Forum* article, asking "what kind of world are we fighting and working for?"[47]

During the Second World War, the outstanding domestic test of such principles was the treatment of the Canadian Japanese. The BC CCF initially pursued long-standing arguments favouring full citizenship for this group. In the immediate aftermath of Pearl Harbor, *The Federationist* "warned against racial prejudice" and "commended the

Japanese Canadians for having helped the war effort."[48] In December 1943, *Maclean's* published Angus MacInnis' denunciation of so-called repatriation:

> We should not forget the ends for which the war is being fought ... human values, human dignity and human relationships ... The taint of the superior race doctrine is not confined to Germany or to the Nazis; we find it on this continent ... I will not be party to discriminating against a people because of race or color ... I advocate granting to those of Japanese origin in Canada all the rights and privileges that I have, on the sole basis that they are human beings. To deny them one iota of the rights and privileges enjoyed by, I shall say, individuals of the race to which I belong would be a denial of the brotherhood of man ... an assertion on my part of the superior race theory for the eradication of which from the minds of men our young men are dying all manner of death in every part of the world.[49]

However, even before MacInnis wrote this brave statement, the CCF had slipped into support for removing Japanese Canadians from the coast and interning them.

In March 1942, provincial CCF leader Harold Winch joined a Citizens' Defence Committee, which "circulated a petition for immediate removal of enemy aliens from all points that the military thought essential for defence and public safety and the immediate 'evacuation of all those of Japanese origin from the Pacific Coast.'" The Vancouver Trades and Labour Council joined the Kiwanis, Rotary, and BC Legion to endorse removal.[50] *The Federationist* echoed the demand.[51] They were far from alone. In February 1944, a Gallup poll revealed that 80 percent of Canadian respondents supported the deportation of all Japanese nationals and that 33 percent favoured the same fate for Japanese Canadians.[52] Also in that year, Grace and Angus MacInnis accepted the ban on coastal residence in their pamphlet *Oriental Canadians – Outcasts or Citizens?*

Even as bigotry mounted, CCFers were divided. In March 1942, Laura joined a small group in organizing the Consultative Council for Cooperation in Wartime Problems of Canadian Citizenship, which took up "justice for the Canadian residents of Japanese origin."[53] Although it accepted dispersal of the BC Japanese population as a means of reducing racial hatred and a spur to integration and assimilation, it rejected "as contrary to the rights of Canadian citizenship" a Vancouver City Council resolution to expel the Japanese from Canada.[54] In 1944, the consultative council joined with the United, Anglican, Roman Catholic, and Baptist churches to warn Ottawa that deportation would be "an act of indefensible tyranny and folly."[55] In the same year, it opposed the removal of "the franchise from all Japanese-Canadians regardless of which province they resided in."[56] In 1945, the committee described disenfranchisement and internment as "the first step toward Naziism ... the principle we have established: Canadian citizens by law can be deprived of certain legal rights on the grounds of race. This is one of the cardinal points of Naziism." Any nation that called itself a democracy should be committed to the removal of all "disabilities" of race.[57]

In 1945, Laura defended Japanese Canadians in the legislature and insisted that their assimilation was no more difficult than that of the Scots. She noted the latter's history of "human sacrifices," "outlandish dress," and "outlandish music." None of that had prevented the Scots from becoming good Canadians, and the Japanese in fact presented less of a challenge.[58] The heightened passions of the times made her semi-humorous comparison offensive to many in the legislature and the press. The *Vancouver Sun* dismissed her remarks as "uncalled-for" and stated that her "ridiculing" of "the Irish and Scots" had left "a bad taste in the mouth of these free, peace-loving people and it shows plainly where your prejudice is pointed."[59]

During the war, the Japanese provoked the greatest discussion of the meaning of race, and the other groups that were excluded from the franchise received little attention. In February 1944, Jamieson nevertheless urged the legislature to enfranchise "East Indians." As she noted, they were "British subjects, they are part of the British Empire ... There is not one valid reason why these people should not have the vote in B.C."[60] The CCF bill to that end, which included giving the vote to all Asians in the armed forces, was defeated the following month.[61] In the 1945 budget debate, Laura connected all such prejudice firmly to capitalism, arguing that "Russia has wiped out competition and has brought 187 racial groups into one national life. A full productive program assuring plenty for all will do away with racial hatred and weld people of all nationalities into a strong socialist nation."[62] The Soviet Union, not the British Empire or the Commonwealth, was, she suggested, often a better model for the future when it came to race relations.

In comparison to Asians, Indigenous people received almost no acknowledgment in the legislature or the press. To be sure, the CCF newspaper occasionally jogged memories about injustice, as in 1943 when a former teacher described the residents of the Inkameep Reserve in the BC Interior as having "much to offer Canadian life."[63] In general, however, such communities were invisible in its pages. Laura herself said little in public, but in 1945, as part of the debate about assimilation and the franchise, she mentioned the general benefits of racial mixing: "Our natives came from Asia and early settlers married them. Some of our best citizens boasted of their Indian blood. Some of the best brains of Europe were a mixture of races."[64] Her arguments on racial integration typically invoked universals rather than specifics. In 1945, *Women Dry Those Tears* pointed out that the "democratic socialist principle of giving equality of opportunity to people of racial origins within its borders" provided the Soviet Union with a "strength and unity that Canadians still deny to themselves." When combined with "adherence to the democratic socialist principle of equality of the sexes,"[65] this approach made Canada's communist ally worthy of emulation.

When Laura contemplated post-war reconstruction, combatting gender and class injustice rather than anti-racism always topped her agenda. Her assessment of the advice furnished in a 1943 pamphlet titled *Security for Canadians* was blunt in this regard. Written by Charlotte Whitton, a conservative, occasionally feminist, social worker and founding director of the Canadian Council on Child Welfare, it was dismissed as offering more "sermonizing" than sense. Whitton had defended private enterprise, which Laura saw as "absurd" because it would never "operate for anything other than the accumulation of profit." She equally condemned the assumption that the great majority of the population should subsist at a minimum level "while a small minority will continue to live at a luxurious standard." That mean-spirited "vision of social security is simply not good enough for Canadians. If that is the best that can be done under capitalism, the only system that Miss Whitton envisions, then Canadians are going to look for a better system."[66] As her disapproval suggested, Laura placed economic restructuring centre front in bettering the post-war world.

When asked in 1943 if "women [had] made the most of their political equality," she outlined the post-war path to relevance. Once more, as during the suffrage campaigns, activists needed to study the "conditions under which underprivileged women and children live, as to housing, nutrition and health, and also wages and conditions of women industrial workers." If women did this, together with considering the policies necessary for peace, they would identify the "social legislation necessary to alleviate bad conditions."[67] That same year, she wondered if women were expected to "turn around after the war and march right back to barbarism" in the workplace.[68] In January 1945, she helped organize the

Women's School for Citizenship conference to investigate post-war job losses. Speaking to unions and women's groups, Jamieson insisted that "to make sure that the place women have earned be maintained, they must refuse to accept unemployment, and together with male workers demand such opportunities as have been provided by a socialized economy in other countries."[69]

Women Dry Those Tears envisioned the new world that social democracy could create. In extended comparisons with New Zealand, which had elected a Labour government in 1937, and Saskatchewan, which had returned Tommy Douglas's CCF in 1944, she emphasized that women's best interests lay with the social welfare state and greater unionization. The nationalization of industries such as electricity and the extension of services in health, education, housing, and employment would found a nation where women no longer had to weep. The skills they had learned in war industries could be used in good peacetime jobs, and their children would discover new opportunities in day nurseries that were linked to the public education system. Neither women nor men would be forced to "endure a 'too-few-jobs' economy."[70] Equal opportunity would extend to racial minorities and new immigrants as well as women.

For all its common sense, that vision remained extremely controversial. In 1944, the *Canadian Home Journal* consulted the nation's elected women on the role of their sex in politics and revealed at best a lack of consensus. Tilly Rolston, introduced as Mrs. J.F. Rolston, urged female readers to protect the homes of the nation by staying out of the labour market. CCFer Agnes Macphail sharply disagreed with that reactionary proposition. The article's author herself largely missed the point: she struggled to occupy a middle ground by stressing that women should be better educated on "current political issues." She employed a metaphor that suffragists could recall: "Government is only housekeeping on a large scale."[71] Although that argument had opened opportunities for a previous generation, it still held one sex largely responsible for homes and families and left little room for state-supported childcare or a fair deal in employment. A Canadian Gallup poll that showed 75 percent of Canadian men and 68 percent of women in support of giving men "the first chance in any competition for postwar jobs" was no happier a portent for Macphail or Jamieson.[72] Similar sentiments emerged in a March 1945 survey conducted by the radio program *Public Opinion:* 83.8 percent of respondents believed that "a woman's place is in the home."[73]

Jamieson strove to make the CCF the antidote for such opinions. As she sought to re-engineer the party as more welcoming and less intimidating, she had reason to appreciate the observations of a female member from Lumby, British Columbia, who addressed its commonplace masculinism: the use of "comrade" was "cliquish" and "childish," narrowing the appeal while savouring of "secrecy, snobbery, dressups and salutes. Of Heils, Honorables, Majesties, and all the clap-trap which progressive people would wipe away. It is conservatives who encourage such conceptions ... as a substitute for the rights of man."[74]

Laura was on the same wavelength in seeking a greater welcome and engagement at all levels. In spring 1944, in private house meetings throughout the Fraser Valley, she told CCFers that "women will come to them [domestic gatherings] who would never go to CCF meetings at a public hall; and that women will take part in the discussions at a house meeting much more readily."[75] She recommended non-partisan gatherings, citing her own invitations from the Old Age Pensioners group of Abbotsford, the Hatzic Parent-Teacher Federation, the Chilliwack Local Council of Women, and the Cultus Lake child nursery co-operative. Such events spread the word that the CCF was practical, not frightening.[76] As she explained to CBC Radio listeners in her February 1945 discussion of the Montreal League for Women's Rights, the Toronto Women's Electors' Association, and the Vancouver Women's School for Citizenship, small groups were best in building effective citizenship and a better democracy.[77]

Within the party, Laura joined ongoing discussion about the relationship of female MLAs to the broader women's community. In a meeting of the CCF Women's Council prior to the 1945 provincial convention, Steeves "contended that CCF women in the legislature want legislation for people, not just for women and children, but since they understand the problems of women and children better than do men in the legislature, social problems become the work of the women MLA's." She added that "women are more intense, more generous, but more intolerant of injustice, and have a real contribution to make on all legislative bodies." Jamieson agreed but, unlike Steeves, she prioritized a women's section of the party to popularize "CCF politics among women, as well as linking up CCF women across the province with the MLAs, and keeping them advised of their problems." Such a section would better mobilize the female voters, who were essential to electoral victory.[78]

Such initiatives were all the more urgent when critics, like polls, gave cause for worry. In March 1944, the editorial director of the Canadian Institute for Public Opinion asserted that women were not using the franchise or had "lost much of the militant crusading spirit of their mothers and are far too diffident and self-deprecatory," remaining "content to parrot the opinions of their menfolk."[79] In late 1944, the Conservative feminist Charlotte Whitton agreed that the CCF was the best major party in offering "more appreciation and partnership to its women," an inclination she attributed to the "general respect in which all but the most prejudiced opinion holds that pioneer woman parliamentarian, Agnes Macphail." More forbiddingly, however, she warned that the CCF, like the Liberals and Conservatives, was succumbing to indifference, a disengagement by female voters that she blamed on both prejudice and a faltering club movement. She particularly singled out the National Council of Women as "no longer an effective operative body," lacking "unified leadership and 'attacking power.'" That failure, she suggested, colluded with pervasive male hostility: "There is deep and silent prayer among most of the males in *all* the political parties" that women will not appear "in the places where policies are made, plans plotted and posts of power assigned." Her conclusion drew a brutal sexual analogy:

> Men tend to use women as ruthlessly in the mass as many would exploit her individually. They want her devotion, her energy, her unquestioned skill for envisaging and executing details in their political organizations. However, they want to purchase it, like her virtue, for a pretty trinket, a passing courtesy, a temporary alliance during the election campaign, but without the entanglement and obligation of a continuing partnership.[80]

A few months later, Whitton nevertheless rejected separate organization and parties. Women, she insisted, did "not want to work out the plan of the future in isolation." Instead, they must storm political parties and refuse to play their assigned parts as "auxiliary forces to carry the light and do the Martha's jobs."[81]

Laura's response, as always, returned to women's raised consciousness and education. This was her message to the Women's School for Citizenship in March 1945:

> In spite of the fact that women today had the vote and the legal right to enter practically all professions and trades, they still suffer the handicap of a strong inferiority complex. This seems to be due to the fact that the attitude toward women is still largely the traditional one: that women are not just people like the rest of society, but a group apart – "the sex"; that because women have a very special function, that of bearing and rearing children, this function, even when it is not used, somehow unfits them for

> performing the various duties and jobs now carried out mostly by men. This attitude ... was a dangerous one, both for women and society. For women, because it causes them to shrink from many of the tasks which would enlarge their perspective and enrich their characters. For society, because, especially now when women are sorely needed for new and unusual tasks, they hesitate to accept these tasks, or find themselves unfitted for them, and the nation is the loser. To educate society to think of women as ordinary people first and as citizens, before it thinks of them specifically as women, is necessary before women can fill their full role as citizens. Women cannot do this alone. They cannot progress normally in face of a false attitude.[82]

In 1945, general elections revealed the views of Canadians and British Columbians on these questions.[83] With its slogan "Build a New Social Order," the federal Liberal Party once again successfully seized the promise of change from the left, and in June 1945 Prime Minister W.L. Mackenzie King won a majority. The CCF emerged with only twenty-eight seats, and the newly named Progressive Conservatives took thirty-nine. For the first time, Social Credit appeared federally with thirteen seats. British Columbia elected five Liberals with 27.5 percent of the vote, five Progressive Conservatives with 30.0 percent, and four CCFers with 29.4 percent, results that suggest the closeness of popular sentiment in the province.

Once the vote was counted, only one woman of the nineteen female candidates nation-wide – eight Labor-Progressive (Communist), six CCF, two Progressive Conservative, two Social Credit, and one Liberal – won her seat. Long-time CCF activist Gladys Strum took the constituency of Qu'Appelle, Saskatchewan.[84] The sole BC CCF female candidate was defeated in Kamloops. The *CCF News* fairly enough concluded that the party record on women was "little better than that of the old-line parties who have never pretended to the degree of equality that we have championed. It is not a situation to be approached in any manner of feminist belligerency but one that should occupy the attention of all true socialists, men and women alike." Shortcomings were all the greater since "with increasing concern of the state for the welfare of its citizens, the field of politics is merely an enlargement of those interests which have been women's chief concern." Unfortunately, "men and women of the CCF still do not place men and women on an equal footing in selecting candidates either for public office or for executive positions within our party. The men go through one 'screening' process, the women through two.

Women, to achieve success, must be twice or even three or four times as good as men."[85]

In October 1945, the BC election again tested the appeal of women and the CCF. With forty-eight candidates of both sexes, the party fielded a complete slate. In all, thirteen women ran for office, a number that the "Women's Views" column in the *CCF News* thought low since "in a democracy it seems fair that the proportion of representatives in the governing bodies should more nearly reflect the proportion in the ordinary population."[86] CCF nominees included the veterans Steeves, MacInnis, and Jamieson, plus three women who wrote for the *CCF News* – Gladys Webster for the South Okanagan, Clare McAllister for Oak Bay, Victoria, and May Campbell for Victoria City. The Labor-Progressive Party nominated two women in the Lower Mainland, both of whom were identified as housewives and mothers, "active in welfare and parent-teachers' association work." One woman contested Victoria as an Independent Conservative. Victoria Liberal Nancy Hodges ran for the Liberal-Conservative Coalition, as did Vancouver Conservative Tilly Rolston. Social Credit chose two female journalists to hoist its colours.[87]

The Liberal-Conservative Coalition once again endeavoured to maximize its vote by rallying anti-Japanese feeling.[88] One of Laura's Vancouver Centre opponents argued that if Japanese residents were allowed to vote, "you'll never get the C.C.F. out as long as you live." Citing the poor treatment of Canadian prisoners of war in Hong Kong, he insisted that "people capable of that should not be allowed in this country."[89] For all its imperfections, Laura's record on the enfranchisement of Japanese Canadians and the defence of civil liberties made her a key target of coalition bigotry, which was also true for Dorothy and Grace.

When the results came in, the CCF increased its share of the vote to 37.62 percent (up by 4.26 percent), but it elected only ten MLAs (a drop of four). The coalition, which collected 55.83 percent of the vote (a decrease of 8.02 percent), collected thirty-seven seats. Rolston won for the coalition Conservatives and Hodges for the coalition Liberals. Jamieson, Steeves, and McInnis,[90] arguably the stars of the legislature, all fell. The *Vancouver Sun* wrote their mainstream epitaph, remarking that the loss of Steeves,

> charming, pretty and witty, whose only son died flying for the RCAF ... will have repercussions all through the CCF structure.
>
> Pretty, diminutive Grace MacInnis ... once boasted the unofficial title of Crown Princess of the CCF ... impressed the Legislature with her earnest and painstaking manner.

> A REFORMIST Mrs. Jamieson ... A lecturer, a clubwoman, a juvenile court judge (1927–38), she was suspected by some CCF people of not being too strict a socialist. Her interests in the House were chiefly social reform, with emphasis on children and the aged.[91]

Another Vancouver editorialist suggested that the Liberals and Conservatives played as a "team" to bring down "powerful, popular C.C.F. spellbinders," among whom he included both Laura and Grace.[92]

Laura came third in the two-member Vancouver Centre constituency, winning 7,549 votes against 10,976 and 10,878 for the coalition candidates. Many factors contributed to her loss. Most obviously, there was the shared determination of the old-line parties to defeat the Reds, as well as the racism they invoked in their attack. Less obvious was Laura's reduced hold on the loyalties of organized women. She had been part of their number since 1911, when she arrived in the province, and her 1939 and 1941 victories had generated significant non-partisan feminist support. In 1945, in contrast, this was less evident. Her labours for the party and the Women's School for Citizenship encouraged loyal CCF supporters, but they lacked the wider appeal of earlier leadership in the Parent-Teacher Association and even the Current Events Clubs. In short, her previous broad female constituency was slipping away. Her efforts to extend the party's appeal did not compensate for her gradual disengagement from many mainstream clubwomen.

The election loss would introduce another stage in the sixty-three-year-old's life, but the BC legislature was the greater loser. Without its CCF women, its debates largely ignored the oppression of women. Only Hodges offered an occasional reminder of democracy's shortcomings. Between 1939 and 1945, the legislature came as close to the promised land of the fair deal as Canadian women would get until the 1970s. Though it may have been an uncertain vehicle for women's equality, the CCF did far better than its mainline rivals.

8
Taking on Post-war Misogyny and Vancouver Politics, 1945–64

When she left the provincial legislature in 1945, Laura Jamieson was sixty-three years old. Nearly two more decades of engagement remained to her. Family continued important as she kept close ties with her daughter, Jean, on the Prairies and back east, her son Stuart in Vancouver, and, in time, eight granddaughters. Although her health occasionally failed, Laura retained her own household and her commitment to public life. Books and newspapers accompanied her everywhere and crowded her home, which often served as a gathering centre for the like-minded. Links with old friends, such as Violet McNaughton, still mattered, but age was reducing their number. Until 1957, she lived in the Kitsilano house she had renovated with a bank loan to better share space.[1] Younger and older women also made their home there, providing both financial support and company. In her seventies, she moved to a small apartment on Adanac Street in East Vancouver, between Commercial and Victoria Drives, a working-class area known for its support of the CCF. Here, much like her suffrage contemporary Helena Gutteridge, she remained fiercely independent until she died of a stroke, aged eighty-one, on June 30, 1964.

Laura used CCF conferences, as well as those of groups such as the United Nations Association and the Canadian Federation of Business and Professional Women, as opportunities to visit family members east of the Rockies and occasionally to go farther, as with a trip to Vienna in 1946. She took pride in her children: a puppeteer, Jean sometimes appeared on the CBC, and Stuart was making his reputation as a progressive political economist studying Indigenous peoples and workers. She also observed the development of her granddaughters, the eldest of whom, Kathleen Shannon, joined the National Film Board in 1956. In the 1970s, she would emerge as a major feminist film producer. As her surviving granddaughters remember, Laura always seemed an unconventional grandmother, deeply committed to the world of ideas and debate, someone whom they admired even as she intimidated. Some thirty years after Laura's death, Kathleen left a brief memory in a paper titled, revealingly, "A Feminist Education": "Mama J was an unresigned activist and politician, but definitely an Older Adult, impatient with the ways of the young. She was busy, impatient, critical, off doing important things in unfashionable hats. She struck terror into the hearts of her children, who passed it on to theirs – me, my sisters and our cousins."[2] Such observations summon up a personality that was rarely seen in public, where Laura normally appeared resolutely upbeat in fighting to arouse consciousness of injustice and practical support for its eradication. However, Kathleen's comments would have corresponded to the jaundiced views of her opponents around the Vancouver City Council table, across the aisle in the legislature, and within the CCF. As a suffragist still standing in politics after the Second World War and the only one elected to a provincial or federal legislature during this time, Laura had survived more than a half-century of ongoing battle. As she soldiered on, she had plenty of reason to keep a stiff upper lip and little inclination to suffer fools.

Like others on the feminist left during the Cold War, Laura Jamieson offered progressive alternatives in the context of pervasive misogyny and red baiting. Female politicians, as in previous decades, were routine targets everywhere. Women's bodies provoked recurring commentary, which, whether unfavourable or favourable, cast doubt on their right to independent politics. A typical dyspeptic observer of the period admitted that the communist Dorise Nielsen might have had "plenty on the ball," but he reduced her ultimately to someone who was "by no means hard to look at." He judged a second woman, Liberal MP Cora Casselman, as insufficiently grateful for his attention, whereas a third, Conservative Ellen Fairclough of Hamilton, Ontario, was assessed as attractive enough but as having "stolen" her riding from a worthier male. CCFer Agnes Macphail passed muster, but the only parliamentarian to gain his unqualified approval was Conservative Martha Black, who had "dressed in pink, kidded the members, radiated charm, didn't let her brains show, and was a great success here in Ottawa, both as a member and a wife." Overall, the report card from this typical critic was dismal: "I think women politically have psittacosis. That's parrot disease. It means that the Little Woman has only one political policy ... John says ..."[3] Beyond enumerating individual shortcomings, he succumbed readily to victim blaming: the real problem after all was female voters – "They will not support a woman against a man."[4]

Canada's commonplace public misogyny underpinned the pervasive fascination with deprived and henpecked husbands, among the most notorious of whom, Dagwood Bumstead, appeared in a popular American comic strip titled *Blondie,* which many Canadian newspapers carried. Wives who had careers in politics or in well-rewarded positions were routinely assumed to leave their ultimately deficient male spouses doing the housework and sacrificing their own names and identities.[5] In other words, female success in public life was directly correlated with male inadequacy. No female politician, or aspirant to the role, could readily ignore such crippling messages. Pervasive contempt was one price that women like Laura had to pay for political ambitions.

Public champions of strong women remained rare. Post-war *Chatelaine,* though still aspiring to speak for English Canadian womanhood, was supremely cautious in endorsing a public role for the "second sex." To be sure, its long-time editor, Byrne Hope Sanders, after returning from wartime secondment as director of the Consumer Branch of the Wartime Prices and Trade Board, sometimes seemed restive. As she observed the masculinist political landscape in 1947, she joined Laura in emphasizing the need for consciousness raising and better political education. In particular, Sanders asked women's groups, most specifically the National Council of Women and its local councils, to reconsider their long-standing bans on explicitly political discussion, obviously hoping for debates such as those that had flourished during the 1930s in the Vancouver Local Council of Women, thanks to CCF delegates. Without such opportunities, the "brightest and best women" would lack essential "support in the way of practical help, and encouragement" in politics.[6] The following year, Sanders recommended *Chatelaine*'s two-thousand-member Consumer Council in an article that included a small picture of Jamieson. As she explained, a survey of its membership revealed that they wouldn't vote for female candidates simply on the basis of their gender, but they would "wholeheartedly support a campaign to encourage more women to go into politics." In fact, 68 percent of participants on the Consumer Council claimed to "prefer women" in public life, and 73 percent agreed with efforts to encourage them: 92 percent felt that female candidates were most suitable for school board, 54 percent for town or city council, 41 percent for provincial legislatures, 35 percent for parliament, and 12 percent for mayoral positions.[7] By singling out Laura, *Chatelaine* also signalled approval of a range of political engagement that included the social democratic left.

The magazine's Consumer Council consisted entirely of women, and its responses to the survey suggested a reservoir of potential backing that political parties might have explored (undoubtedly, its replies would have been far less positive had its membership been male). Such recognition was nevertheless at best modest compensation for the magazine's regular slighting of Laura and female politicians since its inauguration in 1928. Not until Doris McCubbin Anderson became general editor in 1957–58 would *Chatelaine* embrace women's rights more consistently. Even in 1960, Anderson roused considerable controversy when she defended French feminist Simone de Beauvoir and her 1949 exposé *The Second Sex,* long a staple on Laura's recommended reading lists.[8]

Laura's friendship with the veteran Agnes Macphail made her especially sensitive to the special dangers facing feminist trailblazers. In 1949, Macphail used *Maclean's Magazine* to bleakly review the implications of her career in both federal and provincial politics:

> As it is a woman is regarded as a second-rate substitute for a man. The dice is loaded for half the population. The men want to hog everything. They want all the gravy, the gravy boat and the silver ladle ... It's a man's world. Every woman knows that ... Every woman in business, in industry, in public life, has seen men no more able than she getting a higher wage, all the nice promotions, boosted up on the shoulders of their selfish brothers ...
>
> And how the boys stick together! ... Yet women have proved themselves just as capable as men ... to manage the world's affairs; far better suited to serve the people because looking after others is part of their nature ...
>
> If I had known before I entered public life what it meant for a woman to invade a man's world I wouldn't have been able to face it, just as most men wouldn't be able to face war if they knew what it meant, instead of thinking of it as a prolonged binge away from their wives ... A woman in a man's world has to cope at every turn with the danger of wounding the male ego ...
>
> Women have made encouraging progress in the past 20 years, but we still need more women doing more things. We need more women in welfare work, on school boards, on hospital boards and in government. Our House of Commons is now all-male again; I didn't think it would ever go back after my 14 years there.

It was a justifiably bitter assessment of a lifetime devoted to public service.

Macphail did offer a few words of reassurance: "But all men don't like wrestling matches, bull fights and wars. There are civilized men, men with a sense of responsibility, with wisdom and tolerance. There are even some men who think a woman should get a fair break. Not many, but enough to make the struggle seem worth while."[9] Even so, this image hardly stacked up against the contradictory evidence. The fact that Macphail faced near penury after some twenty years of service as an MP and an MLA underscored the overall cost of testing misogynous space.[10]

When Laura looked about her after her electoral defeat in 1945, very few public figures embodied progressive feminist hopes. Ironically, the most visible female interlopers in male politics were often federal Tories, or Progressive Conservatives (PCs) as they were known from 1942 to 2003. The addition of "Progressive" to the party's name signalled its effort to capture the wartime upsurge in support for reform. Although PC candidates were well known to "deny any association with feminist doctrines," they rewarded their adherents with a platform that was committed to "equal pay for equal work and opportunity."[11] In 1957, the former deputy mayor of Hamilton and PC winner of a 1950 by-election, Ellen Louks Fairclough, became Canada's first female federal cabinet minister in the PC government of John G. Diefenbaker. Despite rejecting a feminist label and being generally "male-identified," she took up familiar cudgels in advocating equal pay for equal work.[12] Fairclough might not have shared Laura's political affiliation, but she understood that female politicians faced "criticism on a much broader scale than that meted out to men. They are expected to be well-nigh perfect ... I hope, too, that I won't be the only woman in the House for long." Like the CCFer, she regularly encouraged female candidates to ignore discouragement and to pursue their concerns into active public life.[13]

Charlotte Whitton, a PC activist and previous target of Laura's disdain for her reactionary views on social welfare, entered the post-war spotlight as mayor of Ottawa (1951–60 and 1960–64). After a spirited campaign that engaged clubwomen in ways that resembled Laura's approach during the 1939 and 1941 elections, Whitton challenged the municipal "stag party" and demanded "a new deal. Don't you think it's time you drew a Queen to three Jacks?" She urged women to cease being "sluggards" and to wield the franchise to "claim our freedom."[14] Unlike Jamieson, this ambivalent feminist suggested that women's clubs and the women's auxiliaries of political parties only drained female talent from more important contributions.[15] In the end, Canada's highest-profile Conservative female politicians shared with their BC left-wing counterpart a deep frustration with their party, the electoral system, and a women's community that failed to live up to the promise of suffrage.

Canada's progressive female politicians encountered an additional challenge beyond pervasive misogyny. As was the case for all critics of capitalism, their civil liberties and credibility were ever in doubt and often actively threatened after the Soviet Union moved from Second World War ally to Cold War enemy. The 1945 revelations of espionage by Igor Gouzenko, a clerk in the Soviet Embassy in Ottawa, fired up long-standing prejudice against both the Communist Party and the CCF. Post-war liberal hegemony thrived in a poisonous environment that was largely overseen by the mainstream press. Despite its claims, expressed in its Consumer Council, which was supposedly "balanced as to age, income and locality," to offer an "accurate reflection of the thinking of Canadian women as a whole," "uncolored by prejudice," *Chatelaine* played this game.[16] Even as its coverage of politics remained episodic and generally superficial, progressive views became the target of its frequent red baiting. In 1947, it featured a former Labour voter in Britain who had recanted her 1945 allegiance to the party. She condemned Clement Atlee's Labour government for hard times and recommended Churchill's Conservatives because of their "sound" campaign for "private enterprise."[17] A year later, a former British communist was admired for deserting the left to embrace Roman Catholicism and traditional politics.[18] In 1949, a Cold Warrior *Financial Post* journalist published a *Chatelaine* article titled "Are You a Stooge for a Communist?" In it, he portrayed Canadian communism as infiltrating and corrupting seemingly innocuous campaigns, ranging from peace to civil liberties, racial tolerance, fair prices, day nurseries, and school milk programs, all the while hiding its "Red lights under democracy's bushel." He went so far as to detect rot in an organization that Laura had helped found: "In British Columbia, the Communists admit frankly that they have made inroads in the Parent-Teacher Association." Such infiltration constituted, he thundered, "the greatest danger to democracy in today's national and international crisis."[19]

Amid the poison of the times, the Women's International League for Peace and Freedom (WILPF) was hard hit. Debates over questions such as Canada's role in NATO and the Soviet Union's interventions in Czechoslovakia and Hungary bitterly divided its ranks. During the early 1950s, Laura continued the disengagement from WILPF that had begun during the 1930s. In particular, she was opposed to the appearance of any common front between communists and social democrats such as herself.[20] The Royal Canadian Mounted Police paid little attention to such distinctions. Police officers closely monitored the kind of progressive campaigns – from anti-war to tenants' and workers' rights – that roused Laura and other long-time WILPF members.[21] The daily reality of government surveillance and public attacks, with their echo of the brutal repression of the 1930s, contributed to internecine warfare within the CCF, as members championed various socialist solutions to the attempts of reactionaries to marginalize them. Only women members, however, had to battle misogyny within and without the party.

This double load of prejudice, which kept Laura and others constantly on edge and on guard, was front and centre in the post-war municipal politics of Vancouver. That hotbed further tested her commitment to greater democracy. Both liberal and socialist suffragists had long targeted the reform of cities and towns, gaining their earliest franchises for parks, library, school, and council positions. After 1921, when the majority of Canadians lived in urban areas, and still more after 1951, when towns and cities accommodated 62 percent of the population, they seemed the logical place to start in efforts to engage the electorate. Even as the CCF paid relatively little attention to mobilizing new female voters, key documents in its early history, such as the League for Social Reconstruction's *Social Planning for Canada* (1935), prioritized cities and housing.[22] In 1930s Vancouver, a CCF civic wing had attempted to organize working-class neighbourhoods as a path to provincial success. In 1936, the party ran a full civic slate and elected three of the eight city councillors. In a move that Laura would have applauded, it introduced weekly civic affairs classes to train voters and potential candidates.[23] In March 1937, Helena Gutteridge became the first female councillor on Vancouver City Council and an outspoken critic of urban housing. Together with the Vancouver Housing Association, founded in 1937, she began a long crusade for subsidized low-rental accommodation. She sat on its first executive, and Jamieson soon joined its ranks.[24]

After her forced retirement from the provincial legislature, Laura turned readily to the opportunities in her home city. As always, she reminded sympathizers, "All of us in the CCF ... should remember this: CIVIC GOVERNMENT IS THE BEGINNING OF SOCIALISM. Civic and municipal government is the effort of a group of people in any given area to obtain for themselves by collective effort what they cannot get individually."[25] Nonetheless, women and leftists scrambled to make inroads in municipal bailiwicks dominated by business interests.

Well into the twentieth century, Canada's local governments were far from democratic. Voting was regularly restricted to property owners, living within or outside city boundaries, and corporate and personal property holding could convey multiple franchises. Since women were less likely than men to own property in their own name, many did not appear on voting lists. In contrast, many corporations that owned municipal property had the vote, a privilege once again favouring men. When it came to excluding Asian and Indigenous voters, BC municipal governments differed little from their provincial counterpart; these groups were not enfranchised until the late 1940s and the 1950s. In short, the democratic deficit thrived in cities and towns. Reform was especially difficult in Vancouver, where council had to obtain Victoria's permission to change the city charter, which also determined the franchise. Given that the elected councillors benefitted from the existing voting system, few, unsurprisingly, called for such revisions. Voting restrictions were not the only deterrence to a fair deal. When the CCF began to organize municipally, the province's business and political elites countered with the Non-Partisan Association (NPA) as "their first line of defence against the CCF at the local level." That initiative was shored up by an at-large voting system and deep corporate pockets.[26] "Reds" were the explicit targets, but the NPA also avoided equity when it came to workers, women, and the poor.

However, by the Second World War, the federal Liberal government, pushed by the rising CCF polls, had become more sensitive to urban failings. In 1941, it created the Wartime Housing Limited (1941–49) and in 1946 the Central Mortgage and Housing Corporation. Such fine-sounding initiatives appeared to answer popular demands for greater equality. In fact, they soon provided "massive public subsidies to stimulate and reorganize a private development industry" while leaving municipalities and provinces "ineligible for much of the funding."[27] In post-war Vancouver, this helped to keep the pro-private-development NPA in power and frustrated the hopes of housing activists such as Laura. In 1946, homeless war veterans occupied the Hotel Vancouver, and the Little Mountain Squatters' Association demanded that vacant army huts be used for housing. Both incidents expressed the widespread frustration and anger about the ongoing shortage of affordable accommodation, but they found few champions on city council.[28]

The CCF worked to offset its legislative losses in Victoria by further mobilizing such discontent. In December 1946, Laura stood as one of the four CCF female candidates who ran for BC aldermanic or council positions. After a hard-fought campaign, she topped the Vancouver city-wide CCF list at 19,553 votes. That count left her, however, just short of victorious

NPA office-seekers.[29] The following December, both Grace MacInnis and Jamieson tried for council, whereas Dorothy Steeves sought election to the parks board.[30] In their drive, which no city newspaper saw fit to approve, the CCFers endorsed public ownership of utilities and low-cost housing, the issues they had pursued in Victoria, as solutions to inefficiency, corruption, and poverty. As Laura canvased alongside other CCF hopefuls, NPA contenders self-confidently missed all-candidate meetings.[31]

Rather to her surprise, Laura won a seat at city hall. Grace too did well but ultimately could not close the gap.[32] At the same time, the strong showing of Effie Jones, co-founder of the Housewives' League and mayoral candidate for the communist-linked Civic Reform Association, seemed promising for the left in general. Known as Effie "low fare" Jones due to her stand on public transit, she took 19,218 ballots against NPA candidate Charles "high fare" Jones, who strode to victory with 24,135.[33] Her high numbers suggested that the NPA might be vulnerable.

Responding from her hospital bed, recovering from what she termed a "minor operation," Laura thanked supporters, indicating, "I am looking forward to promoting the program on which I campaigned – low-rental housing, public ownership of light and power, and extension of the franchise."[34] Even as she recuperated, she went into action. During her first month in office, she condemned NPA priorities: "Right now car owners in Vancouver have far more influence on the council than the homeless families hunting for houses." She dismissed her new political colleagues as sharing "a sinister cynicism about civic housing." Laura herself took heart from a warm response from the municipal staff, who seemed "genuinely pleased to see a woman on the council again. They all remember Helena Gutteridge with affection – and the men speak of her with admiration."[35]

A week later, she supported her old favourite, the Vancouver Housing Association, in calling for an application to Victoria to revise the municipal charter so that the city could address its ongoing accommodation crisis.[36] She next initiated a spirited debate on the possibility of "local housing authorities undertaking low-rental schemes."[37] Laura soon told the city's building and town planning committee that "slum areas, recently toured by aldermen, would not benefit from recent provincial-federal discussions on housing because only amendments to speed new building were being considered." The result, she suggested, served only "those who can afford homes" while ignoring the most desperate and deserving. In a pattern that soon became all too familiar, the NPA-dominated Civic Committee resorted to delaying tactics, sending her call for action

Vancouver City Council members, 1947–48. Top row, left to right: Laura Jamieson, John D. Cornett, Roland K. Gervin. Middle row: George C. Miller, Charles E. Thompson. Bottom row: Halford D. Wilson, Alex W. Fisher, Samuel P. Cromie | City of Vancouver Archives, COV-S62-: CVA 296-011

off to Victoria and settling down to business as usual.[38] Laura, however, proposed as her first project a "low–rental housing scheme," modelled on initiatives in Britain, Scandinavia, and New Zealand. She also insisted that city council should lobby Ottawa and the Central Mortgage and Housing Corporation to help house Vancouver citizens.[39] The other council members were determined to avoid such initiatives, a stance that was aided and abetted by the mainstream press, with the *Vancouver News-Herald* typically condemning Laura's championship of so-called charity homes.[40] Community centres, child study initiatives, and co-operative play groups were similarly part of her plans for grassroots revitalization. Very unusually for her time, she recommended early childhood programs for fathers, who would thus learn to share domestic duties and contribute to functioning family democracies.[41]

When the majority of councillors proved unwilling to concede an inch in such battles, the former MLA quickly proved impatient. She found that council meetings were burdened with tedium and minutiae, and she was regularly reported to be at odds with the all-male assembly. The onset of the long terminal illness of the NPA mayor, Charles E. Jones, almost immediately after the election only added to the recurring inertia that dogged council affairs. In the meantime, Laura seized every opportunity to raise consciousness about unmet needs and recalcitrant or absent office-holders. In a strategy that was understandable, if unpersuasive, she regularly lectured her colleagues on the bigger picture that they preferred to sidestep. As convenor of the Social Service Committee, she initiated "a discussion of the proposed amendments to the Deserted Wives' Maintenance Act, so that city council members would know under what provisions (or lack of them) deserted wives now seek justice."[42]

In May 1948, with the hospitalized mayor still out of town and no city manager in charge, the exasperated Jamieson again condemned council's slowdown and resistance to making decisions. She highlighted the understaffing and sidelining of Vancouver's sole planning agency, the Town Planning Commission, which could not play its rightful role as "the vital centre of civic action." Council failings were both large and small. Citing an example of the latter, the irrepressible Laura drew a damning comparison between officialdom's abundant professions of sympathy for the mayor and its brutal indifference to a city street sweeper who had been killed by a "careless motorist." Visiting his widow, Laura inquired about financial and other assistance, only to learn that help consisted solely of a final paycheque and a letter of sympathy from the city engineer. Knowing full well what it meant to lose the family breadwinner, she asked council to ensure that, at the very least, future condolences would come from the mayor, council itself, and the head of the relevant department. She attributed the lack of concern to the fact that municipal employees were "looked upon as necessary evils." She made a similar point in another story for CCF readers: "The day after the firemen had won their wage award I met two of them in a corridor and was congratulating them. They remarked that mine were the first congratulations they had received from a Council member; but a few black looks had come their way."[43] In short, the NPA majority was indifferent or hostile to the welfare of the very people who kept Vancouver functioning.

When it came to serving ordinary citizens, Jamieson proved no happier with the BC Union of Municipalities. Its September 1948 convention resolved to ask the province for an increase in the residential poll or head tax, a decidedly unprogressive measure by which cities could resist raising levies on property.[44] Laura ridiculed the proposal, which was bizarrely defended by its champions as no more than a short-term adjustment to revenue that would eventually be eliminated. The *CCF News* reported more honestly of the cash grab that

> its very name is misleading, since many people who are forced to pay it, do not even receive the right to vote in civic elections. It is levied on men and not on women, which is in itself an indefensible situation. Even the feminists will admit that injustice should be shared as well as privilege ... If the municipalities believe that the poll tax should be abolished, why do they not go to the government and ask for its repeal, instead of indulging in silly prevarications?

Vancouver's acting mayor refused to accept Laura's demand that the poll tax initiative be dropped. The NPA council ultimately agreed to ask Victoria for its abolition but only if "an alternative revenue could be found ... [which had the] effect of nullifying the motion."[45] It then toyed with a possible amendment to the Public School Act, which would enable it to levy an education tax upon "gainfully employed women," among others, without also giving them the right to vote. The fact that the employed wives of property owners would be exempt from the tax, whereas married female tenants would not, simply confirmed class as well as gender prejudices.[46] No wonder that Jamieson condemned it as just "as discriminatory as the poll tax."[47]

Extension of the franchise to all adult property owners and tenants, including the long-excluded Chinese, Japanese, and East Indians, was a core part of the CCF civic program. In dealing with opponents such as the Downtown Business Association, the Vancouver Real Estate Board, the Vancouver Board of Trade, the Association of Property Owners, and the Suburban Business and Property Owners, Laura, in a replay of an old suffragist question, "asked if those who already had the vote should decide whether the vote should be extended."[48] Council meetings became so contentious that the mayor threatened to eject Laura if she continued "to disobey the chair." Her outrage at obvious breaches of democracy was all the greater when NPA alderman and former mayor George Miller endeavoured to kill the extension of voting rights by sending the motion away for further study, a delay that she labelled "the most disgraceful thing I've ever heard of."[49] Rallying her troops beyond the council, Laura cited both suffragists and the English Chartists to argue that disenfranchisement undermined social peace and well-being.[50]

Vancouver finally eliminated the racial ban, but 47 percent of adult residents still lacked the municipal franchise in 1949.[51] Nor did other forms of discrimination disappear. Vancouver alderman Halford D. Wilson, Laura's Conservative opponent in the 1939 Vancouver Centre by-election, maintained his racist ways. In a return to familiar anti-Asian proclivities, he singled out a "Chinese Club recently granted a licence" as the possible subject of a police inquiry in 1949. Jamieson suggested that if there were justifiable concerns, "all licenced social clubs" should be investigated. After much discussion, the beleaguered council voted that it had no power to request any such report.[52] When it came to directly tackling the prejudice of Wilson's proposition, Laura stood largely alone.

She was equally direct in attacking the civic corporate franchise as no more than "a hangover from the time when only persons who owned property could vote in any election." In sum, "the whole procedure is distinctively undemocratic." When the NPA defended the Hudson's Bay Company, the Canadian Pacific Railway, and other businesses resident in the city, Laura insisted that

> the corporations comprise a group easily manipulated in voting by certain interests. Every year letters go out to them from the Non-Partisan Association, urging them to vote and "keep politics out of City Hall" ... A few years ago only a small number of corporations took the trouble to register. Today 496 corporations are registered as owners and 1384 as tenants – 1880 in all.[53]

However, her isolation on council meant that her motion found no seconder, and the battle was lost once again. The struggle nevertheless continued until 1973, when the corporate vote was eliminated by the provincial New Democratic Party government. It was reinstated in 1976, when the Social Credit Party, with its close ties to the NPA, returned to power. Only that administration's defeat and the return of a social democratic government in 1993 secured the final abolition of Vancouver's corporate vote.

The franchise was not Jamieson's only business target. Just as in the legislature, she condemned the monopoly of private power and transport utilities. She urged council to take over the BC Electric Railway as a community resource whose profits and planning should not safely be trusted to private hands. Male NPA councillors resisted fiercely, censuring her proposal as "a bad move" that threatened the financial market for city bonds.[54] Just before the 1949 election, she called for a plebiscite to consider the future of all utilities, but again no colleague would second her motion. In an attempt to circumvent that obstacle, she took the proposal to the city's utilities and airport committee, where she did not require a seconder, but discussion again failed to generate sufficient support.[55]

In the same spirit, the undeterred Laura campaigned to force property developers to pay for the benefits conferred to them by civic rezoning.[56] And when the 1947 report of the Commission on Provincial-Municipal Relations in British Columbia recommended that a city business tax be instigated, she approved of it. Council grudgingly offered the usual delaying tactic of further study, and her proposal ultimately went nowhere lest it upset "big business" and its support for the NPA.[57] Laura's battle against corporate power included proposing a tax on property transactions, which, after all, had increased in value due to civic improvements. She also denounced city council's failure to tender contracts publicly.[58] These efforts too went nowhere.

Even as she assailed corporate giveaways, Laura called for attention and sympathy to be focused on inadequate services to poorer residents. This spurred her criticism when council accepted fare and rate increases by BC Electric and BC Telephone.[59] In one of her last efforts as a city councillor to augment democracy, Laura opposed the exclusion of the press from meetings of the Vancouver Airport Board.[60] Once again, she failed. Frustrated, she could only charge council with relying on both the ignorance and "the continuing apathy of citizens."[61]

In opposing special interests and demanding a better deal for ordinary citizens, Jamieson stressed the proper contribution of highly trained staff. She retained her old League for Social Reconstruction faith that experts could counter traditional government cronyism, which often favoured the well connected and the frequently incompetent. During an early Social Service Committee meeting, in which the Women's New Era League argued for more female restaurant inspectors, Laura proposed that notice of job vacancies be sent to UBC so as to "find the best people."[62] When she concluded that council devoted too much time and attention to the politics of property assessment and too little to the needs of juvenile courts, she urged that the courts be turned over to knowledgeable practitioners and that time and resources be concentrated on the welfare of needy youngsters.[63] The same emphasis infused her attempts, in concert with the local United Nations Association, to which she belonged, to establish a civil defence organization for Vancouver to study the impact of nuclear warfare. Council grumpily agreed to yet another study but rejected Laura's accompanying request for a library of books on municipal government to help guide the councillors themselves and citizens in general.[64] They wanted no advice from suspect experts.

Jamieson's efforts at modernization and accountability similarly met a stonewall, when a majority of council members substituted a far less rigorous examination for her proposed "objective survey" of "the civic administration," last performed in the mid-1920s. She rightly feared that the resulting in-house report would keep failings under wraps and thus invisible to public scrutiny.[65] Her preference was to employ the existing Town Planning Commission to make an up-to-date assessment of civic services. The NPA-dominated council ensured instead that the commission was hived off on remote premises and handicapped by minimum staffing.[66]

Observing that all but one of her civic colleagues belonged to the business class, Laura identified them as the real source of council's failure to embrace modern planning and democratic principles.[67] Since most had "never read anything fundamental about their work," they were ill-equipped to address contemporary problems, such as "factories being crowded together in a huge city with the people living great distances from their work."[68] Her frank conclusions found little hearing. In typical fashion, partisan city journalists lined up with the civic old guard. They were saluted as "public spirited men" whom "no fair-minded person can accuse ... of having subordinated the public interest to their private concerns." In the midst of the firestorm created by Laura's charges, the *Vancouver News-Herald* admitted that the city "has paid and is paying a heavy price for lack of planning in the earlier stages of its development, and it will pay a heavy future price for the inadequacies of present planning." It agreed that "there is some point to Mrs. Jamieson's plea for more fundamental reading and thinking, not only on the subject of civic planning but on the whole subject of economic policy." However, it suggested that no one could be held responsible for present problems, because "the transformation in civic development brought about by motor transportation could hardly have been foreseen two generations ago even by the most far-seeing civic planners." The newspaper then attacked the CCF, and thus Jamieson, for "costly but abortive palliatives in socialist programs of public policy," initiatives presumably held at bay by business-dominated city leaders.[69]

While noisy council meetings saw Laura facing "a swarm of hornets about her ears," proud CCFers comforted themselves that "Mrs Jamieson is used to hornets ... She will not be unduly disturbed."[70] In campaigning for a second term, she was not shy in reiterating the shortcomings of "so-called Non-partisans at every opportunity," notably their partisanship and non-attendance at council meetings.[71] It was to no avail. In December 1949, she was toppled. Dorothy Steeves, running again for civic office, similarly failed to make the cut. The sole successful female candidate was NPA businesswoman Anna Sprott, who remained in office until 1959, becoming the first woman to serve as acting mayor. Democracy in Vancouver would have to await another generation of reformers.

In reviewing Laura's defeat, the *CCF News* editorialist was bitter:

> The tragic part is that those for whom Laura Jamieson has worked so hard in the last two years stayed away from the polls in their thousands, too lazy and indifferent to cast the ballots ... It is only by the exercise of the greatest measure of Christian charity that we can suppress a caustic smile of anticipation as we consider these good people turning to the "outstanding business woman" who has replaced Mrs. Jamieson on the council, for the sympathy and help they will need and which they always received from Laura.[72]

Laura herself tried to make the most of a bad hand. Whatever the cause – apathy or the restricted franchise – the CCF hadn't taken "any worse defeat than we have had before. It does mean that we fight an up-hill battle, as we have always fought. If it is more uphill than usual for a time that should not surprise or dismay us." To rally the downhearted, she pointed to Burnaby, where progressive persistence had paid off with the election of a CCF reeve and two councillors. She also confessed to enjoying "the comradeship" and the "good fun" of the battle for "the broadened civic franchise, public ownership of public utilities, and housing for low-income groups." Supporters needed to accept "that the only worth while way of life is to fight for convictions; and, by struggle, to gain both individual strength and social progress." The CCF should "begin by telling them [voters] that only live fish swim against the stream."[73]

In the meantime, Laura showed no sign of surrender. In January 1950, just weeks after her defeat, she visited an eighty-five-year-old pensioner who had recently been discharged from hospital. Neighbours found him hungry and chilled to the bone in an unheated residence, huddled in inadequate bedclothes. Only Laura proved determined enough to secure a nurse, food, and relief from social services.[74] She likewise remained an advocate for loggers and fishermen, the same vulnerable group who had attracted her sympathies in the 1930s. Their needs for access to city resources, "where they can find good, wholesome entertainment instead of being forced to go to phony dives where they are fleeced and then thrown out," supplied the litmus test of a good city.[75] In the same spirit, Laura backed the December 1950 "Open Sundays" plebiscite on opening taverns and clubs as well as "commercial sports, cultural events and theater performances between the hours of 2 pm and midnight on Sunday."[76] Ordinary people deserved diverse opportunities to relax.[77]

In such continuing advocacy, Laura always returned to the benefits of a reformed franchise. Just a few months after the 1949 election, she spoke to the Civil Liberties Union on its importance.[78] In March, she again informed readers of the *CCF News* about the injustice of the corporate vote.[79] Despite the repeated setbacks for democracy, she told Vancouverites not to "be discouraged by antiquated rules" but to seize the future. The veteran suffragist kept her own hopes high because "our CCF women have carried the resolutions on extension of the civic franchise into the most important women's groups in the city. These groups have learned that women are discriminated against severely in this field and they are preparing to take appropriate action." Such campaigns for greater democracy won the support of the Vancouver Trades and Labour Council.[80] A female journalist for the *Vancouver Sun*, occasionally a progressive newspaper, applauded Laura's persistence, observing that BC cities and towns "are behind the times" and remarking that the limited adult franchise was not real democracy.[81]

Such sustained advocacy helped place Jamieson at the top of the CCF slate in the 1950 civic election, but it proved insufficient to return her to council. However, a municipal plebiscite that granted the vote to wives of property owners did pass during the contest, albeit with a bare majority. By the time of the next election, these newly enfranchised women had not been added to the voters list.[82] Once again, Laura's name was on the ballot, her credentials further strengthened as a board member of the Canadian Federation of Business and Professional Women, convenor of the Laws Committee of the Vancouver Local Council of Women, and a member of the program committee of the Women's School for Citizenship. And once again, she reminded the electorate that "civic government is a bit of socialism, now being run by 'free enterprisers,' who do not believe in what they are doing." In reply, the NPA "cast doubt on the efficiency and economy of all publicly owned light, power and transportation across Canada." Laura failed to convince enough voters and went down to defeat. Ultimately, neither she nor the left in general could break the business hold on Vancouver politics.[83] After the 1951 election, she never again tested Vancouver voters.

Despite defeat, Laura remained publicly buoyant about Vancouver's prospects for better government. Just before its 1952 municipal election, she cheerfully reported the addition of spouses to the voters list and the promise of close scrutiny by the Women Electors' Association. Though admitting that "canvassers will all tell you that women in general are quite unawakened politically," she presented that failure as a call to action: CCF women needed to organize "a persistent campaign to educate women in democracy and its institution. It's bound to bear fruit."[84] Even when her city hall days were well in the past, her volleys against bad governance continued. In 1953, she defended housing subsidies for the poor against the attack of the president of the Canadian Real Estate Board. Jamieson highlighted the benefits of the Little Mountain public housing community, a first in British Columbia. She noted that

> on the basis of dollars and cents the city gains in every way. It cannot lose. The housing will be built of the best materials, as it will be amortised over a long period of time. It will enable many slum dwellers to get decent housing, and, above all, it will allow families with several children to bring them up in clean surrounds.[85]

She would have been pleased to hear a former young resident of the Little Mountain project later confirm that it was "affordable, decent housing for regular people." It had been won after "a hard fought battle ... against formidable opponents in the real estate industry ... and ... sometimes reluctant partners at the federal and provincial levels and escalating construction costs due to the Korean War."[86]

Ottawa's reluctant support for housing the elderly poor inspired the veteran campaigner to pursue other initiatives.[87] Laura succeeded CCF colleague Ernie Winch as a long-time president of the New Vista Society. This non-profit organization was originally set up to address the housing needs of female patients who were discharged from the Provincial Mental Hospital. After the war, assisted by a property grant from the CCF-governed municipality of Burnaby, it shifted its mandate to the housing of vulnerable senior citizens.[88] Of special interest to Laura was New Vista's role in becoming "the first project of its kind to offer accommodation for the single old person."[89] Her earlier experience with co-operative housing was put to good use when she set in motion such New Vista initiatives as the Tenant Recreation Association.[90]

In 1957, well versed as she was in the bleak realities facing the city's poor, Laura returned, now aged seventy-five, to endorsing professional planning as a way to stop the BC Lower Mainland from "becoming a more or less permanent slum town," unable to offer decent housing to many residents. As always, she dismissed the possibility that private enterprise might provide meaningful help. After all, capitalism had helped create "the mess we have allowed to form in downtown areas." A much better solution was "heavier taxes" that could generate new opportunities to make areas such as Strathcona "attractive for both light industry and homes, so that workers can find pleasant places to live close to their work, and in addition be near down-town (and have a fine view)."[91] The fact that she lived in East Vancouver gave her a special appreciation of what was needed to create a livable urban environment. However, Laura never restricted her post-war hopes solely to mobilizing better government in British Columbia's biggest city. As the next chapter demonstrates, she always kept an eye on her province and beyond.

9
Faithful Social Democrat, 1945–64

Even as she laboured on city matters, Laura Jamieson played an active role in CCF politics more generally. The Cold War years proved a major disappointment for progressive Canadians of all persuasions as they faced the resurgence of the political right. In British Columbia, the 1950s saw Social Credit, not the CCF, benefit from popular skepticism about the old alliance between big business and the Conservative and Liberal Parties. In the CCF, frustration and rage at its limited success spurred internecine battles between moderates, or democratic socialists, and hard-liners, or radical socialists. Laura stood on the front lines of contests, both against other parties on the right and against the far left in the CCF. And as always, she set her standard for gender fairness everywhere.

The June 1949 provincial election gave the Liberal-Conservative Coalition government 61.35 percent of the popular vote and thirty-nine seats, whereas the CCF won 35.10 percent and seven seats. Both parties ran full slates, but the coalition nominated only two women, incumbents Tilly Rolston and Nancy Hodges, and the CCF only four, one in Vancouver-Point Grey and three in Greater Victoria. The new Social Credit League and the Social Credit Party fielded three and one, respectively. Jamieson, Dorothy Steeves, and Grace MacInnis did not run, and their replacements had much lower public profiles. This dismal showing returned only Rolston and Hodges. To be sure, feminism did not completely disappear. A former *Victoria Times* journalist with close links to the Canadian Federation of Business and Professional Women and the National Federation of Liberal Women of Canada, Hodges was a lonely beacon for equal pay and married women's property rights. In 1950, she would become the Commonwealth's first woman speaker, the position refused by Mary Ellen Smith almost three decades earlier. A Fraser Valley columnist sympathetically summed up Hodges as "at her best when five women were in the House." The Victoria MLA herself expressed disappointment with the absence of Steeves in particular, whom she described as a good friend. Hodges called for more "women in public life. Their political stripe doesn't matter."[1]

The federal election, which was also held in June 1949, proved just as unsatisfactory. Liberal prime minister Louis St. Laurent romped to 191 seats. The Conservatives gained 41, and the CCF fell from 28 to 13, tying in British Columbia with the former at 3 seats. Nationally, Social Credit dropped from 13 to 10. Across the country, there were only eleven female candidates, none of whom was elected: five CCFers, three Progressive Conservatives, two from the Union of Electors (a spin-off of Social Credit), and one Liberal.[2] Notably, there was no communist, despite Dorise Nielsen's plea for "promotion of women comrades to leading positions in the party."[3] The sole serving female MP, Saskatchewan CCFer Gladys Strum, went down to defeat, and no woman replaced her.[4] The losses of Labour governments in Australia and New Zealand, like drops in BC CCF membership in these years, furthered malaise on the left.[5]

British Columbia's CCFers mobilized two principled but opposing responses to electoral disappointment. Many of their differences were long-standing, rooted in the mosaic of forces that had existed at the party's founding and in subsequent policy debates, notably over participation in the Second World War and, later, the United Nations, relations with Canadian communists, and receptivity to reforms in capitalism as necessary stages on the path to socialism. On the far left stood those who could be dubbed radical, hard-line, or Marxist socialists, often associated with origins in the Socialist Party of Canada. Under leaders such as Dorothy Steeves and Harold Winch, they demanded loyalty to Marxism and resistance to concessions to capitalism, liberal reformism, and collective security. Mustered against them were the variously named gradualists, moderates, democratic socialists, or social democrats (the last two terms were used pretty much interchangeably), such as Jamieson and Grace MacInnis in British Columbia and federal party leaders M.J. Coldwell, Tommy Douglas, and David Lewis. They tied their banner to the promise of universal enfranchisement, parliamentary democracy, the United Nations, and incremental change.

The often acrimonious battles between these two poles never occurred in isolation: the Cold War sharpened all tempers. On the one hand, the entire spectrum of progressive politics was subject to red baiting and surveillance by the RCMP.[6] On the other, the CCF regularly became the take-over target of communists, hopeful of leap frogging to electoral or popular competitiveness. Internal differences in British Columbia were accentuated by the efforts of Canadian Trotskyists (the Revolutionary Workers' Party) to take revolutionary socialism into the CCF.[7] Opponents within the party thus struggled in a highly charged ring of action.

Jamieson joined the fray as a social democrat who was confident of long-term success in a democracy. She understood this position as both principled and pragmatic, but her CCF opponents and some later scholars frequently saw only a slippery slope to the endorsement of liberal reformism.[8] This was the position of Nanaimo activist Mildred MacLeod in a series of exchanges that appeared in the *CCF News* during the early 1950s. As MacLeod explained,

> a socialist of the old school who hangs on to his theories, is considered by some to be a fuddy-duddy. While I realize that one must be a little flexible in one's outlook ... and that changing conditions must be met with new approaches, I still strongly believe that there must be a set of socialist principles which are sacrosanct, which will allow of no whittling away. Otherwise socialism, which set out to change society into a new order, will find that it has itself been changed into a vague and nebulous cult for reforming capitalism.[9]

The biographer of Eve Smith, one of the most charismatic of Laura's adversaries, summed up CCF radicals' opinion of party moderates: "The 'social democrats,' always in control of the CCF's party machinery, cared little for political education, cared even less for socialist terminology and rhetoric, and earnestly set to work signing up members and campaigning to win seats in provincial legislatures and the federal parliament."[10] That conclusion treated Laura and other gradualists as little more than "liberals in a hurry."[11]

Ultimately, however, Jamieson does not fit that picture. She remained committed to socialist education, albeit one that she situated firmly in co-operative principles rather than solely in Marxist doctrine. From her perspective, the proletariat was not the sole source of progressive self-consciousness; that possibility existed for women and indeed for all groups whose awareness of oppression could be raised by education. Laura nevertheless regularly used the terminology of class to locate special interests and understood that class prejudice, like that of gender and race, was very difficult to dislodge. Only extended programs of popular education and practical engagement in co-operative enterprises could broaden minds and ensure a non-capitalist future. There was far more to be done than signing up recruits and winning elections. In sum, Laura remained a CCF socialist but not of the type preferred by other left-wing critics of capitalism.

In 1950, immediately after the onset of the Korean War, the CCF held its national convention in Vancouver. Splits within the provincial party were on full display. When social democrats like Jamieson ultimately controlled the convention, the left wing formed the Socialist Caucus (soon the Socialist Fellowship). Dorothy Steeves typified this faction in refusing to tailor policy to electoral prospects.[12] Her opponent David Lewis, the powerful national secretary, attributed her hard-line stance to "isolation from the studies and research and discussion which go on at this end."[13] To be fairer, the company in which the Dutch-born activist was studying differed from that preferred by the pragmatic Rhodes scholar. Unlike Lewis, with his attachment to the British Labour Party, or the Ontario-born Jamieson, with her key links to Prairie co-operators and suffrage feminists, Steeves grafted a European radical sensibility onto the left-wing faction in the CCF.

Though it is impossible to know the gender breakdown, many party members, perhaps especially those from suffragist or feminist backgrounds such as Jamieson, ultimately found little appeal in "an aristocracy of old Socialists," with their penchant for Marxist theory, not to mention frequent disrespect for women.[14] This seemed the case for a CCF activist who wrote to Grace MacInnis, a leading moderate, in 1946:

> Since I joined the Movement four years ago I have worked very actively from the first month, tried to keep up with current CCF literature & thought, also with current events and then tried to study Socialism and make up for not having been born in a Socialist background ... Yet I can't help thinking that I am a good Socialist & CCFER. We cannot raise a whole race of Socialists in time to do something now. We must convert & use people that are in the world now.[15]

Jamieson adopted much the same line, suggesting that the BC party needed to "take a more constructive action" rather than fuss about ideological purity.[16] In the real world, socialists, like suffragists before them, should seize every opportunity to make inroads against capitalism. Even small improvements could enhance individual lives and enlarge the electoral base of socialism. This faith informed Jamieson's willingness to support the revision of the Regina Manifesto and then the 1956 Winnipeg Declaration of Principles, which forsook anti-capitalist language and accepted a mixed economy.[17]

CCFers like Laura sustained their own brand of radical politics, sometimes characterized as militant mothering,[18] which drew on women's experience of the party and life in general. As in the past, women were likely to have fewer opportunities than men to read and debate socialism's historic texts. In any case, most were directed to a male working class and rarely drew on female experience and exploitation to make sense of how to develop consensus and confront patriarchy. Although there were occasional departures from male suzerainty, as in 1948 when the BC CCF elected Steeves as its first female president, the frequent lack of equal opportunity gave feminists a reason to generate their own standard for socialist relevance, especially in the CCF Women's Council, which was dominated by democratic socialists. As the secretary of the BC council explained in 1949,

> In spite of our profession of progressive thinking, too many men and women are still conditioned to the belief that women's place is in the home. If this is not the case, why is it that when a choice has to be made as to who shall attend a club meeting and who shall put junior to bed, Dad goes to the club and mom stays home?[19]

Another feminist likewise chastised the BC left for its "male domination." Too many male activists took babysitting for granted: "They are out night after night at meetings, while wifey sits home with the bairns. No wonder some of them turn violently anti-labor! (I mean the wives – but sometimes the bairns do too.)" She urged the "CCF, trade unions and other working-class organizations" to "adopt the policy of urging the men to take a different attitude."[20]

Not all blame was assigned to the male side of the ledger. The suffrage campaigns still resonated in many memories, and disappointment was clear. One CCFer exhorted her sisters:

> Many women feel that they have no time for politics. Perhaps they haven't, but in that case they should make time. To keep up with current events is essential. Otherwise one cannot vote intelligently ... The women who worked to get the vote for us didn't do that because they had nothing else to do. They did it because they felt that to be the most important thing that they had to do.

> No woman can possibly do all the work that appears to be ahead of her ... The hand that rocks the cradle may be the hand that rules the world but if so we have been making a very poor job of it by just staying home, rocking. If we are going to train our children to be good citizens we must be good citizens ourselves ... Have we forgotten the camps in the thirties with the crowning indignity at Regina when the police used guns and clubs to prevent the boys continuing to Ottawa?[21]

Female reticence or resistance made Laura continue to insist on special efforts at mobilization. However, even among the moderates this strategy did not find universal support, with the powerful Grace MacInnis, like the radical Steeves, expressing skepticism.

Indeed, feminist efforts were regularly poorly received. When women became too visible in the pages of the *CCF News,* one disgruntled male reader voiced a commonplace complaint: from his perspective, "the wage-slaves and earners – the backbone of the nation" – were badly served by the party and its press. Men, he thundered were "pushed out to the garage, or crouched in the doghouse from winter's wild blast." The editor retorted by suggesting that if he himself were to "write a suitable article we will be pleased to publish it. That might help to restore the 'balance.' Women, it seems, are, on sheer ability and industry, outshining the men."[22] Male hostility among the CCF rank-and-file and leadership was part and parcel of continuing "systemic barriers to women's participation," unless they worked to get out the vote or manage the office and raise funds.[23]

Supposedly progressive governments were not exempt from this pattern. In Saskatchewan, the CCF restricted married women's employment in the civil service: they could be removed in "emergencies" unless they had "special need, circumstances or particular skills." Nor did its otherwise pioneering 1947 Bill of Rights include sexual discrimination.[24] At the federal level, the CCF National Women's Committee floundered, a victim of lack of commitment and funding.[25] In British Columbia, factional fights swept women's rights all the more to the sidelines.[26]

Democratic socialist control of the provincial party could not be taken for granted. In 1948, Steeves was elected provincial president, and another leftist, Rodney Young, became the MP for Vancouver Centre (1948–49), Laura's old bailiwick. Although Laura was elected first vice-president of the BC CCF, defeating the hard-line candidate at the 1950 provincial convention, Steeves defeated her for a National Council seat.[27] However, Jamieson and her allies had the decided advantage of the active support of most of the federal executive. Parliamentary democracy, not factional or class war, was sacrosanct to leaders such as Tommy Douglas, M.J. Coldwell, and David Lewis. Laura agreed in insisting that "the slow transformation of capitalism is only compatible with the consent of the electorate."[28] At the 1950 national convention, she endorsed dropping much anti-capitalist language from the 1933 Regina Manifesto.[29] She also demanded a hard line, wishing to "name specific people and have them expelled" if they refused such revision.[30] Ejection was the cost of saving the CCF from political irrelevance.

Jamieson's post-war politics as a democratic socialist sometimes meant travelling considerable distance from her roots in the Women's International League for Peace and Freedom (WILPF). She accepted Canadian military involvement in the Korean conflict (1950–57) and membership in NATO as part of a commitment to the United Nations and collective security. Such acceptance, in agreement with similar shifts in the Socialist International (formed in 1951), frequently positioned the CCF against WILPF and the Vancouver Peace Council, with their demands for a stronger "Ban the Bomb" position.[31] Jamieson cited Lucy Woodsworth in opposing socialists who chose pacifism above collective security. She asked CCFers to contemplate the outcome if Britain had declined to resist Hitler on the grounds that the war would be a capitalist conflict. The result "would be the miserable country depicted in Noel Coward's 1946 [play], 'Peace in Our Time,'" which portrayed the United Kingdom under German occupation. At the same time, Stalin's purges and treatment of nations in the Soviet sphere undermined confidence in communism. Ultimately, she held that pacifism offered only an inadequate response to totalitarianism on the right or the left. Her conclusion that communist members had too much influence provided another reason for her departure from WILPF in these years.[32]

As she surveyed the world, Laura stood with Frank Underhill, League for Social Reconstruction member, historian, and future Liberal, who wrote for the *Canadian Forum.* She explained,

> at this stage in the world crisis we cannot escape power politics if we are to keep our liberty to work for socialism. Russia has a right to her own ideology, but not to expand and swallow up other countries and suppress freedom until we too are in danger. We must have a world balance that will insure freedom of thought and action for those who want such freedom. The U.N. must bring about that balance of power, and we must help it.
>
> Mr. Underhill goes on to face the most unpleasant truth of all for many socialists. We must not only take part in power politics, but we must

> work with the United States in doing so. To many socialists this seems the crowning indignity. We are so close to the U.S. that we see all her glaring faults ... Actually the Western world has gone a long step forward when it says that we must help backward nations to acquire and keep a decent standard of living, if we wish to live in a safe world ... Those who say "We don't like Russia, but we don't trust the U.S." and refuse to take part in the struggle are retreating from reality and letting liberty go by the board. Where and when do they hope to retrieve it? Or do they care?
>
> Do we really want a democratic socialist world? If we do, we first have to make sure that we have a world now in which free propaganda for democratic socialism can be carried on until the threat of Soviet totalitarianism has been removed by some balance of power in the world. Freedom is the fundamental issue of our time.[33]

Her stress on relative freedom under capitalism merely confirmed her opponents' suspicions of liberal reformism. What critics left unmentioned or probably never noticed was that freedom had a special meaning for some suffragists and New Women. Male privilege required a courageous assertion of female independence and autonomy. Like grassroots co-operation, liberty for women involved a radical change to ways of doing business in every aspect of life. Laura would not readily surrender that deeper politics even as she admitted capitalism's power over both sexes.

Jamieson set her standard for the social democratic wing of the party in a series of *CCF News* articles. The Second World War informed her controversial argument that "most of the democratic procedures and individual freedom which we have came to us through capitalism." In particular, she credited "the liberal tradition" and "the improved standard of living provided by the machine age" as allowing "men and women to drag from an unwilling capitalist regime" both "democratic government and civil liberty." Subsequent "democratic socialist governments" had accelerated that process. She chided her opponents on the farther left as hating capitalism so much that they ignored its full legacy, notably "the tradition of freedom, which has enabled us to gain so much in the past, and will continue to gain if we work along with that tradition instead of against it." Democracy had to be preserved en route to socialism. This slow, painful, and unglamorous method required "adding brick by brick to an edifice, part of which is old and part new, an edifice in which we must go on living while the rebuilding proceeds."[34] She claimed to be undeterred by the defeat of New Zealand's Labour government: a period in opposition could be fruitful. The alternative was a one-party regime, which she rejected, and she accused those on the left, such as Colin Cameron (MLA 1937–53), as effectively sanctioning a "police state."[35]

As always, Laura's arguments took as their leitmotif the practical test of theory. The experience of the Soviet Union under Stalin showed that hard-liners had failed the test. In Canada, the CCF needed to root its ideas and practices in democratic laboratories. In particular,

> every CCF member should belong to a trade union or co-operative, or a farmers' organization, or some group where concrete action is discussed and acted upon. This discipline of concrete action in a group other than the purely political, helps to clarify our political thinking, and tends to more constructive conclusions.
>
> We former elected representatives, who have been defeated, have lost our special workshop. We should make haste to find a substitute so that we will not turn into defeatist, destructive influences in our movement. It needs now, especially, fresh and constructive thinking.[36]

And once again, she warned against slavish dependence upon other nations for appropriate policies, whether the Soviet Union or the United Kingdom. Canada should create its own progressive politics:

> Actually in Canada we are still in the process of forming our parliamentary democracy. We shall not have even the form of it until all the citizens in every municipality have the local vote. Let us work a little harder to get full parliamentary democracy, before we dismiss it as unsuitable for any particular task. Let's have a sense of history.[37]

The association of "democratic" with "socialism" was vital. Without it, the public could not readily distinguish the CCF from Soviet communism or Hitler's national socialism. Unlike totalitarian regimes, democratic socialism united a global community that was committed to "democratic methods in seeking constitutional power to set up a regime where the means of production are owned and operated by the people."[38] One model on the world stage was the pragmatic socialism that Jamieson identified with India's Jawaharlal Nehru, "for whom human life and human welfare are socialist principles, and wherever and with whom he can best serve those principles, there he will go."[39]

Such conclusions left many concerns unaddressed. As Mildred MacLeod, Laura's Nanaimo critic, observed, gradualism might be preferable, but "trying to change the system by reform is like riding two horses going in opposite directions ... Is that all these leaders in our movement ask of a labor party, that it administer capitalism more efficiently?" Like Steeves, MacLeod favoured alternative principles: "Let us not worry too much about getting the votes. We were defeated last election on a platform of mild reform ... We should honestly advocate our socialist policies; capitalism is disintegrating rapidly, and the time will come when people will welcome a real change."[40] A Yellowknife CCFer was equally "taken aback" by Laura's approval of what he termed "Underhillian liberalism." Why, he fairly asked, "stress the value of free speech, when freedom of action is so sharply curtailed?" He rejected Laura's defence of labour governments in New Zealand and Australia, urging members, "Let us remember that while liberal-socialists talk, compromise, plan, capitulate, monopoly capitalism goes on its merry way; children are born, live and die in slums and a new generation is prepared for another war."[41] Laura replied by asking how change was to occur if socialists did not employ "the democratic procedures and civil liberties that we now have as tools."[42] The Socialist Fellowship provided no answer, offering only dangerous "fanaticism."[43]

These disagreements among BC CCFers emerged clearly in what was termed the Rod Young affair. Young was a prominent leader of the CCF left wing and an opponent of NATO.[44] He forthrightly rejected Jamieson's claim that

> capitalism has been accompanied by the tradition of freedom. I do see that each one of the privileges we now enjoy under capitalism has been sprung from the reluctant politicians of the exploiting class by the personal sacrifices, yes, and blood of a tiny group of advanced thinkers and valiant fighters in each generation who sprang from or descended into the ranks of workers ... Yes, Laura, we do have an abiding hatred of capitalism, for into the soul of each of us the hot iron of personal injustice has been seared. But we're not glowering and growling, we're working and singing ...
>
> Yes, Laura, we do want to put the Boss into overalls and we do think the best is none too good for the workingman, and our favorite part of the Regina Manifesto is still the last paragraph, "No CCF Government will rest content until it has eradicated capitalism."[45]

Another CCFer, Alex B. Macdonald, a future New Democratic Party MLA and cabinet minister, came immediately to Laura's defence, dismissing Young as one of those "people in the CCF, especially between elections," who "beat their breasts and roll their eyes, and proclaim themselves better socialists than anyone else." They were, he insisted, far less conspicuous where it counted: "by signing up members, raising funds, and spreading the hope and promise of socialism among fellow citizens." He firmly told Young that "the CCF is not the Socialist Labor party, which is tied to a doctrinaire approach and an insignificant role in public affairs. Let's get on with the job of making our fellow citizens think, act and feel democratic."[46] From the perspective of Grace MacInnis, "the Steeves-Young axis" fed the BC party's isolation in the national CCF. Like Laura, with her strong ties to the Prairies, Grace opposed efforts that she interpreted as dividing British Columbia and Canada.[47]

The case for democratic socialism finally won the day. By May 1951, the Socialist Fellowship had been forced to disband, although some members, including Steeves, retained their CCF membership to pursue arguments within the party. A few years later, Rod Young was expelled from the CCF. Laura and others who "genuinely believed that a change in policy was needed to lift the CCF out of its electoral doldrums" had faced down their radical socialist opponents.[48] Though persisting frustration on both sides did not bode well for effectiveness in mobilizing the provincial electorate in the 1950s, the democratic socialist victory prepared the way for the New Democratic Party in 1961.

For a brief time, post-war CCF divisions were matched on the real right in provincial politics. The Liberal-Conservative Coalition in Victoria gradually came unstuck. In June 1952, a provincial election raised the prospect of a three-way race in which the CCF might do very well. To offset this possibility, the coalition amended the BC Elections Act to replace the first-past-the-post system with alternative voting. On election day, instead of selecting a single name on the ballot, voters ranked all the candidates according to their preference (first, second, third, and so forth). Any candidate who won a clear majority would be elected. However, if there was no clear majority in a riding, the contender with the fewest votes would be dropped, and the second choices would be distributed until a winner emerged. The Liberal Party assumed that Conservative voters would pick a Liberal candidate as their second choice, and the Conservatives expected that Liberal voters would opt for a Conservative. Thus, one or other of the coalition parties would triumph. Such calculations, however, went awry when the BC Social Credit League entered the hustings. The CCF unexpectedly found itself with a provincial rival for dissident voters who rejected both Liberals and Conservatives. When forced to choose, however, CCFers and Social Creditors might well be each other's second choices.[49]

Laura had been cultivating grassroots support in the CCF Women's Council and in constituencies around the province since her 1945 defeat.[50]

In particular, she championed co-operatives as marshalling grounds for a practical leftist politics. She regularly chastised the CCF for indifference, insisting that co-ops

> are much nearer socialism than any government ownership under capitalism. Yet we allow our opponents to confuse socialism with present-day government ownership, and get away with it.
>
> Of course "pure" socialists [by which she meant her opponents in the CCF] do not want any practice in administration, since any practice must be under capitalism. But all socialists who are working to bring in the new social order realize that a transition is an inevitable period when we must for a short time administer capitalism in such a way as to make the transfer to socialism with the least confusion ... Collective thinking and theory should be sufficient to make every socialist wish to put his or her collectivism into every day practice in ordinary life. The first avenue for such action is to buy the family groceries at a co-op store. In the resulting expansion the Vancouver Co-op should be the training ground for future business and administrators under a CCF government.[51]

She organized similar arguments to inspire CCFers who attended the party's summer assemblies: in these settings they would become "better Socialists [and would] learn the answers to confound their political enemies."[52] Like Steeves and MacInnis, she readily used new media, employing local radio to promote the CCF message on housing, health, employment, and good government.[53] She held party meetings at her home in Kitsilano, where CCF member and WILPF activist Mildred Fahrni gave a 1951 talk titled "Women and the Social Revolution in India."[54] She addressed the Co-op Women's Guilds of Aldergrove, Lochdale, North Vancouver, and Vancouver on parliamentary procedure and how to conduct a meeting.[55] She organized Sunday teas at her house, bringing together CCF leaders with sympathetic UBC professors, such as her son, Stuart, social work expert Leonard Marsh, anthropologist Harry Hawthorne, and town planner Peter Oberlander. When she wasn't in Vancouver, she might be stumping the province. In fall 1951, she toured the Okanagan for ten days. In Vernon, she "stressed the part which women could play in politics," pointing out that some municipalities still barred them from "the basic democratic right of voting." No wonder that Vernon still lacked a public library.[56] A month later, she appeared in Ocean Falls, making the same case for heightened democracy.

In 1951, Laura again sought CCF colours in the provincial dual-member constituency of Vancouver Centre. Critics lined up to say that she was too old. In defending her candidacy, Laura cited her grassroots credentials and pointed out that her rival for the party nomination had no equivalent. She suggested that he "get out & join some community organizations & get himself known."[57] Her profile as a former MLA and alderman, vice-president of the Local Council of Women, and executive member of the Community Planning Association and the Vancouver Housing Association eventually made her the CCF flag-bearer. However, the comments about her age, though grounded in ageism and misogyny, were also reminders that her activist days were numbered as she approached her seventieth year.[58] In the meantime, Laura worked her constituency like a veteran. This included cultivating new voters in the Asian community, whom she encouraged to appreciate "the great crusade which the CCF had carried through so successfully on behalf of minority racial groups, ending with the granting of full voting rights, not only to Chinese but to other peoples who have chosen Canada and B.C. as their homeland."[59]

During the 1952 campaign, Laura attacked the outgoing coalition government for its abortive hospital insurance scheme and close corporate ties. And on every platform, she stressed the revitalization of democracy. She referred to Saskatchewan's CCF government, re-elected in a massive majority that month, as a model of efficiency and fairness. In contrast, the BC administration mismanaged healthcare and toadied to the forest giant MacMillan Bloedel. She told voters to ignore the company's threat to move to Alberta,

> for the simple reason that the trees will still be in B.C. Investors will come to this province because the natural resources are here ... These resources belonged to the people under the British North America Act, but ... the B.C. government has been handing them over as fast as they can, rather than administering them for the people and conserving them for the future. The CCF ... planned to build permanent rather than temporary boom payrolls.[60]

Laura took familiar aim at the BC Electric Railway, which she charged "always" had "a government to see that it got what it wanted," unlike ordinary citizens. She also made it clear that "publicly owned power in British Columbia depends on the election of a CCF government."[61]

The alternative voting system produced nineteen Socred MLAs, eighteen CCFers, six Liberals, four Conservatives, and the usual Independent Labour MLA from Fernie. Only eleven women had been nominated: three for the Social Credit League, two for the Liberals, three for the Conservatives, one for the Christian Democratic Party, and two – Jamieson and Steeves – for the CCF. Laura seized Vancouver Centre with 33.17 percent of initial and 53.80 percent of final votes. Her leading opponent, prominent Liberal Coalitionist Gordon Wismer, moved from 24.34 percent to 46.20 percent, suggesting that Laura had taken much support that had earlier gone to Social Credit. Indeed, British Columbians often linked the CCF and Social Credit as foes of failing conventional politics and did not yet distinguish the latter as a champion of the right. CCF and Social Credit voters regularly selected each other as second choice. Given that Laura and the other CCF victor in Vancouver Centre each spent only $441 on the election, in contrast to their coalition Conservative and Liberal opponents' expenditure of over $6,000 each, their achievement was all the more remarkable.[62]

CCF victories occurred despite the familiar anti-socialist views of the leading Vancouver papers. The *News-Herald* was unusual only in its blunt declaration of its "Liberal leanings of which it is unashamed."[63] Though it devoted precious little coverage to female candidates, it encouraged readers to choose Laura's old NPA foe, Alderman Anna Sprott (1879–1961), who ran for the Liberals in Vancouver Centre, and Victoria Liberal Nancy Hodges. In a typical patronizing aside, the editor wished "other brilliant women" good luck, among whom he included Rolston, Steeves, the Conservative Emma Tinsman in Vancouver East running against Harold Winch, and Jamieson. That was the best he could offer since they belonged to "the wrong parties." Despite such prejudices, the journalist still claimed that "at least six women" should be "in the vitally important legislature the people will elect Thursday." As he reminisced,

> We look back to 1941–45 when there were five women members, of varying political beliefs. In all honesty, it must be admitted they ... added much to debate, were never lazy, generally helped progress in British Columbia.
>
> So, good luck to the women on Thursday![64]

On election day, Rolston, now associated with the Social Credit League, took Vancouver-Point Grey, the Liberal Hodges won Victoria City, and Jamieson was successful in Vancouver Centre. The *Vancouver Sun* saluted Rolston as the "Queen in Social Credit headquarters," and it declared Jamieson "a Princess" in the CCF. Laura was jubilant about "a fantastic election" in which she beat the Coalitionist attorney general. While the second-choice ballots were counted, she went home to do some gardening. In a nod to the media fascination with female dress, she reported that she hadn't bought a new hat for election night, because she was "more

BC MLA 1952 | *Vancouver Province,* June 12, 1952, Vancouver Public Library, 61369

concerned about what's under the hat." She also embraced a bit of feminist non-partisanship: "I welcome women into the government," she said, "and the more we have the better it will be for the Province." *Vancouver Sun* readers were told that Alderman Sprott, defeated in Vancouver Centre, was "completely in accord with this attitude."[65]

Jim Nesbitt, a lively observer on BC politics who wrote for the *Chilliwack Progress,* put Laura's victory in the context of the pitiful number of female MLAs:

> She's also a good fighter in the House. She was there before, and she could take on mesdames Hodges and Rolston at one and the same time. No-one

> could ever decide who won, but everyone enjoyed the scrap. Those were the good old days, when there were five women in the House ... They fought among themselves, sometimes, but every now and then they ganged up on the men – and the five of them could usually get their way.[66]

For the election, the *Vancouver Province* ran a photograph of Laura reading Britain's social democratic journal, the *New Statesman,* which reminded knowledgeable readers of the broader progressive community to which she belonged.[67]

The 1952 election produced considerable uncertainty. Laura immediately foresaw a bright future and promised to barnstorm the province, but the CCF soon ran into difficulty. Its provincial leader, Harold Winch, sought the approval of the lieutenant-governor to form the government "on the grounds that his party had more experienced legislators, a bigger percentage of the popular vote, and the support of the single pro-labour independent member." In fact, this independent member, the Fernie MLA Tom Uphill, proved disappointing. He had committed himself to the former Conservative, W.A.C. Bennett, who became British Columbia's first Social Credit premier. Other than Bennett, Tilly Rolston, who became minister of education, was the only government MLA who had legislative experience.[68]

The eventual sitting of the legislature in spring 1953 produced relatively little action as all parties positioned themselves for the inevitable renewal of combat. In the meantime, with only a few weeks of service in Victoria, Laura occupied herself with spreading the CCF message. She might have been on her party's right wing, but in writing about Uruguay in the *CCF News,* she reminded supporters that "the class struggle expresses the very essence of the capitalist system." The CCF role was to lead "the working class along the road towards emancipation, showing it the way which is dictated by the development of social forces," and she hit hard at the "privileged classes, which hold the power of the state, use it for the defense of their own interests by means of legislation, and by brutal repression of popular movements."[69]

In Victoria, Jamieson mapped wide interests. On the one hand, she urged the government to aid flood-ravaged Europe. On the other, she highlighted the failures of the juvenile justice system: "Every year in the life of a boy of that age is doubly important, and for those who go wrong the Government of B.C. will have a greater bill to pay." In condemning the lowered salaries offered to staff of the Girls' Industrial School and the insufficient allowances paid to foster parents, she made her priorities clear: "This economy with efficiency may be all right in handling roads but not when dealing with human beings and especially the loving care necessary for homeless children." Another plea for provincial parks underscored their significance for recreation and relaxation among ordinary people. Nor did Laura ignore her old opponent, the new Social Credit minister Rolston. She congratulated Rolston "on her pilgrimage from the Conservatives to the Coalition, to the Independent Conservative, and now to the Social Credit benches" but asked why, "knowing her love of free enterprise," she had accepted the education portfolio. After all, education was "a truly Socialist department, run by the state for the people." Laura transfixed the legislature when, tongue in cheek, she confessed amazement at Rolston likening her situation to that of the Old Testament patriarch Jacob forced to wait to make Ruth his wife: "Surely the Hon. Member recalls what happened to Jacob ... for at the end of seven years Jacob did not get Ruth, but the short-sighted Leah ... even as the lady Member has got the Social Credit Government." MLAs dissolved in laughter as Rolston had to admit Jamieson's "superior knowledge of the scriptures."[70]

Laura used another speech to argue that because there were so few female MLAs, it was all the more necessary for her to speak out "for the women of the province" to demand greater fairness from the Civil Service Commission in allocating and rewarding employment.[71] Supported by her CCF partner in Vancouver Centre, trade unionist Jim Bury, she presented the province's first Bill for Equal Pay for Equal Work to the legislature. In stressing that pay equality was not for identical labour but for work of equal value, she sought to avoid the weak precedent set in Ontario. After visiting women back east, she had learned that "some employers were re-classifying all jobs in a plant in such a way as to make it impossible to prove that any job a woman was doing was the SAME as even a similar job done by a man." She also heard of the difficulties that employees encountered in presenting their cases to the Industrial Relations Board, thereby risking retaliation. Despite such homework, her bill was ruled out of order. Only in fall 1953 would a new Social Credit government introduce an Equal Pay Act. It retained Ontario's flaws, but Jamieson concluded that the Socreds "received credit from those who did not read it carefully."[72] As Laura later reflected,

> Of course it is unfair to make any person, male or female, with dependents live on the same income as a person without dependents. But it does not cure that situation to assume that all men have dependents and no women

> have, and so always pay men more than women, as the rule was for so long. The family allowances help to correct that, and the old age pensions. Both will have to be increased considerably to even things up. Most School Boards manage by giving the men all the best positions. That is if pay must be equal, promotions don't have to be ... even when merit is the same. Lack of promotion, where merit is superior is a kind of discrimination of course. And when laws against discrimination become strong enough I think women may begin to invoke them in regard to promotion. It will be a long time, probably, because women are very timid in standing up for their rights, partly because they have played second fiddle so long; but even more because they are so afraid of robbing men of their self-confidence and self-esteem.[73]

The veteran suffragist's admission that change would be a long time coming suggested waning confidence in the face of post-war conservatism.

Other familiar causes also appeared in her arguments. She made a plea on behalf of the Doukhobors, asking for greater "understanding of their religion, their marriage laws ... and for the legitimacy of their children." In the same spirit, she used her few weeks in the legislature to criticize budget cuts to adult education, infirmaries, and physiotherapy for the elderly, and she slammed the BC Electric Railway for its abuses.[74] The range of the old University of Toronto debater's contributions intimidated her opponents. As the observant Nesbitt reported for Fraser Valley readers,

> So far CCF Mrs. Jamieson hasn't been rude – or rather, pert. But she's good when it comes to biting sarcasm. She packs a sting, and now and then she lets it go – and those she stings squirm, and hesitate to answer her. The male MLA's are getting pretty good at snapping back at the female MLA's. Gallantry has just about disappeared in legislative debate. Which is the way it should be.[75]

In short, Laura quickly resumed her earlier position as an outspoken MLA, albeit now on her own rather than as one of three talented female CCFers.

When Social Credit faltered before such challenges, Harold Winch once again appealed to the lieutenant-governor to be allowed to assume the premiership. When he was denied, he resigned the leadership of the BC CCF and eventually ran successfully in the 1953 federal election. As it turned out, the party, disgruntled though it was with his sometimes boozy direction, could not easily find a replacement. His successor, schoolteacher Arnold Webster, was a "gentle and dignified" man who "felt terribly uncomfortable in the legislature."[76] This was hardly the right leader to fight the June 1953 election, which the *CCF News* brightly hailed with a headline bolded and in caps "CCF VICTORY IMMINENT."[77] Indeed, the contest, acclaimed as "the roughest, toughest, name-callingest election campaign in B.C. political memory," did not bring good news.[78]

Once again, the press spurned the CCF. Social Credit, in contrast, got a good hearing, with Vancouver's Tilly Rolston taking a prominent place in party ads. Rarer media appeals from the CCF did not single out Jamieson. Although there were twenty-three female candidates in all, many ran for parties and in ridings where there was no hope of victory. Two represented Social Credit, three each stood for the Christian Democratic Party and the Progressive Conservatives, four each for the Liberals and the CCF, and seven for the Labor-Progressive (Communist) Party. No party appeared to treat women and their standard-bearers as a key constituency. The CCF emphasized its (male) team, described as "Honest, Capable, Experienced," and its progressive platform, which included working "FOR a better deal for the aged. FOR an end to racial inequality. FOR better educational opportunities without increased property tax. FOR auto insurance at one-half present costs. FOR a 40-hour week and two weeks holiday for all." Women's rights were conspicuously absent.[79]

Most female candidates did not make the second count in the preferential ballot. Of those who did, Socred Tilly Rolston was defeated by a male Liberal in Vancouver-Point Grey; the Liberal Hodges ran afoul of Socred Lydia Augusta Arsens in Victoria City; and Laura moved from 32.87 percent of the popular vote to a strong but inadequate 47.03 percent against a Social Credit businessman. Steeves stood third in the first count and did not reach the last. No female candidate for the Labor-Progressive Party managed more than a tiny percentage of the first count. In short, only the newcomer, Arsens, won. A populist opponent of bars, fluoride, war, social welfare, communism, and working wives, she would serve for one term and then disappear.[80] All five women veterans of the 1941 election were now gone, and no one committed to gender equality replaced them. That same year, Prime Minister St. Laurent appointed the defeated feminist Liberal Hodges to the Senate.

Overall, CCF seats fell to fourteen and the party's share of the popular vote in the final count to 29.48 percent. By 1956, Webster had been replaced by Glaswegian carpenter Bob Strachan. Dubbed the "breeze from the Hebrides," he could not extinguish Social Credit's pluralities in 1956, 1959, and 1963. The CCF stayed at about one-third of the popular vote. That outcome coincided with shifts in the Social Credit Party. In 1953, it "moved – or at least was seen to move – considerably to the right of the 1952 location when it had been implicitly allied with the CCF."[81] That journey, with its accommodation of big business as the dominant partner in resource development, would capture most of the anti-socialist vote that had clung to the Conservatives or Liberals. Women's rights inevitably suffered.

The August 1953 federal election increased CCF seats in British Columbia from 3 to 7, including Winch for Vancouver East, but offered little consolation. The Liberals won 50.0 percent of the popular vote and 171 seats; the PCs took 31.0 percent and 51 seats; the CCF dropped from 13.4 percent to 11.3 percent, although its total seats increased from 13 to 23; and Social Credit received 5.4 percent and 15 seats. An unprecedented forty-seven women, the highest number until 1972, ran in that election. Four of the twenty-two Labor-Progressives came from British Columbia, as did two of the ten PCs, three of the ten CCFers (including Gladys Strum, former Saskatchewan MP), and one of the three Liberals. Neither of the remaining two, from the Independent Liberals and the Socreds, was from the province. In Ontario, four women were elected: three PCs and one Liberal.[82] Only Ellen Fairclough was visible as a feminist.

After 1953, Laura never again ran for public office. She nonetheless remained a feisty elder activist on behalf of the CCF, internationalism, and women. These causes were always intertwined in her writing, talks, tours, and office-holding. Service on the board of the Federation of Business and Professional Women's Clubs, on the executive of Vancouver's United Nations Association, as president of the Vancouver CCF Women's Council, and as president of the provincial CCF Women's Council showed her persisting passion. When the New Democratic Party emerged in 1961, she was still fighting for democratic socialism. However, the fact that someone in her late seventies was chosen to fill CCF positions was grounded in more than admiration for Laura herself. It disclosed a shortfall of eligible candidates in age groups that might have more resources of time and energy.

Many of Laura's contributions in the last years of her life suggest that she was contemplating the future of democratic socialism. In 1954, she favourably reviewed Richard H.S. Crossman's chapter "Toward a Philosophy of Socialism," which appeared in *New Fabian Essays* (1952). She agreed with the British Labour MP's emphasis on the need for a theory of history that recognized no inevitable progress, that periods of freedom are to be prized, and that socialism should aim "to prevent the concentration of power of either industrial management or the state bureaucracy."[83] From her perspective, democratic socialists had to guard against both the left and the right for the dangers of totalitarianism. A review of American writer Wallace Stegner's *The Preacher and the Slave* (1950), which debunked the myth of radical hero Joe Hill, revealed her continuing preoccupation with class conflict. She accepted Stegner's critical assessment but confessed to preferring John Steinbeck's "warm human writing" in *The Grapes of Wrath* (1939) and *In Dubious Battle* (1936).[84] She also recommended *The History of Socialist Thought,* by G.D.H. Cole, the British historian and advocate of participatory democracy. She shared his belief that "schools, hospitals, refuges for the aged and disabled, and centres of working class culture" were key in rallying and strengthening workers in the battle with capitalism. She singled out Cole's treatment of Flora Tristan as a strong feminist who stood head and shoulders above her contemporaries, in seeing the necessity of international unity.[85] She noted matter-of-factly Tristan's rejection of marriage and praised her stress on the education and employment of women.[86] After all, these latter concerns were Laura's own priority.

Jamieson was equally attentive to Canadian subjects. She regularly scrutinized the economy and rejected claims of good times in the 1950s and 1960s. Post-war profits far outpaced wages and social security:

> Official figures of the DBS [Dominion Bureau of Statistics] show that the share of the national income used for payments like old age pensions, family allowances, workmen's compensation, etc., is scarcely more than was being paid during the worst part of the depression ... Corporations, and that means the individuals who own them, are enabled to grab an even larger share of the national income – fewer and fewer people obtaining more and more of the national wealth.[87]

In 1961, she recommended *Social Purpose for Canada,* the sequel to the League for Social Reconstruction's *Social Planning for Canada* (1935). In a familiar refrain, she emphasized the left's need to reject dogmatic solutions: "We must give up the old idea that socialism is inevitable. Progress is, rather, dependent upon the enlightened acts of free men ... The old 'worker' class is disappearing (by automation) into the new technical and professional class. Our principles and policies must appeal to these people." Equality remained the key value of socialism, but she feared that it was being "smothered in the very structure of mass society." The era's enhanced encouragement of apathy in both men and women, a failing she had always tackled as a suffragist, undermined freedom and fairness. The old veteran was not shy in issuing a call to battle for the successor to the CCF:

"Democratic planning means decentralization instead of regimentation. We must change the 'image' of democratic planning. It can be done, and the New Democratic Party must do it."[88]

As she cast about for ways to increase party support, Jamieson worried about the new middle class, many of whom lived in what she, like other critics of mass society, saw as "new small 'match-box' houses, loaded with crushing mortgages." Whereas Marx might have trusted that this group would side with workers, such post-war voters often resisted the left. Drawing on the ideas of radical American sociologist C. Wright Mills, Laura spotlighted alienation, the effective stand-in for false consciousness during these years, as a spur to acquiescence in capitalism: "How could it be otherwise, with the old class structure gone, and the continuous blaring of consumer advertising, which promises them ease and prestige if they buy the right things – no decisions to make, no effort, just do as the advertiser tells them. What wonder that the new middle class in B.C. votes largely for Santa Claus!"[89] Jamieson's critique of popular culture as crippling women in public life had extended to its impact on both sexes.

For solutions, Laura considered the possibility that the great religions offered antidotes to materialism. Though she was variously identified with agnosticism and the United and Unitarian Churches, she returned to teaching Presbyterian Sunday School classes during her seventies. What this meant in terms of her personal moral anchor is unknown, but she admired Dr. George Grant's critique of the era's tolerance of poverty and threats to freedom. She described this McMaster theologian and idealist philosopher as "one of our best educators."[90] Her review of *The Meaning of the Dead Sea Scrolls* (1956), by the Unitarian minister and civil rights and anti-nuclear activist A. Powell Davis, typically suggested that it was important to focus on Christ's humanity and not to succumb to modern "commercialism."[91] Though her archived personal papers indicate that she was intrigued by faith as a guide to individual ethics, religion appeared at most a flirtation to this committed socialist.

Laura preferred to direct dissatisfaction with the status quo into engagement with the CCF and then the NDP. Well into her late seventies, she remained active as a party recruiter. In 1956, she spent more than two weeks touring the West Kootenays and Okanagan ridings, addressing house gatherings and public meetings. She set out to supplement the current issues addressed by candidates with "the other aspects of socialist philosophy, ethical, moral and psychological, which are apt to receive little attention at election time; and to find out how the rank and file members felt about these things." That tour prompted local requests for

"Study Packages," which she helped the Education Committee assemble, showing that her message still resonated with some voters.[92]

Wherever she spoke, Laura sought out female members. In a call reminiscent of her activism with WILPF, she led discussions about how "we could help our sisters in the underdeveloped countries, in the cause of peace." Such concerns ought to be central to the modern left, and she insisted that the public needed to "know where we stood in this time of the decay of ethical and spiritual standards."[93] In the same spirit, she condemned General Gamal Nasser of Egypt as a nationalist but no socialist.[94] As a committed member of the United Nations Association, which like the CCF was often a "'boy's club' in this era," despite a majority of female members,[95] Laura applauded the Economic and Social Council of the United Nations. It fostered greater global equality by encouraging supporters to dig "down to find the sources and causes of war and then ... remove causes and resolve problems." Socialists needed to support the UN in combatting totalitarianism. When the General Assembly asked members to cut diplomatic ties with fascist Spain, she commended the move, and she was appalled when Argentina, which maintained relations with the Franco government, was elected to the Security Council. She applauded a woman delegate, Mrs. L.V. Pandit, chairman of the Indian delegation, for pointing out that this flouting of collective decisions "was the surest way to ruin the U.N."[96]

Laura regularly credited Canada "with a record clean of any attempt to exploit other countries."[97] This stance was common among her more progressive contemporaries, including Liberal prime minister Lester B. Pearson, who espoused the doctrine of Canada as "the middle power as negotiator, peacekeeper, donor, humanitarian."[98] As in the past, progressive women had a special role to play in extending Canada's essentially benign influence. The support of the Vancouver CCF Women's Council for UNESCO was a case in point. Canadians should act through that body and other groups such as the National Council of Women of Canada (NCWC) to "help their sisters in less favored lands to obtain education and opportunity for action in the community" and thus contribute "the greatest work possible for democracy and peace." As Laura believed, Canada's lack of (external) colonies meant that it was uniquely placed to aid women elsewhere. That naiveté ignored Canada's record with the First Nations and generally allowed Laura to overlook the shortcomings of international assistance. It also made her far from unique in the left or the mainstream.

Very much a veteran of WILPF's founding philosophy, Jamieson trusted that a global sisterhood could ultimately mobilize the respect and resources necessary for emancipation. In this great cause, the left had a special role to play. She seized occasions to highlight the Socialist International and the global perspective of socialists around the world.[99] In 1957, readers of the *CCF News* were alerted to the work of the International Council of Democratic Socialist Women, with which the CCF was affiliated. At its London conference, delegates from eighteen nations considered how to assist women in underdeveloped countries. It is a misreading of her record to suggest that she ever "endorsed Western colonialism in the Middle East, Africa, and Asia."[100] During the post-war years, she persisted in the condemnation of Western imperialism that she had embraced as a WILPF activist. Very typically, she supported a CCF Women's Council proposal that the Vancouver Local Council of Women ask the NCWC to establish the "Canadian Women's Fund for Assisting in the Education of the Women of the Underdeveloped Countries" to be administered by the UN.[101]

As with the proposed fund, Laura's interest in global issues frequently focused on women's economic opportunities. In a review of a 1950 study of British industry, she condemned low wages and regretted that many women accepted men's "superiority." Ultimately, patterns of economic exploitation linked women around the world. She nevertheless refused to be pessimistic as she concluded her assessment of British women workers:

> This book makes me quite proud of my sex, even though I could wish that these particular women were more alive to their own potentialities, and to the larger issues of life in the world around them. But, for women of a distinctly narrow experience, they met life at the level at which they found it, with courage and cheerfulness, and they hardly ever seemed daunted or defeated.[102]

In general, Laura's attention to economic life concentrated on the home front. She was deeply disappointed by the Social Credit government's Equal Pay Act of fall 1953.[103] Speaking for the Vancouver Local Council of Women, she denounced its vagueness. What was required was equal pay for work of "comparable nature."[104] Ultimately, the new act was just as much a sham as the 1931 Sex Disqualification (Removal) Act, whereby no married woman could lose her job but provided no mechanism for enforcement.[105] Eager to gather ammunition for better policy, Laura wrote to other provincial governments, asking for their policies regarding the employment of married women. She was appalled but unsurprised when the replies suggested that wives retained or gained government jobs only on a temporary basis and regularly lost their pension rights.[106] In 1959, she heard more bad news. Some time after she had lost her aldermanic seat, Vancouver City Council,

> finding that continuity on its staff was broken frequently by its women members who left to get married, had made a "Gentlemen's Agreement"; among themselves, at a secret meeting, that every female member of the City Hall staff should have to work for fifteen years for the city before she could even get permission to apply for a senior position!

Laura's solution was familiar: she turned to the local Federation of Business and Professional Women to lodge a protest. At first, the city's lawyer said that the provincial Sex Disqualification (Removal) Act did not apply, but upon a motion from a sympathetic new alderman, not to mention public shaming, the mayor and council voted to cancel the agreement.[107]

As she surveyed the economic landscape in the last years of her life, Laura lamented the complacency of too many women. Ultimately, only those on the left "have always been aware that they should know the wages and working conditions of the women who made the clothes which they, as customers, buy and wear, at least in our own province." That hardy group was not enough. Consumers in general should know key truths such as the fact that "women employees in the garment industry in Vancouver were working for a minimum wage of 60c per hour, which, in many cases was the maximum." This contrasted with the male minimum of seventy-five cents.[108] Buyers should boycott products and protest to governments.

Jamieson's last personal reflections stressed unions as much as the CCF/NDP. She anticipated good results from the 1956 merger of the Trades and Labour Congress of Canada and the Canadian Congress of Labour to form the Canadian Labour Congress. The latter could recruit white-collar workers, including women, and establish a conduit into the CCF. The inclusion of such members would be far from unprecedented, a fact insufficiently appreciated by party radicals. As she reminded readers, the CCF "founder was middle class, and [so too were] many others who have guided the CCF through the years. The middle classes may be harder to win than the old; but we have always been willing to accept difficult challenges."[109] For edification, she pointed to the recent history of BC nurses. For years, the Registered Nurses Association had "considered itself a professional organization rather than a group of workers," but after 1944 it faced an effective rival in the Hospital Employees' Union. When approached by nurses who were upset by conflict between the two bodies, she emphasized the benefits won at Vancouver General Hospital by the union and recommended that the association swallow its pride and become "a bona fide Trade Union."[110] Nurses might be professionals, but they were workers first of all, and they had a vested interest in challenging labour relations as dictated by the liberal state and private enterprise.

Jamieson continuously monitored BC labour conditions. She still counted on the Local Council of Women to broaden public support for better legislation, as "the appearance of a few women from well-established organizations is salutary." In 1962, as a member of the Vancouver NDP Women's Committee, she urged the local council to ask the BC Board of Industrial Relations to raise the minimum wage. In some occupations, such as fish canning and fruit processing, the rate had remained the same for decades. When the BC Federation of Labour and the Needle Trades Council of Greater Vancouver submitted a brief, she produced a two-page memo, "Women Should Know," as part of their educational campaign.[111]

Jamieson's BC Archives papers are rich with mimeographed material from the Retail Clerks' Union, the Bank Employees' Association, the Retail, Wholesale and Department Store Workers' Union, and the Needle Trades Council. When the BC Industrial Relations Board refused to increase the minimum wage in the 1950s, she attributed such recalcitrance and low female unionization to the persistence in a "disillusioning world" of the dream that marriage and a man offered rescue from subordination in the labour force. Despite that bleak conclusion, she insisted that modern young women were beginning to "realize now how easy it is for employed women to be exploited without the public, and the main body of women, knowing it." Women's clubs and the left still needed to educate and agitate.[112]

Laura's papers reveal other familiar causes. She identified the elderly poor who had contributed to Canada's post-war wealth, "but through illness or misfortune were not able to retain their share of it," as victims of private enterprise. Only public authorities could provide the necessary resources.[113] When she endorsed an NDP resolution favouring a capital gains tax, it was clear where the money could be found.[114] As Laura herself aged, her interests in the elderly extended to consideration of their political impact. Ultimately, old women and men were an untapped resource. Once mobilized through education, co-operation, and expertise, they need not be reactionary. Poverty explained much of their resistance to taxes. Nor did Laura let the rich off the hook. There was "little excuse" for elders in that privileged group: "Instead of being under-fed, they are overfed. Too often they overeat, over-drink and over-smoke. They become so flabby-minded that they conform to the current fashion, which just now is 'King size' ... If they survive at all their value to the community is practically nil." In assessing the impact of aging, she made gender distinctions:

> You will notice that here I speak particularly of the males in our population. The women, with the strong motive of keeping their good looks and their youth, in the main avoid over-eating and careless health habits. So they survive longer than the men. If in their superior survival they become just as unprogressive and reactionary as the men at 65 I wouldn't like to say. Incidentally, since there are more women than men in the 65 and over age group, the men can almost always count on having a woman to nurse them through their ulcers and coronaries, whether they deserve their good fortune or not.

Just as in party politics, women's energies were hijacked to subsidize men. None of this was necessary. With sufficient community and economic support, combined with a good dose of socialist education, older adults of both sexes could remain "active, alert, and capable." "A massive adult education program" for the "atomic age" could ensure that the elderly were a force for good. Drawing on the ideas of McGill neurosurgeon Wilder Penfield, she also took inspiration from the lifelong learning initiatives in Scandinavia.[115] Aging minds and bodies could be retrieved to make a better world.

Though international development, women workers, housing, and the situation of the elderly were well-trodden activist paths, Laura's personal papers include a rare and apparently unpublished reflection on the Indigenous peoples of British Columbia. In the late 1950s or early 1960s, she wrote some four pages on the subject, probably for a talk. Largely uncritically, she discussed settler efforts to integrate Inkameep children into Okanagan schools and the artistic talent displayed in the reserve's day school, run by the Department of Indian Affairs. She approvingly cited the Oliver Parent-Teacher Association, local principals, and the Indian agent, all of whom she credited as working "slowly and carefully ... in favor of integrating the Indian children into the local schools." As a result, "the whole town was behind the project." She accepted that progressive sympathizers were "determined to see that our native Indians be given the same opportunities as other Canadians. They were quite certain that if this was done we should find our culture enriched, and our human relations expanded."[116] Such trust in authority was uncharacteristic. Ultimately grounded in ignorance, it starkly contrasted with the cynicism that Laura demonstrated when she assessed the treatment of working women by governments and industry. In failing to move beyond a sympathetic humanitarianism, the woman from the Saugeen Peninsula had still to learn the full lessons of homegrown colonialism and racism.

The stalled progressive agenda of post-war Canada appeared in Laura's *CCF News* review of historian Catherine Cleverdon's pioneering study, *The Woman Suffrage Movement in Canada* (1950). As a veteran of the BC suffrage campaign, she applauded Cleverdon's awareness of "the grinding work, the heart-breaking disappointments suffered by group after group of women, year after year, in province after province, before the vote was won by them across Canada." She recommended Cleverdon's discussion of enfranchisement but suggested that the author was

> slightly wrong in attributing the welfare legislation entirely to the votes cast by the new women voters. The fact is that in order to get the vote we suffragists dug up all the inequalities and injustices under which women suffered. We pointed out that this was the result of having only men voters. We paraded these injustices on every possible occasion, long before we got the vote. We needed to do very little after. The old line parties were so anxious to get the women's vote that they promised it all, and we held them to their promises.

After reminding readers that socialist legislators had introduced many of the first suffrage bills, she charged early crusaders with a blinkered vision:

> One thing very noticeable in this book is that the women asked only for equality with men and seemed satisfied when they got it. But in doing so most of them failed to see that they were implicitly putting their stamp of approval on the "status quo." When they got the vote they did not say to men, in effect: "Now that we've caught up with you in franchise and legislative rights, let's go forward together and win new freedoms for us all." (A few small groups tried to do this but only in the CCF did any development of any size take place.)
>
> That, to my mind, was the place where the woman suffrage movement lost a great opportunity.

Jamieson did not accept Cleverdon's explanation that campaigners were exhausted: the author failed to note that many suffragists were blind to the pervasive lack of democracy.

Laura pointed out that Nellie McClung, "able and witty writer that she was, never seemed to see beyond temperance and the franchise for women." The noted Alberta suffragist Emily Murphy should also have worked for "worthier ends" than Senate appointments. That institution still blighted Canadian democracy. Laura nevertheless concluded her review positively, with the hope that "intelligent women will also begin to think, after reading it, of what women can achieve if they study society, and choose the worthwhile objectives to fight for. The task of CCF women is to help other women to see these objectives by their own thinking, and then get them to want to work for them."[117] This was the goal that she had set herself after enfranchisement: communities of her own sex needed to raise consciousness of oppression.

By the close of the 1950s, however, the *CCF News* confirmed the sad state of feminism through its rare inclusion of articles by or about women. In 1955, a contribution to that publication by the first chair of Ontario's Provincial Women's Council argued that organizational habits retained in "vast networks of 'safe' non-political organizations" dating from the suffrage campaigns hobbled effective "political interest and understanding." To promote democracy, women should enter the CCF, which offered women's committees or sections. She admitted, however, that separate women-only groups encountered hostility and that some women feared being pushed into them and out of real power.[118] The NDP nevertheless established a Women's Committee in 1962, a year after its founding, to "stimulate interest among women, to develop their capabilities in the field of organization and education by providing opportunities to improve their skills and qualifications so they will be more effective as people, as supporters, members, active party officers, or as potential representatives." Laura joined its BC group. It quickly faltered. Not until after the Royal Commission on the Status of Women produced its 1970 report did feminists in the BC NDP again benefit from separate organization.[119]

The general malaise of women's groups that were committed to politics was confirmed by the disappearance of Laura's old standby, the Vancouver Women's School for Citizenship. Not even its effort at a wide range of topics, "from a study of British Guiana with its recent communist plotting, to a panel on Hospital Facilities in Vancouver, to an evening entitled 'What's Wrong with Women?'" when its members "paused to examine ourselves objectively," kept it going.[120] From 1955, its roll call did not include Laura's name. Three years later, the school disbanded, and it proved unable even to sustain hopes of continuing with a monthly book review club. This too disappeared in 1959.

Now in her late seventies, Laura was clearly on the margin of women's and leftist politics. In 1958, her contributions to the *CCF News* included advertising the annual CCF rummage sale, hardly the sign of a key player in party politics.[121] The 1960 luncheon held by the provincial CCF Women's Council seemed successful enough, but the presence of Lucy Woodsworth as a distinguished guest and the observation that CCF groups in "larger centres are affiliated with Local Councils of Women and United Nations Associations" spoke more of the past than the future.[122] A year later, the NDP held its founding convention in Ottawa, which was covered by the *New Democrat,* successor to the *CCF News.* It published a photograph of "the Literature Table," staffed by Laura and others, which it identified as "one of the busiest locations during the Convention." Laura was one of several "faithful members" who attended the event.[123] Despite looking very frail, she also presided over a "meeting of 300 women from provinces" and urged people to study *Social Purpose for Canada* as "their educational task."[124] She did not stop there. In January 1962, she was elected to chair the publicity committee of the Vancouver Women's Committee.[125] The efforts of an eighty-year-old were not enough. She was soon asking about absentee members and how to revive the committee.[126] Less than a year later, Laura was dead and effectively so too was the committee. There was, however, good reason to remember her.

Conclusion

Even before her death on June 30, 1964, Laura Emma Marshall Jamieson had largely disappeared from public memory. While attending an Ottawa meeting with Vancouver NDP MPs that month, she had learned of an error-filled article on her life in the party newspaper. The *New Democrat* published a gentle correction from her on July 1: she was a judge not of the family court but of the juvenile court, not in Vancouver but in Burnaby, and she had represented Vancouver Centre not Burrard. Upbeat to the last, the octogenarian put a comic turn on the misrepresentation, adding, "I am happy so long as I am not forced to complain, as Mark Twain once did, that the reports of his death were greatly exaggerated!"[1] Within days of writing, she was dead.

In early July 1964, she was memorialized in a crowded service at Vancouver's Unitarian Church. The party newspaper tried to make up for its earlier misstep by noting the large numbers of NDPers in attendance as well as the "boys and girls (now men and women) [who] came to tell Laura good-bye. They were the same youths who remembered her understanding heart, and hand of friendship in time of need. For Laura Jamieson, a former juvenile court judge, was much respected and liked." She was saluted as having "devoted her life to fighting for women's rights" and as having been roused by the "Terrible '30s" to join the CCF. Here too was one of the "early suffragettes [sic] in B.C. who were vocal about their ideals. She fought not with emotion alone, but with energy, logic, a cool head, research and statistics. Laura Jamieson is remembered as one of the outstanding women, not only of the New Democratic Party, but of British Columbia." Speaking for an age that had a huge investment in ladylike behaviour, even among the left, the editorialist added the reassurance that "everything that Laura Jamieson did was made doubly effective by the fact that she looked, acted, spoke, thought and was, a lady – in the most complete sense of the term. When she came into the office of the New Democratic Party in Vancouver, her concise thinking and pleasant manner made her extra welcome. We shall miss her."[2]

Grace MacInnis offered a personal testament from a younger comrade in arms. She praised her former benchmate for combining idealism and pragmatism:

> Laura Jamieson wasted no time in cursing the darkness of the world. Her whole life was devoted to lighting candles wherever she could and holding them high ... Throughout her life she held a profound belief that if people knew the facts they would take the proper action. So she held classes and filled speaking engagements on the topics close to her heart. But she was also a woman of action, organizing several cooperative boarding homes for single girls in Vancouver.
>
> During the 1930s Laura's beliefs and activities led her naturally into politics and she took her full share in the formative period of the CCF ... Laura Jamieson was what she seemed – a fine human being of wide sympathies who devoted her life to making her particular corner of society into a fairer, kinder place for people to develop their best abilities.[3]

Though undeniably partisan, Grace's observations seem apt. Her emphasis on Laura's commitment to education and outreach and her generous sympathies captured a lifetime of evolving dedication to a better deal for everyone. Above all, Laura had trusted in the potential of a collaborative politics of intelligence, compassion, and feminism to remake the world.

Laura Jamieson soon disappeared from sight as a significant expression of the CCF's past. Not until the recovery of women's and labour history in the 1970s and 1980s would she, her feminist sisters, and their male allies begin to be rediscovered. Even then, recognition remained uncertain. Suffragists have readily been frozen in time, too often dismissed by later commentators as solely preoccupied with middle-class problems and prejudices. This view tends to leave unnoticed both the left's general unwillingness to foster a feminist wing in its campaigns and the pervasive misogyny and anti-feminism of Canadian life. No wonder Jamieson's importance was easily disavowed some twenty years after her death. During a 1982 interview, former CCF leader Harold Winch casually dismissed his frequent social democratic critic: Laura, he intoned for the edification of scholars who would listen to his recorded epitaph, was "not a student of socialism in any way." She was only "a follower not a leader" and was ultimately "a quiet rather shy person."[4] In underscoring these supposed shortcomings of intellect, of leadership, and of presence, this veteran labour socialist affirmed familiar claims to male political superiority that largely erased female rivals. Subsequent accounts of CCF politics, which fixated on the Socialist Party of Canada vision to the detriment of other dreams of equality or reduced Laura to little more than a doppelganger of Social Credit women, similarly dodged the radical questioning of gender politics that she represented.

Laura is far better remembered as a Canadian New Woman whose ideas of freedom and equality evolved to espouse a left-wing politics grounded in the human rights of women. Her political education began in Ontario and continued in the west, where she abandoned liberalism and backed socialism. That evolution sprang directly from her own experiences and observations of the vulnerability of girls and women in matters from education and employment to family planning and housing. In the suffrage movement and the Women's International League for Peace and Freedom, she built on the sisterhood within her own family, in her days at the Vancouver Normal School, at the University of Toronto, and in the YWCA. Though incomplete, her vision ultimately embraced a far more liberatory politics than that taken up by most of her contemporaries. The result was a well-read and outspoken activist who deserted the Liberal Party favoured by her husband and moved to radical circles that placed her on the margins of the BC women's movement. Those margins were nevertheless sufficient to sustain Jamieson's leadership in civic education initiatives and to launch her legislative career.

As she shifted to the left, Laura Jamieson spotlighted the oppression of workers, but she never identified this group as uniquely placed. Her life and reading affirmed women's particular vulnerability and potential. As a feminist, she insisted that women, like the proletariat so honoured by revolutionary socialists, had untapped capacity for progressive action. Both women and workers could be nurtured through ongoing programs of consciousness raising and political education. Her decades of experience in the women's movement taught this cautious radical to rely upon gradual illumination and empowerment rather than hopes for a revolutionary moment. Above all, she counted on grassroots organizing in clubs, co-operatives, unions, and the CCF as offering passage "step by step to the new social order."[5]

Laura portended, at least in germ, a leftist politics grounded in local communities of mutual respect and shared resources. Perhaps it is not coincidental that her daughter, Jean, went to work for the Company of Young Canadians, with its passion for neighbourhood organizing, that her son, Stuart, collaborated with Indigenous fishers and farm workers, and that her granddaughters involved themselves in diverse progressive causes, from radical filmmaking to public housing, Marxist-Leninism, racially inclusive choreography, and feminist public art. By the time Laura died, a new generation of radical women and men was emerging.

In the decade of her death, the English Canadian New Left explored its own vision of the local education, activism, and politics she had so long championed. Skeptical and often ignorant about the old socialists and organized labour, it knew even less of feminism. Ultimately, it too often privileged white middle-class male intellectuals and university youth in its hopes for a progressive politics. That orientation provided no escape from the limitations of the past. Just as women had not figured as agents of change for enough socialists in Laura's lifetime, they, like other groups marginalized by race in particular, meant too little for most New Leftists in the decade and more after her death.[6] From whatever plane she observed the renewed contest for the hearts and minds of Canadians, Laura would have had good reason to applaud a 1967 pamphlet titled *Sisters, Brothers, Lovers ... Listen*, the feminist effort to raise the consciousness of the New Left.[7]

In the twenty-first century, Canadian feminists and socialists have yet to construct a fully inclusive vision of human liberation. From her childhood on the Saugeen Peninsula until her final moments in East Vancouver, the last suffragist standing laboured on that great project. In challenging the politics of gender and class, and beginning to consider racism, Laura Jamieson was highly unusual. For all the incompleteness of her perspective on equality and human rights, she expanded the old suffragist faith in the possibility of a brighter, fairer day for everyone. Her brave legacy forms part of the history of women worthies whom Laura trusted to inspire Canadians to transform the world.

Postscript from Four Granddaughters

Laura Jamieson was fortunate enough to have eight granddaughters, four born to Jean Jamieson and Jack Shannon and four to Stuart Jamieson and Jean Collins Jamieson. I invited those who remain to contribute reflections on their grandmother. The four who knew her as teenagers and young adults share their thoughts here. I'd also like to recognize the youngest, Laura, who was only a small child when her grandmother died and does not write here, for the interviews she conducted in her memory, especially with her mother and father. Thank-you all!

Dorothy O'Connell (Ottawa)

I remember reading an op-ed article in my local newspaper, where a young female lawyer stated that she had succeeded entirely on her own merits and owed nothing to any women who had come before her. I wondered how she had possibly reached that conclusion, since if it had not been for the women who went before, no women would be in law school, or medicine, or any of the other fields not open to women, who were not even considered persons.

We tend to forget all the struggles that lie behind us, the advances we have come to calmly accept; the right to vote, to work outside the home, to have control of our own bodies and our own decisions about sex and childbirth. And yet, these are all very recent accomplishments, and some of these battles are still being fought.

It took a great deal of fortitude to fight for these things, as control of ourselves was not easily ceded. Women are still not proportionately represented in parliament, for instance, and we are reminded of why many are not interested in running, when we hear the slurs and threats received by successful women in this field. And for many women, whose background is not white, Anglo-Saxon, upper middle class, those freedoms still don't exist.

Mama J fought for those women. Well ahead of her time, she did not fight just for university-educated women like herself, but also for those whose basic needs were not being met, for those whom some of the better-off women did not consider should be eligible for the freedoms that they themselves deserved. Mama J showed her granddaughters that women can fight and succeed. When she was elderly, and not as physically fit, she still fought, sending pictures of children to world leaders when it sometimes seemed that nuclear war was inevitable.

The fight still goes on. Sometimes, when it seems that it will never end, we need to remember women like Mama J. Well done, Laura Jamieson.

Anne Jamieson (Vancouver)

Some of my memories of Mama J are linked to the political person she was, which had a great influence on my own development as a political person. Every Sunday (or at least some Sundays per month), we went for an afternoon dinner at her apartment on Adanac Street, near the corner of Victoria Drive. This is where she lived after selling her house on Trafalgar Street in Kitsilano. As in her house on Trafalgar, there were objects in her apartment from all over the world, where she had travelled as a delegate of a progressive women's group. For example, she had a rattan coffee table from Thailand and an intriguing ivory carving from China of three little monkeys pantomiming "see no evil, hear no evil, speak no evil." And there were books, including collections of Shakespeare, and of course, books by George Bernard Shaw, whom she admired immensely. For those Sunday dinners, she always prepared the same dish – Chinese cuisine – that included water chestnuts, sprouts, and some other things. The crunch of the water chestnuts was most satisfying.

Mama J would have prepared a list of topics that she wanted to cover during dinner conversation with my parents, and these topics were most interesting – about current events and political personages. I learned from Mama J that the employees at Supervalu in North Vancouver (and elsewhere?) had been prevented from joining a union, and thus I decided that I would not buy my groceries there (once I reached the age of doing such shopping). Obviously, our father had soaked up some of her philosophy despite himself, because I distinctly remember that while we were travelling by car through the United States, my parents refused to cross the picket line of a store that we had been about to enter. Mama J encouraged me to join the Young CCFers and showed me publications.

She promoted love of music, giving me a book about the musical instruments in an orchestra. One Christmas, her presents to we three girls (Laurie was not yet born) consisted of certificates saying that she had donated money in our names to some good cause (perhaps UNICEF). Our parents were indignant, but I admired her sense of principle, promoting altruism in us.

She had had a hard life and had to struggle to get educated, which I did not fully appreciate until adulthood. The harshness of losing parents to influenza at age nine, losing an infant son, losing her husband to septicemia – all this and more did not vanquish her indomitable spirit but rather inspired her to work for the betterment of women's lives, for the working class, and for all disadvantaged people. She had tuberculosis and had to stay in a sanatorium for around a year, I believe, so that her husband and two children at home had to be cared for by a housekeeper.

She introduced us to women who were among the first MLAs in British Columbia. She instilled in me the idea that women taking part in politics was a normal part of life. I remember a saying of hers, with respect to how she handled heckling in public meetings, which did not intimidate her in the least: "If you can't stand the heat, get out of the kitchen!"

I always found her to be a most interesting person and a model for womanhood! Of course, my ideas on what constituted progressive politics diverged from those of Mama J once I started university, where exciting political ideas were flourishing. But I cannot deny the profound influence she did have on me as a child and as a young woman.

Karen Jamieson (Vancouver)

When I think of my Grandmother Mama J, what I remember is the talking. Conversations, discussions, debates, and arguments, whenever the family got together, always arising from the fundamental principles of equality, social and economic justice, human rights and worker's rights, the value of work and the importance of unions, the rights and empowerment of women, and universal suffrage. In the living room of our house, she and my father would debate this or that economic policy or direction. We children grew up marinated in these conversations that swirled constantly around us. The names of all the architects of socialist policy in Canada were as familiar as family names. My friends found their heroes in movie stars, but my adolescent hero was wee Tommy Douglas, as Mama J called him, whom she described as fighting like a lion for what was right.

Looking back, I see her socialism as constantly evolving through this crucible of discussion and argument, her process of bringing ideas into the light to be examined and wrestled to the ground. I think that, working from a solid foundation in principles of justice, she must have used dialogue to come ever closer to truth. When I went to university, studied philosophy, and discovered Socrates in my first year, I was excited and felt at home in his dialogical method of moving back and forth between the poles of an argument to come to the truth of the matter.

I became disillusioned with the world of left-wing politics and the UBC philosophy department. I felt myself, as a woman, to be disempowered, and I could find no place in the hierarchical structures and top-down decision making of that milieu. After graduating from UBC at age twenty-one, I discovered dance. I gave myself completely to this art form, believing this was what I was meant to do with my life. I left the life of spoken language and discourse for what I felt was a more truthful language: the language of the dancing body. I was inspired by Martha Graham, who said that "the body never lies." I followed a path that seems, on one level, to have been a radical departure from Mama J's. But as the years passed, I found my path converging more and more with hers, and the values she had communicated to us as children became the foundation of my work. I had come full circle. My leadership style was one of leading from the middle or from behind, and I developed ideas for my dances through dialogical processes. Although the language is that of dance, the process of distilling the truth through multiple perspectives engaged in discourse is the same. I believe I absorbed it from my grandmother. It has become more and more evident that she influenced me enormously, and in many ways I have followed in her footsteps. I understood dance as a powerful tool for social change, for dialogue between cultures, as a means to build community and to empower individuals.

I remember the Christmas when we girls were informed that our present from her would be gifts for children whose needs were greater than ours, children who lacked warm clothing. I distinctly remember having two different reactions. One was unhappy: I wanted a present for me. The other was happy: under our tree, I saw very beautiful hand-knit woollen garments, in red and green, that we would give to the children who needed them. My sister insists that those garments existed only in my imagination, but reflecting on this event led me to understand how much politics is an act of imagination. I imagined the outcome of the act of giving up my present to become a greater present for others. It was my introduction to art as political and the power of art to effect profound change.

Mama J's feminism was ahead of her time. She advocated for universal enfranchisement during a period when many feminists were locked into the ethnicity and class of the dominant culture. Mama J included working-class women and disenfranchised Asian and First Nations men and women, understanding that enfranchisement was the cornerstone of democracy. To me, many of her ideas seem ahead of their time. For many years a pacifist, she understood that peace could not come without economic change and universal enfranchisement. She understood how deeply class and economic injustice fed war. I recently spoke with a young woman who sees herself as the new kind of feminist, with new and radical ideas of inclusivity. I had to draw her attention to the fact that my grandmother not only advocated for an inclusive feminism but also understood the empowerment of women as connected to economic justice.

Rather than diminishing or embittering her, the terrible losses in her life and the hardships she endured seemed to have fuelled her extraordinary will and determination, and she was an indomitable optimist. Orphaned very young, she and her siblings somehow managed to survive on an Ontario scrub farm. There was no social safety net, no support for them. When my sisters and I were young, she wrote stories for us of her childhood. One told of a day spent in the hayloft in the barn, reading and eating nothing but apples. I remember wondering if she had enough to eat at home. I still wonder. She was felled by tuberculosis as a relatively young woman, a disease associated with poverty. I wondered also whether these experiences supported her drive for democratic socialism.

Marion-Lea Jamieson (Vancouver)

I am deeply indebted to Veronica Strong-Boag for writing this biography of my grandmother, Mama J, as it has greatly expanded my knowledge of her life and works, and has redoubled my pride in being her descendant. I am also grateful for this reminder that the rights of women can never be taken for granted but must continually be defended with intelligence and determination, as Laura Jamieson did.

Though I was sixteen when Mama J died, this biography has also made me question why I knew very little about her and why my relationship with her was not close. Part of the answer is that my grandmother was not a smiling, cookie-baking, child-hugging old lady. She did not resemble a stereotypical granny in any way. When we visited, she and my father carried on lively discussions of politics, which was her passion to the last. We granddaughters had not yet developed an interest in politics, or had only uninformed opinions.

But another part of the answer is that there was a tension between my parents and Mama J that is more difficult to explain from a child's view. It's possible that, like any woman who devotes herself to a compelling life outside the home, her children resented that her focus was elsewhere. Or perhaps my father felt that in becoming a successful and highly regarded academic, he had disappointed her hope that he would be a politician. As an adult looking back on her accomplishments, I regret not having known her better.

Though Mama J's staunch feminist beliefs did not overtly shape the way in which my parents brought us up, our family life was strongly influenced by her socialist ideals. Her activism, opposition to consumerism, and pursuit of social equality and justice were important in my parents' philosophy of life, and they impressed these values on us. Though politics is not my passion, I have been politically active since my early teens. Since retiring, I have devoted considerable time and energy to political issues, especially at the local level.

So I can't provide an intimate portrait of Mama J but feel her strong influence in my assumption that we all have a responsibility to question the status quo and to insist on a better, more equitable world. I have tried to pass on this basic assumption to my own children, and I hope they will pass it on to theirs so that Mama J lives on.

Abbreviations

BA	*Burnaby Advertiser*
BB	*Burnaby Broadcast*
BCA	British Columbia Archives
BCF	*British Columbia Federationist*
BCS	*BC Studies*
CCFN	*CCF News*
CF	*Canadian Forum*
CHR	*Canadian Historical Review*
CP	*Chilliwack Progress*
FFP	*Fernie Free Press*
GRMA	Grey Roots Museum and Archives
LEMJ	Laura Emma Marshall Jamieson
L/LT	*Labour/Le Travail*
MM	*Maclean's Magazine*
ND	*New Democrat*
PAS	Provincial Archives of Saskatchewan
SN	*Saturday Night*
TC	*The Champion*
TF	*The Federationist* (CCF)
TGM	*Toronto Globe and Mail*
UBCRBSC	University of BC Rare Books and Special Collections
VDW	*Vancouver Daily World*
VM	Violet McNaughton
VNH	*Vancouver News-Herald*

VP	*Vancouver Province*
VPL	Vancouver Public Library
VS	*Vancouver Sun*
WP	*Western Producer*
WT	*Winnipeg Tribune*
WWW	*Western Woman's Weekly*

Notes

Introduction

1 The other legislators were Louise Crummy McKinney and Roberta Catherine MacAdams (Alberta 1917), Mary Ellen Smith (British Columbia 1918), Edith McTavish Rogers (Manitoba 1920), Agnes Macphail (Ottawa 1921), Nellie L. McClung and Irene Parlby (Alberta 1921), Helen Douglas Smith (British Columbia 1933), and Dorothy Gretchen Steeves (British Columbia 1934).

2 Irene Howard, *The Struggle for Social Justice in British Columbia: Helena Gutteridge, the Unknown Reformer* (Vancouver: UBC Press, 1992), 157.

3 She embodies the unpredictability of allegiances, as described by two major commentators on Vancouver society in the late nineteenth and early twentieth centuries. See Mark Leier, *Red Flags and Red Tape: The Making of a Labour Bureaucracy* (Toronto: University of Toronto Press, 1995); and Robert A.J. McDonald, *Making Vancouver: Class, Status and Social Boundaries, 1863–1913* (Vancouver: UBC Press, 1996).

4 Laura Emma Marshall Jamieson (LEMJ), *Women Dry Those Tears* (Vancouver: CCF Women's Council of BC, with assistance from Ontario CCF Women, 1945), 32.

5 Joan Sangster, "Creating Popular Histories: Re-interpreting 'Second Wave' Canadian Feminism," *Dialectical Anthropology* 39 (2015): 383.

6 Among the most well known in Canada are Carol Lee Bacchi's *Liberation Deferred? The Ideas of the English-Canadian Suffragists* (Toronto: University of Toronto Press, 1982); and Mariana Valverde, *The Age of Light, Soap and Water: Moral Reform in English Canada, 1885–1925* (Toronto: University of Toronto Press, 1991).

7 Mary Kinnear, *Female Economy: Women's Work in the Prairie Provinces, 1870–1970* (Montreal and Kingston: McGill-Queen's University Press, 1991), 150.

8 LEMJ, "Book Review … When Women Won the Vote," *CCF News*, January 7, 1953.

9 Karen M. Offen, *European Feminisms, 1700–1950: A Political History* (Stanford: Stanford University Press, 2000), 11. On Canadian conservatism, see Linda Kealey, "Canadian Socialism and the Woman Question," *Labour/Le Travail (L/LT)* 13 (Spring 1984): 77–100.

10 Constance Errol [Elizabeth Kerr], "Women's Views," *The Federationist,* December 29, 1939.

11 See James Naylor, *The Fate of Labour Socialism: The Co-operative Commonwealth Federation and the Dream of a Working-Class Future* (Toronto: University of Toronto Press, 2016). A May 2017 conference, held at Mount Royal College and titled "Social Democracy, the Left and the CCF/NDP in Canada: Past, Present, and Future," is a case in point. Among the seventeen-point topics in its call for papers were "Canadian Women and the Left," along with "Indigenous activism" and "the Social Gospel and Christian Socialism." The final program made no reference to feminism, and the titles of twenty-four papers did not mention women, though papers focusing on the New Left or McCarthyism might have included them.

12 See Robert McDonald, "'Variants of Liberalism' and the Liberal Order Framework in British Columbia," in *Liberalism and Hegemony: Debating the Canadian Liberal Revolution,* ed. Jean-François Constant and Michel Ducharme (Toronto: University of Toronto Press, 2009), 322–46; and James Naylor, "The British Columbia CCF's Working-Class Moment: Socialism Not Populism," *L/LT* 71 (Spring 2013): 101–21.

13 See Veronica Strong-Boag, "Independent Women, Problematic Men: First and Second Wave Anti-Feminism in Canada from Goldwin Smith to Betty Steele," *Histoire sociale/ Social History* 57 (May 1996): 1–22.

14 Agnes Macphail, "Men Want to Hog Everything!" *Maclean's Magazine,* September 15, 1949.

15 See Veronica Strong-Boag, "'Men Want to Hog Everything': Women in Canadian Legislative Politics after Suffrage Victories," ActiveHistory.ca, May 17, 2017, http://activehistory.ca/2017/05/men-want-to-hog-everything-women-in-canadian-legislative-politics-after-suffrage-victories/.

16 Ibid.

17 "Total and Ruthless Matriarchy, Male Already Obsolete," *Vancouver News-Herald,* December 8, 1949.

18 Susan Walsh, "Equality, Emancipation and a More Just World: Leading Women in the B.C. CCF" (master's thesis, Simon Fraser University, 1984).

Chapter 1: The Girl from the Saugeen Peninsula, 1882–1911

1 On this usage, see Edwin Koenig, *Cultures and Econologies: A Native Fishing Conflict on the Saugeen-Bruce Peninsula* (Toronto: University of Toronto Press, 2005); and Norman Robertson, *The History of the County of Bruce* (Toronto: William Briggs and Bruce Co. Historical Society, 1906).

2 See Phil Henderson, "Worlds on the Edges: The Politics of Settler Resentment on the Saugeen/Bruce Peninsula" (master's thesis, University of Victoria, 2016), 166.

3 See Peter S. Schmalz, *The History of the Saugeen Indians* (Toronto: Ontario Historical Society, 1977); Peter S. Schmalz, *Ojibway of Southern Ontario* (Toronto: University of Toronto Press, 1911); and Stephanie McMullen, "Disunity and Dispossession: Nawash Ojibwa and Potawatomi in the Saugeen Territory, 1836–1865" (master's thesis, University of Calgary, 1997).

4 McMullen, "Disunity and Dispossession," 7.

5 Robertson, *History of the County of Bruce,* 16.

6 McMullen, "Disunity and Dispossession," 98.

7 Robertson, *History of the County of Bruce,* 132.
8 See "Black History in Grey County," Grey Roots Museum and Archives, https://greyroots.com/story/black-history-grey-county; "Black History," City of Owen Sound, https://www.owensound.ca/en/black-history.aspx; and Sylvia Hasbury, *Bruce County's Black Pioneers* (Kincardine: privately printed, 2013).
9 Robertson, *History of the County of Bruce,* 139.
10 Ramsay Cook, "Presidential Address: Tillers and Toilers: The Rise and Fall of Populism in Canada in the 1890s," *Historical Papers* (Canadian Historical Association) 19, 1 (1984): 1–20. https://www.erudit.org/fr/revues/hp/1984-v19-n1-hp1119/030915ar.pdf.
11 Darren Ferry, *Uniting in Measures of Common Good: The Construction of Liberal Identities in Central Canada, 1830–1900* (Montreal and Kingston: McGill-Queen's University Press, 2008), 239–40.
12 Allan Bartley, *Alexander McNeill: A Political Life* (Wiarton: Bruce County Historical Society, 1990), 28.
13 Ibid., 45.
14 Jennifer Trant, "The Victorian Furniture Industry in Grey and Bruce Counties, Ontario" (master's thesis, Queen's University, 1987), 36.
15 Sharon Ann Cook, *"Through Sunshine and Shadow": The Woman's Christian Temperance Union, Evangelicalism, and Reform in Ontario, 1874–1930* (Montreal and Kingston: McGill-Queen's University Press, 2014), 7.
16 Ibid.
17 See "Prayers," *Journals of the Legislative Assembly of Ontario,* May 16, 1893, 136. See also David M. Fahey, *Temperance and Racism: John Bull, Johnny Reb, and the Good Templars* (Lexington: University Press of Kentucky, 2015), which briefly notes that the "chief officer for Ontario" ruled that "no lodge should be 'without a fair proportion of female applicants'" and that "1877 Ontario claimed about fifteen black lodges in its western districts and a total black membership in the thousands." Ibid., 25, 110.
18 *Ontario Commercial Year Book and Gazetteer* (Toronto: n.p., 1906), 750, https://archive.org/details/ontariocommerciaooslsnuoft.
19 Robertson, *History of the County of Bruce,* 78.
20 See ibid., 130.
21 "To Town with Uncle Tom in the 1890s," Laura Emma Jamieson fonds (LEMJ fonds), British Columbia Archives (BCA).
22 Robertson, *History of the County of Bruce,* 76.
23 Though religious faith could be empowering, as can be seen in the life of Ishbel, Lady Aberdeen, it is not often discussed in association with New Women. Nonetheless, religion was significant. See Veronica Strong-Boag, *Liberal Hearts and Coronets: The Lives and Times of Ishbel Marjoribanks Gordon and John Campbell Gordon, the Aberdeens* (Toronto: University of Toronto Press, 2015); and Jean Matthews, *The Rise of the New Woman: The Women's Movement in America, 1875–1930* (Chicago: Ivan R. Dee, 2003).
24 On the role of deaconesses in channelling "female energies in the proper direction," see John D. Thomas, "Servants of the Church: Canadian Methodist Deaconess Work, 1890–1926," *Canadian Historical Review (CHR)* 65, 3 (September 1984): 374. About one-third of the students who trained as deaconesses were nurses. Ibid., 381.

25 "Twenty-One Years of Mission Work in Toronto, 1886–1907: The Story of the Fred Victor Mission," 1907, http://uccdeaconesshistory.ca/wp-content/uploads/biopics/Twenty-One-Years-of-Mission-Work-in-Toronto-Fred-Victor-Mission-1907.pdf.
26 Thomas, "Servants of the Church," 386-87.
27 "The Book That Saved Me for Higher Education," typescript, n.d., LEMJ fonds, BCA.
28 Ibid.
29 OSCI Attendance Registers, 1896–1902, Owen Sound Schools, box 24B, S5F1, SBF19, Grey Roots Museum and Archives (GRMA).
30 Owen Sound Collegiate Institute: Announcement 1896–97, Pamphlets 1896, GRMA.
31 Ibid.
32 See Paul White, *Owen Sound: The Port City* (Toronto: Dundurn Books, 2000).
33 "Everything Was for the Mind in the 1890s," LEMJ fonds, BCA.
34 "My First Year as School Teacher," LEMJ fonds, BCA.
35 Quoted in "A Builders' Exchange," *Vancouver Daily World (VDW),* August 18, 1899.
36 See "Employers' Association Elects New Officers," *VDW,* March 17, 1909; and "Good Government League Elect Executive and Determine upon Campaign for Civic Betterment during the Coming Year," *VDW,* March 13, 1911.
37 "Supporters of Mayor Organize," *VDW,* December 29, 1917.
38 *VDW,* February 28, 1920; "World Ready for a Moses Declaration of Minister," *VDW,* May 3, 1923.
39 "Climbing Grouse Mountain, 62 Years Ago," LEMJ fonds, BCA.
40 "Carter, Neal M.," Memory BC, https://www.memorybc.ca/neal-m-carter. Mount Neal in Garibaldi Park is named after him. W.E. Ricker, "Neal Marshall Carter, 1902–1978," Obituary/Nécrologie, *Journal of the Fisheries Research Board of Canada* 36, 5 (1979): 595–96.
41 See John Calem, "Teaching the Teachers: Establishment and Early Years of the B.C. Provincial Normal Schools," *BC Studies* 61 (Spring 1984): 30–63.
42 "Teachers' Examinations," *VDW,* July 26, 1901.
43 "Gazette," *VDW,* October 3, 1902.
44 For a discussion of the significance of women's education and independence in Canada, see Linda M. Ambrose and Kristin Hall, "A New Woman in Print and Practice: The Canadian Literary Career of Madge Robertson Watt, 1890–1907," *History of Intellectual Culture* 7, 1 (2007): 1–19. For an indication that the New Woman had arrived, to a very uncertain welcome, in British Columbia during the previous decade, see Françoise Le Jeune, "The American New Woman and Her Influence on the Daughters of the Empire of British Columbia," in *New Woman Hybridities: Femininity, Feminism and International Consumer Culture, 1880–1930,* ed. Ann Helmann and Margaret Beetham (London: Routledge, 2004), 74–89.
45 Susan M. Lambeth, "A Short History of Fernie," typescript, Lambeth Jeune Dang Research Group, January 29, 1979, 2.
46 "Riding Trails in the Crow's Nest Pass," typescript, LEMJ fonds, BCA.
47 See "The Scarlett Woman," *Fernie Free Press (FFP),* August 4, 1899. See also "Police Court," *FFP,* February 6, 1900; and "Local and General," *FFP,* August 17, 1900.
48 Wayne Norton and Chris Chala, "A Century of Education in the Elk Valley," in *A World Apart: The Crowsnest Communities of Alberta and British Columbia,* ed. Wayne Norton and Tom Langford (Kamloops: Plateau Press, 2002), 33.
49 Ibid., 33–35.
50 "The Labour Question in B.C." *FFP,* August 15, 1899.

51 Ross McCormack, *Reformers, Rebels, and Revolutionaries: The Western Canadian Radical Movement, 1899–1919* (Toronto: University of Toronto Press, 1977), 9; Leslie A. Robertson, *Imagining Difference: Legend, Curse, and Spectacle in a Canadian Mining Town* (Vancouver: UBC Press, 2005), 8.
52 See "Local and General," August 24, 1900; "The Solution of the Labor Problem," September 21, 1900; "Worse than Chinamen," October 19, 1900; and "The Slav and Woman," April 5, 1901, all in the pro-unionist and generally reform-minded *FFP.*
53 Robert McDonald, "'Simply a Working Man': Tom Uphill of Fernie," in Norton and Langford, *A World Apart,* 105.
54 Ibid., 104.
55 "Riding Trails in the Crow's Nest Pass," typescript, LEMJ fonds, BCA.
56 "The Student from Mexico," Part One, "Climbing the Lizard Range in 1904," typescript, LEMJ fonds, BCA.
57 "Early Summer Schools on the Prairie," LEMJ fonds, BCA.
58 See Anne Rochon Ford, *A Path Not Strewn with Roses; One Hundred Years of Women at the University of Toronto, 1884–1984* (Toronto: Governing Council, University of Toronto, 1985); and Nancy Ramsay Thompson, "The Controversy over the Admission of Women to University College, University of Toronto" (master's thesis, University of Toronto, 1974).
59 See Sara Burke, "New Women and Old Romans: Co-education at the University of Toronto, 1884–95," *CHR* 80, 2 (June 1999): 219–41.
60 Ibid., 221.
61 Alyson E. King, "The Experience of the Second Generation of Women Students at Ontario Universities, 1900–1930" (PhD diss., Ontario Institute for Studies in Education, 1999), 134.
62 Ibid., 130.
63 Ibid., 74.
64 Ibid., 79.
65 LEMJ, "The Women's View Point," *The Federationist,* July 25, 1940.
66 King, "The Experience of the Second Generation," 223.
67 Diana Pederson, "'The Call to Service': The YWCA and the Canadian College Woman, 1886–1920," in *Youth, University and Canadian Society: Essays in the Social History of Higher Education,* ed. Paul Axelrod and John Reid (Montreal and Kingston: McGill-Queen's University Press, 1989), 187.
68 King, "The Experience of the Second Generation," 201.
69 Ibid., 201.
70 Ibid., 232.
71 Pederson, "'The Call to Service,'" 199.
72 *Torontonensis,* 1908, 390.
73 See Kathy James, "Reforming Reform: Toronto's Settlement House Movement, 1900–1920," *CHR* 82, 1 (March 2001): 55–90; Diana Pederson, "Keeping Our Good Girls Good: The YWCA and the 'Girl Problem' 1870–1930," *Canadian Women's Studies* 7, 4 (Winter 1986): 20–24; and Carolyn Strange, *Toronto's Girl Problem: The Perils and Pleasures of the City, 1880–1930* (Toronto: University of Toronto Press, 1995).
74 J.S. Woodsworth, *Strangers within Our Gates: Or, Coming Canadians* (Toronto: F.C. Stephenson, 1909; repr. Toronto: University of Toronto Press, 1972); and *My Neighbor: A Study of City Conditions* (Toronto: Missionary Society of the Methodist Church, 1911; repr. Toronto University of Toronto Press, 1972).

75 James, "Reforming Reform," 76.
76 Cathy Leigh James, "Gender, Class and Ethnicity in the Organization of Neighbourhood and Nation: The Role of Toronto's Settlement Houses in the Formation of the Canadian State, 1902 to 1914" (PhD diss., University of Toronto, 1997), 345.
77 James, "Reforming Reform," 65.
78 Alberta Bastedo, from the 1905 *Varsity*, quoted in ibid., 61.
79 King, "The Experience of the Second Generation," 208. See also Kathy James, "Practical Diversions and Educational Amusements: Evangelia House and the Advent of Canada's Settlement Movement, 1902–09," *Historical Studies in Education* 10, 1–2 (1998): 49; and Pederson, "'Keeping Our Good Girls Good.'"
80 The speaker may well have been Sara Carson, the American director of Evangelia House, who, at a January 1904 University Women's Club meeting, said that "the workers must not think that the benefit will all be on one side," although she did not spell out the benefits. Laura Jamieson quoted in James, "Reforming Reform," 60.
81 Laura Marshall, "Our Heritage," *Torontonensis*, 1908, 81.
82 "Marshall, Laura E," *Torontonensis*, 1908, 78. See also the important study by PearlAnn Reichwein, *Climber's Paradise: Making Canada's Mountain Parks, 1906–1974* (Edmonton: University of Alberta Press, 2014).
83 "First Summer Camp in Yoho Park," GMC [General Mountaineering Camp] Report, 1906.
84 LEMJ, "Climbing Crow's Nest Mt. in 1907," LEMJ fonds, BCA.
85 Ibid.
86 "Marshall, Laura E.," *Torontonensis*, 1908, 78.
87 Only five members of the Women's Literary Society executive between 1891 and 1921 took part in the settlement movement (and it is not clear if Laura was among them). See Charles Morden Levi, "Where the Famous People Were? The Origins, Activities and Future Careers of Student Leaders at University College, Toronto, 1854–1973" (PhD diss., University of Toronto, 1998), 284.
88 James, "Reforming Reform," 64.
89 Quoted in Susan Walsh, "Equality, Emancipation and a More Just World: Leading Women in the B.C. CCF" (master's thesis, Simon Fraser University, 1984), 126fn8.
90 Robert Stamp, "Teaching Girls Their 'God Given Place in Life,'" *Atlantis* 2, 2 (Spring 1977): 24.
91 "The Former Grand Trunk/Canadian National Railway Property," Building Stories, http://www.buildingstories.co/report.php?ListType=bheritage_data&ID=3767&lang=en.
92 See Adelaide Leitch, *Floodtides of Fortune: The Story of Stratford and the Progress of the City through Two Centuries* (Stratford: City of Stratford, 1980).
93 "I.A.M. Local Lodge 1660. History of the Local Lodge," http://www.aim1660.org/historiqueEN.html; Betty Jo Belton, "Stratford's Proud Labour History," *Stratford Beacon Herald*, September 4, 2010, http://www.stratfordbeaconherald.com/2010/09/04/stratfords-proud-labour-history.
94 See Leitch, Chapter 6, "Six Decades of the YWCA," in *Floodtides of Fortune*. See also the impact of YWCA employment with girls on another future CCFer and member of the Women's International League for Peace and Freedom in Nancy Knickerbocker, *No Plaster Saint: The Life of Mildred Osterhout Fahrni* (Vancouver: Talon Books, 2001), 37.
95 "John Stuart Jamieson," *Torontonensis*, 1905, 71.
96 Levi, "Where the Famous People Were?" 135.

97 Brian J. Fraser, *Church, College, and Clergy: A History of Theological Education at Knox College, Toronto, 1844–1994* (Montreal and Kingston: McGill-Queen's University Press, 1995), 91.
98 Ibid., 103. Another influential Knox disciple of Drummond was Professor T.B. Kilpatrick, who arrived from Scotland in 1905. Ibid., 116.
99 Ibid., 91. See also Strong-Boag, *Liberal Hearts and Coronets,* 83.
100 Table 3.8, "Location after 5 Years for Lit. Officers 1891–1921," in Levi, "Where the Famous People Were?" 223.
101 "Cattle Thieves Get 2-Year Sentence," *VDW,* April 20, 1911, 19.
102 "Social and Personal," *VDW,* April 1, 1911, 9.
103 [Alice Ashworth Townley], *Points in the Laws of British Columbia regarding the Legal Status of Women* (Vancouver: A.A. Ashworth, 1911), 3.

Chapter 2: The New Woman as Wife, Suffragist, and Activist, 1911–18

1 "Queen Charlotte Islands," *Encyclopedia Britannia,* 1911, 730.
2 On the significance of ethnicity and class in asserting white superiority, see Sarah Carter, "Britishness, 'Foreignness,' Women and Land in Western Canada 1890s–1920s," *Humanities Research* 13 (November 2006): 43–60.
3 *Vancouver Daily World (VDW),* May 9, 1915.
4 *VDW,* January 26, 1916.
5 "Reg Smith," in *Pioneer Tales of Burnaby: Early Burnaby as Recalled by the Settlers Themselves,* ed. Michael Stone (Burnaby: Corporation of the District of Burnaby, 1987), 80.
6 "John Boberg," in Stone, *Pioneer Tales of Burnaby,* 47.
7 See *Vancouver Sun (VS),* March 10, 1918; and *VS,* March 18, 1918.
8 Laura Jamieson (LEMJ) to C. Cleverdon, April 19, 1944, Catherine L. Cleverdon Papers, Library and Archives Canada.
9 On this development in Vancouver, see Robert A.J. McDonald, *Making Vancouver: Class, Status and Social Boundaries, 1863–1913* (Vancouver: UBC Press, 1996), 125.
10 Catherine L. Cleverdon, *The Woman Suffrage Movement in Canada* (Toronto: University of Toronto Press, 1950; rept. Toronto: University of Toronto Press, 1974), 86; and Linda Louise Hale, "The British Columbia Woman Suffrage Movement, 1890–1917" (master's thesis, University of British Columbia, 1977), 29.
11 See Veronica Strong-Boag, "The Citizenship Debates: Race and Gender in the 1885 Franchise Act," in *Constructing Canadian Citizenship: Historical Readings,* ed. R. Adamoski, D. Chunn, and R. Menzies (Toronto: Broadview Press, 2002), 69–94.
12 See William O'Neill, *Everyone Was Brave: The Rise and Fall of Feminism in America* (New York: Times New Books, 1969). The need for courage has too often been ignored and deserves emphasizing.
13 See Jenny Roth and Lori Chambers, "Introduction," in Minnie Smith [1874–1934], *Is It Just?* (Toronto: Methodist Book and Publishing House, 1911; repr., Toronto: University of Toronto Press, 2011), vi.
14 The first pamphlet was *Daughters, Wives and Mothers in British Columbia: Some Laws regarding Them* (Vancouver: Moore Printing, 1913); the last was *Laws for Women and Children in British Columbia* (Vancouver: McBeath-Campbell, 1939). The revealing title change shifted its subjects from dependants to autonomous subjects.
15 McDonald, *Making Vancouver,* 117.

16 Quoted in Peter Campbell, *Canadian Marxists and the Search for a Third Way* (Montreal and Kingston: McGill-Queen's University Press, 2000), 38.
17 McDonald, *Making Vancouver,* 118.
18 For an initial appraisal, see Veronica Strong-Boag, "Precedents for Today's 'Big Tent' Liberalism: British Columbia's First Woman MLA, Mary Ellen Spear Smith (1863–1933)," *Activehistory,* February 2, 2018, http://activehistory.ca/2018/02/precedents-for-todays-big-tent-liberalism-british-columbias-first-woman-mla-mary-ellen-spear-smith-1863-1933/.
19 Hale, "The British Columbia Woman Suffrage Movement," 59.
20 Ibid., 52.
21 "Women's Names Will Go on Voters' List," *Vancouver Province (VP),* August 26, 1911.
22 On the complications presented by Alfred, Lord Tennyson, for feminists, see Marion Shaw, *Alfred Lord Tennyson* (Brighton: Harvester, 1988).
23 See the front cover of *The Champion (TC),* April 1913.
24 Margaret Ormsby, *British Columbia: A History* (Vancouver: Macmillan, 1958), ch. 13.
25 B. Pullen-Burry, *From Halifax to Vancouver* (London: Mills and Boons, 1912), 343.
26 Doreen Madge Weppler, "Early Forms of Political Activity among White Women in British Columbia, 1880–1925" (master's thesis, Simon Fraser University, 1971), 106.
27 See Joan Sangster, *Dreams of Equality: Women on the Canadian Left, 1920–1950* (Don Mills, ON: McClelland and Stewart, 1989).
28 "The Political Equality League (Victoria Branch)," *TC,* August 1912, 6. See also Hale, "The British Columbia Woman Suffrage Movement," 60.
29 Maria Grant, "The Editor of 'The Week,'" *TC,* May 1913, 8.
30 "In Club Circles," *VDW,* October 2, 1914.
31 See *VP,* October 21, 1914. See also *VP,* October 20, 1914.
32 "Ask Suffrage in South Vancouver," *VS,* September 28, 1917.
33 See Gillian M. Weiss, "'As Women and as Citizens': Clubwomen in Vancouver, 1910–1928" (PhD diss., University of British Columbia, 1983), 88.
34 *VP,* December 4, 1915.
35 LEMJ, "Getting the Vote for Women Forty Years Ago," n.d., LEMJ fonds, British Columbia Archives (BCA).
36 *VP,* April 24, 1915.
37 *VP,* January 27, 1915.
38 *VDW,* January 13, 1915.
39 *VDW,* May 9, 1915.
40 *VDW,* August 29, 1915.
41 *VW,* April 27, 1916. See also Mrs. W.A. McConkey's address on proportional representation to the University Women's Club, VW, November 13, 1916, and her address to the Woman's Forum of South Vancouver, ibid., March 24, 1917.
42 "Must Practice Close Economy," *VDW,* July 14, 1916.
43 LEMJ, "Getting the Vote for Women Forty Years Ago," LEMJ Fonds, BCA.
44 "In Club Circles," *VDW,* January 13, 1916.
45 "Laws for Women," *VDW,* March 22, 1916.
46 *VP,* March 22, 1916.
47 *VP,* September 11, 1916.
48 *VP,* November 28, 1916.
49 "Women Must Prepare to Serve Humanity When Ballot Secured," *VS,* November 27, 1916.

50 "Women Want Minimum Wage," *VDW,* June 20, 1917. See endorsement by New Era League of mother's pensions and minimum wage in "League Urges Food Economy," *VDW,* January 16, 1918.
51 LEMJ, "Getting the Vote for Women Forty Years Ago."
52 *VP,* January 17, 1916; *VP,* August 5, 1916. Evidently, this instruction met with the approval of the Union of B.C. Municipalities. *VP,* November 28, 1916. See also Laura's speech to the Women's Forum of South Vancouver, held in the Liberal Club rooms, supporting the municipal vote for wives of absent soldiers. *VP,* September 25, 1916.
53 *VP,* September 20, 1916; "Social Notes," *VDW,* January 29, 1917.
54 "In Club Circles," *VDW,* December 9, 1916.
55 "Conscription of Profits Urged," *VDW,* May 2, 1917.
56 *VP,* September 11, 1915; *Western Clarion,* April 7, 1916.
57 *VDW,* November 14, 1916. She was also involved with the local Arbor Day Committee. See "Vancouver Arbor Day Committee – Its Composition and Work," *VDW,* March 17, 1917.
58 Elsie MacGill, *My Mother the Judge* (Toronto: Ryerson Press, 1955), 142.
59 See "Liberal Meeting," *VDW,* April 19, 1916; "Liberals Form Federal Body," *VDW,* January 22, 1917; and *VS,* December 6, 1916.
60 "Burnaby," *VS,* July 6, 1917.
61 "Reception Is Given by Liberal Women," *VDW,* March 10, 1916.
62 "Woman Suffrage Is Assured in Province," *VDW,* November 27, 1915.
63 "Women Must Prepare to Serve Humanity When Ballot Secured," *VS,* November 27, 1916.
64 McDonald, *Making Vancouver,* 119.
65 "Strong Pleas Made for Woman's Suffrage," *VDW,* February 22, 1916. See also her "Women and the Franchise" address to the open meeting of the Women's Educational Club of New Westminster's Columbia College. *VDW,* September 19, 1916.
66 "Women Wanting the Vote Have Nothing to Expect from Conservatives," *VS,* March 14, 1916.
67 Dr. Ryan, "Are Opposed to Referendum," *Daily Colonist,* April 27, 1916.
68 "Women Working Hard for Empire," *VDW,* June 10, 1916.
69 "Mrs. Pankhurst Tells Local Suffragists of Women's Work in War," *VS,* June 10, 1916.
70 "Thwarting the Women," *VS,* April 19, 1916.
71 Veronica Strong-Boag, "Reading Referendums: From Brexit in the U.K. to Women Suffrage in Canada," *BC Studies Blog,* August 2016, http://www.bcstudies.com/?q=blog/recurrent-voices-part-2-reading-referendums-brexit-uk-women-suffrage-bc.
72 See *Electoral History of British Columbia, 1871–1986* (Victoria: Elections BC, 1988).
73 "What Will They Do with It?" *Maclean's Magazine,* July 1, 1916.
74 *VP,* September 22, 1916.
75 Robin Fisher, *Duff Pattullo of British Columbia* (Toronto: University of Toronto Press, 1991), 129–30.
76 See "Suffrage Leaders Are Opposed to Franchise Act as Now Proposed," *VS,* September 11, 1917; "More Entitled to Vote Than Before," *VS,* September 23, 1917; and "May Women Vote in Federal Elections," *VS,* October 18, 1917.
77 "Mr. H.H. Stevens, M.P., Justifies Position," *Victoria Colonist,* October 2, 1917.
78 Anne Anderson Perry, "Some Facts regarding the Federal Franchise for Women," *Western Woman's Weekly,* March 8, 1919.

79 LEMJ to Violet McNaughton (VM), June 8, 1933, Violet McNaughton fonds (VM fonds), Provincial Archives of Saskatchewan (PAS).
80 "John Waplington," in Stone, *Pioneer Tales of Burnaby*, 336.
81 LEMJ to VM, July 1, 1934, VM fonds, PAS.
82 Quoted in Marilyn J. Harrison, "The Social Influence of the United Church of Canada in British Columbia, 1900–1960," (master's thesis, University of British Columbia, 1975), 27fn36.
83 LEMJ, "Galsworthy at His Best," *British Columbia Monthly*, month unidentified, 1918.
84 George Watson, *The Lost Literature of Socialism* (Cambridge: Lutterworth Press, 1998), 11.
85 Eric Damer, "Town and Gown: The Early History of the Vancouver Institute" (master's thesis, University of British Columbia, 1995), 13.
86 Ibid., ix.
87 Ibid., 48.
88 "Come on Reds," *Ubyssey*, December 2, 1920.

Chapter 3: Still Bettering the World, 1918–26

1 Nellie McClung, *In Times Like These* (New York: D. Appleton, 1915; University of Pennsylvania Digital Library, n.d.), http://digital.library.upenn.edu/women/mcclung/times/times.html.
2 "Law Students Prove Splendid Dance Hosts," *Vancouver Daily World (VDW)*, February 5, 1921.
3 "Social Evening at Home of Mrs. Farris Is Enjoyed by Club," *VDW*, December 10, 1923.
4 See "Annual Concert Held at Industrial Home Wednesday Evening," *VDW*, December 20, 1923.
5 "University Women Present Series of Diminutive Dramas," *VDW*, March 26, 1923.
6 "Nations League Branch Formed," *VDW*, November 3, 1923, lists him as a member of the general committee. On the executive were politician H.H. Stevens as honorary president, Mary Ellen Smith as second vice-president, and Professor Mack Eastman of UBC as secretary.
7 See *Report of the Fourth Congress of the Women's International League for Peace and Freedom* (Washington, DC: Women's International League for Peace and Freedom, 1924), https://archive.org/details/reportoffourthco24wome; and Laura Emma Marshall Jamieson (LEMJ) to Violet McNaughton (VM), undated letter, Violet McNaughton fonds (VM fonds), Provincial Archives of Saskatchewan (PAS).
8 "Boys' Summer School Planned by Y.M.C.A.," *VDW*, June 16, 1921.
9 "In 'Y' Circles," *VDW*, August 5, 1922. See also "Forty Boys Spend Vacation in School," *VDW*, July 23, 1921.
10 "Burnaby Magistrate Addresses P.-T.A. at Nightingale School," *VDW*, November 29, 1922.
11 "Changing Ideals of Youth of Today Are Subject of Address," *VDW*, April 18, 1923.
12 "Interesting Addresses Are Feature of P.T.A. Meeting," *VDW*, October 1, 1923. See also Veronica Strong-Boag, "Intruders in the Nursery: Childcare Professionals Reshape the Years One to Five," in *Childhood and Family in Canadian History*, ed. Joy Parr (Toronto: McClelland and Stewart, 1982), 160–78.
13 "Has Been Beaten for 19 Years Wife Tells Magistrate," *VDW*, June 10, 1922.
14 Angus McLaren, *Our Own Master Race: Eugenics in Canada, 1885–1945* (Toronto: McClelland and Stewart, 1990), 96n42.

15 Quoted in Mary Kinnear, *Margaret McWilliams: An Interwar Feminist* (Montreal and Kingston: McGill-Queen's University Press, 1991), 118.
16 Quoted in *Vancouver Sun,* December 1, 1918.
17 "A Woman's Party," *Western Woman's Weekly (WWW),* March 28, 1918.
18 Editorial, *WWW,* August 10, 1918.
19 Gillian M. Weiss, "'As Women and as Citizens': Clubwomen in Vancouver, 1910–1928" (PhD diss., University of British Columbia, 1983), 135–36.
20 See Veronica Strong-Boag, "Mary Ellen Spear Smith," Women Suffrage and Beyond, http://womensuffrage.org/?p=21014.
21 See Margaret Fairley, "The Women's Party," *The Rebel,* November 1918, 27–29.
22 "Mrs. Ralph Smith Opens Her Election Campaign," *VDW,* January 18, 1918.
23 Ibid.
24 See Margaret Little, "Claiming a Unique Place: The Introduction of Mothers' Pensions in B.C.," *BC Studies (BCS)* 105–6 (1995): 80–102.
25 *Victoria Daily Colonist,* April 10, 1920, quoted in Lisa Pasolli, "'Talkin' Day Care Blues': Motherhood, Work, and Child Care in Twentieth-Century British Columbia" (PhD diss., University of Victoria, 2012), 81. Although I have relied on her dissertation here, Lisa Pasolli has revised it as the excellent *Working Mothers and the Child Care Dilemma: A History of British Columbia Social Policy* (Vancouver: UBC Press, 2015).
26 *VDW,* April 30, 1918.
27 Helen Gregory MacGill, *Laws for Women and Children in British Columbia* (Vancouver: McBeath-Campbell, 1928), 3.
28 Untitled typescript, first line "What were the laws like a hundred years ago in B.C.?" p. 4, LEMJ fonds, British Columbia Archives (BCA).
29 Mrs. Ralph Smith, "Legislation and the Lady," *WWW,* March 29, 1919.
30 "Women Are Coming into Their Own," *WWW,* November 1, 1919.
31 Christopher A. Clarkson, "Remoralizing Families? Family Regulation and State Formation in British Columbia, 1862–1940" (PhD diss., University of Ottawa, 2002), 349.
32 "Meeting to Discuss Minimum Wage," *VDW,* November 27, 1918.
33 Anna Gooding, "Policing Women: Clubwomen, Policewomen, and Delinquent Girls in Vancouver, 1910–1930" (BA hons. thesis, University of British Columbia, 2015), 39.
34 "Forum Committee Suggests Women for City Council," *VDW,* March 16, 1918.
35 "Political Equality League Luncheon," *VDW,* June 28, 1920.
36 See "Nominations Made by New Era League," *Vancouver Province (VP),* September 9, 1921; "Women's Forum Commences Work," *VP,* September 16, 1921; and "New Era League Endorses Action of Mrs. MacGill," *VP,* January 20, 1922.
37 "The Dawn of a New Era," *WWW,* December 28, 1918.
38 *British Columbia Federationist,* August 30, 1918.
39 J.S. Woodsworth, *Re-construction from the Viewpoint of Labour* (Winnipeg: Hecla Press, 1919), 13.
40 Ibid., 14.
41 "Announcements," *VDW,* November 13, 1920.
42 "Announcements," *VDW,* June 28, 1920.
43 "Announcements," *VDW,* March 2, 1921.
44 Quoted in Gail Cuthbert Brandt et al., *Canadian Women: A History,* 3rd ed. (Toronto: Nelson, 2011), 408. For similar sentiments, see Anonymous, "The Confessions of a She-Politician," *Maclean's Magazine,* June 1, 1922.

45 Joan Sangster, "Canadian Women in Radical Politics and Labour, 1920–1950" (PhD diss., McMaster University, 1984), 164–65. Smith won 3.2 percent of the vote and 6,078 votes. See also Sheila Nickols, "Up with the Petticoats! Down with the Trousers! From Suffragist to Political Candidate: Mary Graves of Victoria," *British Columbia Historical News* 34, 3 (Summer 2001): 2–7. On Woodsworth's support for deaconesses, see Matthew G. Newfeld, "'To Lead Them to the Higher Life': Women Workers at All People's Mission, 1907–1917," *Historical Papers* (Canadian Society of Church History) (1994): 91.

46 Robert K. Burkinshaw, "Conservative Protestantism and the Modernist Challenge in Vancouver, 1917–1927," *BCS* 85 (Spring 1990): 24–42.

47 See "Dr. N.S. Hardikar," *Victoria Daily Colonist,* March 23, 1921.

48 "No Disloyalty in Seeking Good," *VDW,* March 21, 1921.

49 "Mrs. Jamieson Addresses P.-T. on Peace League," *VDW,* December 14, 1921. See also "Women's International League for Peace," *WWW,* November 26, 1922. In 1933, Angell won the Nobel Peace Prize even as he condemned fascism and endorsed collective security. On WILPF and its affinity for Angell's arguments, see Lucian M. Ashworth, "Women and War: The Women's International League for Peace and Freedom (WILPF) and the Problem of Collective Security" (paper presented at the Transnational Actors in War and Peace Conference, St. John's, Newfoundland, July 14–15, 2014), 9.

50 LEMJ, "The Will to Peace and the Will to War," *WWW,* January 7, 1922.

51 "The World's Mail. India Pays Its Own Civil Service," *VDW,* September 11, 1922.

52 "Peace League Hears Review of War Book," *VDW,* February 8, 1923.

53 Donald A. Wright, *The Professionalization of History in English Canada* (Toronto: University of Toronto Press, 2015), 84. See too "Come on Reds," *Ubyssey,* December 2, 1920, 3, which features Eastman as the honorary president of the Student Socialist Party when it was addressed by Woodsworth and Jamieson. S. Mack Eastman (1882–1968) was a contemporary of Laura's at the University of Toronto and studied in Paris and at Columbia. Eastman moved to UBC in 1915 and remained until 1925 (interrupted by war service 1916–1918). From 1919–25, he headed History, before leaving for the International Labour Office in Geneva. He retired to Vancouver in 1949, becoming active alongside Laura in the United Nations Association and the Canadian Institute of International Affairs. See the Mack Eastman fonds, Rare Books and Special Collections, University of British Columbia.

54 "War Pictures Start Dispute," *VDW,* February 15, 1923.

55 "Women's Lit," *Ubyssey,* February 14, 1924.

56 Melinda Plastas, *A Band of Noble Women: Racial Politics in the Women's Peace Movement* (Syracuse: Syracuse University Press, 2011), 10. See also Thomas Socknat, *Witness against War: Pacifism in Canada, 1900–1945* (Toronto: University of Toronto Press, 1987); Veronica Strong-Boag, "Peace-Making Women: Canada, 1919–1939," in *Women and Peace: Theoretical, Historical, and Practical Perspectives,* ed. Ruth Roach Pierson (London: Croom Helm, 1987), 170–91: and Ashworth, "Women and War."

57 LEMJ to Emily Greene Balch, August 12, 1922, quoted in Irene Howard, *The Struggle for Social Justice in British Columbia: Helena Gutteridge, the Unknown Reformer* (Vancouver: UBC Press, 1992), 246–47. On Balch, who won the Nobel Prize for Peace in 1946 for her work with WILPF, see Kristen E. Gwinn, *Emily Greene Balch: The Long Road to Internationalism* (Urbana: University of Illinois Press, 2010).

58 *The Totem,* 1925, 73.

59 Sheilagh L. Steer, "The Beliefs of Violet McNaughton: Adult Educator, 1909–1929" (master's thesis, University of Saskatchewan, 1979), 134.

60 Terry Crowley, "Parents in a Hurry: The Early Home and School Movement in Ontario," *Histoire sociale/Social History* 19, 38 (November 1986): 324.
61 LEMJ to VM, June 12, 1924, VM fonds, PAS.
62 LEMJ to VM, April 24, 1925, on PTA Office of President letterhead, VM fonds, PAS.
63 "A Public Library," *Burnaby Broadcast,* June 23, 1927; see also N.F. Black, "A Library Survey in British Columbia," *The B.C. Teacher,* April 1927, 41–45.
64 Dave Obee, *The Library Book: A History of Service to British Columbia* (Vancouver: B.C. Library Association, 2011), 90.
65 Marjorie C. Holmes, *Library Service in British Columbia* (Victoria: Public Library Commission, 1959), 15.
66 LEMJ, "Canada First," *Canadian Trade Unionist,* October 21, 1926, 2. This seems to be a reworked and secularized version of a 1924 poem entitled "American First" by Bishop George Ashton Oldham (see United States, Library of Congress, https://www.loc.gov/resource/rbpe.20803800/).
67 Ibid.
68 Weiss, "'As Women and as Citizens,'" 110.
69 *Chilliwack Progress,* December 2, 1926.
70 "A Friend of Youth: Jamieson, John Stuart," *VP,* quoted in *New Outlook,* December 22, 1926, A73–0026//175 (29), Student Files, University of Toronto Archives.
71 John Stuart Jamieson, Probate P-11643, GR-1415.12535, microfilm B08736, accession no. 91–4202, BC Supreme Court (Vancouver), BCA. My thanks to Ashley Forseille for retrieving this file.

Chapter 4: Widowed Judge and Progressive Activist, 1927–39

1 Quoted in Walter Volovsek, "Time Windows: Lilette Mahon: Art in Living," *Castlegar News,* October 22, 2015, updated October 24, 2015, https://www.castlegarnews.com/opinion/time-windows-lilette-mahon-art-in-living/.
2 Laura Jamieson (LEMJ) to Violet McNaughton (VM), June 8, 1933, Violet McNaughton fonds (VM fonds), Provincial Archives of Saskatchewan (PAS).
3 LEMJ to VM, August 19, 1936, VM fonds, PAS.
4 LEMJ to VM, July 28, 1935, VM fonds, PAS.
5 LEMJ to VM, January 3, 1930, VM fonds, PAS.
6 LEMJ to VM, July 28, 1935, VM fonds, PAS.
7 LEMJ to VM, April 9, 1935, VM fonds, PAS.
8 "Duties of Husband Assumed by Wife," *Toronto Globe and Mail (TGM),* March 10, 1927.
9 Anne Anderson Perry, "Our Women Magistrates: An Examination of Their Point of View," *Chatelaine,* July 1929, 11, 38–41, 50.
10 "Women and Their Work," *Chatelaine,* October 1930, 24.
11 H.M. Cassidy, "Report of the Advisory Committee on Juvenile Delinquency", October 3, 1936.
12 See Pernille Jakobsen, "Bench–Breakers? Women Judges in Prairie Canada, 1916–1980" (PhD diss., University of Calgary, 2014). Her list of office-holders doesn't include Laura Jamieson. See 12n40.
13 Marilyn Callahan and Christopher Walmsley, "Rethinking Child Welfare Reform in British Columbia, 1900–60," in *People, Politics, and Child Welfare,* ed. Leslie T. Foster and Brian Wharf (Vancouver: UBC Press, 2007), 24.

14 M. Moscrop, "The Life and Times of Amy Leigh," *Canadian Welfare* 34, 3 (1958): 120–25. See also her views, as director of social services for Vancouver, on the evacuation of Japanese Canadians as an unfortunate necessity in Ann Gomer Sunahara, *The Politics of Racism: The Uprooting of Japanese Canadians during the Second World War* (Toronto: J. Lorimer, 1981), ch. 4.
15 "Juvenile Court Committee," *Burnaby Broadcast (BB),* June 30, 1927.
16 British Columbia, *Report of the Royal Commission on Mental Hygiene* (Victoria: King's Printer, 1927), http://www.llbc.leg.bc.ca/public/pubdocs/bcdocs_rc/338733/338733_report_rc_mental_hygiene.pdf. See also Angus McLaren, *Our Own Master Race: Eugenics in Canada, 1885–1945* (Toronto: McClelland and Stewart, 1990); and Nic Clarke, "'Sacred Daemons': Exploring British Columbian Society's Perceptions of 'Mentally Deficient' Children, 1870–1930," *BC Studies (BCS)* 144 (2004–05): 61–89.
17 All quotes come from Laura E. Jamieson, *Sex Education in the Child Welfare Programme* (Victoria: Provincial Board of Health, 1928). See also her chairing of the Burnaby Woman's Forum discussion of tuberculosis, "Tuberculosis," *VW,* November 17, 1915.
18 Jamieson, *Sex Education,* 16–17.
19 *BB,* August 28, 1930, 2.
20 Callahan and Walmsley, "Rethinking Child Welfare Reform," 15.
21 E. Paulson, G. Zilm, and E. Warbinek, "Profile of a Leader: Pioneer Government Advisor: Laura Holland RN RRC, CBE LLD (1883–1956)," *Nursing Leadership* 13, 3 (September 2000): 36–39.
22 "Social Group Work: A Panel Discussion," *Proceedings of the 6th Canadian Conference on Social Work* (Vancouver, June 21, 22, 23, 1938).
23 "Mrs. Jamieson Tells about California," *Vancouver News-Herald (VNH),* June 15, 1938.
24 "Parent-Teacher Group Wants Health Insurance," *VNH,* April 14, 1939.
25 LEMJ to VM, November 18, [193?], VM fonds, PAS. See also Mary Kinnear, *Woman of the World: Mary McGeachy and International Co-operation* (Toronto: University of Toronto Press, 2004).
26 LEMJ to VM, October 14, 1928, VM fonds, PAS.
27 LEMJ to VM, March 27, 1929, VM fonds, PAS, quoted in Terence Crowley, *Agnes Macphail and the Politics of Equality* (Toronto: J. Lorimer, 1990), 64–65.
28 See LEMJ, "Hands Off China: Vancouver Committee," *Western Producer,* March 24, 1927. See also Tom Buchanan, "China and the British Left in the Twentieth Century: Transnational Perspectives," *Labor History* 54, 5 (2013): 541–44.
29 Thomas Socknat, "Witness against War: Pacifism in Canada, 1900–1945" (PhD diss., McMaster University, 1981), 214. See, for example "Mrs. Jamieson to Speak on 'Nations and Peace,'" *Winnipeg Tribune (WT),* October 22, 1927.
30 Michael Welton, "Echoes of Those Now Silent: Canadian Women's Associations as Learning Sites," 8, http://www.populareducation.co.za/sites/default/files/ECHOES%20OF%20THOSE%20NOW%20SILENT%202(1).pdf.
31 Sheilagh L. Steer, "The Beliefs of Violet McNaughton: Adult Educator, 1909–1929" (master's thesis, University of Saskatchewan, 1979), 134.
32 "Suggests Peace Conference of Canadian Women," *The U.F.A.,* December 15, 1928. This publication was the official organ of the United Farmers of Alberta, the Alberta Wheat Pool, and other provincial marketing pools.
33 LEMJ, "Education for Peace," *Western Producer (WP),* January 24, 1929.
34 Socknat, "Witness against War," 216.

35 "Says Wider Vision Is Present Need of Canadian Women," *TGM,* July 9, 1929. See also "Such a Small World!" *TGM,* July 9, 1929.
36 See "Westerners' Work for Peace Praised," *Montreal Gazette,* July 10, 1929.
37 Quoted in "Homey Little Talks to Settle Questions of World Import: Mrs. Jamieson Has Small Faith in Chilly Diplomatic Conferences," *TGM,* September 10, 1929.
38 "Machine for Peace Is Object of Women: Speeches in Discard," *TGM,* September 9, 1929.
39 VM to LEMJ, October 9, 1930, VM fonds, PAS, quoted in Christa L. Scowby, "'Divine Discontent': Women, Identity, and the *Western Producer*" (master's thesis, University of Saskatchewan, 1996), 31.
40 See "Events Club Hears about Communism," *VNH,* February 21, 1934.
41 "Systems of Countries Form Lecture Subject," *VNH,* November 21, 1933.
42 LEMJ to VM, July 3, 1932, VM fonds, PAS.
43 McNaughton's introduction to Laura Jamieson, "Education for Peace," *WP,* January [day unknown], 1929. Thanks to Georgie Taylor for reminding me of this and the following quote.
44 LEMJ to VM, June 11, 1933, VM fonds, PAS.
45 Lucian M. Ashworth, "Women and War: The Women's International League for Peace and Freedom (WILPF) and the Problem of Collective Security" (paper presented at the Transnational Actors in War and Peace Conference, St. John's, Newfoundland, July 14–15, 2014), 5.
46 Ibid., 3.
47 Byrne Hope Sanders, "The Challenge of 1934," *Chatelaine,* January 1934, 2 (capitalization in original).
48 Byrne Hope Sanders, "Why Not a Dramatic Peace?" *Chatelaine,* February 1934, 2.
49 Irene Parlby, "Unthinking Women and Peace," *Chatelaine,* May 1934, 2.
50 Ibid.
51 Byrne Hope Sanders, "Home Women in the World," *Chatelaine,* November 1934, 2.
52 See Vera Brittain, "Youth and Peace," *Chatelaine,* June 1935, 22–23; and Vera Brittain, "Can Youth Win the Peace?" *Chatelaine,* September 1935, 16–17.
53 "Women's Progress Most Vital Event during Past 100 Years," *VNH,* December 3, 1935. The speaker was Mary Dignam.
54 LEMJ to VM, March 4, 1938, VM fonds, PAS.
55 LEMJ, "Developing Public Opinion on Peace (1937)," *Vancouver Province (VP),* May 14, 1937, in Nancy M. Forestell and Maureen Monagh, eds., *Documenting First Wave Feminisms,* vol. 2, *Canada: National and Transnational Contexts* (Toronto: University of Toronto Press, 2014), 316.
56 "Internationalism and Peace Day," *VNH,* March 5, 1937.
57 LEMJ, "Developing Public Opinion on Peace (1937)," 316–18 (emphasis in original).
58 Socknat, "Witness against War," 332–33.
59 "League Takes Up Cudgels for Unemployed Single Men," *VNH,* October 27, 1936.
60 Ashworth, "Women and War," 12.
61 *VNH,* June 20, 1937.
62 "W.I.L. to Ask Government to Give Credits to China," *VNH,* February 28, 1939.
63 "Mrs. C.B. Sissons Named Head of Women's League for Peace and Freedom," *WT,* June 3, 1937.
64 LEMJ, "Vancouver's Folk Art Festival," *Canadian Forum,* December 1933, 105. For a sympathetic liberal perspective, see also Nellie L. McClung, "The Value of a Handicraft

Festival," in *Leaves from Lantern Lane* (Toronto: Thomas Allen, 1936; Project Gutenberg, n.d.), https://gutenberg.ca/ebooks/mcclung-leavesfromlanternlane/mcclung-leavesfromlanternlane-00-h.html#chap057.

65 LEMJ, "Vancouver's Folk Art Festival," 105.

66 Candida Rifkind, *Comrades and Critics: Women, Literature, and the Left in 1930s Canada* (Toronto: University of Toronto Press, 2009), 150. See also Patricia Hews Everett-Kabut, "The Cooperative Commonwealth Federation and Amateur Theatricals in 1930's Vancouver, BC" (PhD diss., University of British Columbia, 2016). Relying on the archival papers of Arthur J. Turner, a CCF activist and MLA, Everett-Kabut emphasizes the contributions of three men, perhaps not surprisingly: Turner himself, Denny Kristiansen, and Hubert Evans. However, she does acknowledge the significance of women's contribution to the cultural agenda of the CCF. She also notes that Evans, a Quaker, had a particular appreciation for "the agency and the strength of women" (230).

67 Irene Howard, *The Struggle for Social Justice in British Columbia: Helena Gutteridge, the Unknown Reformer* (Vancouver: UBC Press, 1992), 162; "Waiting for Lefty," Past Tense: Vancouver Histories, October 29, 2010, https://pasttensevancouver.wordpress.com/2010/10/29/waiting-for-lefty/. See also Bonita Bray, "Chapter 12. Against All Odds: The Progressive Arts Club's Production of *Waiting for Leftie*," in *Canadian Working-Class History: Selected Readings*, 3rd ed., ed. Laurel S. MacDowell and Ian Radforth (Toronto: Canadian Scholars' Press, 2006), 250-70.

68 On the Progressive Arts Club and the play, see "Waiting for Lefty," *Past Tense: Vancouver Histories.*

69 See Hugh Johnston, *Jewels of the Qila: The Remarkable Story of an Indo-Canadian Family* (Vancouver: UBC Press, 2011), 95, 149; and LEMJ to VM, June 11, 1933, VM fonds, PAS.

70 "League of Peace Hears Speaker on Japanese Question," *VNH,* April 16, 1934.

71 "International League Passes Resolutions on Votes and Peace," *VNH,* March 23, 1937.

72 LEMJ to VM, March 4, 1938, VM fonds, PAS.

73 "League Sponsors Panel Discussion," *VNH,* April 28, 1937.

74 "Women Favor Civic Rights for B.C. Born Orientals," *VNH,* June 19, 1934.

75 See Walter E.W. Ellis, "Some Aspects of Religion in British Columbia Politics" (master's thesis, University of British Columbia, 1959), 144; and "From Telephone Interview with Laura Jamieson February 24, 1958," in ibid., 227n185.

76 Fiona Paisley, *Glamour in the Pacific: Cultural Internationalism and Race* (Honolulu: University of Hawaii Press, 2009), 37.

77 Ibid., 138.

78 "Against Exporting of War Materials," *Ottawa Citizen,* July 7, 1939.

79 "Chinese 'Joan' to Speak Here," *VP,* April 21, 1939. The student was Loh Tsei.

80 "Government Asked to Consider Finding Homes for Jews," *VNH,* December 6, 1938.

81 Quoted in Anne Elizabeth Wilson, "A Pound of Prevention – Or an Ounce of Cure: A Plea for National Legislation on a Growing Problem," *Chatelaine,* December 1928, 13.

82 "Protest against Oriental Colony," *BB,* December 18, 1930.

83 "Canadian Fascisti Now Has over 700 Members," *VNH,* May 15, 1933. Despite the title, the article notes the claim of "nearly 1300" members.

84 See "Women's International League for Peace and Freedom Resolutions of the Zurich Conference," in *The Essential Feminist Reader*, ed. Estelle Freedman (New York: Modern Library, 2007), 199–203.

85 LEMJ to VM, July 3, 1932, VM fonds, PAS.

86 "Time for Women to Act – Men Been Talking for Years," *VNH,* October 22, 1937.
87 VM to LEMJ, July 6, 1932, VM fonds, PAS. Jamieson's ill health also worried McNaughton, who hailed her as "a most important person, and we can't afford to have you laid aside."
88 "Vancouver Review: The Archeology of Metrotown," Terry Glavin: Chronicles and Dissent, July 26, 2006, http://transmontanus.blogspot.ca/2006/07/vancouver-review-archeology-of.html.
89 Quoted in M. Theresa Healey, "'Trouble Enough': Gender, Social Policy and the Politics of Place in Vancouver and Saskatoon, 1929–1939" (PhD diss., Simon Fraser University, 1998), 232.
90 LEMJ to VM, July 3, 1932, VM fonds, PAS. A self-published volume, Partridge's *War on Poverty* has been described as a "virulent attack on capitalists, big industry, and poverty and a clarion call to underpaid labourers and the exploited poor." K. Murray Knuttila, "Partridge, Edward Alexander," in *Dictionary of Canadian Biography,* vol. 16 (Toronto/Quebec City: University of Toronto/Université Laval, 2003), http://www.biographi.ca/en/bio/partridge_edward_alexander_16E.html.
91 LEMJ to VM, June 11, 1933, VM fonds, PAS.
92 LEMJ to VM, July 3, 1932, quoted in Socknat, "Witness against War," 265.
93 Ronald Grantham, "Some Aspects of the Socialist Movement in British Columbia, 1898–1933" (master's thesis, University of British Columbia, 1942), 171.
94 See Gillian Creese, "The Politics of Dependence: Women, Work and Unemployment in the Vancouver Labour Movement before World War II," *Canadian Journal of Sociology* 13, 1–2 (Spring 1988): 121–42.
95 Quoted in Alexander Guy Richmond, "Stand by Your Man: An Examination of Women's Participation in the Ontario and British Columbia Cooperative Commonwealth Federation, 1933–1950" (master's thesis, Queen's University, 2000), 98.
96 Creese, "Politics of Dependence," 135.
97 "The Jobless Woman," *Chatelaine,* September 1930. See also MacGill's "What of the Wage-Earning Wife?" *Chatelaine,* March 1930.
98 Mary Patricia Powell, "Response to the Depression: Three Representative Women's Groups in British Columbia" (master's thesis, University of British Columbia, 1967), abstract.
99 Richmond, "Stand by Your Man," 82.
100 Healey, "'Trouble Enough,'" 220. For the New Era League, see "Great Advance," *VDW,* June 14, 1923. For a generally negative treatment of the league, see Gillian M. Weiss, "'As Women and as Citizens': Clubwomen in Vancouver, 1910–1928" (PhD diss., University of British Columbia, 1983).
101 See "Council of Women to Press for Recognition," *VNH,* September 12, 1933.
102 Richmond, "Stand by Your Man," 73.
103 See Shirley Tillotson, *Contributing Citizens: Modern Charitable Fundraising and the Making of the Welfare State, 1920–1966* (Vancouver: UBC Press, 2008), 85.
104 Untitled typescript, first line "What were the laws like a hundred years ago in B.C.?" p. 6 (capitalization in original), LEMJ fonds, BCA.
105 "Western World's Low Birth Rate," *Saturday Night,* August 4, 1928.
106 Médéric Martin, "Go Home, Young Woman," *Chatelaine,* September 1933, with a response by Agnes Macphail, "Go Home, Young Woman, Ha! Ha!" *Chatelaine,* October 1933; and William D. Tait, "Some Feminisms," *Dalhousie Review* 10, 1 (1930–31): 51–56. See also Margaret Hobbs, "Equality and Difference: Feminism and the Defence of

Women Workers during the Great Depression," *Labour/Le Travail* 32 (Fall 1993): 201–23; and Joan Sangster, *Earning Respect: The Lives of Working Women in Small-Town Ontario, 1920–1960* (Toronto: University of Toronto Press, 1995).

107 "Laws for Women in the Last Hundred Years," typescript, LEMJ fonds, BCA.

108 Editorial, "Paper Rights for Women," *CCF News*, August 17, 1949.

109 Lisa Pasolli, "'Talkin' Day Care Blues': Motherhood, Work, and Child Care in Twentieth-Century British Columbia" (PhD diss., University of Victoria, 2012), 91.

110 "Ald. Wilson Fails in Effort to Oust Working Married Women," *VNH*, February 14, 1939.

111 *VP*, June 30, 1939, quoted in Michaela Freud, "The Politics of Naming: Constructing Prostitutes and Regulating Women in Vancouver, 1934–1945" (master's thesis, Simon Fraser University, 1995), 45.

112 "Prominent Club Women Extend Felicitations," *VNH*, December 20, 1933.

113 Irene Howard, "The Mother's Council of Vancouver: Holding the Fort for the Unemployed, 1935–38," *BCS* 69–70 (Spring–Summer 1986): 249.

114 See Victor Howard, *We Were the Salt of the Earth: A Narrative of the On-to-Ottawa Trek* (Regina: University of Regina Press, 1985), 38; and "Church Mob Howls Down McGeer," *VNH*, May 20, 1935.

115 Howard, "Mother's Council of Vancouver," 282.

116 Richmond, "Stand by Your Man," 102.

117 See "Smoke Out the Reds" and "Planned Destructiveness of Communists to Be Exposed," *VNH*, May 30, 1935. See also James Dyer, "Looking around: While the Battle Waged," *VNH*, June 20, 1935.

118 Delmage was also known for her support for the education of Indigenous people. In recognition of her work for the PTA, the UBC Senate approved the Margaret Delmage Award in 1962, which was granted to children of BC Indigenous people who were entering a BC university or college. "Prizes, Scholarships and Bursaries: Margaret Delmage Award," in minutes of the UBC Senate meeting, October 17, 1962, http://www.library.ubc.ca/archives/pdfs/senate/UBC_Senate_Minutes_1962_10_17.pdf.

119 RCMP, "Appendix No. II: Reports by Provinces I: British Columbia," in "Report on Revolutionary Organizations and Agitation in Canada," No. 848, March 17, 1937, 133, marked secret, https://journals.lib.unb.ca/index.php/RCMP/article/view/9534/9589.

120 "Police Arrest More Jobless 'Tin-Canners,'" *VNH*, May 27, 1938.

121 Howard, "Mother's Council of Vancouver," 279–80.

122 Ibid., 280.

123 "Police Arrest More Jobless 'Tin-Canners'"; Howard, *Struggle for Social Justice*, 250.

Chapter 5: The Challenge of Electoral Politics, 1927–39

1 Not to be confused with the BC Reconstruction Party, a CCF-affiliated group.

2 Robert A.J. McDonald, "'Telford Time' and the Populist Origins of the CCF in British Columbia," *Labour/Le Travail (L/LT)* 71 (Spring 2013): 87.

3 See James Naylor, *The Fate of Labour Socialism: The Co-operative Commonwealth Federation and the Dream of a Working-Class Future* (Toronto: University of Toronto Press, 2016).

4 Quoted in James Naylor, "The British Columbia CCF's Working-Class Moment: Socialism Not Populism," *L/LT* 71 (Spring 2013): 105.

5 On this, see McDonald, "'Telford Time.'"
6 See the rather inconclusive description of Jamieson's talk on the subject in "Technocracy and Its Implications," *Burnaby Broadcast,* January 26, 1933. On the *Vancouver Sun*'s coverage, see David Adair, "The Technocrats 1919–1967: A Case Study of Conflict and Change in a Social Movement" (master's thesis, Simon Fraser University, 1970), 45. See also William Akin, *Technocracy and the American Dream: The Technocracy Movement, 1900–1941* (Berkeley: University of California Press, 1977).
7 Naylor, *The Fate of Labour Socialism,* 172.
8 Naylor, "The British Columbia CCF's Working-Class Moment," 104.
9 Naylor, *The Fate of Labour Socialism,* 80.
10 Ibid., 82.
11 See Christine Price, "'A Very Conservative Radical': Reverend Robert Connell's Encounter with Marxism in the BC CCF" (master's thesis, Simon Fraser University, 2006).
12 Ibid., 79.
13 Naylor, "The British Columbia CCF's Working-Class Moment," 120.
14 "Socialism Takes a Bow," *Vancouver News-Herald (VNH),* August 2, 1933.
15 Laura Jamieson (LEMJ) to Violet McNaughton (VM), June 8, 1933, Violet McNaughton fonds (VM fonds), Provincial Archives of Saskatchewan (PAS).
16 See "Mrs. Jamieson Forecasts Outlook," *VNH,* January 20, 1938.
17 LEMJ to VM, June 11, 1933, VM fonds, PAS.
18 SPC leaders feared that without an educated membership, "a vangardist cult of leadership" would be created. See Naylor, "The British Columbia CCF's Working-Class Moment," 105.
19 Quoted in LEMJ to VM, June 11, 1933, VM fonds, PAS.
20 LEMJ to VM, July 3, 1932, VM fonds, PAS.
21 Joan Sangster, *Dreams of Equality: Women on the Canadian Left, 1920–1950* (Don Mills, ON: McClelland and Stewart, 1989), 92.
22 Joan Sangster, "'Women and the New Era': The Role of Women in the Early CCF, 1933–1940," in *"Building the Co-operative Commonwealth": Essays on the Democratic Socialist Tradition in Canada,* ed. J. William Brennan (Regina: Canadian Plains Research Center, University of Regina, 1984), 84.
23 Elizabeth Kerr, quoted in Sangster, "'Women and the New Era,'" 84.
24 "Mrs. J.S. Jamieson Addresses Club," *VNH,* October 14, 1938.
25 "Woman to Carry on Campaign by Plane and Radio," *Winnipeg Tribune* (WT), July 6, 1928.
26 Anne Anderson Perry, "Women Begin to Speak Their Minds," *Chatelaine,* June 1928, 6, 61. See also H.F. Gadsby, "Letters of a Woman M.P.," *Maclean's Magazine (MM),* February 15, 1929.
27 Helen Gregory MacGill, "Are Women Wanted in Public Life? And the Important Question Is, 'Are They Really Needed?'" *Chatelaine,* September 1928, 1, 4, 50.
28 E.C. Buchanan, "The Last Fortress Fallen," *Saturday Night (SN),* February 22, 1930, which condemned King for "this surrender of the citadel of men's privilege."
29 Anne Anderson Perry, "Stag Politics," *Chatelaine,* May 1930, 10–11, 61.
30 Grattan O'Leary, "Is Women's Suffrage a Success?" *Chatelaine,* September 1930, 12.
31 Terence Crowley, *Agnes Macphail and the Politics of Equality* (Toronto: J. Lorimer, 1990), 105.
32 "Freedom of Women Now Unwanted Toy," *VNH,* August 14, 1933.

33 "Article on Freedom of Women Creates Comment in Clublife," *VNH,* August 17, 1933. See also the meeting organized by the Business and Professional Women's Club, "Women Candidates Air Many Campaign Views," *VNH,* October 3, 1933.

34 Neil Sutherland, "T.D. Pattullo as a Party Leader" (master's thesis, University of British Columbia, 1960), 54.

35 "Eleven Women in B.C. Election Race," *Montreal Gazette,* October 30, 1933. See also Nancy Knickerbocker, *No Plaster Saint: The Life of Mildred Osterhout Fahrni* (Vancouver: Talon Books, 2001).

36 "Only One Woman Is Elected in B.C.," *Montreal Gazette,* November 4, 1933.

37 "League Urges Portfolio for City Woman," *VNH,* November 16, 1933.

38 "New Era League Still Argues Relief Methods," *VNH,* January 24, 1934.

39 Editorial, "The Challenge of 1934," *Chatelaine,* January 1934, 2.

40 On the two latter phenomena, see Constance Templeton, "Shall I Go into Service?" *Chatelaine,* July 1933, 17, 49; and Médéric Martin, "Go Home, Young Woman," *Chatelaine,* September 1933.

41 Benge Atlee, "Should Women Be Men?" *MM,* September 15, 1934.

42 "Second Woman in B.C. Legislature," *Montreal Gazette,* July 17, 1934.

43 "Eleven Women in B.C. Election Race," *Montreal Gazette,* October 30, 1933.

44 Sutherland, "T.D. Pattullo as a Party Leader," 67. See also "Dictatorship in B.C. Special Powers Act Gives Pattullo Full Control of Province," *VNH,* March 17, 1934; and Robin Fisher, *Duff Pattullo of British Columbia* (Toronto: University of Toronto Press, 1991), 262.

45 Editorial, "A Sad Plight," *VNH,* September 27, 1935.

46 See Parliament of Canada, "Women Candidates in General Elections – 1921 to Date," https://lop.parl.ca/About/Parliament/FederalRidingsHistory/hfer.asp?Election=18&Language=E&pa=84&Search=WomenCandidate.

47 Walter Volovsek, "Time Windows: Lilette Mahon: Art in Living," *Castlegar News,* October 22, 2015, updated October 24, 2015, https://www.castlegarnews.com/opinion/time-windows-lilette-mahon-art-in-living/; Parliament of Canada, "Women Candidates in General Elections – 1921 to Date." Despite possessing the same name as the earlier RP associated with the League for Social Reconstruction, the 1935 party mobilized dissident conservatives led by H.H. Stevens, a former cabinet minister under R.B. Bennett.

48 Edith Kerr Macdonald, "'Women in Politics' – But Are They?" *Chatelaine,* October 1936, 4, 86.

49 "Women Hear Current Events," *VNH,* November 6, 1935.

50 Liberal ad, "C.C.F. and the Oriental Vote," *VNH,* October 9, 1935 (capitalization in original).

51 Donald K. Alper, "From Rule to Ruin: The Conservative Party of British Columbia, 1928–1954" (PhD diss., University of British Columbia, 1975), 144n130; *Vancouver Sun (VS),* December 8, 1938.

52 See *Electoral History of British Columbia, 1871–1986* (Victoria: Elections BC, 1988).

53 From a general meeting of the Vancouver Local Council of Women, as reported in *VS,* December 7, 1937, 6; and "Women to Stand by Feminine Election Candidates," *VNH,* December 7, 1937. See Andrea Smith, "The Origins of the NPA: A Study in Vancouver Politics 1930–1940" (master's thesis, University of British Columbia, 1981).

54 Richmond, "Stand by Your Man," 84–85.

55 *Winnipeg Free Press,* June 4, 1937.

56 *Burnaby Advertiser (BA),* October 1, 1937. See also "Mrs. Stuart Jamieson to Speak at Capital Hill Community Hall," *BA,* May 27, 1938, with her talk titled "Organization of Community Centres and the Advantages of Same."

57 "Mrs. Laura Jamieson Resigns Judgeship," *BA,* April 1, 1938.
58 Pernille Jakobsen, "Bench–Breakers? Women Judges in Prairie Canada, 1916–1980" (PhD diss., University of Calgary, 2014), 44.
59 "City Campaign Speeds Up," *VS,* April 22, 1939.
60 "Woodsworth Message to Centre Riding," *The Federationist (TF),* April 27, 1939.
61 "Mrs. Jamieson Wins 'Centre' at By–Election," *VS,* May 1, 1939.
62 "More Candidates Announced," *VS,* April 20, 1939; "Conservatives Pick Wilson, C.C.F. Mrs. Jamieson for Vancouver Centre," *Vancouver Province (VP),* April 20, 1939.
63 See "Mrs. Jamieson C.C.F. Candidate in Centre," *VNH,* April 20, 1939.
64 Bruce Hutchison, "Our Politicians Get Ready for an Unwelcome Battle," *VS,* April 10, 1939.
65 Ibid.
66 "C.C.F. Candidate Wants Issues Defined," *VNH,* April 25, 1939. See also "Liberals Take Beating at C.C.F. Meeting," *VNH,* April 27, 1939.
67 On the important Texada Island conflict, see Andy Parnaby, "'We'll Hang All Policemen from a Sour Apple Tree!': Class, Law, and the Politics of State Power in the Blubber Bay Strike of 1938–39" (master's thesis, Simon Fraser University, 1995). Unfortunately, Parnaby offers no details on the role of Corey or Jamieson.
68 "C.C.F. Claims Credit for Social Laws," *VNH,* April 28, 1939.
69 "Citizens Urged to Cast 'Vote of Protest' by C.C.F. Leaders," *VNH,* April 29, 1939.
70 See "Mrs. Jamieson Scores Rivals," *VP,* April 27, 1939; and "Mrs. Jamieson Fears Fascism," *VP,* April 22, 1939.
71 Campaign poster on woman's page, *VNH,* April 26, 1939.
72 For this ecumenical list, see "Mrs. Jamieson to Be Honored at Tea," *VNH,* April 27, 1939.
73 "Women Sink Political Differences to Get behind One of Their Own Sex," *VS,* April 27, 1939.
74 "Now Is Your Chance," *VNH,* May 1, 1939.
75 Editorial, "The By-Election," *VNH,* May 1, 1939.
76 "Mrs. Jamieson Scores Rivals."
77 "Mrs. Jamieson Fourth Woman M.L.A. in B.C.," *VNH,* May 2, 1939.
78 Editorial, "Vancouver Centre," *VNH,* May 3, 1939.
79 "Feminine Trio Wins Support for the C.C.F.," *VP,* October 22, 1941.
80 "Admirers of Victorious C.C.F. Candidate Stage Victory Walk," *VP,* May 2, 1939.
81 "C.C.F. WINS VANCOUVER CENTRE," *VNH,* May 2, 1939 (capitalization in original).
82 "CCF Victory Speeds Drive to Elect Hurry," *TF,* May 4, 1939.
83 George Weir was the cabinet minister. See Sutherland, "T.D. Pattullo as a Party Leader," 113; and Fisher, *Duff Pattullo of British Columbia,* 309.
84 Bruce Hutchison, "By-Election Vote May Cast Shadow Long Way Ahead," *VS,* May 1, 1939.
85 "Mrs. Jamieson Thanks You," *TF,* May 4, 1939.

Chapter 6: Suffragist in the BC Legislature, 1939–41

1 Three untitled pages beginning "lately, I've been having a new experience," Kathleen Shannon fonds, R5469, folder "Miscellaneous," Library and Archives Canada (LAC).
2 See "S. Jamieson Is CCF Research Director," *CCF News (CCFN),* February 24, 1944.
3 W. Craig Riddell, Gideon Rosenbluth, and Mark Thompson, "Tribute to Stuart Marshall Jamieson, 1914–2002," *Relations industrielles/Industrial Relations* 59, 2 (2004): 231.

4 See "Teamwork in House Where Eight Girls Live on Co-operative Basis," *Ottawa Citizen,* September 10, 1946.
5 Laura E. Jamieson, "Co-op Living in Vancouver," *Canadian Forum (CF),* April 1943, 19.
6 Ibid.
7 "Club Women Can Help Solve Many Problems," *Vancouver Province (VP),* October 30, 1944.
8 Helen Bannerman, "Member of the Legislature: Former Park Head Girl Visits Here," *Owen Sound Sun Times,* undated clipping but summer 1942, Park Head Women's Institute, Tweedsmuir History, binder Xeroxed copies of history, vol. 1, Bruce County Museum and Archives.
9 Clare McAllister, "Women's Views," *CCFN,* November 16, 1944.
10 Constance Errol, "Women's Views," *The Federationist (TF),* December 7, 1939.
11 Elizabeth Kerr, "Women's Views," *TF,* December 29, 1939.
12 Errol, "Women's Views," *TF,* January 25, 1940.
13 Ibid.
14 Irene Howard, *The Struggle for Social Justice in British Columbia: Helena Gutteridge, the Unknown Reformer* (Vancouver: UBC Press, 1992), 35.
15 Benjamin Isitt, *Militant Minority: British Columbia Workers and the Rise of a New Left, 1948–1972* (Toronto: University of Toronto Press, 2011), 87.
16 Laura Jamieson (LEMJ) to Grace MacInnis, July 28, 1940, Grace MacInnis fonds, Correspondence 1940–45, University of BC Rare Books and Special Collections (UBCRBSC).
17 Three-page typescript, unidentified but from these years, pp. 3–5 in blue scribbler, LEMJ fonds, box 1, British Columbia Archives (BCA).
18 See Colin Campbell, "J.L. Ilsley and the Transition to the Post-war Tax System: 1943–1946," *Canadian Tax Journal* 63, 1 (2005): 4.
19 Quoted in James Naylor, "The British Columbia CCF's Working-Class Moment: Socialism Not Populism," *Labour/Le Travail* 71 (Spring 2013): 108.
20 LEMJ, "The World at a Glance," *TF,* August 31, 1939. See also Mary Hallett, "The Social Credit Party and the New Democracy Movement: 1939–1940," *Canadian Historical Review* 47, 4 (December 1966): 301–25.
21 LEMJ, "The World at a Glance," *TF,* September 14, 1939.
22 James Naylor, *The Fate of Labour Socialism: The Co-operative Commonwealth Federation and the Dream of a Working-Class Future* (Toronto: University of Toronto Press, 2016), 257.
23 Georgina Murray, "Woman M.L.A. Opposed to Pomp," *Vancouver News-Herald (VNH),* February 14, 1935.
24 Martin Ceadel, "The Peace Movement between the Wars: Problems of Definition," in *Campaigns for Peace,* ed. R. Taylor and N. Young (Manchester: Manchester University Press, 1987), 84.
25 Thomas H. McLeod and Ian McLeod, "T.C. Douglas," in *Saskatchewan Premiers of the Twentieth Century,* ed. Gordon L. Barnhart (Regina: Canadian Plains Research Center, University of Regina, 2004), 173.
26 Naylor, *The Fate of Labour Socialism,* 279.
27 Donald K. Alper, "From Rule to Ruin: The Conservative Party of British Columbia, 1928–1954" (PhD diss., University of British Columbia, 1975), 154n17.
28 LEMJ, "Educating toward Peace," handwritten, no date but c. 1939, LEMJ fonds, BCA.
29 Naylor, *The Fate of Labour Socialism,* 276.

30 "Anscomb Flays C.C.F. Members for Anti-War Statements in House," *VP,* November 14, 1939.

31 "Steeves, Jamieson Address CCF Women's Central Group," *BCF,* October 24, 1940; LEMJ, "The B.C. Legislature Sits," *CF,* January 1941, 308.

32 "C.C.F. Speakers Advocate New Socialist Democracy," *Chilliwack Progress (CP),* February 19, 1941.

33 LEMJ, "The B.C. Legislature Sits," 307.

34 "Bitter Personal Attacks Mark New Debate on War," newspaper clipping, November 14, 1939, BC Legislative Assembly Sessional Clippings Books, roll 14, Vancouver Public Library (VPL).

35 See Jeffrey Keshen, "Wartime Jitters over Juveniles: Canada's Delinquency Scare and Its Consequences, 1939–45," in *Age of Contention: Readings in Canadian Social History, 1900–45,* ed. Jeffrey Keshen (Toronto: Harcourt Brace, 1997), 364–86.

36 Quoted in "Mrs. Jamieson's Speech," *TF,* November 9, 1939.

37 Bruce Hutchison, "Across the Bay," *VS,* November 8, 1939, BC Legislative Assembly Sessional Clippings Books, roll 14, VPL.

38 "Improved Social Conditions Would Relieve Delinquency: Mrs. Jamieson Scores Liberal Appointments to Juvenile Courts and Institutions," *TF,* November 28, 1940.

39 LEMJ, "Women's Views," *TF,* January 6, 1941.

40 "C.C.F. Speakers Advocate New Socialist Democracy," *CP,* February 19, 1941.

41 "Mrs. Laura Jamieson Spends Busy Week in Prince Rupert," *TF,* May 15, 1941.

42 "Go to Business Women's Convention," *Spokesman-Review,* May 16, 1940.

43 See LEMJ, "Women's Views," *TF,* October 14, 1940.

44 Quoted in Ramona Marie Rose, "'Keepers of Morale': The Vancouver Local Council of Women, 1939–1945" (master's thesis, University of British Columbia, 1990), 44.

45 LEMJ, "Women's Views," *TF,* January 2, 1941.

46 LEMJ, "Women's Views," *TF,* August 22, 1940.

47 LEMJ, "Women's Views," *TF,* October 24, 1940.

48 LEMJ, "Women's Views," *TF,* November 28, 1940.

49 LEMJ, "Women's Views," *TF,* November 14, 1940.

50 LEMJ, "Women's Views," *TF,* August 8, 1940.

51 LEMJ, "Women's Views," *TF,* December 26, 1940.

52 LEMJ, "Women's Views," *TF,* July 25, 1940.

53 LEMJ, "Women's Views," *TF,* August 1, 1940.

54 LEMJ, "Women's Views," *TF,* December 19, 1940.

55 LEMJ, "Women's Views," *TF,* August 1, 1940.

56 LEMJ, "Women's Views," *TF,* September 19, 1940 (capitalization in original).

57 LEMJ, "Women's Views," *TF,* September 26, 1940.

58 LEMJ, "Mainly for Women," *TF,* February 13, 1941.

59 LEMJ, "Women's Views," *TF,* October 17, 1940.

60 LEMJ, "Women's Views," *TF,* August 29, 1940.

61 Ibid.

62 While practising in British Columbia, Lindenfeld would write that "the most serious problem of our time is the difficulty of cooperation for the common good of the community (family, nation, etc.)." Elda Lindenfeld and Marion MacDonald, "Adler's Contribution to Social Adjustment," *Individual Psychology Bulletin* 6, 1 (January 1947): 22.

63 LEMJ, "Women's Views," *TF,* September 13, 1940.

64 LEMJ, "Women's Views," *TF,* August, 15, 1940.
65 LEMJ, "Women's Views," *TF,* December 12, 1940.
66 LEMJ, "Women's Views," *TF,* August 22, 1940.
67 LEMJ, "Women's Views," *TF,* September 6, 1940.
68 LEMJ, "The Foreign Engineer," *Canadian Forum (CF),* January 1941, 350–51.
69 LEMJ, "Women's Views," *TF,* November 21, 1940.
70 LEMJ, "Women's Views," *TF,* December 5, 1940.
71 LEMJ, "Mainly for Women," *TF,* February 6, 1941. Note the new title of the column, with its suggestion of a mixed audience.
72 See Faith Johnston, *A Great Restlessness: The Life and Politics of Dorise Nielsen* (Winnipeg: University of Manitoba Press, 2006).
73 LEMJ, "Women's Views," *TF,* October 10, 1940.
74 LEMJ, "Women's Views," *TF,* October 31, 1940.
75 Isabel M. Reekie, "Vancouver Women's School for Citizenship," July 1956, typescript, file 466–1-5, City of Vancouver Archives.
76 "Citizenship School for Women," *TF,* May 1, 1941.
77 Elizabeth Kerr, "Women's Views," *TF,* May 22, 1941.
78 Elizabeth Kerr, "Women's Views," *TF,* June 5, 1941.
79 LEMJ, "Women's Views," *TF,* January 30, 1941.
80 See William G. Robbins and Katrine Barber, *Nature's Northwest: The North Pacific Slope in the Twentieth Century* (Tucson: University of Arizona Press, 2011), 204–5.
81 See Gordon Hak, *Capital and Labour in the British Columbia Forest Industry, 1934–74* (Vancouver: UBC Press, 2011), 74.
82 See Jeffrey A. Keshen, *Saints, Sinners, and Soldiers: Canada's Second World War* (Vancouver: UBC Press, 2004), 57.
83 LEMJ, "When White and Brown Men Meet," *CF,* August 1941, 146–47.
84 "Social Security at Home Big Post-war Problem," *TF,* November 14, 1940.
85 LEMJ, "The B.C. Legislature Sits," *CF,* January 1941, 307–8.
86 "C.C.F. Speaker Asks New Order," unnamed newspaper clipping, November 9, 1940, BC Legislative Assembly Sessional Clippings Books, roll 14, VPL.
87 M.L. Young, "Marriage Is My Career," *Chatelaine,* January 1941, 33.
88 "Marriage Is My Career," *Chatelaine,* March 1941, 2–3.
89 LEMJ, "Women's Views," *TF,* January 23, 1941.

Chapter 7: Legislative Veteran, 1941–45

1 "Sees Uprising If C.C.F. Wins," *Vancouver Province (VP),* October 16, 1941.
2 "Meet the Candidate – No. 12: Fluent on the Platform, Grace MacInnis Is Still a Homemaker," *Vancouver News-Herald (VNH),* October 6, 1941.
3 "Meet the Candidate – No. 6: Mrs. Steeves Believes Time Has Come for 'New Order of Things,'" *VNH,* September 30, 1941.
4 "Meet the Candidate – No. 2: Welfare, Courts, Teaching Gave Mrs. Jamieson Political Urge," *VNH,* September 24, 1941.
5 "'It's Lopsided to Have Only Men Make Laws' Says Mrs. Rolston," *VNH,* October 5, 1941.
6 Pat Wallace, "The Woman's Touch: That's What's Needed, Think the Eight Feminine Candidates for the Provincial House," *Vancouver Sun (VS),* October 18, 1941. See also

"Twelve Women Seek B.C. Seats: Provincial Election Draws New Candidates: Three Veterans Also," *Toronto Globe and Mail,* October 14, 1941.

7 See Table 3.1 "Women in the BC Legislature, by Election," in Jocelyne Praud, "When Numerical Gains Are Not Enough: Women in British Columbia Politics," in *Stalled: The Representation of Women in Canadian Government,* ed. Linda Trimble, Jane Arscott, and Manon Tremblay (Vancouver: UBC Press, 2013), 59.

8 "British Columbia Creates Record by Electing Five Women to the House," *VS,* October 22, 1941.

9 See Marion Isabel Angus, "B.C. Elected All Five of Them!" *Chatelaine,* February 1942, 20–21, for its trivial treatment.

10 "Election Results Vote of Censure on Liberal Governments," *VS,* October 22, 1941.

11 Laura Jamieson (LEMJ), "Women's Views," *The Federationist (TF),* November 6, 1941.

12 LEMJ, "Women's Views," *TF,* December 24, 1941.

13 George M. Abbott, "Duff Pattullo and the Coalition Controversy of 1941," *BC Studies (BCS)* 102 (Summer 1994): 34.

14 Dorothy G. Steeves, "British Columbia Moves Leftwards," *Canadian Forum (CF),* December 1941, 266.

15 See Susanne Klausen, "The Plywood Girls: Women and Gender Ideology at the Port Alberni Plywood Plant 1942–1991" *Labour/Le Travail* 41 (1998): 199–235.

16 Wendy Cuthbertson, *Labour Goes to War: The CIO and the Construction of a New Social Order, 1939–45* (Vancouver: UBC Press, 2012).

17 Bruce Hutchison, "Ladies' Day," *VS,* January 9, 1942. See also Elmore Philpott, "As I See It," *VS,* February 6, 1940.

18 See Donald K. Alper, "From Rule to Ruin: The Conservative Party of British Columbia, 1928–1954" (PhD diss., University of British Columbia, 1975), 217–18.

19 LEMJ, "Women's Views," *TF,* August 27, 1942.

20 Quoted in "Have Canadian Women Made the Most of Their Political Equality?" *Chatelaine,* September 1943, 9.

21 LEMJ, "Women's Views," *TF,* February 26, 1942.

22 LEMJ, "Women's Views," *TF,* April 9, 1942.

23 LEMJ, "Women's School for Citizenship," *CF,* March 1945, 277.

24 Ibid.

25 Ibid., 275–77.

26 "Federal Housing in Esquimalt Attacked in B.C. Legislature," *Victoria Daily Colonist,* January 29, 1942.

27 LEMJ, "Women's Views: Sees Fruit Packing Houses and Canneries," *TF,* August 20, 1942.

28 See also "Mrs. Jamieson Defends Women in Industries," *VP,* February 12, 1944.

29 LEMJ, "Will Women Workers Organize?" *TF,* May 28, 1942, 3.

30 B.A. McKelvie, "Wage Scale Study Planned for Domestics," newspaper clipping, March 16, 1944, BC Legislative Assembly Sessional Clippings Books, roll 15, Vancouver Public Library (VPL).

31 LEMJ, *Women Dry Those Tears* (Vancouver: CCF Women's Council of BC, with assistance from Ontario CCF Women, 1945), 22.

32 LEMJ, "Postwar Employment Prospects for Women," *CCF News (CCFN),* August 23, 1945.

33 Jamieson, quoted in "Club Women Can Help Solve Many Problems," *VP,* October 30, 1944.

34 "Mrs. Jamieson Boosts Adult Education Demands Better Wages for Women," *TF*, March 11, 1943.
35 "New Day Seen for Women," *VS*, March 2, 1943.
36 "Women MLA's Battle over Day Nurseries," *VS*, March 4, 1943.
37 "Mrs. Jamieson Defends Women in Industries," *VP*, February 12, 1944.
38 "'Sermonizing' Judge Scorned," *VP*, February 10, 1943.
39 B.A. McKelvie, "Babies' Milk, Hope Highway and Whether Pigs Have Smell," *VP*, February 10, 1943.
40 Thelma Lecocq, "Fashion for War," *Maclean's Magazine (MM)*, January 15, 1942.
41 Thelma Lecocq, "Woman Power," *MM*, June 15, 1942.
42 Lotta Demsey, "They're Still Feminine!" *MM*, January 1, 1943.
43 Lotta Demsey, "Sisters in Arms," *MM*, April 15, 1943.
44 LEMJ, "Women's Views," *TF*, April 9, 1942.
45 Ibid.
46 LEMJ, *Women Dry Those Tears*, 32.
47 Grace MacInnis, "Wanted: Country," *CF*, June 1942, 76.
48 Werner Cohn, "The Persecution of Japanese Canadians and the Political Left in British Columbia, December 1941–March 1942," *BCS* 68 (Winter 1985–86): 11. Ultimately, however, Cohn concludes that the CCF failed to stand by the Japanese.
49 "Should We Send the Japs Back? NO says Angus MacInnis," *MM*, December 1, 1943.
50 Patricia Roy, *The Triumph of Citizenship: The Japanese and Chinese in Canada, 1941–67* (Vancouver: UBC Press, 2014), 58.
51 Cohn, "The Persecution of Japanese Canadians," 13.
52 Marilyn J. Harrison, "The Social Influence of the United Church of Canada in British Columbia, 1930–1948" (master's thesis, University of British Columbia, 1975), 184.
53 Ibid., 178.
54 Ibid., 179.
55 Quoted in Christopher MacLennan, *Toward the Charter: Canadians and the Demand for a National Bill of Rights, 1929–1960* (Montreal and Kingston: McGill-Queen's University Press, 2003), 38. See also Laura's rejection of "race prejudice and color discrimination" in Roy, *Triumph of Citizenship*, 121.
56 Harrison, "Social Influence of the United Church," 183.
57 Howard Norman and the Consultative Council, *What About the Japanese Canadians?* (Vancouver: Vancouver Consultative Council for Cooperation in Wartime Problems of Canadian Citizenship, 1945), 6, 11–12, 14. See also Stephanie Bangarth, *Voices Raised in Protest: Defending North American Citizens of Japanese Ancestry, 1942–49* (Vancouver: UBC Press, 2008).
58 "Scots, Irish of Canada Can Assimilate Japanese," and J.K. Newbitt, "Day in the House," newspaper clippings, March 6, 1945. See also "Bagpipes Skirl as Scot Denounces Mrs. Jamieson's Racial Comments," newspaper clipping, March 8, 1945. All in BC Legislative Assembly Sessional Clippings Books, roll 14, VPL.
59 "Mrs. Jamieson's Remarks," *VS*, March 10, 1945.
60 Quoted in Gordon Root, "City Member's Plea: East Indians' Vote Pressed," *VP*, February 24, 1944. In October 1942, the national executive committee of the CCF asked Ottawa to lead in ensuring a "democratic settlement in India," rather

than maintaining the empire. J.F. Hilliker, "The British Columbia Franchise and Relations with India in Wartime, 1939–1945," *BCS* 46 (Summer 1980): 55.

61 "Defeat Vote for East Indians," newspaper clipping, March 16, 1944, BC Legislative Assembly Sessional Clippings Books, roll 14, VPL.

62 Our Own Correspondent, "Mrs. Jamieson Denounces All Racial Discrimination," *CCFN,* March 8, 1945.

63 Jean Webber, Penticton, "B.C. Indians Have Rich Cultural Heritage: Native Handicrafts, Arts and Rama Have Much to Offer Canadian Life," *TF,* July 15, 1943.

64 "Assimilation of 'Wild Highlanders' Argument against Racial Prejudice," newspaper clipping, March 6, 1945, BC Legislative Assembly Sessional Clippings Books, roll 14, VPL.

65 LEMJ, *Women Dry Those Tears,* 32.

66 LEMJ, Review of Charlotte Whitton, *Security for Canadians, CF,* October 1943, 167.

67 Quoted in "Have Canadian Women Made the Most of Their Political Equality?" *Chatelaine,* September 1943, 9.

68 "Better Deal for Women Workers Asked in the House," *VP,* March 2, 1943.

69 Mildred Fahrni, "Request Improved Labor Laws for Women," *CCFN,* January 25, 1945. See also Vancouver School for Citizenship: Conference Report (1945), AM1519: PAM 1945–71, City of Vancouver Archives; and "Mrs. Jamieson Requests Better Social Services," *TF,* February 11, 1943.

70 LEMJ, *Women Dry Those Tears,* 28.

71 Alexander Guy Richmond, "Stand by Your Man: An Examination of Women's Participation in the Ontario and British Columbia Cooperative Commonwealth Federation, 1933–1950" (master's thesis, Queen's University, 2000), 40.

72 Quoted in Clare Boothe Luce, "Women Can Win the Peace," *Chatelaine,* February 1944, 5.

73 S.P. Lewis, *Grace: The Life of Grace MacInnis* (Madeira Park, BC: Harbour, 1993), 180.

74 Grace M. Worth, Lumby, "Women's Views: The Derivation and Connotation of 'Comrade,'" *TF,* April 8, 1943.

75 "Mrs. Jamieson Meets Valley Farm Wives," *CCFN,* May 25, 1944.

76 LEMJ, "Mrs. Jamieson Enthused by Fraser Valley Tour," *CCFN,* May 11, 1944.

77 LEMJ, "Notes: How Freedom Works (3:18 P.M.)," *CBC Program Schedule: Prairie Region,* week of February 18, 1945, p. 4, http://www.otrr.org/FILES/Magz_pdf/CBC%20Program%20Schedule/CBC%20Program%20Schedule%20450218.PDF.

78 "CCF Women's Rally Here Attracts Many Visitors," *CCFN,* April 19, 1945. See also Charlotte Whitton's rejection of a women's party or separate political organization as representing much less than equality in her "Women Hold the Balance of Power," *Chatelaine,* May 1945, 7, 53, 55–56.

79 Wilfred Sanders, "Women Are Disappointing," *Chatelaine,* March 1944, 59.

80 Charlotte Whitton, "What's the Matter with Us?" *Chatelaine,* December 1944, 39–40 (emphasis in original).

81 Whitton, "Women Hold the Balance of Power," 7, 55.

82 LEMJ, "Women's School for Citizenship," *CF,* March 1945, 276.

83 For one of *Chatelaine*'s rare interventions in the election, see "Why I Intend to Vote For: – ," *Chatelaine,* June 1945, which offered justification from three partisan women, one each from the Liberal, Progressive Conservative, and CCF Parties.

84 See her manifesto for a future in which "husbands will outgrow pettiness and fear" and "women themselves will accept and discharge the duties, rights, and responsibilities in a democracy." Gladys Strum, "Girl Meets Boys," *Chatelaine,* January 1947, 49.
85 Editorial, "Women in the House (of Commons)," *CCFN,* June 21, 1945.
86 Clare McAllister, "Women's Views," *CCFN,* September 20, 1945.
87 Kathleen Rex, "Thirteen Women Candidates in B.C.," *Lethbridge Herald,* October 23, 1945.
88 See Alpert, "From Rule to Ruin," especially 248–50.
89 "C.C.F. Jap Policy, Socialism Lashed by Coalitionist," *VNH,* October 19, 1945.
90 "Women Candidates Fare Badly in B.C." *Lethbridge Herald,* October 26, 1945.
91 "'13 Unlucky for Women' Only Two Are Elected," *VS,* October 26, 1945 (capitalization in original).
92 "Coalition Gain in Power Seen in B.C. Vote Outcome," *VNH,* October 20, 1945.

Chapter 8: Taking on Post-war Misogyny and Vancouver Politics, 1945–64

1 See Jill Wade for a sensitive discussion of housing options for those with little income. She includes the example of a widow who "avoided relief by operating a lodging house in Kitsilano" in 1938. Jill Wade, "Marginal Housing in Vancouver, 1886–1950," *Urban History Review* 25, 2 (March 1997): 23.
2 "A Feminist Education," Kathleen Shannon fonds, R5469, folder "Miscellaneous," Library and Archives Canada.
3 Austin Cross, "Women in Politics Haven't Much Sense," *Chatelaine,* September 1950, 56–58.
4 Ibid., 13.
5 Ken Johnstone, "I Married a Corporation," *Chatelaine,* May 15, 1953.
6 Byrne Hope Sanders, "The Women of Canada," *Chatelaine,* January 1947, 16.
7 Chatelaine Consumer Council Reports, "Do Women WANT Women in Public Life?" *Chatelaine,* January 1948, 12, 55.
8 For a more positive view of *Chatelaine* that stresses traditions of dissent, see Valerie Korinek, *Roughing It in the Suburbs: Reading Chatelaine Magazine in the Fifties and Sixties* (Toronto: University of Toronto Press, 2000), especially 311–13 on the de Beauvoir controversy.
9 Agnes Macphail, "Men Want to Hog Everything!" *Maclean's Magazine (MM),* September 15, 1949.
10 Lotta Demsey, "Editorial: She Wouldn't Have Been Elected Dog-Catcher," *Chatelaine,* April 1952.
11 Margaret Conrad, "'Not a Feminist, but ... ': The Political Career of Ellen Louks Fairclough, Canada's First Female Federal Cabinet Minister," *Journal of Canadian Studies* 31, 2 (Summer 1996): 5–28.
12 See Conrad, "'Not a Feminist,'"; and Ellen Louks Fairclough, *Saturday's Child: The Memoirs of Ellen Louks Fairclough, Canada's First Female Federal Cabinet Minister* (Toronto: University of Toronto Press, 1995), with an introduction by Margaret Conrad.
13 Ellen Fairclough, "Nonsense," *Chatelaine,* September 1950, 60.
14 Quoted in Eva-Lis Wuorio, "Last of the Battling Suffragettes," *MM,* March 1, 1951.

15 See P.T. Rooke and R.L. Schnell, *No Bleeding Heart: Charlotte Whitton – A Feminist on the Right* (Vancouver: UBC Press, 1987).

16 *Chatelaine* Consumer Council Reports, "Do Women WANT Women in Public Life?" *Chatelaine,* January 1948, 12–13.

17 Gwen Skinner, "I'm Sick of Socialism," *Chatelaine,* December 1947, 26–27, 103.

18 Jodi Hyland, "I Renounced Communism," *Chatelaine,* June 1948, 26–27.

19 Ronald Williams, "Are You a Stooge for a Communist?" *Chatelaine,* April 1949. See the remarks by the editor, Byrne Hope Sanders, "The Cancer of Communism," *Chatelaine,* May 1949. See also T.G. McManus, "The Reds," *MM,* November 15, 1950; Blair Fraser, "How Dr. Endicott Fronts for the Reds," *MM,* July 15, 1952; "The Reds Are Ready to Wage War inside Canada," *MM,* June 15, 1951; Wallace Goforth and Sidney Katz, "If the Russians Attack Canada," *MM,* June 15, 1952; and McKenzie Porter, "The Empire's Dutiful Daughters," *MM,* August 15, 1952.

20 Other WILPFers, including Gutteridge, remained faithful. See Irene Howard, *The Struggle for Social Justice in British Columbia: Helena Gutteridge, the Unknown Reformer* (Vancouver: UBC Press, 1992), ch. 11.

21 See Julie Guard, "Women Worth Watching: Radical Housewives in Cold War Canada," in *Whose National Security? Canadian State Surveillance and the Creation of Enemies,* ed. M. Steedman, G. Kinsman, and D.K. Buse (Toronto: Between the Lines, 2000), 73–88.

22 *Social Planning for Canada* devoted a chapter to housing. For a discussion that emphasizes the managerial and paternalist orientation of much planning, see Sean Purdy, "Industrial Efficiency, Social Order and Moral Purity: Housing Reform Thought in Canada, 1900–1950," *Urban History Review* 25, 2 (March 1997): 30–40.

23 Andrea Smith, "The CCF, NPA, and Civic Change: Provincial Forces Behind Vancouver Politics, 1930–1940," *BC Studies* (*BCS*) 53 (Spring 1982): 57–58.

24 John C. Bacher, *Keeping to the Marketplace: The Evolution of Canadian Housing Policy* (Montreal and Kingston: McGill-Queen's University Press, 1993), 185.

25 Laura Jamieson (LEMJ), "At the City Hall," *CCF News (CCFN),* November 1949, 23 (capitalization in original).

26 Smith, "The CCF, NPA, and Civic Change," 62.

27 Thomas Gunton, "The Evolution of Urban and Regional Planning in Canada: 1900–1960" (PhD diss., University of British Columbia, 1981), 272–73.

28 See Jill Wade, "'A Palace for the Public': Housing Reform and the 1946 Occupation of the Old Hotel Vancouver," *BCS* 69–70 (Spring–Summer 1986): 288–310; and Thomas M. Thomson, "The Death and Life of the Little Mountain Housing Project: BC's First Public Housing Community" (master's thesis, University of British Columbia, 2010), 75–76.

29 See "CCF Nominates Civic Candidates," *CCFN,* October 31, 1946; and "Local Civic Vote Results," *CCFN,* December 12, 1946.

30 "CCF Civic Candidates," *CCFN,* December 4, 1947.

31 "NPA Regime Blamed for Fare Increase," *Vancouver News-Herald (VNH),* December 9, 1947.

32 "Mrs. Jamieson Elated; Thought She Had Lost," *Vancouver Province (VP),* December 11, 1947.

33 Ben Isitt, *Militant Minority: British Columbia Workers and the Rise of a New Left, 1948–1972* (Toronto: University of Toronto Press, 2011), 205–6. The nicknames reflect their responses to the BC Electric Railway increasing fares and eliminating

weekly passes. See also Bert Whyte and Larry Hannant, *Champagne and Meatballs: Adventures of a Canadian Communist* (Edmonton: Athabasca University Press, 2011), 244; and Fern Miller, "Vancouver Civic Political Parties: Developing a Model of Party-System Change and Stabilization," *BCS* 25 (Spring 1975): 6.

34 "Mrs. Jamieson Extends Thanks to Supporters," *CCFN*, December 18, 1947.
35 LEMJ, "At the City Hall," *CCFN*, January 15, 1948.
36 "Vancouver to Seek Housing Authority," *CCFN*, January 22, 1948.
37 Laura Jamieson, "At the City Hall," *CCFN*, February 5, 1948.
38 "City Raps PUC Again on Hearing," *VP*, September 7, 1949. See also "Low-Rent Home Plan Called Vital," *VP*, September 7, 1949.
39 "Council Won't Enter Fraserview Argument," *VP*, February 15, 1949.
40 "Ownership Preferred," *VNH*, September 13, 1949. See her response, "Housing for People Who Can't Afford It," *VNH*, September 21, 1949.
41 "Second Alderman Well Versed in Civic Facts," *VNH*, December 12, 1947.
42 "The City Council Putters Along," *CCFN*, April 16, 1948.
43 LEMJ, "At the City Hall," *CCFN*, May 20, 1948. See also "Committee Will Study City Poll Tax Problem," *VP*, February 11, 1949.
44 On this relic, see Shirley Tillotson, "Relations of Extraction: Taxation and Women's Citizenship in the Maritimes, 1914–1955," *Acadiensis* 39, 1 (Winter–Spring 2010): 27–57.
45 "The Lady was Right," *CCFN*, September 14, 1948.
46 LEMJ, "At the City Hall," *CCFN*, October 19, 1949; "Council Postpones School Tax Scheme," *VNH*, October 18, 1949.
47 LEMJ, "At the City Hall," *CCFN*, October 19, 1949.
48 "City Franchise Stirs Tempest," *VP*, January 12, 1949.
49 "Women Will Get City Vote: Mrs. Jamieson in 'Scene,'" *VP*, January 17, 1949.
50 *CCFN*, January 19, 1949.
51 "Civic Aldermen Again Reject Full Adult Civic Franchise," *CCFN*, October 5, 1949.
52 "Poll Tax Discussion Slated for February 8," *VP*, February 1, 1949.
53 LEMJ, "The Company Vote," *CCFN*, September 30, 1948.
54 "Council Downs BCER Purchase," *VNH*, March 22, 1948.
55 LEMJ, "At the City Hall," *CCFN*, September 14, 1949.
56 See the instance in "City Likely to Discard Town Planning Viaduct," *VNH*, April 13, 1948.
57 LEMJ, "City Fathers Reject Jamieson Proposal for Real Estate Tax," *CCFN*, October 14, 1948.
58 LEMJ, "At the City Hall," *CCFN*, October 19, 1949.
59 See "CCF Hits 'Interim' Fare Rise," *VP*, July 9, 1949; and "Council Rejects Phone Plan," *VP*, July 5, 1949.
60 "Aldermen Champion the Press," *VP*, December 29, 1949.
61 LEMJ, "At the City Hall," *CCFN*, October 19, 1949.
62 "City Should Hire More UBC Grads, Says Alderman," *VNH*, January 27, 1948.
63 "Council Rapped for 'Neglect' of Welfare Work," *VNH*, February 25, 1948.
64 "City Fathers Decline Study of Atomic Bomb," *VNH*, June 10, 1948.
65 See LEMJ, "Why Did 7 Aldermen Block Move for Survey?" *VNH*, April 27, 1949.
66 LEMJ, "At the City Hall," *CCFN*, May 20, 1948.
67 "Community Planning Goal of C.C.F. Party," *VNH*, July 22, 1948.
68 "Community Planning Goal of C.C.F. Party," *VNH*, July 26, 1948.
69 "'Not City Planners, But Businessmen,'" *VNH*, July 27, 1948.
70 "Parking-Lot Politics," *CCFN*, December 7, 1949.

71 LEMJ, "At the City Hall," *CCFN,* November 23, 1949; LEMJ, "At the City Hall," *CCFN,* November 30, 1949.
72 Editorial, "Civic Apathy," *CCFN,* December 21, 1949.
73 LEMJ, "Public Apathy Blamed for Poor Civic Vote," *CCFN,* December 21, 1949.
74 "Former Alderman Comes to Aid of Aged Pensioner," *CCFN,* February 1, 1950.
75 "Speaker Advocates Recreation Centres," *CCFN,* November 30, 1950.
76 "Vancouver Votes Down Open Sunday," *Ottawa Citizen,* December 10, 1951. Though this article deals with the second plebiscite, of 1951, it discusses the 1950 plebiscite as well.
77 See "Speaker Advocates Recreation Centres," *Ubyssey,* November 30, 1950.
78 LEMJ, "Civic Franchise and Civil Liberty," *CCFN,* February 8, 1950. See also her explanation of how to get on the voting list. "Voting under B.C. Municipal Act," *CCFN,* February 15, 1950; and her "Almost Half of Vancouver Citizens Have No Vote in Civic Elections," *CCFN,* March 1, 1950.
79 LEMJ, "The Company Vote," *CCFN,* March 15, 1950.
80 LEMJ, "Now's The Time to Get on the Vancouver Voters' List," *CCFN,* April 26, 1950.
81 Mamie Moloney, "In One Ear," *Vancouver Sun,* April 28, 1950.
82 *VP,* November 25, 1951. See also LEMJ, "Greater Effort Needed in Drive to Extend Municipal Franchise," *CCFN,* May 2, 1951.
83 LEMJ, "Why Citizens Should Elect CCF Members to City Council," *CCFN,* November 21, 1951; and "Meet Your Aldermanic Candidates," *CCFN,* November 28, 1951.
84 LEMJ, "Vote of Vancouver Women Be Decisive," *CCFN,* November 26, 1952.
85 LEMJ, "Subsidized Housing," *CCFN,* July 22, 1953. The property taxes on the finished project more than paid for the civic subsidy. See also the observation that Laura was the only alderman, past or present, to support the Little Mountain housing project. Thomson, "The Death and Life," 85.
86 Thomson, "The Death and Life," 70.
87 On this opposition, see ibid., 83–85.
88 See LEMJ, "Subsidized Housing," *CCFN,* July 22, 1953; and Dorothy Joan Barberie, "'New Vista': A Housing Project, Burnaby, B.C.: A Review of Its Welfare and Administrative Experience" (master's thesis, University of British Columbia, 1959). Barberie thanks Laura for her assistance.
89 Barberie, "'New Vista,'" 31.
90 Ibid., 57.
91 LEMJ, "Planning at the City Hall," *CCFN,* October 30, 1957.

Chapter 9: Faithful Social Democrat, 1945–64

1 Jim Nesbitt, "She's the Only One of Her Kind," *Maclean's Magazine,* September 1, 1950, 22. See also Margaret Boyes, "Nancy Hodges: Speaker and Trailblazer," *Canadian Parliamentary Review* 20, 2 (1997): 14–15.
2 "Women Candidates: Canadian Federal Elections, 1921–2011," Elections, Simon Fraser University, https://www.sfu.ca/~aheard/elections/women-elected.html.
3 Quoted in Faith Johnston, *A Great Restlessness: The Life and Politics of Dorise Nielsen* (Winnipeg: University of Manitoba Press, 2006), 210.
4 See her hopes in Gladys Strum, "Girl Meets Boys," *Chatelaine,* January 1947, 49.
5 See Benjamin Isitt, "Confronting the Cold War: The 1950 Vancouver Convention of the Cooperative Commonwealth Federation," *Canadian Historical Review* 91, 3 (2010): 465–501.

6 See Reg Whitaker and Gary Marcuse, *Cold War Canada: The Making of a National Insecurity State, 1945–1957* (Toronto: University of Toronto Press, 1994); and Ron Verzuh, "Remembering *Salt:* How a Blacklisted Hollywood Movie Brought the Spectre of McCarthyism to a Small Canadian Town," *Labour/Le Travail (L/LT)* 74 (Fall 2015): 165–98.
7 See Isitt, "Confronting the Cold War," 466.
8 See ibid.; and Ian McKay, *Rebels, Reds, Radicals: Rethinking Canada's Left History* (Toronto: Between the Lines, 2005).
9 Mildred MacLeod, "A Word to the Wives," *CCF News (CCFN),* July 18, 1951.
10 Arthur Cathers, *Beloved Dissenter: Eve Smith* (Blyth, ON: Drumadravy Books, 1997), 59. Smith left the CCF to join the Socialist Party of Canada in 1953 and would go on to become a significant figure in the peace and environmental movements.
11 Scholars have sometimes agreed. See, for example, Robert A.J. McDonald, "'Variants of Liberalism' and the Liberal Order Framework in British Columbia," in *Liberalism and Hegemony: Debating the Canadian Liberal Revolution,* ed. Jean-François Constant and Michel Ducharme (Toronto: University of Toronto Press, 2009), 322–46. See the critique in James Naylor, "The British Columbia CCF's Working-Class Moment: Socialism Not Populism," *L/LT* 71 (Spring 2013): 101–21.
12 Ibid., 473.
13 David Lewis to Angus MacInnis, October 25, 1948, quoted in Isitt, "Confronting the Cold War," 474.
14 "Muriel" to G. MacInnis, April 19, 1946, in Isitt, "Confronting the Cold War," 471.
15 Ibid.
16 Laura Jamieson (LEMJ) to Grace MacInnis, July 28, 1940, quoted in Isitt, "Confronting the Cold War," 471n14.
17 On these shifts, see Isitt, "Confronting the Cold War."
18 See Joan Sangster, *Dreams of Equality: Women on the Canadian Left, 1920–1950* (Don Mills, ON: McClelland and Stewart, 1989).
19 "Women in Politics," *CCFN,* January 26, 1949.
20 Mildred MacLeod, "A Word to the Wives: Do Our Men Need Reforming?" *CCFN,* August 1, 1951.
21 Vera Loucks, *CCFN,* December 16, 1948.
22 "Our Readers Write," *CCFN,* January 21, 1953.
23 Benjamin Isitt, "Tug-of-War: The Working Class and Political Change in British Columbia, 1948–1972" (PhD diss., University of New Brunswick, 2003), 215.
24 The quoted passage, from Saskatchewan's amended Public Service Act, is in Sangster, *Dreams of Equality,* 214. Esyllt W. Jones discusses such shortcomings in her "Mindel Cherniack Sheps and the Founding of Medicare in Canada," unpublished ms., 28.
25 Sangster, *Dreams of Equality,* 202.
26 Ibid., 212.
27 Isitt, "Confronting the Cold War," 479n33.
28 Quoted in Ivan Avakumovic, *Socialism in Canada: A Study of the CCF/NDP in Federal and Provincial Politics* (Toronto: McClelland and Stewart, 1978), 160.
29 Isitt, "Confronting the Cold War," 487.
30 LEMJ to Grace MacInnis (April 17, 1951), Grace MacInnis fonds, box 4-10, University of BC Rare Books and Special Collections (UBCRBSC).
31 Isitt, "Confronting the Cold War," 488.
32 Irene Howard, *The Struggle for Social Justice in British Columbia: Helena Gutteridge, the Unknown Reformer* (Vancouver: UBC Press, 1992), 254.

33 LEMJ, "Freedom Necessary for Socialism," *CCFN,* November 8, 1950. See Frank Underhill, "Canadian Socialism and World Politics," *CF,* October 1950, 151. See also Kenneth C. Dewar, *Frank Underhill and the Politics of Ideas* (Montreal and Kingston: McGill-Queen's University Press, 2015).
34 LEMJ, "The Emphasis Is on Democracy," *CCFN,* January 4, 1950.
35 Ibid.
36 Ibid.
37 LEMJ, "Socialist Approach," *CCFN,* October 31, 1951.
38 LEMJ, "Our Readers' Forum," *CCFN,* December 13, 1950.
39 LEMJ, "Congress Party" and "Our Readers' Forum," *CCFN,* February 14, 1951.
40 Mildred MacLeod, "From Capitalism to Socialism," *CCFN,* January 25, 1950.
41 Chuck Crate, Yellowknife, "Socialism or Liberalism," *CCFN,* February 8, 1950.
42 LEMJ, "Reply to Crate," in "Our Readers' Forum," *CCFN,* March 1, 1950.
43 LEMJ, "What Purpose Dissolution?" *CCFN,* April 4, 1951.
44 See Elaine Bernard, "The Rod Young Affair in the British Columbia Co-operative Commonwealth Federation" (master's thesis, University of British Columbia, 1979).
45 "Our Readers Write," *CCFN,* January 25, 1950.
46 Alex B. Macdonald, "Our Readers Write," *CCFN,* February 8, 1950.
47 Grace MacInnis to David Lewis, July 13, 1950, copy, Grace MacInnis fonds, box 4–5, UBCRBSC.
48 Isitt, "Confronting the Cold War," 500–1.
49 See Gordon Hak, "Populism and the 1952 Social Credit Breakthrough in British Columbia," *CHR* 85, 2 (June 2004): 277–96, for the best discussion of this popular or populist response.
50 See "Women's Council Reports Progress," *CCFN,* March 7, 1946; "Women's Council Protests Federal Service Layoffs," *CCFN,* March 7, 1946; and "Women's Council Hold Garden Fete at Boag Property," *CCFN,* July 11, 1946.
51 LEMJ, "The CCF and the Co-operative Movement," *CCFN,* February 28, 1946.
52 These were envied by Conservatives and Liberals. See "CCF Camp Amazes Old Parties," *Vancouver News-Herald (VNH),* July 12, 1948.
53 See Alexander Guy Richmond, "Stand by Your Man: An Examination of Women's Participation in the Ontario and British Columbia Cooperative Commonwealth Federation, 1933–1950" (master's thesis, Queen's University, 2000), 99.
54 "Coming Events," *CCFN,* March 7, 1951.
55 Mollie Jenkins, "Co-op Women's Guilds," *B.C. Credit Unionist,* June 1950, 10.
56 Margaret Jones, "Women's Council Column," *CCFN,* October 2, 1951.
57 LEMJ to Grace MacInnis, May [1952?], Grace MacInnis fonds, box 4–6, UBCRBSC.
58 "CCF Candidates in June 12 Election," *CCFN,* May 28, 1952.
59 LEMJ, "Meeting at Yee Home," *CCFN,* April 2, 1952.
60 "Resentment to Beat Gov't, CCF'er Says," *Vancouver Sun (VS),* June 5, 1952.
61 "BCE Unsafe from CCF Forum Told," *Vancouver Province (VP),* May 19, 1952.
62 See "Least Got Most: 1952 Election Expenses Filed," *VS,* May 23, 1953.
63 "Never Overlook the Women," *VNH,* June 10, 1952.
64 Ibid.
65 Thelma Root, "Old Campaigners: Tilly and Laura Parties' Queens as Lead in Polls," *VS,* June 13, 1952.
66 James K. Nesbitt, "Capital Viewpoints," *Chilliwack Progress (CP),* October 1, 1952.
67 Photo of Laura Jamieson, *VP,* June 12, 1952.

68 See H.F. Angus, "Note on the British Columbia Election in June 1952," *Western Political Quarterly* 5, 4 (December 1952): 585–91.
69 LEMJ, "News of Socialists the World Over," *CCFN*, February 4, 1953.
70 "Economy for Efficiency Soulless Says Jamieson," *CCFN*, February 11, 1953.
71 "Laura Jamieson against Cut of Pro-Rec Funds," *CCFN*, March 4, 1953.
72 "Laws for Women in the Last Hundred Years," typescript, p. 6, LEMJ fonds (capitalization in original), British Columbia Archives (BCA).
73 Untitled typescript, first line "What were the laws like a hundred years ago in B.C.?" p. 11, LEMJ fonds, BCA.
74 "Laura Jamieson against Cut of Pro-Rec Funds," *CCFN*, March 4, 1953.
75 James K. Nesbitt, "Capital Viewpoints," *CP*, March 11, 1953.
76 Frank Howard, *From Prison to Parliament* (Victoria: Trafford, 2003), ch. 21.
77 "CCF VICTORY IMMINENT," *CCFN*, May 27, 1953.
78 Jack Webster, "Roughest B.C. Election," *VS*, June 8, 1953.
79 CCF election ad, *VS*, June 8, 1953 (capitalization in original).
80 For a rare discussion of Arsens, see Brian T. Thorn, *From Left to Right: Maternalism and Women's Political Activism in Postwar Canada* (Vancouver: UBC Press, 2016), 55–57, 101–4.
81 David J. Elkins, "Politics Makes Strange Bedfellows: The B.C. Party System in the 1952 and 1953 Provincial Elections," *BC Studies* 30 (Summer 1976): 14.
82 "Women Candidates in General Elections – 1921 to Date," Parliament of Canada, https://lop.parl.ca/About/Parliament/FederalRidingsHistory/hfer.asp?Language=E&Search=WomenCandidate&Election=22.
83 Crossman, quoted in LEMJ, "Toward a Socialist Philosophy," *CCFN*, March 3, 1954.
84 LEMJ, "Book Review," *CCFN*, March 3, 1954.
85 LEMJ, "Women's Council Column: Flora Tristan," *CCFN*, June 8, 1955.
86 LEMJ, "Women's Council Column: Flora Tristan (Conclusion)," *CCFN*, July 6, 1955.
87 LEMJ, "Our Buoyant Economy," *CCFN*, October 12, 1955.
88 "Notes on Social Purpose for Canada," typescript, notes for reading groups, n.d., LEMJ fonds, BCA.
89 LEMJ, "The Middle Class and the White Collar," *CCFN*, October 10, 1956.
90 "Problems of an Aging Population," undated typescript, LEMJ fonds, BCA. Grant was a controversial but influential figure for the Canadian left from the 1960s onward. For a discussion of his view that capitalism was "empty freedom," see Robert Meynell, *Canadian Idealism and the Philosophy of Freedom: C.B. Macpherson, George Grant, and Charles Taylor* (Montreal and Kingston: McGill-Queen's University Press, 2011).
91 LEMJ, "Christmas and the Scrolls," *CCFN*, December 1, 1957.
92 "Education Committee Study Outline Ready," *CCFN*, January 23, 1957.
93 LEMJ, "Journey into the Interior," *CCFN*, July 25, 1956.
94 LEMJ, "Nasser No Socialist," in "Letters to the Editor," *CCFN*, August 27, 1958.
95 Tarah Brookfield, *Cold War Comforts: Canadian Women, Child Safety, and Global Insecurity* (Waterloo: Wilfrid Laurier University Press, 2012), 102.
96 LEMJ, "Women and the United Nations," *Business and Professional Woman*, January–February 1948, 10.
97 LEMJ, "Women's Council Column: Sisters in Faraway Places," *CCFN*, February 22, 1956.
98 Andrew Cohen, "Pearsonianism," in *Pearson: The Unlikely Gladiator*, ed. Norman Hillmer (Montreal and Kingston: McGill-Queen's University Press, 1999), 153. Compare this

idealistic view with Yves Engler, *Lester Pearson's Peacekeeping – The Truth May Hurt* (Black Point, NS: Fernwood, 2012).

99 See LEMJ, "News of Socialists the World Over," *CCFN,* April 29, 1953; "News of Socialists the World Over," *CCFN,* September 2, 1953; "Socialist Women of the World Meet," *CCFN,* September 25, 1957; "News of Socialists the World Over: Report on Franco-Spain," *CCFN,* January 20, 1954; and "News of Socialists the World Over: New Life for the Villages of India," *CCFN,* February 17, 1954.

100 Thorn, *From Left to Right,* 36. Neither the source citations in *From Left to Right* nor the thesis upon which it is based provide any evidence for this claim by the author.

101 LEMJ, "Women's Council Column: Sisters in Faraway Places," *CCFN,* February 22, 1956.

102 LEMJ, "Women's Council Column: Women's Life and Labour," *CCFN,* October 29, 1952.

103 On her hopes, see LEMJ, "FIGHT FOR EQUAL PAY ALMOST WON," *CCFN,* October 14, 1953 (capitalization in original).

104 See Dominique Clément, *Equality Deferred: Sex Discrimination and British Columbia's Human Rights State, 1953–84* (Vancouver: UBC Press, 2014).

105 See Julia Stockett, "The Case of the Five Married Women," *CCFN,* August 1, 1951.

106 See letters from Jamieson to Quebec (October 24, 1958) and to Manitoba (October 9, 1958), LEMJ fonds, BCA.

107 "The Mysterious Legislation," typescript, n.d., LEMJ fonds, BCA.

108 "Women Should Know," typescript, n.d., LEMJ fonds, BCA.

109 LEMJ, "The Middle Class and the White Collar," *CCFN,* October 10, 1956.

110 LEMJ, "Women's Council Column: Nurses Vote to Stay with Local 160," *CCFN,* September 30, 1953.

111 "Resolutions Convener" to Miss B. Williscroft, Secretary, Vancouver Local Council of Women, April 23, 1963, LEMJ fonds, BCA.

112 "Women's Wages," handwritten, 1963, LEMJ fonds, BCA.

113 LEMJ, "Subsidized Housing is Un/Canadian," c. 1960, LEMJ fonds, BCA.

114 LEMJ, "Letter to Editor," *VS,* May 29, 1963.

115 "Problems of an Aging Population," c. 1960s, LEMJ fonds, BCA.

116 LEMJ, "Integration in the Okanagan," n.d., LEMJ fonds, BCA.

117 LEMJ, "Book Review: When Women Won the Vote," *CCFN,* January 7, 1953.

118 Marjorie Mann, "Women in the CCF," *CCFN,* October 26, 1955.

119 Lynda Erickson, "Women and Political Representation in British Columbia," in *Politics, Policy and Government in British Columbia,* ed. R. Kenneth Carty (Vancouver: UBC Press, 1996), 110.

120 Helen Racine (Mrs. L.G.), "Report on Women's School for Citizenship to Vancouver Council of Women, 1953–54," copy typescript, folder Annual Reports 1947–57, 564-D-1, City of Vancouver Archives.

121 LEMJ, "CCF Women's Council Exposes Socred Policy," *CCFN,* February 26, 1958; "Saskatchewan Scores Again," *CCFN,* September 24, 1958; "A Special Message," *CCFN,* February 26, 1958.

122 "CCF Women's Luncheon Draws Huge Crowd," *CCFN,* April 27, 1960.

123 *New Democrat (ND),* November 1961.

124 "Women Delegates Hold Special Meet," *ND,* November 1961.

125 "Women's Group Active," *ND,* January 1962.

126 LEMJ, "The Faceless Crowd: The Forum," *ND,* August 1963.

Conclusion

1 "Talk Back!" *New Democrat (ND),* July 1, 1964.

2 "Laura Jamieson, Women Dry Those Tears," *ND,* August 1, 1964.

3 Attached notes from Grace MacInnis, September 23, 1977, Vancouver Business and Professional Women's Club fonds, folder "Notes on Club History," box 588–2, City of Vancouver Archives.

4 Interview with Harold Winch, May 18, 1982, Susan Walsh Oral History Collection, Simon Fraser University Archives, quoted in Brian Thorn, "'Visions of the New World Order': Women and Gender in Radical and Reactionary Movements in Post-World War II Western Canada" (PhD diss., Trent University, 2006), 85.

5 Laura Jamieson to Grace MacInnis, July 28, 1940, quoted in Benjamin Isitt, *Militant Minority: British Columbia Workers and the Rise of a New Left, 1948–1972* (Toronto: University of Toronto Press, 2011), 88.

6 See Ian Milligan, *Rebel Youth: 1960s Labour Unrest, Young Workers, and New Leftists in English Canada* (Vancouver: UBC Press, 2014), 65–66.

7 Judi Bernstein et al., *Sisters, Brothers, Lovers ... Listen* (Boston: New England Free Press, 1967), Rise Up! A Digital Archive of Feminist Activism, http://riseupfeministarchive.ca/activism/issues-actions/organizing-documents-of-the-early-womens-liberation-movement/sistersbrotherssloverslisten-bernsteinmortonseesewood/.

Selected Bibliography

Full notes regarding archival and other sources are available throughout this volume, but this bibliography highlights the key scholarly writing.

Alper, Donald K. "From Rule to Ruin: The Conservative Party of British Columbia, 1928–1954." PhD diss., University of British Columbia, 1975.

Ambrose, Linda M., and Kristin Hall. "A New Woman in Print and Practice: The Canadian Literary Career of Madge Robertson Watt, 1890–1907." *History of Intellectual Culture* 7, 1 (2007). http://www.ucalgary.ca/hic.

Ashworth, Lucian M. "Women and War: The Women's International League for Peace and Freedom (WILPF) and the Problem of Collective Security." Paper presented at the Transnational Actors in War and Peace Conference, St. John's, Newfoundland, July 14–15, 2014.

Bacchi, Carol Lee. *Liberation Deferred? The Ideas of the English-Canadian Suffragists, 1877–1918.* Toronto: University of Toronto Press, 1982.

Bangarth, Stephanie. *Voices Raised in Protest: Defending North American Citizens of Japanese Ancestry, 1942–49.* Vancouver: UBC Press, 2008.

Barman, Jean. *The West beyond the West: A History of British Columbia.* Toronto: University of Toronto Press, 2007.

Brookfield, Tarah. *Cold War Comforts: Canadian Women, Child Safety, and Global Insecurity.* Waterloo: Wilfrid Laurier University Press, 2012.

Callahan, Marilyn, and Christopher Walmsley. "Rethinking Child Welfare Reform in British Columbia, 1900–60." In *People, Politics, and Child Welfare,* ed. Leslie T. Foster and Brian Wharf, 10–33. Vancouver: UBC Press, 2007.

Campbell, Peter. *Rose Henderson: A Woman for the People.* Montreal and Kingston: McGill-Queen's University Press, 2010.

Carter, Sarah. "Britishness, 'Foreignness,' Women and Land in Western Canada 1890s–1920s." *Humanities Research* 13 (November 2006): 43–60.

Clément, Dominique. *Equality Deferred: Sex Discrimination and British Columbia's Human Rights State, 1953–84.* Vancouver: UBC Press, 2014.

Cleverdon, Catherine L. *The Woman Suffrage Movement in Canada*. Toronto: University of Toronto Press, 1950. Reprinted with introduction by Ramsay Cook. Toronto: University of Toronto Press, 1974.

Crowley, Terence. *Agnes Macphail and the Politics of Equality*. Toronto: J. Lorimer, 1990.

Fisher, Robin. *Duff Pattullo of British Columbia*. Toronto: University of Toronto Press, 1991.

Ford, Anne Rochon. *A Path Not Strewn with Roses: One Hundred Years of Women at the University of Toronto, 1884–1984*. Toronto: Governing Council, University of Toronto, 1985.

Fraser, Brian J. *Church, College, and Clergy: A History of Theological Education at Knox College, Toronto, 1844–1994*. Montreal and Kingston: McGill-Queen's University Press, 1995.

Hale, Linda Louise. "The British Columbia Woman Suffrage Movement, 1890–1917." Master's thesis, University of British Columbia, 1977.

Hobbs, Margaret. "Equality and Difference: Feminism and the Defence of Women Workers during the Great Depression." *Labour/Le Travail* 32 (Fall 1993): 201–23. https://doi.org/10.2307/25143731.

Howard, Irene. "The Mother's Council of Vancouver: Holding the Fort for the Unemployed, 1935–38." *BC Studies* 69–70 (Spring–Summer 1986): 249–87.

–. *The Struggle for Social Justice in British Columbia: Helena Gutteridge, the Unknown Reformer*. Vancouver: UBC Press, 1992.

Isitt, Benjamin. *Militant Minority: British Columbia Workers and the Rise of a New Left, 1948–1972*. Toronto: University of Toronto Press, 2011. https://doi.org/10.3138/9781442690158.

–. "Tug-of-War: The Working Class and Political Change in British Columbia, 1948–1972." PhD diss., University of New Brunswick, 2003.

James, Kathy. "Practical Diversions and Educational Amusements: Evangelia House and the Advent of Canada's Settlement Movement, 1902–09." *Historical Studies in Education* 10, 1–2 (1998): 48–66.

–. "Reforming Reform: Toronto's Settlement House Movement, 1900–1920." *Canadian Historical Review* 82, 1 (March 2001): 55–90. https://doi.org/10.3138/CHR.82.1.55.

Johnston, Faith. *A Great Restlessness: The Life and Politics of Dorise Nielsen*. Winnipeg: University of Manitoba Press, 2006.

Kealey, Linda. "Canadian Socialism and the Woman Question." *Labour/Le Travail* 13 (Spring 1984): 77–100. https://doi.org/10.2307/25140401.

–. *Enlisting Women for the Cause: Women, Labour, and the Left in Canada, 1890–1920*. Toronto: University of Toronto Press, 1998.

Keshen, Jeffrey A. *Saints, Sinners, and Soldiers: Canada's Second World War*. Vancouver: UBC Press, 2004.

King, Alyson E. "The Experience of the Second Generation of Women Students at Ontario Universities, 1900–1930." PhD diss., Ontario Institute for Studies in Education, 1999.

Kinnear, Mary. *Female Economy: Women's Work in the Prairie Provinces, 1870–1970*. Montreal and Kingston: McGill-Queen's University Press, 1991.

–. *Margaret McWilliams: An Interwar Feminist*. Montreal and Kingston: McGill-Queen's University Press, 1991.

Knickerbocker, Nancy. *No Plaster Saint: The Life of Mildred Osterhout Fahrni*. Vancouver: Talon Books, 2001.

Korinek, Valerie. *Roughing It in the Suburbs: Reading Chatelaine Magazine in the Fifties and Sixties*. Toronto: University of Toronto Press, 2000.

Leier, Mark. *Red Flags and Red Tape: The Making of a Labour Bureaucracy.* Toronto: University of Toronto Press, 1995.

Levi, Charles Morden. "Where the Famous People Were? The Origins, Activities and Future Careers of Student Leaders at University College, Toronto, 1854–1973." PhD diss., University of Toronto, 1998.

MacGill, Elsie. *My Mother the Judge.* Toronto: Ryerson Press, 1955.

Matthews, Jean. *The Rise of the New Woman: The Women's Movement in America, 1875–1930.* Chicago: Ivan R. Dee, 2003.

McDonald, Robert A.J. *Making Vancouver: Class, Status and Social Boundaries, 1863–1913.* Vancouver: UBC Press, 1996.

–. "'Telford Time' and the Populist Origins of the CCF in British Columbia." *Labour/Le Travail* 71 (Spring 2013): 87–100.

–. "'Variants of Liberalism' and the Liberal Order Framework in British Columbia." In *Liberalism and Hegemony: Debating the Canadian Liberal Revolution,* ed. Jean-François Constant and Michel Ducharme, 322–46. Toronto: University of Toronto Press, 2009.

McLaren, Angus. *Our Own Master Race: Eugenics in Canada, 1885–1945.* Toronto: McClelland and Stewart, 1990. https://doi.org/10.3138/9781442623316.

Naylor, James. "The British Columbia CCF's Working-Class Moment: Socialism Not Populism." *Labour/Le Travail* 71 (Spring 2013): 101–21.

–. *The Fate of Labour Socialism: The Co-operative Commonwealth Federation and the Dream of a Working-Class Future.* Toronto: University of Toronto Press, 2016.

Norton, Wayne, and Tom Langford, eds. *A World Apart: The Crowsnest Communities of Alberta and British Columbia.* Kamloops: Plateau Press, 2002.

Paisley, Fiona. *Glamour in the Pacific: Cultural Internationalism and Race.* Honolulu: University of Hawaii Press, 2009. https://doi.org/10.21313/hawaii/9780824833428.001.0001.

Pasolli, Lisa. "'Talkin' Day Care Blues': Motherhood, Work, and Child Care in Twentieth-Century British Columbia." PhD diss., University of Victoria, 2012.

–. *Working Mothers and the Child Care Dilemma: A History of British Columbia Social Policy.* Vancouver: UBC Press, 2015.

Pederson, Diana. "'The Call to Service': The YWCA and the Canadian College Woman, 1886–1920." In *Youth, University and Canadian Society: Essays in the Social History of Higher Education,* ed. Paul Axelrod and John Reid, 187–215. Montreal and Kingston: McGill-Queen's University Press, 1989.

Plastas, Melinda. *A Band of Noble Women: Racial Politics in the Women's Peace Movement.* Syracuse: Syracuse University Press, 2011.

Reichwein, PearlAnn. *Climber's Paradise: Making Canada's Mountain Parks, 1906–1974.* Edmonton: University of Alberta Press, 2014.

Richmond, Alexander Guy. "Stand by Your Man: An Examination of Women's Participation in the Ontario and British Columbia Cooperative Commonwealth Federation, 1933–1950." Master's thesis, Queen's University, 2000.

Rooke, P.T., and R.L. Schnell. *No Bleeding Heart: Charlotte Whitton – A Feminist on the Right.* Vancouver: UBC Press, 1987.

Rose, Ramona Marie. "'Keepers of Morale': The Vancouver Local Council of Women, 1939–1945." Master's thesis, University of British Columbia, 1990.

Roth, Jenny, and Lori Chambers. "Introduction." In *Is It Just?* by Minnie Smith. Toronto: University of Toronto Press, 2011. First published 1911 by Methodist Book and Publishing House (Toronto).

Roy, Patricia. *Boundless Optimism: Richard McBride's British Columbia*. Vancouver: UBC Press, 2012.

–. *The Triumph of Citizenship: The Japanese and Chinese in Canada, 1941–67*. Vancouver: UBC Press, 2014.

Sangster, Joan. *Dreams of Equality: Women on the Canadian Left, 1920–1950*. Don Mills, ON: McClelland and Stewart, 1989. https://doi.org/10.3138/9781442623491.

Schmalz, Peter S. *The History of the Saugeen Indians*. Toronto: Ontario Historical Society, 1977.

Socknat, Thomas. *Witness against War: Pacifism in Canada, 1900–1945*. Toronto: University of Toronto Press, 1987.

Strong-Boag, Veronica. "The Citizenship Debates: Race and Gender in the 1885 Franchise Act." In *Constructing Canadian Citizenship: Historical Readings*, ed. R. Adamoski, D. Chunn, and R. Menzies, 69–94. Toronto: Broadview Press, 2002.

–. "Independent Women, Problematic Men: First and Second Wave Anti-Feminism in Canada from Goldwin Smith to Betty Steele." *Histoire sociale/Social History* 57 (May 1996): 1–22.

–. "Intruders in the Nursery: Childcare Professionals Reshape the Years One to Five." In *Childhood and Family in Canadian History*, ed. Joy Parr, 160–78. Toronto: McClelland and Stewart, 1982.

–. "Peace-Making Women: Canada, 1919–1939." In *Women and Peace: Theoretical, Historical, and Practical Perspectives*, ed. Ruth Roach Pierson, 170–91. London: Croom Helm, 1987.

Thorn, Brian T. *From Left to Right: Maternalism and Women's Political Activism in Postwar Canada*. Vancouver: UBC Press, 2016.

Trimble, Linda, Jane Arscott, and Manon Tremblay, eds. *Stalled: The Representation of Women in Canadian Government*. Vancouver: UBC Press, 2013.

Wade, Jill. "'A Palace for the Public': Housing Reform and the 1946 Occupation of the Old Hotel Vancouver." *BC Studies* 69–70 (Spring–Summer 1986): 288–310.

Walsh, Susan. "Equality, Emancipation and a More Just World: Leading Women in the B.C. CCF." Master's thesis, Simon Fraser University, 1984.

Weppler, Doreen Madge. "Early Forms of Political Activity among White Women in British Columbia, 1880–1925." Master's thesis, Simon Fraser University, 1971.

Whitaker, Reg, and Gary Marcuse. *Cold War Canada: The Making of a National Insecurity State, 1945–1957*. Toronto: University of Toronto Press, 1994.

Index

Note: "(i)" after a page number indicates an illustration; BC stands for British Columbia; CCF stands for Co-operative Commonwealth Federation; LEMJ stands for Laura Emma Marshall Jamieson; WILPF stands for Women's International League for Peace and Freedom.

Aberdeen, Lady Ishbel, 31, 38, 50, 225*n*23
Aberhart, William, 103–4
Adams, Jane, 87, 133
African Americans, 15
Alpine Club of Canada, 25, 35, 142
Anderson, Doris McCubbin, 165
Anscomb, Herbert, 127
Arkanasy, Anna Helene, 134–35
Arsens, Augusta, 199
Asians: Chinese immigration, 42, 67, 74; and the franchise, 42, 43, 59, 93, 113, 154, 160, 169, 173–74, 193, 219; racism toward, 28, 42, 67, 70, 94, 95, 174; removal and internment of Japanese during the Second World War, 152–54
Asiatic Exclusion League, 95

Balch, Emily Greene, 75, 92, 234*n*57
BC Conservatives, 6, 43, 46, 55, 72, 74, 114, 119, 141–42; opposition to the franchise, 59, 102–3. *See also* MacGill, Helen Gregory; Non-Partisan Association; Social Credit Party
BC Electric Railway: LEMJ on, 174, 193, 198; rates, 175, 251*n*33
BC Home and Domestic Employees Union, 47
BC Liberal Party, 6, 7, 51, 73, 102, 108, 112, 113–14. *See also* Jamieson, John Stuart (Jack); Liberal-Conservative Coalition; Non-Partisan Association; Smith, Helen Douglas; Smith, Mary Ellen
BC Reconstruction Party, 102, 103, 111, 112, 240*n*1
BC Socialist Party, 44–45
Bell-Irving, H.O., 40
Bennett, R.B., 100, 102, 108, 109, 112
Bennett, W.A.C., 142, 196
Bethune, Norman, 16
birth control, 76, 84, 107; LEMJ's views on, 131, 139. *See also* sex education
Black, George, 82
Black, Martha, 82, 112, 163
black people, 15–16, 25, 30, 225*n*17
Bollert, Mary, 142
Bolshevik Revolution, 61, 62

Bondfield, Margaret, 107
Borden, Robert Laird, 50, 54, 58–59
Bourassa, Henri, 8
Bowser, William John, 46, 55
Brigden, Beatrice, 107
British Columbia Equal Franchise Association, 50
Brittain, Vera, as influence on LEMJ, 60, 91
Bruce Peninsula. *See* Saugeen Peninsula
Burnaby Women's Forum, 49(i), 49–50, 52, 231*n*52
Bury, Jim, 197

Callaghan, Morley, 96
Cameron, Colin, 189
Campbell, Colin, 124
Campbell, May, 160
Campbell, Peter, 9
Canadian Communist Party, 103
Canadian Federation of Business and Professional Women, LEMJ and, 94, 178, 200
Canadian Patriotic Fund, 52
Canadian Social Hygiene Council, 84
Canadian Socialist League, 44
Capilano, Joseph, 41
Carson, Sara, 228*n*80
Carter, Albert E., 24–25
Carter, Cassie, 24, 25
Carter, Kezia Marshall, 24
Carter, Neall Marshall, 25
Casselman, Cora, 138, 163
The Champion, 46, 47(i), 48
Chatelaine: Consumer Council of, 164–65, 167; editor Byrne Hope Sanders, 111, 164; editor Doris McCubbin Anderson, 165
childcare, 156
Chown, Alice, 21
Clark, Susie Lane, 106, 123
Cleverdon, Catherine L., 5, 9, 43, 208–9
Cohn, Werner, 248*n*48
Coldwell, M.J., 182, 187
Cole, G.D.H., 106, 126, 201
Communist Party, 92, 94, 103, 106, 167; Dorise Nielsen and, 136–37; as the Labor-Progressive Party, 137, 147, 159, 160, 199, 200
communists, 6, 94, 100, 167, 170, 183. *See also* Mother's Day Committee; Nielsen, Dorise
Connell, Robert, 104, 113
Conservative Party, 54, 63, 102, 112; as Progressive Conservatives (1942–2003), 159, 166, 182, 199. *See also* Bennett, R.B.
Consultative Council for Co-operation in Wartime Problems of Canadian Citizenship, 153–54
Co-operative Commonwealth Federation: BC CCF Women's Central Group, 124, 130; endorsement of enfranchisement of Asians, 113, 173; and equal pay for equal work, 45, 72, 107, 150, 197; and feminism, 6–7, 123–25, 186; formation of, 103; and minimum wage, 117, 148, 149; National Women's Committee, 186; and radical vs practical socialism, 103, 125, 182, 190–91, 192; Socialist Fellowship, 184, 190, 191; support for removal and internment of Japanese Canadians, 153; and woman suffrage, 7. *See also* Co-operative Commonwealth Federation Women's Council; Woodsworth, James Shaver
Co-operative Commonwealth Federation Women's Council: British Columbia, 107, 147, 157, 185, 191, 200, 203, 204, 210; Ontario, 209; Vancouver, 203, 204, 210
co-operatives, 16, 96, 106, 125, 135–36, 192; LEMJ living in, 121–20, 122
Corey, H.L., 116, 117
Cornett, John D., 171(i)
Cripps, Isobel, 135
Cromie, Samuel P., 171(i)
Cross, Gladys Elspeth, 108
Current Events Clubs, LEMJ and, 106, 115

day nurseries, 148, 150–51, 156
de la Roche, Mazo, 138–39
deaconesses, 21, 225*n*24. *See also* Marshall, Eliza
Delmage, Margaret, 100, 240*n*118

Dhillon, Anup Singh, 93
Diefenbaker, John G., 166
Douglas, Tommy, 182, 187, 218
Doukhobors, 149, 198
Drummond, Henry, 38, 229*n*98

Eastman, S. Mack, 75, 232*n*6, 234*n*53
Eaton, Fraudena Gilroy, 90, 109
education: LEMJ on, 51–52, 67, 75–76, 106, 125, 148, 152, 183–84, 197, 207; spending, 98, 146, 198. *See also* Parent-Teacher Association of British Columbia; sex education
enfranchisement. *See* suffrage movement
equal pay for equal work, 45, 49, 67–68, 72, 107, 150, 151, 166, 197–98, 204–5
Errol, Constance. *See* Kerr, Elizabeth
eugenics, 65, 84
Evangelia House, 33–34, 228*n*80
Evans, Hubert, 139, 238*n*66
Everett-Kabut, Patricia Hews, 238*n*66

Fahrni, Mildred Osterhout, 37, 96, 110, 192
Fairclough, Ellen Louks, 163, 166, 200
Farris, Evlyn Fenwick, 45, 60, 63
fascism, 126–27. *See also* Women's International League for Peace and Freedom
Fascists of Canada, 95, 238*n*83
Federated Labour Party, 6, 28, 61, 62, 72, 74, 103; campaigning as the Canadian Labour Party, 73, 83. *See also* Independent Labour Party
Fernie, BC, 26(i), 26–27
First World War: anniversaries, strategic use of, 91; effect on suffrage campaign, 48, 50, 52, 55. *See also* Women's International League for Peace and Freedom
Fisher, Alex W., 171(i)
the franchise: property qualifications for, 43, 70, 144–45, 168–69, 173, 174, 178; women's lack of use of, 5–6, 109–110, 157–58, 185–86. *See also* Asians; Indigenous peoples
Fry, Marjory, 146

general strikes, 61, 62, 95
Gervin, Roland K., 171(i)
Ginger Group, 6, 74
Grant, George, 202, 256*n*90
Grant, W.L., 75
Green, T.H., 38
Gutteridge, Helena: and birth control, 76; and the CCF, 104, 114, 123; election to Vancouver City Council, 5, 70, 114, 168; and global co-operation, 94–95; lecture to the Vancouver Institute, 60–61; and the Local Council of Women, 97; and the Minimum Wage League, 50; and the 1941 BC provincial election, 142; and suffrage, 6, 45, 46, 57; support for unemployed workers, 100–1; as Vancouver City Council alderman, 98–99, 101, 116–17, 118, 123; and the Women's Employment League, 48; and the Women's International League for Peace and Freedom, 251*n*20; and the Women's Social and Political Union, 45

Hardikar, Dr., 74
Harrison, Peggy, 100
Hart, John, 141
Henderson, Rose, 73
Hodges, Nancy: and the Liberal-Conservative Coalition, 146, 160; and the 1941 BC provincial election, 142–44, 143(i); and the 1945 BC provincial election, 161; and the 1949 BC provincial election, 181–82; and the 1952 BC provincial election, 194; and the 1953 federal election, 199
Holland, Laura, 86
Holtby, Winifred, 134
housing, 122, 145, 146, 147, 168, 169, 170–71, 177, 179–80, 250*n*1, 251*n*22, 253*n*85
Howard, Irene, 9
humanism, 47–48
Hundal, Jerry, 93
Hutchison, Bruce, 8–9, 116, 119, 128, 146

Imperial Order Daughters of the Empire, 67, 75, 114
Independent Labour Party, 73, 74, 103

India, 74–75, 93
Indigenous peoples, 12–15, 13(i), 17, 20, 26, 41–42, 154–55, 240*n*118; and the franchise, 59, 169; LEMJ writings on, 207–8
industrial relations. *See* unions
International Association of Machinists, 37
International Council of Women, 91
International Organization of Good Templars, 17–18, 225*n*17
internationalism. *See* League of Nations Society; Women's International League for Peace and Freedom

Jamieson, Angus Bruce, 43, 53, 59
Jamieson, Anna, 60
Jamieson, Anne Marie, 121; memories of LEMJ, 216–17
Jamieson, John Stuart (Jack), 39(i); death of, 11, 22, 78; and League of Nations Society, 63, 232*n*6; and the Liberals, 53, 63, 65; as magistrate, 63, 64–65; marriage to LEMJ, 10, 37–38, 41–43, 46, 63; speeches to the Parent-Teacher Association, 64; and the YMCA, 63–64
Jamieson, Karen, 42, 121; memories of LEMJ, 217–19
Jamieson, Laura (daughter of Stuart and Jean Jamieson), 121
Jamieson, Laura Emma Marshall: address to the Canadian Conference on Child Welfare, 84–85; address to the Student Socialist Party, 234*n*53; as BC MLA, 120–40, 143–61, 143(i), 144(i); childhood of, 3, 10, 12–24, 19(i); on day nurseries, 150–51; death and memorial of, 211–12; on Doukhobors, 149, 198; election to BC legislature, 5, 7, 11, 116–19; on equal pay, 49, 150, 197, 204; founding of West End Community Centre, 86, 93, 129; illness, 43, 59, 239*n*87; as juvenile court judge, 10, 27, 81, 82, 83–84, 85–86, 114–15, 161; and the Local Council of Women, 97, 193; marriage to Jack Jamieson, 10, 37–38, 41–43, 46, 63; on Marx and Marxism, 11, 71, 107, 125, 183–84; on minimum wage, 49(i), 117, 205, 206; and mountain climbing, 10, 28, 34–35; and the New Vista Society, 122, 179; and the 1941 BC provincial election, 142–44, 143(i), 144(i); and the 1945 BC provincial election, 160–61; and the 1952 BC provincial election, 192–96, 195(i); parents (*see* Marshall, Joseph; Smith, Lucinda); and practical socialism, 146–47; presidency of the Burnaby Women's Forum, 49(i), 49–50; presidency of the Parent-Teacher Association, 76–77, 82, 161; on racism, 4, 93–95, 152, 154–55; response to fascism, 91–92, 126–27, 129, 134, 135, 203; student at Owen Sound College Institute, 21–22, 23–24; student at the University of Toronto, 28–32, 32(i); as teacher, 25–26, 28–29; on unions, 117, 132, 135, 149, 150, 185, 189, 205–6; and University College Women's Literary Society (University of Toronto), 29(i), 32, 36; and Vancouver Arbor Day Committee, 231*n*57; as Vancouver City Council alderman, 70, 170–75, 171(i); *Women Dry Those Tears*, 147, 150, 152; and women's employment, 48–49, 97, 138, 149, 150–51, 155–56, 204–5. *See also* Co-operative Commonwealth Federation; suffrage movement; University Women's Club; Vancouver Folksong and Dance Festival; Vancouver Women's School for Citizenship; Women's International League for Peace and Freedom
Jamieson, Laura Jean (Jean, daughter of LEMJ). *See* Shannon, Jean (Laura Jean Jamieson)
Jamieson, Marion-Lea, 121; memories of LEMJ, 219–20
Jamieson, Stuart Marshall: birth of, 43; collaboration with Indigenous peoples, 42, 214; research, 121, 162; university education, 81, 120–21
Johnson, E. Pauline, 15, 41–42
Johnston, Ellen, 80
Jones, Charles E., 170, 172, 251*n*33
Jones, Effie, 170, 251*n*33

Kerr, Elizabeth, 100, 123–25
Kidd, Benjamin, 31
Kilpatrick, T.B., 229*n*98
King, Garfield, 92
King, William Lyon Mackenzie: electoral loss in 1930, 109; and the Persons Case, 108, 241*n*28; return to power in 1935, 112; return to power in 1945, 159; selection as federal leader of the Liberal Party, 62
Kinnear, Mary, 5
Komagata Maru, 42
Korean War, 179, 187, 198
Kristiansen, Denny, 238*n*66
Ku Klux Klan, 74, 120

Labor Temple, Vancouver, 46, 48, 114
Labor-Progressive Party. *See* Communist Party
Laurier, Wilfrid, 50
League for Social Reconstruction: similarity of arguments with those of Technocracy, 104, 175; *Social Planning for Canada*, 103, 106, 168, 201, 251*n*22; *Social Purpose for Canada*, 201, 210
League of Nations Society, 63, 88–89, 91, 100, 111, 232*n*6
Leavy, Nora, 110
Lefeaux, Wallace, 141
Leigh, Amy, 83, 236*n*14
LeSueur, Evelyn, 138
Lewis, David, 182, 184, 187
Liberal-Conservative Coalition, 141–42, 143, 146, 160, 181, 191
Liberal-Labour alliances, 45–46. *See also* Smith, Mary Ellen; Smith, Ralph
Lindenfeld, Elda, 134–35, 245*n*62
Ling, Catherine Emily, 142
Little Mountain project, LEMJ support for, 179, 253*n*85
Little Mountain Squatters' Association, 169
Livesay, Dorothy, 91, 93, 100
living wage, 52
Local Councils of Women, 44, 89, 210. *See also* Vancouver Local Council of Women

MacAdams, Roberta Catherine, 65, 223*n*1
Macdonald, Alex B., 190–91
Macdonald, John A., 43
MacGill, Helen Gregory: firing by BC Conservatives, 82; on gender and economic inequality, 97; on the lack of women in public life, 108; on laws affecting women and children, 44, 51, 68, 109, 229*n*14; on racism, 95; renouncing of Tory allegiance, 55; and suffrage, 45
MacInnis, Angus, 73, 74, 113, 127, 142, 153
MacInnis, Grace: and bill for minimum wage, 149–50; and campaign for equal pay, 150; and democratic socialism vs Marxism, 182, 184, 191; disappointment with low female political participation, 186; marriage to Angus MacInnis, 73; and the 1941 BC provincial election, 142–44, 143(i), 144(i), 1945; and the 1945 BC provincial election, 160–61; and the 1947 Vancouver civic election, 170; on racism, 152; support for ban on coastal residence of Japanese Canadians, 153; tribute to LEMJ, 212
MacKay, Laura, 110
Macleod, Mildred, 183, 189–90
Macphail, Agnes Campbell: Charlotte Whitton on, 158; childhood, 16; election to Ontario legislature, 134; election to Parliament, 73, 109, 112, 113, 223*n*1; misogynistic views on, 163; and suffrage, 6, 8; on women in politics, 108, 156, 165–66; and the Women's International League for Peace and Freedom, 73
Macphail, Andrew, 8
Mahon, Lilette, 80, 112
Maitland, Royal Lethington, 141
Marshall, Aubrey Milton, 59
Marshall, Edward, 18, 20, 29
Marshall, Eliza: birth, 18; employment in Toronto, 24, 31; financing of LEMJ's education, 21–22, 79; Methodism and missionary work, 20–21, 33, 40
Marshall, Ellen (Ellen Johnston), 18, 20, 80
Marshall, Gilbert, 18, 20, 24, 59–60, 80
Marshall, Joseph, 15, 18

Marshall, Stanley, 18
Marx, Karl, LEMJ's views on, 125
McAllister, Clare Nulalinda, 142, 160
McBeath, Peter, 25
McBride, Mary Douglas, 142
McBride, Richard, 46, 55, 57
McClung, Nellie Letitia, 16, 17, 50, 57, 63, 223*n*1; *In Times Like These*, 130; LEMJ's views on, 6, 208–9; and non-partisanship, 66
McGeachy, Mary, 87
McGregor, Mrs. J., 108
McIntosh, J.W., 83, 84
McKinney, Louise Crummy, 65, 223*n*1
McNaughton, Violet, 6, 89, 239*n*87
McNeill, Alexander, 16–17
Methodist Church and temperance, 17, 18
Michel, BC, 26, 27
militant mothering ideology, 47–48
Military Voters Act, 58–59
Miller, George C., 171(i), 173
minimum wage: domestic minimum wage bill, 149–50; Helen Gregory MacGill on, 109; LEMJ on, 49(i), 117, 205, 206; Mary Ellen Smith on, 67
Minimum Wage League, 50
Mother's Council. *See* Mother's Day Committee
Mother's Day Committee, 5, 99–100, 99(i), 100–1, 102, 113
mothers' pensions, 67, 97, 98, 113, 146
Murphy, Emily, 6, 70, 209

Nahneebahweequa (Catherine Sutton), 15
National Council of Women of Canada, 38, 65, 66, 90, 203, 204; ban on political discussion, 164; Charlotte Whitton's criticism of, 158; endorsement of suffrage, 44
nationalization, 51, 135, 156
Native Daughters of British Columbia, 70, 110, 112
Native Sons of British Columbia, 95
Naylor, James, 7
Nehru, Jawaharlal, 189
Nesbitt, James K. (Jim), 195–96, 198
New Democracy movement, 126
New Democratic Party, 142, 174; founding of, 11, 191, 200, 210; Women's Committee, 206, 209
New Era League, 70, 72, 97, 109, 111, 175
New Vista Society, 122, 179
New Women, 20, 21, 25, 45
Nielsen, Dorise, 136–37, 163, 182
Non-Partisan Association, 103, 144, 172, 176–77; business support for, 114, 169–70, 175, 178; ties to Social Credit, 174
Non-Partisan League, 6, 65
North-West Rebellion, 15
Norton, Mary, 109–110
nurses: enfranchisement of, 58–59; training as deaconesses; 225*n*24; and unionization, 205–6

O'Connell, Dorothy. *See* Shannon, Dorothy
Oldham, George Ashton, 235*n*66
O'Leary, Grattan, 8, 109
Osterhout, Mildred. *See* Fahrni, Mildred Osterhout
Owen Sound College Institute, 22(i), 22–23

Pankhurst, Emmeline, 55
Pan-Pacific Association of Women, 91, 94
Parent-Teacher Association of British Columbia, 52–53, 86, 167; Jack Jamieson speeches to, 64; LEMJ presidency of, 76–78, 82, 161, 240*n*118
Parker, Elizabeth, 35
Parlby, Irene, 90–91, 223*n*1
Partridge, Edward Alexander, 96, 239*n*90
Paterson, Mrs. A.J., 69
Patrons of Industry, 16
Pattullo, Dufferin, 99, 110, 111, 112, 119, 141
Pearson, Lester B., 203
Perry, Anne Anderson, 65, 108
Political Equality League: address by Jack Jamieson, 40; *The Champion*, 46, 47(i), 48; hosting of Emmeline Pankhurst, 55; and municipal franchise campaign, 46; speech by Augusta Stowe-Gullen, 70; and women's employment, 48–49
Progressive Conservatives. *See under* Conservative Party

Progressive Party, 6, 108, 109, 112
Provincial Normal School (Vancouver), 25
Pullen-Burry, Bessie, 46

Regina Manifesto, 185, 187, 190
religion, 198, 202, 225*nn*23–24
Revolutionary Workers' Party, 103, 183
Riel, Louis, 15
Rogers, Edith McTavish, 223*n*1
Rolston, Tilly, 146, 160, 181, 199; election to the BC legislature, 142–43, 143(i), 194, 196; LEMJ's criticisms of, 147–48, 150–51, 197; on minimum wage, 149–50; on role of women in politics, 156
Roosevelt, Eleanor, as example to LEMJ, 131–32, 133, 136
Royal Commission on Dominion-Provincial Relations (the Rowell-Sirois Commission, 1937–40), 106, 127, 129

Sanders, Byrne Hope, 111, 164
Sanger, Margaret, 76
Sangster, Joan, 4–5, 9
Saugeen Peninsula: black residents of, 15–16; history of, 12, 14–15; Indigenous peoples of, 12, 13(i), 14–15, 20
Second Socialist International (1889–1916), perspective on feminism, 7
Second World War, 126, 145–46; removal and internment of Japanese Canadians, 152–54; and women's employment, 149–50, 155–56. *See also* Women's International League for Peace and Freedom
Sex Disqualification (Removal) Act 1931, 98, 204, 205
sex education, 45, 84. *See also* birth control
Sexual Sterilization Act, 1933, 65, 84
Shannon, Dorothy, 120; memories of LEMJ, 215–16
Shannon, Elizabeth, 120
Shannon, Jack, 80, 81
Shannon, Jean (Laura Jean Jamieson), 43, 80–81, 120, 162, 214
Shannon, Kathleen, 81, 120, 163
Shannon, Mary Ruth, 120
Smith, Eve, 183, 254*n*10
Smith, Goldwin, 8
Smith, Helen Douglas: as BC MLA, 102, 110–11, 114, 119, 122, 223*n*1; LEMJ's views on, 136; loss in the 1941 BC provincial election, 142; opposition to Asian immigration, 70
Smith, Janet, murder of, 74
Smith, Lucinda (Lucy), 15, 18
Smith, Mary Ellen: as BC MLA, 5, 50, 55, 66–69, 72, 82, 102, 182, 223*n*1; and League of Nations Society, 232*n*6; and Liberal-Labour politics, 45–46; loss in the 1928 provincial election, 108, 110; on non-partisanship, 68; and racism, 67, 95
Smith, Minnie, *Is It Just?*, 44
Smith, Priscilla Janet, 73, 83, 234*n*45
Smith, Ralph, 43, 45–46
Snowsell, Felicia, 142
Social Credit clubs, 102
Social Credit League (BC), 83, 113, 160, 181, 191, 193, 194, 196, 197, 198, 199
Social Credit Party, 112, 126, 142, 159, 181, 182, 199–200, 204; ties to the Non-Partisan Association, 174
Social Democratic Party, 44, 45
social welfare state, LEMJ's views on, 156
Socialist Party of Canada, 103, 104, 105, 106, 115, 118, 241*n*18
socialists: attitude toward the CCF, 103; attitude toward feminists, 5–6, 107, 123; attitude toward LEMJ, 4, 7, 104, 125
Sprott, Anna, 176–77, 194, 195
St. Laurent, Louis, 182, 199
Steeves, Dorothy Gretchen: as BC MLA, 119, 122, 123, 124, 136, 152, 157; and birth control, 131; and the CCF, 11, 111–12, 144(i), 145, 160, 170, 176; election to the BC legislature, 91, 111, 114; and founding of the League for Social Reconstruction, 105; and the Local Council of Women, 97, 114; and Marxism, 184; and the 1941 BC provincial election, 142–44, 143(i), 144(i); and the 1945 BC provincial election, 160–61; and the 1949 BC

provincial election, 181; and the 1952 BC provincial election, 193–94; and the 1953 federal election, 199; and pacifism, 126–27; and political organizing, 133; as president of the BC CCF, 182, 185, 186, 191; and the Socialist Party of Canada, 105; support for LEMJ's by-election campaign, 116, 118; support for the Vancouver Folksong and Dance Festival, 92; support for unemployed workers, 100–1; views regarding LEMJ, 145
Stevens, H.H., 59, 232*n*6, 242*n*47
Stevenson, Harry Attwood, 59
Stowe, Emily Howard, 36
Stowe-Gullen, Augusta, 70
Strachan, Bob, 199
Strum, Gladys, 159, 182, 200, 250*n*84
Student Socialist Party, 234*n*53
Su-á-pu-luck (Joseph Capilano), 41
suffrage movement, 5, 43–61, 47(i), 56(i)
suffragettes, 6, 45, 48, 55

Technocracy, 104
Telford, Lyle, 103–4
temperance. *See* International Organization of Good Templars; Woman's Christian Temperance Union
Thompson, Charles E., 171(i)
Tinsman, Emma, 194
Tolmie, Simon Fraser, 108
Townley, Alice, 110, 111
Trades and Labour Congress of Canada, 16, 205
Tristan, Flora, 5, 201
Turner, Arthur J., 238*n*66

Underhill, Frank, LEMJ and, 187, 190
unions, 4, 26, 28, 37, 47, 95, 97, 132, 149–50, 205–6. *See also* Gutteridge, Helena; minimum wage
United Farm Women of Ontario, 80
United Farmers of Alberta, 112, 236*n*32
United Farmers of Canada, 87–88, 109
United Farmers of Ontario, 80, 112
United Nations, LEMJ support of, 182, 187, 203
United Nations Association, LEMJ involvement in, 162, 175, 200, 203, 210, 234*n*53
United Suffrage Societies, 59
University of British Columbia Women's Literary Society, 75
University Women's Club: address by Jack Jamieson, 40; Evlyn Farris and, 45, 60, 63; and formation of the Parent-Teacher Association, 76; LEMJ and, 48, 51, 52, 53, 54–55, 61, 63, 74; and suffrage, 44, 51; of Toronto, 30
Uphill, Tom, 8, 28, 196

Vancouver Folksong and Dance Festival, 92–93
Vancouver Housing Association, 168, 170, 193
Vancouver Institute, 60–61, 62
Vancouver Local Council of Women, 25, 40, 90, 109, 178, 204, 206; and broadening the municipal franchise, 130; CCF delegates in, 123, 164; LEMJ as vice-president of, 123, 193; and representation of women in public affairs, 70–71, 97; support for the Vancouver Folksong and Dance Festival, 92; and women's political platform, 66
Vancouver Trades and Labour Council, 55, 61, 73, 150; support for franchise reform, 178; support for removal and internment of Japanese Canadians, 153
Vancouver Women's Emergency Committee to Aid the Single Unemployed, 5, 100, 115
Vancouver Women's Forum, 70
Vancouver Women's Liberal Association, 51, 53, 57
Vancouver Women's School for Citizenship, 135, 155–56, 158–59, 161, 178; aims of, 137–38; annual conference, 148–49; disbanding of, 209
Victoria, BC, 44
Victorian Order of Nurses, 73, 83

Wade, Jill, 250*n*1
Wartime Elections Act, 58–59

Weaver, Arthur Oliver, 35
Weaver, George, 125
Webster, Arnold, 198, 199
Webster, Gladys, 160
Weir, George, 243*n*83
Whitton, Charlotte, 86, 158, 166; LEMJ criticism of, 155
widows: and the franchise 43, 59; laws regarding, 67, 79; succeeding husbands in politics and appointed office, 82
Wilson, Alex D., 39–40
Wilson, Halford D., 116–17, 118, 171(i), 174
Winch, Ernest, 45, 103, 111, 122, 179
Winch, Harold: criticism of LEMJ, 212–13; as president of the BC CCF, 116, 118, 141, 145, 153, 182, 196, 198, 200; and radical vs practical socialism, 103, 125, 182
Wismer, Gordon, 194
Woman's Christian Temperance Union, 16, 17–18, 51, 94, 114
women suffrage. *See* suffrage movement
Women's Canadian Club, address by Jack Jamieson, 40
Women's Employment League, 48
Women's Freedom Union (the "Go Aheads"), 46
Women's International Labor Organizations, 91
Women's International League for Peace and Freedom, 6, 63; and anti-racism, 46, 93–95; Fraudena Gilroy Eaton as president of, 90, 109; LEMJ and, 10, 46, 73, 74, 75–76, 86–89, 101, 124, 167–68, 187, 213; response to fascism, 90, 91–92
Women's Labour Leagues, 6, 87, 95, 100
Women's Literary Society: University College, Toronto, 32, 36, 228*n*87; University of British Columbia, 75
Women's Lyceum. *See* Co-operative Commonwealth Federation Women's Council
Women's Prohibition Society. *See* Woman's Christian Temperance Union
Women's School for Citizenship. *See* Vancouver Women's School for Citizenship
Woodsworth, Grace. *See* MacInnis, Grace
Woodsworth, James Shaver: address to Student Socialist Party, 234*n*53; election to Parliament, 73, 74, 109, 112; endorsement of LEMJ as CCF candidate for election, 115, 116; endorsement of suffrage campaigns, 7; endorsement of suffrage for Asian Canadians, 113; feminism of, 71–72; leadership of CCF, 7, 11, 112; as mentor and friend of LEMJ, 71, 105; organization of the Winnipeg All People's Mission, 34; and pacifism, 87–88, 126; *Strangers within Our Gates*, 42
Woodsworth, Lucy, 71, 73, 140, 187, 210
Wrong, George M., 30

YMCA, 63–64
Young, Rodney, 186, 190–91
YWCA, 33, 36, 91, 92, 97, 114, 149; LEMJ as secretary of, 10, 54